GLOBAL MANDATORY FAIR USE

In a path-breaking work, Tanya Aplin and Lionel Bently make the case that the quotation exception in Article 10 of the Berne Convention constitutes a global mandatory fair use provision. It is global, they argue, because of the reach of Berne and TRIPS, and its mandatory nature is apparent from the clear language of Article 10 and its *travaux*. It relates to 'use' that is not limited by type of work, type of act or purpose, and it is 'fair' use because the work must be made available to the public, with attribution, and the use must be proportionate and consistent with fair practice. By explaining the contours of global mandatory fair use – and thus displacing the 'three-step test' as the dominant, international copyright norm governing copyright exceptions – this book creates new insights into how national exceptions should be framed and interpreted.

Tanya Aplin has been a professor of intellectual property law at King's College London since 2011. She is Director of the Postgraduate Diploma in UK, EU and US Copyright Law and Co-director of the LLM in Intellectual Property and Information Law offered by King's College London, and a door tenant at Three New Square, Lincoln's Inn. Her publications include *Copyright Law in the Digital Society: The Challenges of Multimedia, Intellectual Property: Patents, Copyright, Trade Marks and Allied Rights* (7th, 8th and 9th eds., with Prof. Cornish and Prof. Llewelyn); *Intellectual Property Law: Text, Cases and Materials* (1st, 2nd and 3rd eds, with Dr Davis); and *Gurry on Breach of Confidence: The Protection of Confidential Information* (with Prof. Bently, Prof. Johnson and Mr Malynicz). She has also edited the *Research Handbook on Intellectual Property and Digital Technologies* and is on the Editorial Committee of the *Modern Law Review* and *Current Legal Problems*.

Lionel Bently has been the Herchel Smith Professor of Intellectual Property Law at the University of Cambridge since 2004. He is Co-director of the Centre for Intellectual Property and Information Law at the University of Cambridge and a door tenant at 11 South Square, Gray's Inn. His publications include *The Making of Modern Intellectual Property Law* (with Prof. Brad Sherman); *Intellectual Property Law* (editions 1–4, with Prof. Brad Sherman; 5th ed, with Profs. Sherman, Dev Gangjee and Phillip Johnson); and *Gurry on Breach of Confidence: The Protection of Confidential Information* (with Prof. Aplin, Prof. Johnson and Mr Malynicz). He is General Editor of *International Copyright Law and Practice* (with Burton Ong), co-editor (with Prof. Martin Kretschmer) of *Primary Sources on Copyright* and Editor-in-Chief of the *Cambridge Law Journal*.

CAMBRIDGE INTELLECTUAL PROPERTY AND INFORMATION LAW

As its economic potential has rapidly expanded, intellectual property has become a subject of front-rank legal importance. Cambridge Intellectual Property and Information Law is a series of monograph studies of major current issues in intellectual property. Each volume contains a mix of international, European, comparative and national law, making this a highly significant series for practitioners, judges and academic researchers in many countries.

Series Editors

Lionel Bently
Herchel Smith Professor of Intellectual Property Law, University of Cambridge

Graeme Dinwoodie
Global Professor of Intellectual Property Law, Chicago-Kent College of Law, Illinois Institute of Technology

Advisory Editors

William R. Cornish, Emeritus Herchel Smith Professor of Intellectual Property Law, University of Cambridge

François Dessemontet, Professor of Law, University of Lausanne

Jane C. Ginsburg, Morton L. Janklow Professor of Literary and Artistic Property Law, Columbia Law School

Paul Goldstein, Professor of Law, Stanford University

The Rt Hon. Sir Robin Jacob, Hugh Laddie Professor of Intellectual Property, University College London

Ansgar Ohly, Professor of Intellectual Property Law, Ludwig-Maximilian University of Munich

A list of books in the series can be found at the end of this volume.

Global Mandatory Fair Use

THE NATURE AND SCOPE OF THE RIGHT TO QUOTE COPYRIGHT WORKS

TANYA APLIN

King's College London

LIONEL BENTLY

University of Cambridge

CAMBRIDGE
UNIVERSITY PRESS

CAMBRIDGE
UNIVERSITY PRESS

University Printing House, Cambridge CB2 8BS, United Kingdom

One Liberty Plaza, 20th Floor, New York, NY 10006, USA

477 Williamstown Road, Port Melbourne, VIC 3207, Australia

314–321, 3rd Floor, Plot 3, Splendor Forum, Jasola District Centre,
New Delhi – 110025, India

79 Anson Road, #06–04/06, Singapore 079906

Cambridge University Press is part of the University of Cambridge.

It furthers the University's mission by disseminating knowledge in the pursuit of
education, learning, and research at the highest international levels of excellence.

www.cambridge.org
Information on this title: www.cambridge.org/9781108835459
DOI: 10.1017/9781108884099

First published 2020

A catalogue record for this publication is available from the British Library.

Library of Congress Cataloging-in-Publication Data
NAMES: Aplin, Tanya Frances, 1972– author. | Bently, Lionel, 1964– author.
TITLE: Global mandatory fair use : the nature and scope of the right to quote copyright works
/ Tanya Aplin, King's College London; Lionel Bently, University of Cambridge.
DESCRIPTION: Cambridge, United Kingdom ; New York, NY : Cambridge University Press,
2020. | Series: Cambridge intellectual property and information law | Includes
bibliographical references and index.
IDENTIFIERS: LCCN 2020018242 | ISBN 9781108835459 (hardback) | ISBN 9781108884099 (ebook)
SUBJECTS: LCSH: Fair use (Copyright) | Copyright.
CLASSIFICATION: LCC K1420.5 .B46 2020 | DDC 346.04/82–dc23
LC record available at https://lccn.loc.gov/2020018242

ISBN 978-1-108-83545-9 Hardback

Contents

Acknowledgements

This book has had a long gestation period, and versions of it have previously been presented at multiple seminars, workshops and conferences, including the Fordham Conference on Intellectual Property Law and Policy (Cambridge, UK, April 2015), the workshop on 'Music and Creativity' (Cambridge, UK, April 2015), the IP Bar Association Annual Lecture (Gray's Inn, London, July 2015), the ZiF conference 'Towards an Ethics of Copying' (Bielefeld, Germany, October 2015), a seminar at Emmanuel College, Cambridge (November 2015), the Bournemouth University conference on 'Copyright Reform: The Implications One Year On' (Bournemouth, November 2015), ATRIP (Jagiellonian University, Cracow, June 2016), the conference on 'Comparative Dimensions of Limitations and Exceptions' (Singapore, July 2016), the IViR seminar (IViR, University of Amsterdam, April 2016), the Wolfson Humanities Society (Wolfson College, Cambridge, February 2018), ALADDA Intellectual Property Conference (Salamanca, Spain, June 2018), the 'Age of Stream' Conference (UEA, Norwich, July 2018), 'One Hundred Years of Copyright' (House of World Culture, Berlin, Germany, October 2018), 'Learning on Screen Members' Day: Copyright and Creative Reuse' (London, December 2018, RSA House), 'Owning Expression and Propertizing Speech' (University of Luxembourg, November 2019), CREATe Public Lecture (University of Glasgow, February 2020), and the Harold Fox Memorial Lecture (Toronto, Canada, February 2020). Our thanks go to the many peers who have commented on and debated the questions we have engaged in over several years, including Richard Arnold, Graeme Austin, Amrei Bahr, Jørgen Blomqvist, Kathy Bowrey, Robert Burrell, Richard Danbury, Jennifer Davis, Graeme Dinwoodie, Thomas Dreier, Alan Durant, Sévérine Dusollier, Niva Elkin-Koren, Hector Foucé, Suzy Frankel, Christophe Geiger, Peter Fydler, Daniel Gervais, Jane Ginsburg, Jonathan Griffiths, Henning Grosse Ruse-Khan, Darren Hick, Emily Hudson, Bernt Hugenholtz, Sabine Jacques, Ariel Katz, Barbara Lauriat, Brigitte Lindner, Makeen F. Makeen, Thomas Margoni, Ryszard Markiewicz, Daniel McClean, Bartolomeo Meletti, Chris Morrison, Wee Loon Ng-Loy, Norbert Niclauss, Ansgar Ohly, Ruth

Okediji, Johnson Okpaluba, Claudy Op den Kamp, Eberhard Ortland, James Parish, Alexander Peukert, Sam Ricketson, Pamela Samuelson, Nick Scharf, Jane Secker, Martin Senftleben, Michael Silverleaf, Aram Sinnreich, Will Slauter, Anna Tischner, Mireille van Eechoud and Kim Weatherall.

The manuscript draws on two published articles: 'Whatever Became of Global, Mandatory Fair Use: A Case Study in Dysfunctional Pluralism', in S. Frankel (ed), *Is Intellectual Property Pluralism Functional?* ATRIP Intellectual Property Series (Edward Elgar 2019), ch. 1, and 'Displacing the Dominance of the Three Step Test', in Shyamkrishna Balganesh, Wee Loon Ng-Loy and Haochen Sun (eds.), *Comparative Aspects of Limitations and Exceptions in Copyright Law* (Cambridge University Press, forthcoming 2020), ch. 3.

Thanks also to Malcolm Langley at the QMUL IP Archive for his help in locating sources and to Mr James Parish and Dr Jacqueline Nwozo for their valuable research assistance at different stages of the project. We are grateful to the editors, Cameron Daddis, Matt Gallaway and Rebecca Jackaman, at Cambridge University Press and the production and copyediting team of Richards Paul and Rachel Paul, all of whom greatly assisted in the smooth journey from proposal to publication. Finally, we would like to thank our respective partners, Megan Smith and Clair Milligan, for their constant and patient support.

Table of Legislation

EU DIRECTIVES AND REGULATIONS

TABLE OF NATIONAL LEGISLATION

Table of Cases

EUROPEAN COURT OF HUMAN RIGHTS

WTO PANEL REPORTS

FRANCE

GERMANY

SPAIN

OTHER JURISDICTIONS

1

Introduction

Imagine an international instrument that does not merely oblige contracting parties to confer rights on copyright holders (permitting only optional, narrowly circumscribed, exceptions) but also mandates limitations. *Imagine*, too, that such an instrument requires parties to permit use of material that has been taken from existing works, irrespective of the purpose of so doing, but only on the condition that the use is in accordance with fair practice. *Imagine* that such a mandatory limitation allows the reuse of transformed versions of works, including parodies, and even the whole of a protected work. *Imagine*, indeed, a regime of global mandatory fair use. Surely such a fantasy, or 'thought experiment', is a pointless, 'academic' exercise, given the political economy of international copyright and the dominant place within it occupied by the so-called three-step test, which has long been thought to cast a cloud over the legitimacy of the US fair use defence?[1] Yes and no. Yes, it is pointless to imagine, but no, this is not because it is impossible to achieve; it is pointless to imagine because there is no need to imagine it. *It already exists.*[2] This is precisely the effect of Article 10(1) of the Berne Convention.[3]

---

[1] For continuing discussion, see Justin Hughes, 'Fair Use and Its Politics – at Home and Abroad' in Ruth L Okediji (ed.), *Copyright Law in an Age of Exceptions and Limitations* (Cambridge University Press 2017), ch. 8, 234–74.

[2] See also S Ricketson, *WIPO Study on Limitations and Exceptions of Copyright and Related Rights in the Digital Environment* (2003) SCCR 9/7, 13: 'It is possible, therefore, that Article 10(1) could cover much of the ground that is covered by "fair use" provisions in such national laws as that of the United States of America (USA)' and Graham Greenleaf and David Lindsay, *Public Rights: Copyright's Public Domain* (Cambridge University Press 2018), 363: 'there is scope for greater use of the flexibility allowed by international copyright law for national laws to introduce relatively broad quotation exceptions ... which can extend to some transformative uses.' Cf. Ruth L Okediji, 'Towards an International Fair Use Doctrine' (2000) 39 *Colum J Transnat'l L* 75, 89, arguing that the US conception of fair use is not reflected in international copyright law. Interestingly, in her review of exceptions under Berne, Article 10 is mentioned only in passing – see fns. 99–105 and fns. 133 and 149. Okediji later observes at 113: 'Other exceptions contained in the Berne Convention, such as the right under Article 10 to quote from a protected work, also reinforce core values, such as freedom of speech, that inform the scope of the American fair use doctrine.'

[3] Berne Convention on the Protection of Literary and Artistic Works 1886 (rev. Paris 1971) ('Berne'). For the current text of Berne, see https://wipolex.wipo.int/en/treaties/textdetails/12214 (accessed 20 January 2020).

This much-neglected provision already mandates global fair use.[4] This is a proposition that will seem shocking to some, on both sides of copyright's polarised political spectrum. To so-called 'maximalists', global mandatory fair use is unthinkable because US fair use is itself legally dubious, in the light of the international requirement that exceptions must be confined to certain, special cases. Section 107 of the US Copyright Act 1976 is only maintainable because there is a body of jurisprudence that transforms the open norm of 'fair use' into a series of reasonably clearly understood and well-defined instances. Adoption of such an open norm by other jurisdictions, without such jurisprudence, fails to offer certainty as to the limited scope of the limitation that international law appears to demand. At the opposite end, that of the 'copy-left' movement, the proposition cannot be correct, because, were it so, the international *acquis* would not be as appalling as it is taken to be.

However, while the 'copy-left' movement may be right to highlight the limitations the Berne Convention imposes on the room left to adapt copyright to the digital environment, not every aspect of the Convention should be regarded as a source of dismay. Article 10(1) is just such a provision. On its face, it requires contracting parties to permit quotation from a work, and is subject to a series of conditions, the most important of which is that such quotation be in accordance with 'fair practice'. Importantly, such 'quotation' must be permitted whatever the purpose of the use, as long as the material taken is proportionate to the purpose of its user. We suggest that the term 'quotation', understood in terms of its ordinary use across the entire cultural sphere, describes a broad range of practices of reuse of copyright-protected material, including in some situations the whole of that material. For sure, the 'fair quotation' exception does not encompass every act that currently falls within the US 'fair use' doctrine – in particular, private copying and certain technological uses.[5] However, it does require that many transformative expressive uses be permitted if the use is fair, proportionate and appropriately attributed.

In this book, we explain and justify the proposition that Article 10(1) of Berne constitutes a global mandatory fair use provision. It is global because of the reach of Berne *qua* Berne and *qua* the Agreement on Trade Related Aspects of Intellectual

---

[4]   This was recognised by one of its key proponents, the Swedish judge Torwald Hesser. He explained the proposal expanded the quotation to 'general application, but restates it in terms compatible with the American doctrine of fair use': see Torwald Hesser, 'Intellectual Property Conference of Stockholm, 1967: The Official Program for Revising the Substantive Copyright Provisions of the Berne Convention. The Fifth Annual Jean Geiringer Memorial Lecture on International Copyright Law' (1967) 14 *Bull Copyright Soc'y* 267, 275, fn. 22. For discussion as to why it has been neglected, see Lionel Bently and Tanya Aplin, 'Whatever Became of Global, Mandatory, Fair Use? A Case Study in Dysfunctional Pluralism' in Susy Frankel (ed.), *Is Intellectual Property Pluralism Functional?* (Edward Elgar 2019), ch. 1.

[5]   In turn, therefore, these additional limitations do need to be justified under other parts of the Berne Convention, especially Article 9(2), as well as Article 13 of the Agreement on Trade Related Aspects of Intellectual Property Rights 1994 ('TRIPS') and Article 10(2) of the WIPO Copyright Treaty 1996 ('WCT').

Property Rights ('TRIPS').[6] It creates a mandatory exception because of the clear language of the provision and its *travaux*. It relates to 'use' that is not limited by type of work, type of act, or purpose. Finally, it is 'fair' use because the conditions of Article 10(1) and 10(3) Berne, namely, the work having been lawfully made available to the public, attribution, proportionality and fair practice, must be satisfied. In particular, the requirement of 'fair practice' embraces a range of normative considerations relating to economic and moral harm, distributive justice, and freedom of expression.

We begin in Chapter 2 with the history of Article 10(1) of Berne. This chapter details the evolution of the quotation exception, from its proposal at the 1928 Rome Revision, its incorporation at the 1948 Brussels Revision and key changes made at the 1967 Stockholm Revision, whereby the restriction on 'short' quotations was removed and the exception was extended to all types of works, without any restrictions on the purpose of the quotation. We note that the key to success at Stockholm (compared to prior initiatives) was the abandonment of proposed limitations as to the subject matter, extent or purpose of the re-use in favour of a notion of 'fair practice'. Chapter 3 considers a series of issues relating to the nature of Article 10(1) Berne. First, we examine the mandatory character of Article 10(1), an argument based primarily on the language of the provision and supported by the *travaux* to the 1967 Stockholm Conference. Second, we consider the place of Article 10(1) within the Berne Convention and its relationship to subsequent international treaties, the Agreement on Trade Related Aspects of Intellectual Property Rights ('TRIPS') and the WIPO Copyright Treaty 1996 ('WCT'), in particular, discussing the types of works and types of rights to which the quotation exception is applicable. Finally, this chapter addresses the reasons why the 'three-step test' is not applicable to the quotation exception, which largely stem from the status of Article 10(1) Berne as a mandatory obligation.

The following chapters offer a detailed exploration of Article 10(1) Berne. Chapter 4 examines some of the necessary requirements for Article 10(1) to apply. We start by demonstrating that quotation is not restricted by purpose, as shown by the *travaux* to the Stockholm Revision of Berne. We next consider how the requirement of 'made available to the public' should be understood and how the attribution requirement in Article 10(3) Berne may be satisfied. Finally, we explain that proportionality is an assessment that occurs before evaluating the condition of 'fair practice', which we argue should do the bulk of the work in assessing the permissibility of a quotation. We argue that the proportionality requirement is one of asking whether the length of the quotation is suitable for the purpose for which it is being used and whether a shorter quotation would have been as effective in achieving this purpose.

Chapter 5 examines in detail the meaning of 'quotation'. Drawing on a wide range of sources, legal and cultural, we suggest that 'quotation' is a broad concept, and, most importantly is not limited in ways that some have assumed. In particular, we

---

[6] A copy of this may be found at https://www.wto.org/english/docs_e/legal_e/27-trips_01_e.htm (accessed 20 January 2020).

emphasise that the conception of quotation in the Berne Convention is not limited by the established conventions associated with textual or print quotation, in particular notions of 'dialogue'. Freed from this preconception, it becomes clear that 'quotation' describes a broad range of reuses of materials, and should not be restrictively understood nor limited by length, type of work, its unaltered nature or the purpose for which it is used. Rather, the key constraint on what Berne requires be permitted is the condition of 'fair practice'. Thus, in Chapter 6 we put forward a detailed understanding of 'fair practice' which reflects a pluralistic range of considerations encompassing harm to the author, distributive justice concerns and freedom of expression. Informed by these normative understandings of 'fairness', we argue that 'fair practice' requires an assessment of the nature or purpose of the quotation; the type of expressive use that is involved; the nature of the work that has been quoted; the size of the quotation and its proportion in relation to the source work; and harm to the market for the source work and the integrity interests of the author of the source work.

We then move to Chapter 7 to discuss the considerable significance of our interpretation of Article 10(1) Berne. In particular, we argue that Article 10(1) provides a fresh lens through which to view national copyright exceptions and has the potential to displace the dominance of the three-step test in this arena. We illustrate this point by reference to the US fair use exception and show how, according to Article 10(1), the open-ended, multi-factorial, royalty-free nature of US fair use may be justified as a matter of international copyright law. At the same time, however, to comply with Article 10(1), the US fair use exception may need to pay greater attention to the unpublished status of works that are used and the moral rights of authors. A second consequence is the need to amend national legislation that has not properly implemented the quotation exception. We demonstrate how specific quotation exceptions in several (mainly) civil law jurisdictions are contrary to Article 10(1), either by restricting the types of purposes of the quotation or imposing a quantitative limit of 'short' quotations. The fair dealing exceptions in common law jurisdictions are also problematic to the extent that they restrict quotation to the purposes of criticism or review. A third consequence is on judicial interpretation of quotation exceptions and we illustrate how the EU and UK quotation exceptions should be interpreted by the CJEU and national courts in light of Article 10(1), noting the flaws in the recent CJEU decisions in *Spiegel Online* and *Pelham*.[7] A fourth implication is that Article 10(1) Berne, rather than the three-step test, provides an international legal basis for the parody exception[8] that exists in many national laws and, as such, may require the scope and requirements of this type of exception to be revisited. Finally, we observe the potential for our interpretation of Article 10(1) to animate changes to industry guidelines or the development of codes of best practice. Existing guidelines on quotation usage tend to be risk averse,

---

[7]   Case C-516/17 *Spiegel Online GmbH v. Volker Beck* EU:C:2019:625 (CJEU, Grand Chamber) and
      Case C-476/17 *Pelham GmbH v. Hütter* EU:C:2019:624 (CJEU, Grand Chamber).

[8]   Contrast Sabine Jacques, *The Parody Exception in Copyright Law* (Oxford University Press 2019), ch. 2.

whereas Article 10(1) Berne, properly understood, provides the basis for less restrictive practices by user groups.

In short, we argue that national and regional copyright exceptions should be systematically revisited and interpreted in light of Article 10(1) Berne. Once this is done, we can expect changes to our legal frameworks and different sorts of permitted uses of copyright material to emerge as a result. Until now, global mandatory fair use has been a latent international legal norm: in this book, we expose its force and potential to shape permitted uses of copyright material.

2

The History of Article 10(1) Berne

In this chapter, we explore the history of Article 10(1) Berne, in order to enable the reader to understand the key stages in its evolution that inform or confirm our interpretation of the character and breadth of the provision.[1] As we will see, several important features of Article 10(1) Berne, including the meaning, length and purpose of 'quotation', were explored as part of the *travaux* to the Stockholm Revision of the Berne Convention. These *travaux* offer valuable guidance to clarify the meaning of the text (where its meaning is unclear) and to confirm a meaning deduced in the normal way from the ordinary meaning of the text, viewed in its context and in light of its object and purpose.[2] Moreover, it is also useful to see those *travaux* in the context of three earlier discussions of the right of quotation: in 1885 in Berne, in 1928 at Rome and in 1948 at Brussels. As those involved in the Stockholm Revision would have been cognisant of the previous attempts to introduce a quotation exception, inferences can also be drawn from differences between the Stockholm text and those proposed in Rome and Brussels.

I BERNE (1884–1886)

As agreed in 1886, the Berne Convention contained no express right of quotation. In part, this was unnecessary, as no provision was made as to a right of reproduction.[3] However, a clause was included that clarified that Members could permit the

---

[1] Some of the *travaux* are recorded in two volumes: WIPO, *Records of the Intellectual Property Conference of Stockholm, June 11 to July 14, 1967*, vol. I and II (WIPO, 1971; hereafter 'Records'). Other documents are retained at the World Intellectual Property Organization, referenced under its former acronym 'BIRPI'. We have sourced these documents from series BT209 at the National Archive, Kew, England (hereafter 'TNA'). These are designated 'TNA: BT 209/ . . . '.

[2] Vienna Convention on the Law of Treaties, concluded at Vienna on 23 May 1969, Article 32.

[3] *Documents de la Conférence réunis A Bruxelles du 5 au 26 Juin 1948* (BIRPI 1951), 244. In turn, many commentators have argued that the presence of the exception/limitations meant the Convention *implicitly* recognised a reproduction right: see, for example, Mihály Ficsor, *Guide to the Copyright and Related Rights Treaties Administered by WIPO* (WIPO 2003); Jane Ginsburg, 'Achieving Balance in International Copyright Law' (Review of J Reinbothe and Silke von Lewinski, *The WIPO Copyright Treaties* 1996) (2003) 26 *Columbia Journal of Law and the Arts* 201, 203.

inclusion of extracts from works in collections, particularly for educational purposes. Article 8, as adopted, read:

> As regards the freedom of including excerpts from literary or artistic works for use in publications destined for teaching or scientific purposes, or for chrestomathies, the effect of the legislation of the countries of the Union, and of special arrangements existing or to be concluded between them, is not affected by this Convention.[4]

This itself was a considerably diluted provision from the mandatory exception that had been sponsored by the German delegation in 1884,[5] with flexibility having been specifically extended to maximise the possibility of Great Britain adhering to Berne – a hope that came to be fulfilled.[6] At the conference in 1885, when the desirability of the German proposal was being discussed, the question had also arisen as to the treatment of quotations. According to the Report of that Conference:

> In the discussion that took place on the subject of this Article, it was asked whether it covered the right of quotation, and the Spanish Delegation in particular wished to know whether such quotations as were necessary in commentaries, critical studies or other scientific or literary works were authorized under the Article concerned. The French Delegation said that, in spite of the lack of legal provisions concerning the right of quotation in the legislation of its country, that right had always been recognized by case law. The delegations of the other countries, several of which did have legal provisions on the subject, endorsed the above statement with respect to their countries.[7]

---

[4]   Convention Concerning the Creation of an International Union for the Protection of Literary and Artistic Works of 9 September 1886, Article 8.

[5]   The Draft of a Convention respecting the Formation of a General Union for the Protection of the Rights of Authors, as adopted at the 1884 conference, can be found, in French and English, in *Correspondence Respecting the Formation of an International Copyright Union*, Parliamentary Papers, C.-4606, 19 (in French) and 22 (in English). Although mandatory, the freedom Article 8 of the draft convention secured to publish 'extracts, fragments or entire passages from literary or artistic work… provided that this publication is specifically destined and adapted for instruction, or is of a scientific character' was limited to material 'appearing for the first time in another country of the Union'.

    One feature of Article 8 of the 1884 draft was that there was no limitation on the size or significance of the 'extracts, fragments or entire passages'. Following its modification in 1885, the British delegates reported: 'We regarded the article on this head which appeared in the draft project of last year as being extremely dangerous, and providing a facile means for wholesale appropriation. We therefore proposed its omission with the view of leaving the matter to be settled by the law of each state. We ultimately consented to the insertion of the existing article VIII, which carries out our views on the subject.' No. 58, Inclosure 1, Messrs Adams and Bergne to the Marquis of Salisbury, 25 September 1885, in *Correspondence*, 54.

[6]   Lionel Bently and Brad Sherman, 'Great Britain and the Signing of the Berne Convention in 1886' (2001) 48 *J Copyright Soc'y USA* 311–40 (describing the change in the British position).

[7]   Records of the Second International Conference for the Protection of Literary and Artistic Works found at companion website to Sam Ricketson and Jane C Ginsburg, *International Copyright and Neighbouring Rights: The Berne Convention and Beyond* (2nd ed., Oxford University Press 2006) at https://global.oup.com/booksites/content/9780198259466/ (accessed 10 June 2020), 103–49 at 132; *Actes de la 2ème Conférence internationale pour la protection des oeuvres littéraires et artistiques réunie à Berne du 7 au 18 Septembre 1885* (International Office, Berne, 1885), 47.

The report is thus clear that the right to quote was recognised universally in the laws of Members of the Berne Union. However, the report does not indicate conclusively, as some have suggested, that the right of quotation was encompassed within the freedom left to Members by Article 8.[8] The responses to the Spanish question do not suggest a conclusion as to whether quotation was unaffected because it fell *within* Article 8. Rather, it is simply made clear that all Members regarded the right as unaffected, either because it was encompassed by Article 8 or simply because it fell outside the Convention.

II ROME (1928)

The topic was revisited at the 1928 Rome Revision Conference.[9] The Italian administration and Berne office proposed to distinguish the right to quote, which was to be obligatory, from the freedom of Members to make compilations of extracts recognised in Article 8:[10]

> Art 10 (1) It is permitted to make analyses or short textual quotations of published literary works for critical, polemical or educational purposes.
>
> (2) With regard to the faculty of lawfully borrowing from literary or artistic works, the matter is left to the laws of the countries of the Union and, if it is more favourable to the author, that of the particular arrangements concluded or to be concluded between them.
>
> (3) All borrowings recognised as legal must correspond to the original text and be accompanied by an exact indication of the source (title of the work, name of the author if known).[11]

The explanatory text elaborated that 'le droit d'emprunt' – the 'right to borrow' – was then regulated in the legislation of the countries of the Union in such an inconsistent manner that it was impossible to contemplate a uniform provision. However,

---

[8] According to Ficsor, 'an agreement was reached that, on the basis of that provision, quotations would also be allowed': Ficsor, *Guide to the Copyright and Related Rights Treaties Administered by WIPO* (2003), 61, [BC-10.1]. Ginsburg, 'Achieving Balance', 203, fn. 12, also suggests that 'a quotation exception has existed in some form in the Berne Convention since the original 1886 text'.

[9] Union Internationale pour La Protection des Oeuvres Littéraire et Artistique, *Actes de la Conférence Réunie A Rome Du 7 Mai au 2 Juin 1928* (Berne: Bureau de L'Union, 1929). In advance, the Bureau had prepared a study of 'Les Emprunts Licite' (1924), *Le Droit D'Auteur* 37, 52, 67, 77, 87.

[10] *Conférence de Rome. Propositions avec exposés des motifs préparées par L'administration Italienne et Le Bureau International de Berne* (February 1927) (Berne: Bureau International de L'Union, 1927) in BT 209/741, pp 16–17 and *Actes*, 61 ff, pp. 74–5.

[11] Article 10(1) Il est permis de faire dans un but critique, de polémique ou d'enseignement des analyses ou courtes citations textuelles d'oeuvres littéraire publiées
(2) En ce qui concerne la faculté de faire licitement d'autres emprunts à des oeuvres littéraires ou artistiques, est réservé l'effet de la législation de, pays de l'Union, et, s'il est plus favorable à l'auteur, celui des arrangements particuliers conclus ou à conclure entre eux.
(3) Tous les emprunts reconnus licites doivent être conformes au texte original et accompagnés de l'indication exacte de la source (titre de l'oeuvre, nom de l'auteur s'il est connu).

where the law of borrowing was universally recognised, as is the case for short quotes for the purpose of criticism, controversy or teaching, the development of a uniform rule 'seems appropriate'. Moreover, the proposal indicated it was desirable to insert in the Convention an obligation on any borrower not to alter the text of the original and to indicate the source from which it drew. This was explicitly linked to the moral rights of the author (which 'are nowadays more and more respected'), though the condition was not limited to situations where an alteration would be capable of damaging the writer's literary reputation.[12] The requirement to indicate the source was said to be one of 'pure and simple equity'.

In response, the French proposed a substantial reworking of the Italian/ Berne text based on a text approved at the Lugano meeting of ALAI in June 1927:[13]

(1) In any work of a critical, polemical or teaching nature, it is lawful to include analyses or short textual quotations of any literary, scientific or artistic production, provided, however, that the production analysed or cited has been already published.

(2) For chrestomathies, anthologies and all teaching works, it is lawful to borrow from literary, artistic or scientific works already published, provided that the total of borrowings made from a single work does not exceed three pages of the first edition of this work, or in any case not more than half of this work, if it is a scientific or literary work; a page or a quarter at most of the work, if it is a musical work; in the latter case, the work can never be inserted into another musical composition.

All borrowings recognised as legal must be in full conformity with the original text and be accompanied by the exact indication of the source (title of the work, names of the author and of the publisher if they are known).

(3) The total or partial reproduction of works of plastic and graphic art is only lawful if it takes place, by the process of graphic arts, in publications of a critical or scientific or educational nature, and if these works have already been delivered to the public.

---

[12] A German-proposed qualification would have modified the condition so that it required the borrowing 'conform to the original work, provided that the purpose of the borrowing does not warrant modification': *Conférence de Rome. Propositions quelques-unes avec exposés des motifs présentées par L'administrations Allemande, Autrichienee, Britannique, Française et Suise* (Juillet 1927) (Berne: Bureau International de L'Union, 1927) 4 in BT 209/741.

[13] *Propositions et Contre-Propositions et Observations*, 16; in *Actes*, 100. The ALAI text is set out in 'Voeux se rapportant aux dispositions de la Convention de Berne', (1927–1935) in *Documents* (1951) 433, 447. Note also the discussion of the right of citation at ALAI in (1926) (Nov) *Le Droit D'Auteur* 127–8.

The domestic law of copyright in France was, at this stage, largely judge-made, and the Cour de Cassation (Criminal Chamber) had, in a judgment on 10 March 1926, admitted the potential legality of 'artistic quotation' in a case relating to three small reproductions of works by Auguste Rodin. The case is discussed in H. Desbois, *Le Droit D'Auteur* (3rd ed., 1978), [249]. Desbois notes that the reproductions were small, illustrating a work describing the development of French art, inseparable from the text and unlikely to compete with authorised reproductions.

(4) The Contracting States may subject the exercise of the right defined in paragraphs 2 and 3 of the present article the payment of a royalty.

A few points are worth observing about the French/ALAI proposal, which, in general, foreshadows the peculiarly narrow view of the legitimacy of quotation that has been pushed by a large number of French writers over recent decades. Like the Bureau/Italian proposal, the quotation right was identified as applying only to 'textual quotations' but, in contrast, extended to quotation *from* works of all kinds, not just literary works. However, while broadened in this manner, the French proposal narrowed the quotation right by reference to not the purpose of use but the type of text *in which* the quote was deployed.[14] Second, with respect to the use of borrowings in compilations, the French proposed quantitative limits and some absolute rules. It proposed that musical borrowings were not to be allowed in other music, and artistic works were only to be reproduced in publications if they had already been permitted to appear in such publications. Third, the French proposed to allow Members of the Union to require that remuneration be paid for borrowings that went beyond the narrow exception for short quotations.

In contrast with the French, the Swiss proposed expanding the Italian formulation of the quotation right, explaining that the limitation to literary works was unacceptable and that quotation should be permitted for musical and artistic works.[15] It proposed that the first paragraph of the Italian/Bureau provision be replaced with the following text:

> Art 10 (1) It is permitted to make analyses or short textual quotations from published literary or musical works for critical, polemical or educational purposes. It is permitted, for the same purposes, to reproduce published works of figurative art or photography; this reproduction can only take place, however, insofar as it is necessary to explain the text.

The Dutch limited its response to the Italian/Bureau proposal to the second clause on compilations. It said it would be desirable to arrive at a regulation fixing exactly the quantity of borrowings that, in relation to each work, would be allowed for the benefit of anthologies or other collections intended to serve a teaching or scientific purpose. At the same time, the Dutch response acknowledged the difficulty with arriving at such quantitative stipulation, noting that this would be necessary to allow the possibility of quoting an entire poem, while nevertheless seeking to fix exactly the maximum extent of such a taking.[16]

---

[14]   As we will see in Chapter 5, pp. 110–113, it remains a point of contention how far quotation is limited to the quotation in a later work of authorship, and how far the ordinary meaning of the term permits the freestanding reuse of works or parts thereof.

[15]   *Propositions et Contre-Propositions et Observations*, 20–21; *Actes*, 104.

[16]   *Nouvelle Proposition des Administrations Norvégienne et Suédoise et Observations du Gouvernement Néerlandais* (Mars 1928), 5; *Actes*, 109.

Although the principle of a right of quotation appeared to be approved by all participants at the Conference,[17] differences quickly emerged as to the detail; most jurisdictions regarded the right to quote as too narrowly framed in the Programme proposal, even though the later paragraphs left further flexibility concerning compilations.[18] To begin, the British and Danish delegations doubted the advisability of such a change – the British being keen to retain the existing fair dealing rules from the 1911 Copyright Act.[19] Hungary, for example, would have extended the purposes specified to include 'scientific' purposes.[20] Switzerland and Japan, with which Norway indicated its assent, proposed that the right extend beyond literary material to encompass musical works, figurative arts and photographs, and to recognise it might be appropriate to reproduce the whole of the work 'if this proved necessary to explain the text'.[21] The Norwegian delegate said it shared the opinion of Switzerland but found the word 'explain' too restrictive. The Swiss responded by proposing an alternative formulation, namely that use of the work was 'connected to' the text, a proposition to which Norway assented. Norway also pointed out that, as formulated, the proposed provision omitted oral works and suggested, therefore, that the right to quote be extended to situations where works had been delivered to the public ('livrées au public') rather than requiring that they had been published.[22]

Following these interventions, the Drafting Committee initially accepted a text presented by the Japanese delegation, which reproduced the first paragraph of the Bureau/Italian proposal but extended the right to cover quotation from artistic as well as literary works and removed the limitation that the quotation be textual. However, other problems applicable more generally to the whole of Article 10 meant that the success in finding a suitable formulation was short-lived.[23] As discussion progressed, it became clear that the delegates were unlikely to agree on a text.[24] Proposals limited by type of work or purpose were too narrow; those that abandoned those conditions potentially too broad. In the end, no such provision was adopted, and the discussion was not even mentioned in the final report.[25] The British delegates viewed the failure as 'not surprising . . . having regard to the wide diversity of national legislations and requirements in this matter'.[26]

---

[17] Actes, 250 ('ce droit n'est pas contesté').
[18] Résumé des Propositions et de la Discussion, in Actes, Part IV, 250–4.
[19] Actes, 250. On reactions of UK lobbyists to the proposal, see BT 209/727.
[20] Actes, 250.
[21] Actes, 250 ('si celle-ci se révélait nécessaire pour expliquer le texte').
[22] Actes, 251.
[23] Actes, 251.
[24] In addition, the French delegation expressed concerns that the introductory words 'it is permissible to . . .' (il est permis de . . .) might encourage too much borrowing. See Actes, 251
[25] Ricketson and Ginsburg (2006), at https://global.oup.com/booksites/content/9780198259466/15550027 (accessed 10 June 2020), pp. 223–56.
[26] Rome Copyright Conference, 1928. Report of the British Delegates, 26, in BT 209/734.

III BRUSSELS (1948)

As a result of the initial, if provisional, consensus at Rome, it had been envisaged that there might be support for express recognition of a right of quotation at the next conference, which was immediately scheduled to take place in Brussels in 1935.[27] Preparations were therefore soon set in train, including a 1932 set of provisional proposals and a more formal proposal soon after.[28] However, the convening of the conference was delayed, initially because countries had been slow to ratify the Rome Revision, but also because of ongoing attempts to reconcile the international copyright arrangements operating in the Americas with those largely centred in Europe (i.e. Berne), and then, of course, by the Second World War.[29]

By the time the Burueau was ready to convene a conference, the initial aspiration to deal in detail with quotation had been abandoned, the proposers instead opting for a much less ambitious addition, namely, the recognition of an obligation on those who borrowed from protected works to attribute the source of the material used. The programme explained that limiting the right to quote by reference to the purpose of the work in which the material was included had proved too narrow:

> [I]t was pointed out to the International Literary and Artistic Association that this way of granting the right of quotation to the benefit of only three categories of works was too narrow a solution. This observation seems fair to us. A scientific work, even if it is not strictly speaking critical, must be able to contain quotations. Think of a book of literary history, or just history. Such works are inconceivable without references and quotes. Often the author will reproduce the appreciation of others in order to confront it with his own, but all his work cannot, however, be called a work of criticism or controversy. It is also sometimes said to cover oneself with the authority of a big name to give more weight to one's own judgment. In short, it is obvious that quotation cannot be restricted to the extent provided for in our proposal. So the proposal was dropped.[30]

Another proposal relating to the quotation of artistic works had also been floated but later dropped. Building on discussions at Rome, the Belgian/Bureau group proposed to permit the complete reproduction of works of art, when the image thus published would have been in connection with the text of the work in which it was to be incorporated. The idea was to permit the use of artistic works to illustrate 'scientific works' (works of history, history of art) where reproductions of paintings accompany

---

[27] Union Internationale pour La protection des Oeuvres Littéraires et Artistiques, Conférence de Bruxelles. Tableau des Voeux Émis par Divers Congrès et Assemblés (1927-1935) (January 1947) (Berne: Bureau, 1947) in BT 209/898, 18 (ALAI, Lugano, 2-4 June 1927 and Montreux, 30 January-3 February 1935).

[28] 'Les Travaux Préparatoire de la Conférence de Bruxelles', (1933) (July-September) Le Droit D'Auteur 73, 90, 97, at 98.

[29] Documents de la Conférence réunis A Bruxelles du 5 au 26 Juin 1948 (BIRPI 1951) (hereafter 'Documents (1951)'), 13.

[30] Documents (1951), 244. For a Report of the conclusions of ALAI on the original proposal (in Montreux-Caux, 30 January to 3 February 1935), see (1935) Le Droit D'Auteur 39.

the text. However, this proposal was thought to harm the authors too much, partly because the draft was not expressly limited to such works but also because the idea of a 'connection of the image with the text is a vague notion, which risks opening the door to many abuses'.[31] The danger was thought to lie in the possibility that any reproduction of an artwork might be legitimised merely by adding a little text. The Programme organisers could not see a way through the difficulty: on the one hand, a broadly defined treaty provision might lead countries to expand exceptions beyond their existing breadth; on the other hand, a narrower conception was unlikely to be acceptable to 'countries which widely recognize the right to quote', as well as to those, in particular the Anglo-Saxon countries, which prefer to leave the judge complete freedom in the assessment of what is 'fair dealing' with the work.[32] Thus, the organisers decided to refrain from introducing into the Convention a provision relating to the right of quotation.

In the end, the Programme proposal was very limited: '[e]xtracts shall be accompanied by an indication of their source.'[33] Even here, the organisers had abandoned more ambitious plans. The experiences at Rome had made it clear that a condition of this sort might run into opposition if it were applied to 'small citations', though would likely be accepted for 'didactic and scientific borrowings', so the 1948 programme added the condition only as a qualification of existing Article 10. The 1932 proposal would also have required that any extract must correspond with the work used (*l'emprunt devait être conforme a l'oeuvre utilisée*). However, the organisers had concluded that such a condition 'would have no chance of being accepted'.[34] At Rome it had been clear that countries wanted not only to be free to permit translations of quotations and extracts but also to make other changes to these borrowings deemed necessary, given the purpose of the publication. There was no prospect of agreement on this point.

Various counter-proposals were made. The most ambitious came from France. In preparation for the proposed 1936 conference, it had suggested the following text:

> In any of the countries of the Union it shall be lawful to make short citations from articles in newspapers and periodicals, particularly when such extracts are grouped together under the same heading in a newspaper or periodical for the purpose of giving a brief survey of the whole of such articles.
>
> It is reserved to the national legislations of the countries of the Union and to special arrangements existing or to be concluded between them to permit brief extracts from literary, scientific, musical or cinematographic works to be inserted in

[31] *Documents* (1951), 244.
[32] *Documents* (1951), 245.
[33] *Documents* (1951), 245; Union Internationale pour La protection des Oeuvres Littéraires et artistiques, *Conference de Bruxelles. Propositions avec exposés des motifs préparées par L'administration Belgee et Le Bureau de L'Union* (January 1947) (Berne: Bureau Union, 1947) in BT 209/898, pp. 37–8.
[34] *Documents* (1951), 245.

works and in publications destined for educational purposes and having a scientific or documentary character, as well as in works of criticism or of controversy.

As regards anthologies or chrestomathies, the insertion therein of extracts from literary, scientific or musical works may be authorised by the above-mentioned national legislations or special arrangements, subject to the payment of an equitable royalty.

The citations and extracts mentioned in the preceding paragraphs shall be accompanied by an indication of source (in the case of a citation or extract from a newspaper or periodical, the name of the newspaper or periodical and the name of the author of the article; in other cases, the title of the work and the name of the author and of the publisher.[35]

The French Government explained its thinking: first, that a distinction should be recognised between 'quotations' comprising brief extracts (*'citations de peu éten-dues'*) for specified legitimate purposes and more extensive extracts (*'extraits'*) in anthologies or chrestomathies. For the latter, but not the former, use should only be permitted on payment of an equitable royalty. Although not explained, it is notable that while the French proposal would have extended the right to make extracts to musical and cinematographic works,[36] it did not provide for any such reuse of artistic works. In addition, the French proposed a mandatory and general rule (*'d'une prescription impérative et générale'*) relating to quotation from newspaper and periodicals.[37] This mandatory rule would ensure in all the countries of the Union the freedom to make small quotations from such articles published in newspapers 'when such a quotation appears in the part of a newspaper or periodic collection precisely intended to give a summary of a set of articles' (as was the practice in France in so-called *'revues de presse'*).[38]

By the time of the Conference in 1948, the French had already modified the details of its counter-proposal.[39] The structure remained the same: a mandatory exception,

---

[35] *Documents* (1951), 246–7. This translation from UK Government file, 'International Union for the Protection of Literary and Artistic Works. Brussels Conference, 1948. Instructions to Delegates', 36, in BT209/898. Also in BT209/970 (where a note says 'The French attempt to regulate more precisely the right of making extracts should, I suggest, be resisted').

[36] *Documents* (1951), 247 ('quotations from cinematographic works should also be mentioned and accepted, under the same condition of brief extent, as those from literary and musical works'). In fact, extracts from cinematographic works were to be permitted only under paragraph 2 (i.e. in works having one of the specified purposes), whereas musical works could be subject to both provisions.

[37] *Documents* (1951), 247. It is possible that the idea that the exception should be 'general' indicated a desire that it be applied not just to works with a country of origin in another Member of the Union, but also to domestic works. This would explain the use of language 'in all countries of the Union'. If this is correct, the proposal involved a shift in the logic of the Union towards a supranational code.

[38] *Propositions et Contre-Propositions et Observations Presentées par Les Administrations des Pays de L'Union* (February 1936), 31–2, reproduced in *Documents* (1951), 246–7.

[39] According to the Bureau, these changes were as a result of the influence of *L'Association Juridique Française pour la protection internationale du droit d'auteur: Documents* (1951), 247. It is worth noting that from 1945 through to 11 March 1957, the French legislature was engaged in the process of codifying copyright into legislation. Desbois suggests that the legislative provisions on 'short

applicable in all countries of the Union, for short quotation from newspapers, followed by two provisions allowing national law to permit extracts, one limited primarily by reference to purposes, the other relating to compilations and anthologies. In its explanatory text, the French Government explained that it perceived a distinction between the treatment of small and large quotations (*'petites citations'* and *'grandes citations'*). The former, including quotation for the purposes of criticism and daily information, were widely recognised and obligatory. While not previously treated in the Convention the first paragraph had the objective of partially filling this gap by proclaiming the legality in all countries of short quotations (*'courtes citations'*) of articles from newspapers and periodicals. With respect to the second category, in contrast with the earlier proposal, which sought to differentiate between these based on size *and* purpose, paragraphs 2 and 3 were now to be limited to small extracts (*'courts extraits'*), although acknowledging that for anthologies and chrestomathies these might include entire works (*'les reproductions integrals'*). Moreover, the French reverted to its traditional position and deleted the obligation to condition the exception on the user paying equitable remuneration.

At the Conference, the British delegation said that while it had no difficulty with the mandatory exception on 'revues de presse', it could not support the parts of the French proposal as regard other borrowings. The Bureau's account explains that the British regarded these as too wide (*'trop larges'*) and that, in regard to the issue of quotations, it was not desirable to impose too many charges on the publisher (*'imposer trop de charges à l'editeur'*).[40] Given that in these paragraphs the 'publisher' might be either the owner of copyright in the earlier work or the publisher of the educational work or compilation, the gist of the British objection is not on its face clear; though the most obvious reading is that it objected to the proposals as too generous to users. Other delegations had different objections: the Belgian delegation opposed the limitation to 'short' extracts, observing that the appropriate amount was best assessed by a tribunal in the context of the specific use,[41] while the Danish delegation noted that the provision was unduly limiting, as it precluded the reproduction of the whole work even if it were itself short.[42] The Austrian delegation objected to the removal of Member States' freedom to permit illustrations, in response to which the Director of the Bureau, Bénigne Mentha, observed (contrasting Article 10 with that of Article 9): 'The reproduction of artistic works could be considered as a quotation within the framework of art. 10. . . . It follows that, in works for teaching, for example, artistic works can be reproduced in a reduced form, by way of quotation.'[43]

quotations' derives from Article 35-3 of the 'projet d'ordonnance' of 1945. This linkage could also explain the shift in the logic entailed in the introduction of a 'general' provision not merely formally applicable to foreign works but intended also to be applicable 'in all countries of the Union' and thus to domestic works.

40   *Documents* (1951), 249
41   *Documents* (1951), 248–9.
42   *Documents* (1951), 249.
43   *Documents* (1951), 249

As in 1928, once again the Conference had been unable to find a mechanism to delineate permissible quotation in a manner that accommodated the broad spectrum of uses of works that were thought legitimate without ending up with a provision that was unduly broad. Quantitative criteria and purpose limitations were too constraining. In the end, the Conference only accepted two proposals: one on short quotations from newspapers and periodicals (deriving from paragraph 1 of the French counter-proposal), the other on attribution. In his General Report, the French scholar Marcel Plaisant summed up the difficulty: 'The question of making extracts from known works has always given rise to abuse; on the other hand it is very difficult to limit the right of quotation which, without being of itself a mark of culture, remains a custom of cultured writers.'

While the French delegation had put forward 'an analytical text' regulating the legality of extracts, to avoid disturbing accepted customs, the Conference had to content itself with certain drafting changes, albeit 'of a somewhat substantial character'.[44] The new first paragraph set out the mandatory rule on quotation: 'it shall be permissible in all countries of the Union to make short quotations from newspaper articles and periodicals, as well as to include them in press summaries.'[45] Paragraph 2 retained the traditional freedom, acknowledged since 1886, though added a new qualification that the extent of an extract was to be justified by reference to its purpose. Paragraph 3 adopted the Programme proposal of an obligation to attribute the source of such takings, while incorporating the Hungarian suggestion that the user also acknowledge 'the name of the author, if that name appears on the source'.[46] Plaisant concluded by observing that Article 10 as adopted at Brussels reconciles 'the rights of authors on the one hand with the needs of the public anxious to draw upon the treasures of human knowledge'.[47]

IV STOCKHOLM (1967)

The 1948 text was expanded at the Stockholm Revision in 1967 to take up its current form: the limitations to 'short' quotations, and then only those from newspapers and periodicals, gave way to a broader right of quotation.[48] The key to understanding the development of the quotation right, then, is to take a close look at the developments that led to the Stockholm Revision. As we will see, various attempts were made again

---

[44]   General report of the work of the Diplomatic Conference by Marcel Plaisant, Reporter General at the Plenary Session, Friday, 25 June 1948 in *Documents* (1951) 100, and also in BT 209/900.

[45]   https://wipolex.wipo.int/en/treaties/textdetails/12802.

[46]   *Documents* (1951), 248; Propositions et Contre-Propositions et Observations Presentees par Les Administrations des Pays de L'Union (March 1948) 14 in BT 209/898.

[47]   General report of the work of the Diplomatic Conference by Marcel Plaisant, Reporter General at the Plenary Session, Friday, 25 June 1948, in *Documents* (1951) 100 and BT 209/900.

[48]   The Stockholm Act entered into force on 20 January 1970. For the text, see https://wipolex.wipo.int /en/treaties/textdetails/12801. Article 10(3) Berne reiterated the condition of acknowledgment of source and the name of the author, if 'his name appears thereon'.

to identify the breadth of legitimate quotation by reference to size ('shortness') and purpose. Critical to the success of the revision was deployment of a distinct concept: 'fair practice.'

Moves for the Stockholm Revision began at the very end of the 1950s,[49] with the establishment of a Study Group to formulate a basic proposal. Once this had been done, further consultation occurred with a Committee of Non-Official Experts (1963), and following revisions, consideration by a Committee of Government Experts (1965). The Study Group then developed the draft in response to these Committees, as well as the inputs of various groups including the European Broadcasting Union (EBU), the International Federation of Journalists (IFJ), the International Publishers Association (IPA) and International Gesellschaft Fuer Urheberrecht (INTERGU) as well as a special body, the so-called 'Authors' Consultative Committee' (CCA), set up by BIRPI.[50] The basic proposal was presented at the Diplomatic Conference, and discussed in Main Committee I in June 1967, where the text now present in the Convention was adopted.

A *The Study Group*

The Study Group comprised two Swedish experts and two representatives of the Berne Bureau (at this stage known as the *Bureaux Internationaux Réunis pour la Protection de la Propriété Intellectuelle* (BIRPI)).[51] The Swedish experts were the Supreme Court Judge Torwald Hesser (1917–2004)[52] and Professor Svante

---

[49] Torwald Hesser (1961) (September) *Le Droit D'Auteur* 238 ff, 'Some Questions Concerning the Future Revision of the Berne Convention', (1962) *Le Droit D'Auteur* (English Supplement) 11 (explaining that rapid social and technological progress during the 1950s had brought new problems and made revision more urgent; and referring to decisions made by the Permanent Committee in Munich in 1959 to prepare for a conference in Stockholm with a target date of 1965); C Masouyé, 'The Next Stockholm Conference' (1962) 34 *RIDA* 2, 4; The Editorial Committee (1962) 36–7 *RIDA* 2.

[50] The Authors' Consultative Committee, established in 1962, was composed of seven representatives from ALAI (International Literary and Artistic Association), seven from BIEM (the International Bureau for Mechanical Reproduction) and eleven from CISAC (International Confederation of Societies of Authors and Composers): see Report of the Authors Consultative Committee, BIRPI: DA/22/7, pp. 40-41 (Annex). The 'CCA' issued two reports: one (BIRPI: DA/20/4) on the Study Group's initial proposal; a second (BIRPI: DA/22/7) considering the proposal that was to be considered by the Committee of Government Experts in 1965. The Committee was chaired by Marcel Boutet, the President of ALAI from 1947, and the Rapporteur was Alphonse Tournier of BIEM (an organisation he is said to have founded in 1929).

[51] From 1970, BIRPI became known as the World Intellectual Property Organization.

[52] Seth Carl Erik Torwald Hesser completed his law degree at the University of Stockholm and was made a judge of the Svea High Court in 1949 and of the Supreme Court in 1959. In January 1962, Hesser published 'Some Questions Concerning the Future Revision of the Berne Convention', in the BIRPI-run journal *Droit D'Auteur*, p. 11. Between 1963 and 1979, Hesser was President of the Council of Europe's Legal Committee for Radio and Television. Eva Hemmungs Wirtén described Hesser as the 'architect of the Stockholm conference': see 'Colonial Copyright, Postcolonial Publics: The Berne Convention and the 1967 Stockholm Diplomatic Conference Revisited' (2010) 7(3) *SCRIPT-ed* 532, 537. Both Hesser and Bergström had represented Sweden at the Diplomatic Conference in Rome in 1961 in relation to the Convention for the Protection of Performers, Phonogram Producers and Broadcasting

Bergström (1916–81), a law professor from Uppsala University.[53] The BIRPI experts were its Director, the Dutch law professor Georg Bodenhausen (1905–1997),[54] and the Head of the Copyright Division, French lawyer Claude Masouyé (1924–1986).[55] The Study Group met on several occasions in Stockholm and Geneva and circulated the resulting proposals on 1 June 1963.[56]

Importantly, the Study Group regarded its mandate under Article 24 of the Brussels Act of Berne, which referred to 'improvements intended to perfect the system', as broad and not limited merely to extending rights granted under international law. The Group said it encompassed 'also the general development of copyright by reforms intended to make the rules relating to it more simple to apply, as well as to adapt them to social, technical and economic conditions of the contemporary community'.[57] Under this broad perspective, the Conference would ultimately consider a Protocol dealing with Developing Countries,[58] a matter that was

Organizations. For a photographic portrait of Hesser, see A. Bogsch, *The First Twenty Five Years of the World Intellectual Property Organization from 1967 to 1992* (Geneva: WIPO, 1992) 24.

[53] Widely regarded as the inventor of 'extended collective licensing', Bergström had written a doctoral thesis on collective bargaining at Uppsala in 1948 and published widely on copyright, including issues relating to broadcasting. See S Bergström, 'Current Problems Concerning Broadcasting in the International Field' (1958) 51 *EBU Review (B)* 21–6; (1959) 25 *RIDA* 120-159. On Bergström's background, see Thomas Riis and Jens Schovsbo, 'Extended Collective Licences and the Nordic Experience' (2010) 33 *Col Jo L & Arts* 471, 473, fn. 4; Stig Strömholm, (1981) SvJT 398–9, at https://svjt .se/svjt/1981/398.

[54] Georg Hendrik Christiaan Bodenhausen succeeded Jacques Secrétan as the first non-Swiss director of BIRPI in January 1963 and held that position until 1970 when BIRPI was dissolved and he became Director-General of WIPO, a position he held until 1973. Prior to joining BIRPI, he was a professor of law at the University of Utrecht from 1946 to 1962, as well as a practising lawyer in The Hague. He had received an LLM from the University of Leiden in 1927 and had been Rapporteur-General of the Committee of Experts on Neighbouring Rights (Rome, 1951) and was Vice-President of ALAI (the Association Littéraire et Artistique Internationale). Bodenhausen had represented the Netherlands at the Brussels Revision of Berne in 1948 and at the Universal Copyright Convention conference in Geneva in 1952. Bodenhausen authored a guide to the Paris Convention. He died in Lausanne in 1997. For a portrait, see www.wipo.int/about-wipo/en/dgo/former_dgs.html and WIPO, *The First Twenty Five Years*, 23.

[55] Claude Masouyé, born in 1924, had studied at the Ecole des Sciences Politiques, University of Paris; was Assistant Professor of Law, University of Paris, 1947–9 and was Charge de Mission, Office of the Head of State, France, 1945–8. He seems to have become involved in copyright in the late 1940s, when he took up the post of Director for Foreign Affairs, Society of Authors & Composers, France, a position he held from 1949 to 1961. From there, he moved to BIRPI, where in 1961 he became Head of the Copyright Division, BIRPI, 1961–9; He went on to become Senior Counsellor, Head, External Relations Division, WIPO, 1969–73, and Director, Office of the Director General, WIPO, from 1973.

[56] BIRPI: DA/20/2 (located, inter alia, at TNA: BT209/1244, item 11).

[57] DA/20/2, p. 5. Cf. Sam Ricketson and Jane C Ginsburg, *International Copyright and Neighbouring Rights: The Berne Convention and Beyond* (2nd ed., Oxford University Press 2006) [3.52], 123, who suggest this wider perspective was only adopted in order to accommodate developing countries. It is clear that not all those involved in the process agreed with the broad approach taken by the Study Group: Report of the Authors Consultative Committee, BIRPI: DA/22/7, p. 2 (arguing that reforms should be limited to expanding the protection of authors).

[58] Following the recommendation adopted by the African States at the Brazzaville copyright seminar, in Republic of Congo, 5–10 August 1963. On this, see Ricketson and Ginsburg (2006), [14.08], 888 et seq.

to prove extremely controversial. However, it also informed the Study Group's views on the formulation of limitations.[59]

While Torwald Hesser had not initially thought it would be feasible for the Stockholm Revision to reform Article 10 on quotation,[60] the Study Group decided to do so. The Study Group made a number of proposals that are relevant to the decision to expand the 'quotation right' (though, in contrast with earlier conferences, these did not involve amendment of the provision on educational compilations – Article 10(2) of the Brussels text). First, and most important, was the removal of the right of free reproduction by the press that had been recognised in Article 9(2) of the Brussels Act.[61] 'In consequence of this modification, the Study Group submits a more general drafting of Article 10 relating to the right of quotation.'[62] This was to accommodate cases 'where there is a genuine need for literal reproduction' (whereas recasting the informative content of an article was regarded as not falling within copyright), 'to satisfy the needs of the press as regards giving accounts of the ingredients of articles which have appeared in other newspaper or periodicals'.[63] However, if this was to be achieved, the Study Group proposed that the limitation to 'short quotations' be removed, for three interconnected reasons: first, it might be necessary to reproduce 'fairly considerable proportions' to provide 'sufficient direction' on various subjects of public discussion; further, that lengthy quotation might be 'necessary to ensure the reporting [of another author's] opinions in a proper and exact manner'; and third, 'fairly extensive quotation' may be necessary 'as the point of departure for a reply'. Consequently, the Study Group suggested that the delimitation of the exception would best be achieved by reference to two norms: 'the rules generally accepted and developed in this field'; and that 'the right of quotation can only be exercised to the extent delimited by its purpose'. These were articulated as the conditions of 'fair practice' and that 'the extent [be] justified by the purpose'.[64] In many respects these two concepts, particularly 'fair practice', were to prove the key to reaching consensus.

If the Study Group's reformulation of the quotation exception as regards newspaper and journal articles was part of an overall narrowing of the public domain, its proposal to apply the quotation right to other works looked on its face to be an

---

[59] The Study Group, however, rejected British suggestions for a 'basic re-arrangement of the convention': *General Report of the Swedish/BIRPI Study Group Established at 1st June 1963*, BIRPI: DA/20/2, p.6.

[60] Torwald Hesser (1961) (September) *Le Droit D'Auteur* 238 ff, 'Some Questions Concerning the Future Revision of the Berne Convention', (1962) *Le Droit D'Auteur* (English Supplement) 11 (at 14, suggesting that while the 'advantage of keeping the Convention in tune with reality speaks in favour of the revision of [Article 10(1)] ... it would be too big a task for the Stockholm Conference to settle these complicated questions in detail' but considering that Article 10*bis* 'must ... be studied by the future Conference').

[61] BIRPI: DA/20/2 p. 41. The issue had been raised by the International Federation of Journalists.

[62] BIRPI: DA/20/2, p. 8.

[63] BIRPI: DA/20/2, p. 44.

[64] BIRPI: DA/20/2, p. 45.

extension. However, the Study Group did not view it altogether in this way. Rather, it was only a 'literal interpretation' that limited the quotation right under Brussels to newspaper articles, whereas 'in actual fact it is applied, by analogy, to quotations from other works'.[65] The Study Group proposed that this 'field of universal application' should be recognised *expressis verbis*. It noted that this reflected the recognition 'in the field of science' of such a right in relation to theses, books and so forth. In relation to the quotation defence, the proposal was to broaden the Brussels quotation exception from quotations from newspaper articles and periodicals to quotations in general. Although the Study Group proposal thus seemed to have sought merely to recognise in the express terms of the Convention a quotation exception already acknowledged in law and social norms,[66] it recognised that this was in fact an 'enlargement', and suggested therefore that 'it may be desirable to establish yet another condition', that is, that the work quoted had been lawfully made accessible to the public.[67] The Study Group also suggested that it was possible to retain without modification Article 10(3) 'on the duty of mentioning the source and the name of the author in quotations and extracts'.[68] The proposed reformulation was: 'It shall be permissible to make quotations from a work which has been lawfully made accessible to the public, provided that they are compatible with fair practice, and to the extent justified by the purpose.'[69]

B *Committee of (Non-official) Experts*

This proposal was referred to a Committee of Experts, a twenty-two-person committee from twelve countries,[70] as well as representatives from some NGOs (ALAI, BIEM and CISAC). The Committee was chaired by Eugen Ulmer,[71] the Professor at the Institute of Copyright Law, University of Munich, and met in Geneva, 18–23 November 1963.[72] The Committee of Experts, with two abstentions, 'unanimously expressed itself in favour of a new draft' of Article 10(1),[73] though in notably different terms from that proposed by the Study Group. While it agreed with the removal of the qualification that the quotations should be 'short',[74] the Committee proposed a further qualification: the right to quote be limited to quotation for

---

[65] BIRPI: DA/20/2, p. 45.
[66] Pierre Recht 'Should the Berne Convention include a Definition of the Right of Reproduction?' (April 1965) *Copyright* 82–9, 85 (assenting to this point).
[67] BIRPI: DA/20/2, p. 46
[68] BIRPI: DA/20/2, p. 46.
[69] BIRPI: DA/20/3, p. 6a.
[70] A total of sixteen were invited.
[71] Proposed by Switzerland and seconded by the UK.
[72] Alphonse Tournier, 'Le Comité d'experts de Genève' (1964) 42 *RIDA* 27, 40.
[73] BIRPI: DA/22/2, p. 50. Apparently, this was after 'an exhaustive discussion': Preparatory Documents, S/1, in *Records*, 117. The extract from DA/20/29 refers to a 'detailed discussion'.
[74] A French proposal to reinsert the term was rejected by seven votes to four.

'scientific, cultural, informatory or education' purposes.[75] It suggested the following text:

> It shall be permissible to make quotations from a work which has been lawfully made available to the public, provided that they are compatible with fair practice, and in so far as they are justified by the scientific, commentary, instructional or informative purpose in view, including quotations from newspaper articles and periodicals in the form of press summaries.[76]

According to Masouyé, the introduction of a purpose-limitation was thought important to the experts who found the concept of 'fair practice' to be 'a notion of Anglo-Saxon law which seems to some too general and too vague'.[77] The Committee of Non-official Experts also sought for reinsertion of the provision found in Brussels to the effect that the exception covered 'press summaries'/ 'revues de presse'.

C *Second Report of the Study Group*

On 1 July 1964, the Study Group produced a second report in response to the recommendations of the Committee of (Non-official) Experts.[78] As it explained, the Study Group 'could not rid itself of the impression that the list of purposes [proposed by the Committee] was too restricted – for instance, quotations made for an artistic purpose are not included'.[79] No doubt this observation reflected in part the earlier failures to reach agreement on a quotation exception in Rome and Brussels. As the Study Group thought it was 'practically impossible to indicate satisfactorily all the purposes by which quotations must be justified', it decided to reject the Committee's amended text and instead maintain the original proposal. The Study Group did, however, adopt the Committee's suggestion to reincorporate the reference to press summaries from the Brussels text.

In an important parallel development, the Study Group proposed to reformulate Article 9 so as to recognise expressly a reproduction right, the absence of which it saw

---

75 Claude Masouyé, 'Perspectives de revision de la Convention de Berne' (1964) 43 *RIDA* 5, 26; Alphonse Tournier, 'Le Comité d'experts de Genève' (1964) 42 *RIDA* 27, 40. Tournier represented BIEM (*Bureau Internationals des Sociétés gérant les droits d'enregistrement et de reproduction mécanique*) and was also at the later meeting of the Committee of Government Experts.

76 BIRPI: DA/22/2, p. 54. BIRPI: DA 22/7, p. 10 translates 'fair practice' as 'fair dealing'. The translation of Tournier's account that was published in *RIDA*, at 42, uses quite different language, offering a rather literal translation of the French term 'bon usages': 'Are lawful the quotations taken from a work, already rendered lawfully accessible to the public, on condition that they conform to good usage and to the extent justified by the scientific, critical, educational or informative goal to be attained, including articles from newspapers and periodical collections in the form of press reviews.'

77 BIRPI: DA/22/2, p. 26.

78 Claude Masouyé, 'Perspectives de revision de la Convention de Berne' (1964) 43 *RIDA* 5, 10 (also referring to reports from the Authors Consultative Commission and the European Broadcasting Union). The Study Group met on several more occasions in 1964 in Geneva and Stockholm.

79 BIRPI: DA.22/2, p. 54.

as an anomaly.[80] However, in turn, the introduction of such a right meant consideration needed to be given to permissible exceptions, the Study Group noting at least fourteen such exceptions commonly featuring in national law. Instead of elaborating a list,[81] the Study Group suggested 'a formula allowing Member countries ... the possibility of limiting, in certain cases, the recognition or the exercise of the right'.[82] In Article 9(2) of the proposal, therefore, the Study Group suggested that Members should be permitted to operate exceptions 'for specified purposes and on the condition that these purposes should not enter into economic competition with these works'. As regards the interaction with other exceptions, such as those relating to quotation, educational compilations or reporting current events, the Group proposed that the freedom be subject to a requirement to have 'regard to the provisions of [the] Convention' – that is, the specific limitations permitted (or required) elsewhere. The conditions of those provisions 'must always be respected'.[83]

D *Interest Group Inputs*

The Study Group's second (1964) report was reviewed by a number of international organisations: the European Broadcasting Union (EBU), the International Federation of Journalists (IFJ), the International Publishers Association (IPA) and International Gesellschaft Fuer Urheberrecht (INTERGU), as well as a special body, the so-called 'Authors' Consultative Committee' (CCA), set up by BIRPI.[84] The Reports from each of these groups were included in the documents made available to the Committee of Government Experts in 1965.

The Authors Consultative Committee, which met in October 1964, commented critically on the Study Group's revised proposal.[85] The CCA said it was disquieted by the proposal, which involved a considerable extension of the quotation right. In

---

[80]   BIRPI: DA/22/2, p.47. The Study Group may have been influenced by Professor Maro Fabiani's article 'Le droit de Reproduction et La revision de la Convention de Berne' in (November 1964) *Le Droit D'Auteur* 286. Cf. Pierre Recht 'Should the Berne Convention Include a Definition of the Right of Reproduction?' (April 1965) *Copyright* 82–9 (adding the right in express terms, and then subjecting it to exceptions such as to render the right non-existent, a 'serious error').

[81]   BIRPI: DA/22/2, p. 49, fn. 24.

[82]   BIRPI: DA/22/2, p. 8.

[83]   BIRPI: DA/22/2, p. 48.

[84]   The Authors' Consultative Committee, established in 1962, was composed of seven representatives from ALAI, seven from BIEM and eleven from CISAC. The 'CCA' issued two reports: one (BIRPI: DA/20/4) on the Study Group's initial proposal; a second (BIRPI: DA/22/7) considering the proposal that was to be considered by the Committee of Government Experts in 1965. The Committee was chaired by Marcel Boutet, the President of ALAI from 1947, and the Rapporteur was Alphonse Tournier of BIEM (an organisation he is said to have founded in 1929). Tournier, the father of SACEM director Jean-Loup Tournier, died in 1968. Boutet, who had co-authored with Robert Plaisant a book on the Brussels version, died 12 December 1971: Claude Masouyé, Obituary (December 1972) *Copyright* 61–2.

[85]   Report of the Authors Consultative Committee, BIRPI: DA/22/7, pp. 9–10 (considering the proposal that was to be considered by the Committee of Government Experts in 1965). See below, Ch 3, Section 1, p. 34.

particular, the CCA was concerned that the quotation exception now covered 'all categories of works' and thereby introduced 'dangerous possibilities', such as allowing quotation 'in the domain of musical works'. The CCA opposed the removal of the 'guarantee' provided by the qualification that a quotation be 'short' and stated that it would be preferable were the exception limited to use for specified purposes, as had been proposed by the Committee of Non-official Experts.

The European Broadcasting Union, an association of public service broadcasters that had been founded in 1950 (with the post-war demise of the International Broadcasting Union and failure of the International Broadcasting Organization), also produced a report commenting on the Study Group's proposal, and this was included in the documents circulated to the Committee of Government Experts.[86] Although its main interests lay elsewhere, the EBU indicated that it had concerns over the removal of Article 9(2) from the Brussels text, given that it might be necessary to allow recirculation of press articles in developing countries 'not merely in the form of quotations but in their entirety'. However, given the proposal to add special provisions for developing countries, the EBU indicated that it was content with the new proposed Article 9, given that it would be subject to the limitations in Article 10, 10bis and 11bis.[87] However, it warned that the proposed formula according to which Members were free to operate limitations on the (newly recognised) reproduction right, with its focus on 'economic competition', might prove difficult to apply, and if broadly interpreted might threaten the operation of many exceptions recognised in national laws. It proposed the addition of a qualification, for example, that the economic competition identified be '"adverse", "harmful", "unreasonable", "unfair", or something to the like effect'.[88]

The International Federation of Journalists, an organisation of (then around 30) national professional associations of journalists, said it approved of the extension of the quotation right in Article 10(1),[89] though it sought that some explanations be added to the terms of the text. In particular, it sought to clarify the notion of quotation by reference to the dictionary *Grand Larousse*, according to which (the IFJ stated) 'a quotation means a "brief" statement, the repetition of a passage from a longer text'.[90] The proposed deletion of the word 'short' from the formulation of the quotation exception, it stated, should 'not give rise to the false impression that quotations need no longer be "short" or "brief" in order to be lawful'. The IFJ indicated that it was content with the concept of 'fair practice', stating that 'the constituent factors of this expression are sufficiently familiar to bona fide journalists and applied often enough by them to require no further explanation'. In contrast, it

---

[86]   BIRPI: DA/22/8.
[87]   BIRPI: DA/22/8, p. 14.
[88]   BIRPI: DA/22/8, p. 15.
[89]   Indeed, it quoted approvingly from an earlier report (from 1930) in which it had stated that '[c]opyright protection is limited generally and universally by the right to make quotation, which [Swiss scholar from Lausanne University] de Rham calls an absolute necessity of intellectual life, without which no discussion would be possible'.
[90]   BIRPI: DA/22/9, p. 7.

was more concerned with the notion of 'purpose', reiterating that 'the purpose of the quotation must always to be to clarify the text' not 'simply to reproduce an interesting or amusing text'.[91] The IFJ also sought to articulate a rather narrow conception of 'press summary', distinct from 'pilfering pure and simple', which was characterised by 'the number of cuttings, their brevity, and their methodical arrangement with a view to proving a point'. Indeed, for a good press summary, 'one has to be capable of condensing it in a few words for the benefit of the public'. The Report sought to exclude from lawful press summaries 'the regular reproduction of cuttings, compiled, for instance, by a press agency specializing in this type of service for newspapers wishing to subscribe'.[92]

The International Publishers' Association (IPA), then with members from twenty-eight countries,[93] adopted a report on the Study Group's proposals at its Washington Congress in May/June 1965.[94] This approved of the stipulation of a right of reproduction and also the adoption of (what it called) 'uniform directions' as to permissible limitations thereto. It asked that these describe 'the notions of non professional authorized uses, such as "personal use," "fair use" or "fair dealing"'. It also approved of the general regulation of 'the rights of reproducing excerpts and quotations'.

The International Gesellschaft Fuer Urheberrecht (INTERGU), formed in Berlin in 1954,[95] offered brief remarks on the proposed changes as regards the quotation exception,[96] agreeing that the 'proposal can basically be approved', though in the case of musical works, it suggested that quotation 'should be permissible only in writings'.[97] INTERGU also commented on the proposed changes to Article 10bis, indicating a preference for the Study Group's original proposal, rather than the more flexible version contained in the 1964 Report.

91   BIRPI: DA/22/9, p. 8.
92   BIRPI: DA/22/9, p. 9.
93   Founded in Paris in 1896 with the specific purpose of promoting the protection of copyright, the IPA is an international federation of national publisher associations.
94   BIRPI: DA/22/186.
95   It was then headed by Eric Schultze of the German collecting society, GEMA. INTERGU still exists, with its seat at GEMA, though with a much less obvious international dimension. See www .intergu.de. Schultze was also a CISAC representative on the Authors' Consultative Committee.
96   BIRPI: DA/22/10, p. 9. In relation to proposed Article 9(2), INTERGU argued that 'private recording of sounds or images' not be included within Article 9(2), appearing to suggest that any such exception falls under Article 13(2) and, like that, be subject to a requirement to pay 'just remuneration'.
97   Pierre Recht, President of the Belgian Copyright Commission and a Member of the Legislative Committee of CISAC, noted that Schulze had made this point in a letter to the Authors' Consultative Committee, and indicated his agreement with the point: 'Should the Berne Convention include a Definition of the Right of Reproduction?' (April 1965) Copyright 82–9, 85.

E *Committee of Government Experts*

The conclusions of the Study Group, and the views of the interests groups, were considered by the Committee of Government Experts, which met between 5 July and 14 July 1965. Thirty-five of the fifty-four eligible countries were present (represented by seventy-six delegates), along with seventeen NGOs, the US as an observer, and representatives of the ILO and UNESCO.[98] Many had proposed amendments of the draft Treaty text that had been circulated in advance of the meeting.

France, for example, proposed further limits to the right of quotation, to restore the limitation that quotations be 'short', as well as to require that they be limited 'to the extent justified by the critical, controversial, educational, scientific or informatory nature of the work in which they are incorporated'.[99] It also sought to limit the reference to quotation by way of press summary by a proviso that such use is 'in conformity with established practice'. The Swiss delegation also proposed to impose further limitations on the quotation right, in accordance with the views of the Committee of Non-official Experts.[100] It observed:

> The right to make quotations from all works places a considerable restriction on the protection of authors. The Swiss Delegation is of the opinion that the scope of the right should be determined in as precise a manner as possible, especially in view of the fact that it is proposed to delete the adjective 'short'. The condition formulated in the text proposed by the Study Group ('to the extent justified by the purpose') seems too sweeping to the Swiss Delegation, which would prefer the text adopted in November 1963 by the Committee of Non-Governmental Experts. Indeed, it seems necessary that the purposes for which the quotation may be made should be restricted.

The Committee held 'lengthy discussions' as to the proposed Article 10(1).[101] While the delegations of Belgium, Italy, the Netherlands and Yugoslavia indicated their support for the further refinement of Article 10(1), which was otherwise 'too vague', other delegates supported the Study Group's proposed text. The Report summarises the views of the latter in this way:

> They pointed out, in particular, that the enumeration of the purposes pursued, as submitted in the proposals of Switzerland and France, did not cover all the cases: for example, judicial purposes (India), political purposes (parliamentary speeches), aesthetic purposes (quotation from one musical work in another musical work) and the purposes of entertainment (Federal Republic of Germany); that such an enumeration was too restrictive and that the notion of short quotations could be interpreted by the courts in ways that differed according to the country (Monaco); that it was difficult to win the agreement of the countries on a text that was too strict

---

[98] (1965) *Copyright* 194–7.
[99] BIRPI: DA/22/23.
[100] BIRPI: DA/22/17.
[101] Preparatory Documents, S/1, in *Records*, 117.

(Tunisia); and that the formula adopted by the Study Group had the advantage of being clear and concise (India).[102]

In the end, the Committee rejected the proposed limitations to Article 10(1) – the French proposal by twenty-one to eight, the Swiss proposal by fourteen to ten. It also rejected two further proposals, one from the United Kingdom to make the quotation exception optional rather than mandatory,[103] and another, from Sweden, to give Member States freedom to determine the conditions under which it would be permissible to make quotations (so that the existence of the exception would be required, but its scope left flexible). The former was rejected by nineteen votes to seven, and the latter by sixteen votes to eight. Ultimately, the Study Group's text was supported by twenty-one votes to six.[104]

F *The Draft Treaty*

Following the meeting of the Committee of Government Experts, the text was referred back to the Study Group, which made certain alterations, before circulating the draft text for consideration at the diplomatic conference.[105] Thus, on the issue of the quotation right, the text of the Proposal was identical to that recommended by the Committee of Government Experts.

G *The Intergovernmental Conference*

The final stage at which the quotation right was considered was at the intergovernmental conference itself. The programme draft treaty was subject to a host of tabled amendments. France, Italy and Switzerland sought to narrow the proposed exception. France again proposed amending Article 10(1) by reintroducing the limitation to 'short' quotation.[106] Italy suggested that if the qualification of Article 10(1) to only 'short' quotations was not adopted, there should instead be an express qualification of the purposes for which quotation could be lawful.[107] Switzerland sought further qualification of proposed Article 10(1), emphasising that the quotation must occupy 'a subordinate position', by adding that such quotations only be allowed 'to the extent that they serve as an explanation, reference or illustration in the context in which they are used'.[108] South Africa and the UK, in contrast, were concerned with how the different exceptions

---

[102]   BIRPI: DA/22/33 p. 10.
[103]   Perhaps William Wallace proposed this because he appreciated that the 'fair dealing for criticism or review' exception in the Copyright Act 1956 fell someway short of the mandatory right being proposed. See BIRPI: DA/22/33, p. 10, [53].
[104]   BIRPI: DA/22/33 p. 10.
[105]   Preparatory Documents, S/1, in *Records*, 77.
[106]   Preparatory Documents, S/13, in *Records*, 615.
[107]   Preparatory Documents, S/13, in *Records*, 623.
[108]   Preparatory Documents, S/17, in *Records*, 664.

interacted. South Africa sought clarification that Article 9 was subject to the provisions in Article 2*bis*, 10, 10*bis*, 11*bis*(3) and 13.[109] South Africa and the UK, in contrast, were concerned with how the different exceptions interacted. The UK sought some further clarification of the provision in Article 10(2), which it suggested was rendered superfluous by Article 10(1), proposing that, if maintained, Article 10(2) should not apply to 'complete works'. It also sought a statement clarifying the interrelationship between rights and exceptions, suggesting that where an exception was created to a specific right, that exception should be treated as 'governing all cases with which it deals'. BIRPI circulated a document collating the observations.[110]

The adoption of the quotation right was considered in Main Committee I, where Professor Eugen Ulmer chaired proceedings, with Bergström acting as Rapporteur and Masouyé as Secretary.[111] The Committee began by considering the issue of the reproduction right on 15 June 1967,[112] with the question of quotation in Article 10(1) being dealt with the following day, 16 June 1967. Discussion began with the two proposed amendments to the Programme text, one from Switzerland and the other from France.[113] The Swiss amendment proposed two changes: to re-introduce the qualification that the quotation be short and to define the purpose of the quotation by limiting permissible reuse 'to the extent that they serve as an explanation, reference or illustration in the context in which they are used'.[114] The French delegation indicated its support for the Swiss, explaining that some such qualification was required because the notion of 'quotation' did not of itself 'involve the idea of brevity'.[115] Perhaps surprisingly, given its stance on press articles, the Hungarian delegation supported the Swiss amendment, and the Italian expert Vitorio de Sanctis also spoke in favour of retaining the limitation 'short' from the Brussels text.[116] In contrast, the British, German, Austrian and Swedish delegates spoke against the amendments, noting that quotations might be legitimate but not short,[117] while the Monaco delegate highlighted that the adjective short would raise particular problems in relation to the quotation of artistic works, where moral rights would be implicated if only part was used, and was thus not desirable.[118] Torwald Hesser, a key member of the Study Group, also noted that the Swiss proposal 'did not enumerate sufficient purposes'; it was not sufficiently flexible. If the motive for adding such a condition was fear that the exception would be too capacious, he

[109]   Preparatory Documents, S/13, in *Records*, 629.
[110]   Preparatory Documents, S/18, in *Records*, 665 ff, with Article 9, 10 and 10*bis* dealt with at 669–70.
[111]   Svante Bergström, Report of the Work of the Main Committee I, *Records*, 1131. Also published in (1967) *Copyright* 183 ff.
[112]   Minutes of the Fifth Meeting on Main Committee I in *Records*, 851; Svante Bergström, Report of the Work of the Main Committee I, [83], *Records*, 1145.
[113]   Preparatory Documents, S/45 and S/68, in *Records*, 688 and 690.
[114]   Preparatory Documents, S/68, in *Records* 690.
[115]   Robert Touzery, in Minutes, [762], *Records*, 860.
[116]   István Timár at [763], *Records*, 860; De Sanctis, in Minutes, [770], *Records*, 861.
[117]   William Wallace, Dietrich Reimer, Robert Dittrich and Torwald Hesser, in Minutes, [764]–[767], *Records*, 860–1.
[118]   George Straschnov, in Minutes, [769], *Records*, 861.

noted, the real limitation was to be found in the 'fair practice' condition.[119] The Tunisian, Indian, Irish and Czech delegates all spoke in support of the Programme, as presented, the latter (Vojtěch Strnad) explaining that though Article 10(1) had been linked with the abolition of Article 9(2) from Brussels, the decision to retain Article 9(2) (as Article 10bis(1) of the revised text) that had just been taken by the Committee need not affect the question of Article 10(1). Significantly, he noted, Article 9(2) of the Brussels text had no application where express reservation had been made and only applied to limited types of material. The Swiss amendment was duly rejected by twenty-seven votes to ten. In light of this, the French amendment was not pushed. The fair quotation exception was adopted as proposed in the programme, and it was quickly agreed that the provision should apply to translations.[120]

[119] Minutes, [767], *Records*, 861.
[120] Amendment proposed by Czechoslovakia, Hungary, Poland, Preparatory Documents, S/51, in *Records*, 688; Chairman, Minutes, [780] in *Records*, 861.

3

Preliminary Considerations about the Nature of the Quotation Exception

I THE MANDATORY NATURE OF THE QUOTATION EXCEPTION

A *Article 10(1) Berne as Mandatory*

An important starting point is our claim that Article 10 of the Berne Convention creates an obligation on Members of the Union to recognise a limitation on the copyright that allows for quotation. The proposition is based primarily on the language used: Article 10 begins with the words 'It shall be permissible ... '.[1] This imperative language may be contrasted with Article 10(2) Berne, which, in relation to exceptions for education, states: 'It shall be a matter for legislation in the countries of the Union ... to permit.' Similar permissive language is also found in Article 10*bis* in relation to reporting current events and Article 9(2), which allows exceptions to the reproduction right 'in certain special cases'. The language of Article 10(1) is distinct and clearly reads as mandatory rather than permissive. Although there is barely any reference to the mandatory nature of the exception in the Stockholm *travaux*,[2] the limitation is described in terms that reflect its basis in the entitlement of the user. The BIRPI Study Group (1963), rejecting a prior formulation that limited the exception to short quotation, repeatedly referred to the exception as 'the right to make quotations' or the 'right of quotation',[3] language that was carried through into the proposal for the Stockholm Conference[4] and that is entirely consistent with the

---

[1]   The French 'sont licites' is perhaps even clearer, in that it indicates quotations are permitted rather than permissible. Moreover, Article 10(1) of the Brussels version of Berne stated 'Dans tous les Pays de l'Union sont licites ... '.

[2]   The language reproduced that in the Brussels text. As explained in Chapter 2, pp. 13–14, at Brussels the Bureau had not made any proposal on quotation, but the French did. The French proposal was presented as 'mandatory' and 'proclaiming the legality in all countries' of short quotations of articles from newspapers and periodicals. It is interesting too that a mandatory right of quotation had been proposed at Rome, though the language was different: 'Il est permis ... '. See Chapter 2, Section II, p. 11.

[3]   WIPO, *Records of the Intellectual Property Conference of Stockholm, June 11 to July 14, 1967*, vol. I and vol. II (WIPO 1971) ('*Records*'), 116.

[4]   Document S/1, 'Proposals for Revising the Substantive Copyright Provisions, Articles 1–20 (Prepared by the Government of Sweden with the Assistance of BIRPI)', in *Records*, 117.

mandatory formulation of Article 10(1).[5] Moreover, it based its reasoning on the widespread acceptance of such a right in the 'field of science'.[6] It is likely that the acceptance of the mandatory nature of the quotation right at the Stockholm Conference arose from the fact that at both the Rome[7] and Brussels Revision Conferences, there was apparently acceptance of the notion, even though it was not until the Brussels Act in 1948 that the right of quotation was introduced. The prior version of Article 10(1) (the Brussels Act version of Berne) stated: '(1) It shall be permissible in all countries of the Union to make short quotations from newspaper articles and periodicals, as well to include them in press summaries.'[8] Once again, we note the mandatory language 'it shall be permissible' as well as the fact that the *Rapporteur* to the 1948 Conference, Marcel Plaisant, referred to the 'right of quotation'.[9]

The *travaux* of the Stockholm Revision, which is where the existing Article 10(1) Berne was introduced, do not contain any discussion of the rationale for the mandatory status of Article 10(1); however, they do indicate that it was acknowledged and accepted. Perhaps surprisingly, some resistance came from the United Kingdom,[10] and when the Committee of Government Experts met in Geneva in July 1965, the UK tabled an amendment that would have aligned the status of Article 10(1) with the various other exceptions recognised in the Convention, or then being proposed. However, despite receiving support from the Netherlands, the Committee of Government Experts rejected the UK proposal by nineteen votes to seven and a Swedish proposal to offer Member States the freedom to establish conditions was likewise rejected, this time by sixteen votes to eight.[11] The matter was not raised thereafter, but the special status of Article 10(1) was clear.[12] By way of contrast, at the

---

[5] Annette Kur and Henning Grosse Ruse-Khan, 'Enough Is Enough – The Notion of Binding Ceilings in International Intellectual Property Protection' in Annette Kur and Marianne Levin (eds.), *Intellectual Property Rights in a Fair World Trade System – Proposals for Reform of TRIPS* (Edward Elgar 2011), ch. 8, 359–407, 393, fn. 111.

[6] Preparatory Documents, S/1, in *Records*, 117. See also Pierre Recht, 'Should the Berne Convention include a Definition of the Right of Reproduction?' (April 1965) *Copyright* 82–9, 85 ('I agree to this being stated *expressis verbis*, because this is the de facto situation'). The proposers of the Brussels programme acknowledged the universal quality of the right to quote: *Documents de la Conférence réunis A Bruxelles du 5 au 26 Juin 1948* (BIRPI 1951), 244. ('A scientific work, even if it is not strictly speaking critical, must be able to contain quotations. Think of a book of literary history, or just history. Such works are inconceivable without references and quotes.')

[7] Union Internationale pour La Protection des Oeuvres Littéraire et Artistique, *Actes de la Conférence Réunie A Rome Du 7 Mai au 2 Juin 1928* (Berne: Bureau de L'Union, 1929), 250.

[8] Brussels Act of Berne may be found here: https://wipolex.wipo.int/en/treaties/textdetails/12802 (accessed 21 January 2020).

[9] *Documents de la Conférence réunis A Bruxelles du 5 au 26 Juin 1948* (BIRPI 1951), 99 ('le droit de citation').

[10] This contrasts with the position taken by the UK at the Brussels Conference: *Documents* (1951), 249.

[11] BIRPI: DA/22/33, p. 10, paras. [53]–[54]. See herein Ch 2, Section IV, Part E, p. 26.

[12] See Pierre Recht, 'Should the Berne Convention include a Definition of the Right of Reproduction?' (April 1965) *Copyright* 82–9, 84–5 ('The power to legislate freely on this point was removed from national legislations [*sic*], and the latter have had imposed on them a minimum below which they cannot go on the plea that the quotation must be short'). See also S Gerbrandy and F Klaver, 'La Revision de la Convention de Berne' (1967) 52 *RIDA* 5, 54 ('a coercive limitation on author's

intergovernmental Conference in June 1967, amendments were made to Article 10*bis*(1), which re-enacted Article 9(2) from the Brussels Act, 'to avoid the impression' that it was compulsory.[13] In its Brussels form (inherited from the Rome Revision Conference in 1928), Article 9(2) had stated, in mandatory terms, that 'articles ... may be reproduced ["peuvent être reproduits"]. . . unless the reproduction thereof is expressly reserved', thus seemingly leaving no freedom to Member States as to whether to adopt such an exception.[14] This was altered at Stockholm, but the form of Article 10(1) was left intact.

The mandatory nature of the exception has also been recognised by many of the leading commentaries on the Convention. The WIPO *Guide to the Berne Convention* itself refers to the limitation as arising 'from the Convention itself'.[15] Leading US copyright scholar Paul Goldstein asserts categorically that 'Article 10(1) of the Berne Paris Text obligates member countries to permit "quotations"'.[16] Professors Sam Ricketson and Jane Ginsburg refer to Article 10 as the one Berne exception that comes closest to embodying a 'user right' to make quotation: Article 10(1) exceptions are matters that *must* rather than *may* appear in national laws.[17] Lest it be thought that this is primarily an interpretation offered by Anglo-American scholars, Catalan Professor Raquel Xalabarder,[18] German scholars Annette Kur, Martin Senftleben and Henning Grosse Ruse-Khan[19] and Dutch Professor Bernt

copyright' which Member States cannot reduce). Professor Gerbrandy was on the Drafting Committee at the Stockholm Conference.

13   Bergström, Report, [102], in *Records*, 1149.
14   Ricketson and Ginsburg (2006), [13.53], 800.
15   Claude Masouyé, *Guide to the Berne Convention* (WIPO 1978), 58. The Guide was authored by Masouyé, a member of the Study Group.
16   Paul Goldstein, *International Copyright: Principles, Law, Practice* (Oxford University Press 2001) 303. See also Graeme B Dinwoodie and Rochelle C Dreyfuss, *A Neo-Federalist Vision of TRIPS* (Oxford University Press 2012), 185 ('the Berne Convention includes a mandatory quotation right'); Daniel J Gervais, 'Making Copyright Whole: A Principled Approach to Copyright Exceptions and Limitations' (2008) 5 *U Ottawa L & Tech J* 1, 9 and 20, noting that the quotation right is mandatory.
17   Ricketson and Ginsburg (2006), [13.42], 788–9. See also Jane C Ginsburg, 'The Most Moral of Rights: The Right to Be Recognized as the Author of One's Work' (2016) 8 *Geo Mason J Int'l Com L* 44, 50, and Graham Greenleaf and David Lindsay, *Public Rights: Copyright's Public Domain* (Cambridge University Press 2018), 134, 141, 357, referring to Article 10(1) as a mandatory exception.
18   Raquel Xalabarder, *Study on Copyright Limitations and Exceptions for Educational Activities in North America, Europe, Caucasus, Central Asia and Israel* (WIPO, 5 November 2009), SCCR/19/8, 19-20; R Xalabarder, 'The Remunerated Statutory Limitation for News Aggregation and Search Engines Proposed by the Spanish Government; Its Compliance with International and EU Law' (30 September 2014), IN3 Working Paper Series. Available at SSRN: https://ssrn.com /abstract=2504596 (accessed 28 January 2020), 2; R Xalabarder, 'Press Publisher Rights in the New Copyright in the Digital Single Market Draft Directive', CREATe Working Paper 2016/15 (December 2016), 13; R Xalabarder, 'On-line Teaching and Copyright: Any Hopes for an EU Harmonized Playground?' in Paul Torremans (ed.), *Copyright Law: A Handbook of Contemporary Research* (Edward Elgar 2007), ch. 15, 373–401, 397 and also 398: 'BC sets a *maximum protection* and the quotation exception is part of that ceiling.'
19   Annette Kur and Henning Grosse Ruse-Khan, 'Enough Is Enough – The Notion of Binding Ceilings in International Intellectual Property Protection' in Annette Kur and Marianne Levin (eds.),

Hugenholtz have all made the same point. Co-authoring with Goldstein, Hugenholtz argues that Article 10 represents 'the only instance of a mandatory limitation in an international copyright treaty'.[20] Martin Senftleben has also described the 'right of quotation' recognised in Article 10(1) as a 'mandatory use privilege'.[21]

Nevertheless, it should be noted that a few commentators regard Article 10(1), despite its mandatory language and the supporting *travaux*, as an optional exception.[22] Their central argument is that the mandatory nature of the exception does not sit well with the 'logic' of Berne.[23] This logic is tied to two key principles of Berne: minimum rights for works of foreign authors and the principle of national treatment. First, the Convention purports to lay down minimum standards, Union Members being permitted to create more author-protective rules and to enter into agreements to recognise such rules, according to Articles 19 and 20, respectively.[24] How can a mandatory rule fit with this approach? Second, the minimum standards in the Convention apply only to foreign, Berne-qualifying works. This means that a Union Member, while it would have to apply the quotation exception to foreign

     Intellectual Property Rights in a Fair World Trade System: Proposals for Reform of TRIPS (Edward Elgar 2011), ch. 8, 359–407, 380 (the ordinary meaning of Art 10(1) 'does not lend itself to any other understanding than that it is meant to be binding'); Annette Kur, 'Of Oceans, Islands, and Inland Water – How Much Room for Exceptions and Limitations under the Three Step Test?' (2009) 8 *Rich J Global L & Bus* 287, 290 ('the copyright holder cannot enjoin others from using parts of it for quotation purposes, to the extent this complies with the requirements set out in Article 10(1) Berne'); Annette Kur, 'Limitations and Exceptions under the Three-Step Test – How Much Room to Walk the Middle Ground' in Annette Kur and Marianne Levin (eds.), *Intellectual Property Rights in a Fair World Trade System: Proposals for Reform of TRIPS* (Edward Elgar 2011), ch. 5, 208–61, 217: 'one rare example of a mandatory provisions is found in Article 10.1 RBC'.

20   Paul Goldstein and Bernt Hugenholtz, *International Copyright: Principles, Law, Practice* (Oxford University Press 2010), 379, [11.4.1]. See also Bernt Hugenholtz and Ruth L Okediji, 'Conceiving an International Instrument on Limitations and Exceptions to Copyright', Amsterdam Law School Legal Studies Research Paper No 2012-43 at http://ssrn.com/abstract=2017629 (7 March 2012), 15–16 (accessed 28 January 2020). For another authors' rights scholar, see Lucie Guibault, *Copyright Limitations and Contracts: An Analysis of the Contractual Overridability of Limitations on Copyright* (Kluwer 2002), 32: 'the right to quote is the most important limitation for the safeguard of the user's freedom of expression', which notes the mandatory nature of Article 10(1) Berne.

21   See Martin Senftleben, 'Quotation, Parody and Fair Use' in B Hugenholtz, A Quaedvlieg and D Visser (eds.), *A Century of Dutch Copyright: 1912–2012* (DeLex 2012), 354.

22   Mihály Ficsor, *The Law of Copyright and the Internet* (Oxford University Press 2002), 259 ff., [5.09]; S von Lewinski, *International Copyright Law and Policy* (Oxford University Press 2008), 156, [5.163]; J Blomqvist, *Primer on International Copyright and Related Rights* (Edward Elgar 2014), 159–60.

23   Ficsor, *The Law of Copyright and the Internet*, 260–1, [5.11]. The same point has been raised in relation to the mandatory exceptions introduced by the Marrakesh Treaty to Facilitate Access to Published Works for Persons Who Are Blind, Visually Impaired or Otherwise Print Disabled 2013 ('Marrakesh Treaty'), www.wipo.int/treaties/en/ip/marrakesh/ (accessed 21 January 2020): see Sam Ricketson and Jane Ginsburg, 'The Berne Convention: Historical and Institutional Aspects' in Daniel J Gervais (ed.), *International Intellectual Property: A Handbook of Contemporary Research* (Edward Elgar 2015), ch. 1, 3–36, 32–4.

24   Berne Convention, Article 19 ('The provisions of this Convention shall not preclude the making of a claim to the benefit of any greater protection which may be granted by legislation in a country of the Union') and Article 20 (wherein special agreements are permitted between Members of the Union 'in so far as such agreements grant to authors more extensive rights than those granted by the Convention').

works, might exempt its domestic works from such an exception and, in so doing, offer better protection for its domestic authors.[25] Yet, if this were to happen, the odd situation would arise whereby the Union Member would breach the principle of national treatment contained in Article 5(1) Berne. Thus, indirectly, Union Members would need to introduce the exception for domestic authors,[26] and yet Berne is not usually considered an instrument that regulates how Members deal with domestic authors.[27]

We do not propose to deny that there are oddities here. However, we do not find them surprising, and we certainly do not accept the answer to a logical impasse is to rewrite Article 10(1).[28] To paraphrase Justice Holmes, the life of the law is not logic but experience.[29] Such a proposition must be even more true of a multilateral convention that is subject to repeated revision: when adopting new norms, respect is not always shown for the underlying logic of the treaty. But that does not imply the new norms should be rejected (or read down). Moreover, the adoption of new norms may reflect, or instantiate, changes in the logic. Article 10(1) is just such a case. The adoption of Article 10(1) came at a time when Berne was transforming from a mechanism for co-ordinating national copyright regimes (coupled with minimal harmonisation) into an international code of substantive rules.[30]

---

[25] Cour de Cassation, 10 February 1992, n. 95-19030, translated in J C Ginsburg and E Treppoz, *International Copyright Law: US and EU Perspectives. Texts and Cases* (Edward Elgar 2015) 186 (with the Court rejecting possible application of Article 10(1) rather than Article L. 122-5.3a of the Code of Intellectual Property to the auctioneer's reproduction of an image of a painting on the basis that the country of origin of the painting was France, so domestic law was applicable).

[26] But Kur and Grosse Ruse-Khan (2011), 392, note that '[d]ifferential legal treatment between domestic and foreign right holders seems an impossible task in a globalized world'.

[27] S Ricketson and J Ginsburg, 'The Berne Convention: Historical and Institutional Aspects' in Daniel J Gervais (ed.), *International Intellectual Property: A Handbook of Contemporary Research* (Edward Elgar 2015), ch. 1, 3–36. Article 10(1) of the Brussels version had emphasised that quotation was to be permitted 'in all countries of the Union', implying perhaps that it was to be of universal application. By the time of Stockholm, these words were treated as superfluous.

[28] S Gerbrandy and F Klaver, 'La Révision de la Convention de Berne' (1967) 52 *RIDA* 5, 54 ('a coercive limitation on author's copyright' which Member States cannot reduce). Professor Gerbrandy was on the Drafting Committee at the Stockholm Conference.

[29] Oliver Wendell Holmes Jr, *The Common Law* (Little, Brown 1881), 1.

[30] The Stockholm Revision also saw the adoption of a provision allowing Member States to exclude from copyright 'official documents': Article 2(4) states that '[i]t shall be a matter for legislation in the countries of the Union to determine the protection to be granted to official texts of a legislative, administrative and legal nature, and to official translations of such texts'. As it is difficult to conceive of many situations in which documents that are 'official' for a particular country will not have their 'country of origin' (under Article 5(4)) in that country, so that formally speaking Berne is irrelevant (Article 5(1)), the inclusion of Article 2(4) can be explained by reference to the idea that the Convention was perceived increasingly as a code. See also Sam Ricketson and Jane C Ginsburg, 'The Berne Convention: Historical and Institutional Aspects' in Daniel J Gervais (ed.), *International Intellectual Property: A Handbook of Contemporary Research* (Edward Elgar 2015), ch. 1, 3–36, 24–5, noting that 'successive revisions of the Convention have achieved a high degree of comprehensiveness as to the subject matter and scope of what must be protected, the level of protection to be given, conditions for its availability, and its duration' but noting that 'Berne does not "codify" these matters in the sense of providing a strict template to be applied by all member states'.

In such a context, the Study Group regarded its mandate under Article 24 of the Brussels Revision, which referred to 'improvements intended to perfect the system', as broad and not limited merely to extending rights granted under international law. It said it encompassed 'also the general development of copyright by reforms intended to make the rules relating to it more simple to apply, as well as to adapt them to social, technical and economic conditions of the contemporary community'.[31] As is well known, under this broad perspective, the Conference would ultimately consider a Protocol dealing with Developing Countries,[32] a matter that was to prove extremely controversial. However, it also informed the Study Group's views on the formulation of limitations.[33] Only the Authors Consultative Committee ('CCA'), which met in Paris on 13–15 October 1964,[34] took issue with the Study Group's understanding of its remit, in particular its interpretation of Article 24 of the Brussels version. Rather, the CCA argued that Article 24 needed to be understood in the light of the fact that 'from its inception the Berne Convention's purpose was to protect in as efficient and uniform a way as possible the rights of authors'. Consequently, the CCA would not support any modification that was 'of such a nature as to diminish in any way the protection at present granted to authors by the Convention now in force'.[35] As a result, not surprisingly, the CCA said it was 'disquieted by the considerable extension' to be effected by the proposed Article 10(1)[36] and sought pragmatically to support the limitations proposed by the Committee of Non-official Experts. As things turned out, the broader perspective of the Study Group prevailed.

The drafters had, not surprisingly, put to one side the theoretical possibility that a country might in its laws distinguish between domestic authors and Union works. The quotation exception, mandatory for Berne works, was expected to be applied evenly to domestic and Berne works – and the practice of almost all Members seems to have been to apply exceptions indiscriminately to works, whatever their origin (even if, in respect of formalities, countries subsequently distinguished between domestic and foreign authors – i.e. the US). Indeed, Torwald Hesser described one of the goals of the reforms as providing 'a model for legislation pertaining to the internal conditions of member countries'.[37] Viewed in that light, a mandatory exception seems to be entirely consistent with the reality that Berne now operates as an international

---

[31]   Cf. Ricketson and Ginsburg (2006), [3.52], 123, which suggests this wider perspective was only adopted in order to accommodate developing countries.

[32]   Following the recommendation adopted by the African States at the Brazzaville Copyright seminar, in Republic of Congo, 5–10 August 1963. On this, see Ricketson and Ginsburg (2006), [14.08], 888 et seq.

[33]   The Study Group, however, rejected British suggestions for a 'basic re-arrangement of the convention': BIRPI: DA/20/2, p. 6.

[34]   BIRPI: DA/22/7. See above, Chapter 2, Section IV, Part D, pp. 22–23.

[35]   BIRPI: DA/22/7, p. 2.

[36]   BIRPI: DA/22/7, p. 9.

[37]   T Hesser, 'Intellectual Property Conference of Stockholm, 1967' (1967) 14 *Bull Copyright Soc'y* 267, 275.

code.[38] In addition to the nature of the Berne Convention evolving over time, the international copyright community is also more at ease with recognising and introducing mandatory exceptions, as illustrated by the Marrakesh Treaty.[39] Article 4(1)(a) of the Marrakesh Treaty mandates contracting parties to provide for limitations or exceptions to the rights of reproduction, distribution and making available to the public in relation to accessible format copies for the visually impaired. The Treaty also mandates, in Articles 5 and 6, the cross-border exchange of accessible format copies. As such, the Marrakesh Treaty has been praised by scholars as disrupting the 'dominant "rights only" model of international copyright law'.[40] Given that Article 1 of the Marrakesh Treaty states that it does not affect the rights and obligations under existing treaties (such as Berne), then it cannot be the case that the mandatory provision in the Marrakesh Treaty is contrary to the international copyright landscape established and regulated by Berne.

Finally, the mandatory quality of Article 10(1) is not called into doubt by the European Union's figuring of Article 5(3)(d) of the Information Society Directive[41] as 'optional' (the only mandatory exception under the Directive being for transient and incidental copies in Article 5(1)). Rather, the Commission recognised the mandatory nature of Article 10 of Berne. In the Proposal it is stated: 'The limitations set out to the reproduction right at international level vary. *The Berne Convention provides for a number of compulsory exceptions* (for news of the day, miscellaneous facts, *quotations*,) as well as several exceptions of an optional nature, notably for informational and educational use'[42] (emphasis added).

Article 5(3)(d) of the Information Society Directive clearly needs to be interpreted in light of the international obligations contained in Article 10(1) of Berne. It is therefore rather surprising that the interaction was overlooked by the trio of decisions issued by the Court of Justice of the European Union on 29 July 2019.[43] The Court did accept that while the exceptions listed in Article 5(2) and 5(3) of the Directive

---

[38]   The language of Article 10(1) of the Brussels version of Berne was consistent with the idea that the exception was to be applied universally – that is, to confer a user right irrespective of the country of origin of the work. Then the text stated, 'In all countries of the Union are permitted . . . ' ('Dans tous les Pays de l'Union sont licites . . . ').

[39]   Marrakesh Treaty to Facilitate Access to Published Works for Persons Who Are Blind, Visually Impaired or Otherwise Print Disabled 2013 ('Marrakesh Treaty') www.wipo.int/treaties/en/ip/marra kesh/ (accessed 21 January 2020).

[40]   See Ruth L Okediji, 'The Limits of International Copyright Exceptions for Developing Countries' (2019) 21 *Vand J Ent & Tech L* 689, 731.

[41]   Directive 2001/29/EC on the Harmonization of Certain Aspects of Copyright and Related Rights in the Information Society 22.6.2001, OJ L 167/10 ('Information Society Directive').

[42]   See Proposal for a European Parliament and Council Directive on the Harmonization of Certain Aspects of Copyright and Related Rights in the Information Society (10 December 1997), COM(97) 628 final, p 15, [10].

[43]   Case C-469/17 *Funke Medien NRW GmbH v. Bundesrepublik Deutschland* EU:C:2019:623 (CJEU, Grand Chamber); Case C-476/17 *Pelham GmbH v. Hütter* EU:C:2019:624 (CJEU, Grand Chamber); Case C-516/17 *Spiegel Online GmbH v. Volker Beck* EU:C:2019:625 (CJEU, Grand Chamber).

appear 'optional', some of them are, in fact, mandatory.[44] However, the CJEU seems to understand the obligatory nature of some of the exceptions to be a consequence of the need to establish a fair balance between the interests of rightsholders and the 'interests and fundamental rights of users of protected subject matter, in particular their freedom of expression and information guaranteed by Article 11 of the Charter, as well as of the public interest'.[45]

The reason why Article 5(3)(d) of the Information Society Directive is couched as an optional provision probably relates to the fact that no quotation exception is mandatory for related rights under international law. Article 15 of the Rome Convention, for example, makes no specific reference to quotation, only providing that 'any Contracting State may, in its domestic laws and regulations, provide for the same kinds of limitations with regard to the protection of performers, producers of phonograms and broadcasting organisations, as it provides for, in its domestic laws and regulations, in connection with the protection of copyright in literary and artistic works'.

The reproduction right, harmonised in Article 2 of the Information Society Directive, covers not just Berne Convention works, nor Rome Convention–related rights, but certain rights to which no international arrangements apply (notably, fixations of films). The fact that the quotation exception is couched in optional terms probably reflects the fact that it was intended to be optional for Member States as regards related rights, even though it was mandatory under Berne for authorial works.[46]

Rather surprisingly, given its prior jurisprudence in which the CJEU has not shown any tendency to permit Member States to insert additional conditions or qualifications to harmonised norms, the Court in *Funke Medien* and *Spiegel Online*

---

[44] *Funke Medien*, [58]; *Pelham*, [60]; *Spiegel Online*, [43] ('may, or *even must*, be transposed. . .').
[45] *Funke Medien*, [57]; *Spiegel Online*, [42]; *Pelham*, [59] (though not referring explicitly to Article 11 of the Charter of Fundamental Rights of the European Union 2000).
[46] Raquel Xalabarder, 'On-line Teaching and Copyright: Any Hopes for an EU Harmonized Playground?' in Paul Torremans (ed.), *Copyright Law: A Handbook of Contemporary Research* (Edward Elgar 2007), ch. 15, 373–401, 398, noting that there is no incompatibility between Article 5(3)(d) of the Information Society Directive and Article 10(1) Berne because the former '*allows* Member States to provide for a quotation exception, while the [Berne Convention] *obliges* Member States to provide for it, at least as far as non-national authors/works', but she expresses regret that 'an opportunity to formally integrate such a prior common obligation into the EU *acquis*' was missed. Note that in relation to user-generated content, the EU has made the quotation exception (and criticism, review, parody, caricature and pastiche exceptions) mandatory: see Directive (EU) 2019/790 of the European Parliament and of the Council of 17 April 2019 on Copyright and Related Rights in the Digital Single Market and amending Directives 96/9/EC and 2001/29/EC OJ L 130, 17.5.2019, p. 92–125 ('Digital Single Market Directive'), Art 17(7). The effect of Art 17(7) of the Digital Single Market Directive has been described as 'mandatory breathing space for transformative UGC', thus making the copyright exception 'particularly robust' and requiring 'Member States to introduce these use privileges' if they do not have them already: see Comment of the European Copyright Society on Selected Aspects of Implementing Article 17 of the Directive on Copyright in the Digital Single Market Into National Law 27 April 2020 at https://europeancopyrightsocietydotorg .files.wordpress.com/2020/04/ecs-comment-article-17-cdsm.pdf (accessed 10 June 2020), p. 11.

also went on to indicate that Article 5(3)(d) of the Information Society Directive did not constitute 'full harmonisation' and Member States are left with 'significant discretion allowing them to strike a balance between the relevant interests'.[47] In particular, while the Court indicated that the concept of 'quotation' had an autonomous interpretation, which was 'determined by considering its usual meaning in everyday language, while also taking into account the legislative context in which it occurs and the purposes of the rules of which it is part',[48] it indicated that Member States retain some discretion as to the implementation of Article 5(3)(d),[49] in particular the requirements of 'fair practice' and 'to the extent required by the specific purpose'.[50] This discretion is, however, constrained by European Union law, including 'complying with all the conditions laid down in that provision'[51] and the principle of proportionality in EU law;[52] the need to pursue the objectives of the Directive (or at least not to compromise them);[53] the three-step test in Article 5(5) of the Information Society Directive[54] and allowing for a 'fair balance' between the fundamental rights in the EU Charter[55] (in this case the right to intellectual property and the right to freedom of expression).

We evaluate in Chapter 7 the CJEU rulings in *Pelham* and *Spiegel Online* and, in particular, critique the Court's interpretation of 'quotation'.[56] What is worth pointing out at this juncture is that national implementation of Article 10(1), including what constitutes 'fair practice' and the quotation being 'proportionate', is constrained by Berne to a certain extent. As will be argued in Chapter 4, Section IV, the 'proportionate' nature of the quotation to its purpose is distinct from the requirement of 'fair practice' and involves asking whether a shorter quotation could have achieved the same purpose but in a manner less restrictive of the author's rights, whereas 'fair practice' is where the key normative assessments are made. As will be argued in Chapter 6, 'fair practice' is an international copyright norm that requires consideration – either in national legislation or by national courts – of several factors that emerge from norms of harm, freedom of expression, distributive justice and, in limited circumstances, custom. Where there is discretion for Berne Union Members is in the relative emphasis given to the fairness factors emerging from these norms.[57] Most of the constraints that the CJEU has indicated are not necessarily problematic

---

[47]   *Spiegel Online*, [27]–[28]; *Funke Medien*, [42]–[43]. The CJEU did not deal with this issue in *Pelham* for Article 5(3)(d) but did rule that Article 2(c) of the Information Society Directive dealing with the right of reproduction constituted a measure of full harmonisation: *Pelham*, [85].

[48]   *Pelham*, [70]. See Chapter 7, section III, pp. 211–214.

[49]   *Spiegel Online* [28]–[30]; *Funke Medien*, [40]–[42].

[50]   *Funke Medien*, [43].

[51]   *Funke Medien*, [48]; *Spiegel Online*, [32].

[52]   *Funke Medien*, [49]; *Spiegel Online*, [34].

[53]   *Funke Medien*, [50]; *Spiegel Online*, [36].

[54]   *Funke Medien*, [52]; *Spiegel Online*, [37].

[55]   *Funke Medien*, [53]; *Spiegel Online*, [38].

[56]   Chapter 7, section III, pp. 209–216, below.

[57]   Chapter 6, section III, esp. p. 189, below.

because the conditions in Article 5(3)(d) Information Society Directive mirror those in Article 10(1) Berne, there is the need to give 'effect' to the EU exceptions, and a 'fair balance' between fundamental rights could allow for the normative values of harm to property rights and freedom of expression to be taken into account. However, the three-step test (as will be argued as follows) is irrelevant to the scope and implementation of the right of quotation.[58] Further the EU principle of 'proportionality' should not be confused with the 'proportionate' nature of the quotation, as required by Article 10(1) Berne and Article 5(3)(d) Information Society Directive.

B *Is Article 10(1) Berne Imperative?*

We have argued that Article 10(1) Berne is mandatory in nature, but is it mandatory in the (civil law) sense of being *imperative* rather than *suppletive* (or supplementary)? This distinction is traced back to the Roman law distinction between *jus cogens* and *jus dispositivum*, and in civil law systems, 'imperative' legal rules refer to 'those legal precepts rooted in public policy which may not be set aside by private agreement', whereas 'suppletive' legal rules are those 'legal norms designed to supplement the parties' will in cases wherein its application is not excluded'.[59] In other words, the question is whether Article 10(1) Berne, aside from being an exception that Berne Union Members *must* implement in their national laws, must also be an exception that cannot be derogated from in any way, including by contract or technological protection measures?

When it comes to national and to some extent EU copyright legislation, there has been considerable debate about whether copyright exceptions should be overridden by private ordering measures, such as contract or technological protection measures.[60]

---

[58] Chapter 3, section IV, below. Because some national legislatures have implemented the three step test in domestic legislation, national courts sometimes view it as a constraint on the quotation right: see e.g. Audiencia Provincial Madrid (Section 28) July 25, 2019, Aranzadi Civil 2019, no. 1413 (referring to the three step test in Article 40 bis of Spain's Copyright Act).

[59] Alejandro M Garro, 'Codification Technique and the Problem of Imperative and Suppletive Laws' (1981) 41 *Louisiana Law Review* 1007, 1008. Garro argues that there is no rigorous method of identifying whether a legal provision is imperative or suppletive. He argues that imperative provisions should use the '"shall" form of verb and should state expressly the legislative sanction attached (e.g., "a contrary agreement is null")' (1030).

[60] For a discussion, see Lucie Guibault, *Copyright Limitations and Contracts: An Analysis of the Contractual Overridability of Limitations on Copyright* (Kluwer 2002); Estelle Derclaye and Marcella Favale, 'Copyright and Contract Law: Regulating User Contracts: The State of the Art and a Research Agenda' (2010) 18 *J Intell Prop L* 65; Papers in the *Symposium Intellectual Property and Contract Law for the Information Age* in (1999) 87 *Cal L Rev* 1; Thomas Heide, 'Copyright, Contract and the Legal Protection of Technological Measures – Not the Old Fashioned Way: Providing a Rationale to the Copyright Exceptions Interface' (2002–2003) 50 *J Copyright Soc'y U.S.A.* 315; Guiseppe Mazziotti, *EU Digital Copyright Law and the End-User* (Springer 2008) 27–33, 94–102 and ch. 7, and Pascale Chapdelaine, *Copyright User Rights: Contracts and the Erosion of Property* (Oxford University Press 2017), 52–4, 188–91. Based on empirical work, Jessica Silbey suggests that there is 'the ubiquitous practice of contracting around IP defaults' in order to 'effectuate optimal business relationships in creative and innovative fields': Jessica Silbey, *The Eureka Myth: Creators, Innovators, and Everyday Intellectual Property* (Stanford University Press 2015), 280.

We occasionally see imperative rules in EU copyright law, such as Article 5(3) of the Software Directive:[61]

> The person having a right to use a copy of a computer program shall be entitled, without the authorization of the rightholder, to observe, study or test the functioning of the program in order to determine the ideas and principles which underlie any element of the program if he does so while performing any of the acts of loading, displaying, running, transmitting or storing the program which he is entitled to do.

The imperative nature of this 'reverse engineering' exception for copyright-protected computer programs is made obvious by Article 8 of the Software Directive, which states: 'Any contractual provisions contrary to Article 6 or to the exceptions provided for in Article 5(2) and (3) shall be null and void.'[62] Having said this, the reference to the CJEU in SAS *Institute* and the Court's subsequent ruling[63] demonstrates how assessing the 'overridability' of copyright exceptions can be less than straightforward. In SAS *Institute*, the defendants had relied on the fact that they had studied a licensed computer program in order to independently develop their own software. The claimants, however, argued that the defendants were acting outside the scope of their licence because *inter alia* they had used an edition of the computer program for purposes that were commercial and not 'non-production' purposes. The question, therefore, for the CJEU was whether the licensee could reverse engineer the computer program – that is, 'observe, test or study the functioning' of the program 'if the licence permits the licensee to perform acts of loading, running and storing . . . when using [the program] for the particular purpose permitted by the licence, but the acts done in order to observe, study or test [the program] extend outside the scope of the purpose permitted by the licence'.[64] The CJEU's ruling on this question was unclear and convoluted;[65] however, the UK Court of Appeal held that the CJEU had distinguished between acts permitted by the licence and the purpose for which those permitted acts were carried out. The Court of Appeal concluded, 'Once you have crossed the threshold of being entitled to perform acts for any purpose specified in the licence, article 5(3) permits you to perform those same acts for a purpose which falls within article 5(3).'[66] While the Court of Appeal adopted a workable interpretation of the CJEU's ruling in SAS, it was not without its difficulties and this

---

[61] Directive 91/250/EEC [1991] OJ L122/42 subsequently codified as 2009/24/EC on the Legal Protection of Computer Programs [2009] OJ L 111/16 ('Software Directive').

[62] Article 6 refers to the decompilation exception and Article 5(2) to the right to make back-up copies by a person having a right to use the computer program.

[63] Case C-406/10 SAS *Institute Inc v. World Programming Ltd* EU:C:2012:259 (CJEU, Grand Chamber).

[64] SAS *Institute*, [28].

[65] SAS *Institute*, [59]–[62]. See also the observation of Arnold J in SAS *Institute Inc v. World Programming Ltd* [2013] EWHC 69 (Ch), [2013] RPC 17, [64] and Daniel Gervais and Estelle Derclaye, 'The Scope of Computer Program Protection after SAS: Are We Closer to Answers?' [2012] *EIPR* 565, 570–1.

[66] SAS *Institute Inc v. World Programming Ltd* [2013] EWCA Civ 1482, [2014] RPC 8, [101].

was so despite the express language in the Software Directive that contractual provisions to the contrary would be 'null and void'.[67]

There are also situations where EU copyright law expressly indicates the relationship between copyright exceptions and technological protection measures. Here we can point to Article 6 of the Information Society Directive, which applies to copyright works (other than computer programs)[68] and requires Member States to provide adequate legal protection against the circumvention of any effective technological protection measures or in relation to the manufacture, sale or other commercial distribution of circumvention measures.[69] Of particular relevance here is the fact that Article 6(4) subparagraph 1 obligates Member States to take appropriate measures (in the absence of voluntary measures taken by rightholders) to ensure that rightholders make available to the beneficiary of the listed specific exceptions[70] the means of benefiting from those exceptions, where they have legal access to the protected work. In other words, the 'appropriate measures' to ensure the means of benefiting from exceptions only apply where there are copy-control technological protection measures in use (and not access-control measures). Further, the obligation on Member States only applies in respect of certain exceptions and does not extend to Article 5(3)(d) on quotation. Moreover, the obligation in Article 6(4) subparagraph 1 does not apply where the works or other subject matter have been 'made available to the public on agreed contractual terms in such a way that members of the public may access them from a place and at a time individually chosen by them'. The difficulty is whether we are to infer from Article 6(4) of the Information Society Directive that the quotation exception can be *always* overridden by technological protection measures or whether it simply indicates that an obligation on Member States to facilitate beneficiaries relying on exceptions to copy works subject to technological protection measures applies only to certain exceptions, in which case Member States could go further and ensure that the quotation exception is not prejudiced by the use of technological protection measures. Moreover, Article 6(4) and the remainder of the Information Society Directive is silent about the relationship between contract and the exceptions within Article 5.

This silence may explain why the United Kingdom, when choosing to revise its copyright exceptions in 2014 consistently with Article 5 of the Information Society

---

[67]   Another example of express language indicating the binding nature of certain exceptions is Article 8 of Directive 96/9/EC of the European Parliament and of the Council of 11 March 1996 on the legal protection of databases OJ L 77/20 ('Database Directive'), which states that '[a]ny contractual provision contrary to Articles 6(1) and 8 shall be null and void'. Article 6(1) deals with a copyright exception relation to accessing the contents of a database by a lawful user, and Article 8 deals with a lawful user of a database extracting or reutilising insubstantial parts of the contents of a database.

[68]   For computer programs, see Article 7 of Software Directive. Although there are no anti-circumvention provisions for *sui generis* databases in the Database Directive, Art 6(3) of 2001/29/EC extends to such subject matter.

[69]   For a more detailed discussion, see T Aplin, *Copyright Law in a Digital Society* (Hart 2005), 231–8, and Mazziotti (2008), 94–100 and ch. 7.

[70]   These are Articles 5(2)(a), 5(2)(c), 5(2)(d), 5(2)(e), 5(3)(a), 5(3)(b) and 5(3)(e). Omitted from this list is, of course, Article 5(3)(d) on quotation.

Directive, felt able to insert the following language in section 30(4) of the CDPA: 'To the extent that a term of a contract purports to prevent or restrict the doing of any act which, by virtue of subsection (1ZA), would not infringe copyright, that term is unenforceable.' Section 30(1ZA) of the CDPA refers to the quotation exception. The same provision on unenforceability of contractual terms is also included for the exception for caricature, parody or pastiche in section 30A of the CDPA.[71] Indeed, as Professor Adrian Aronsson-Storrier has explained, the relationship between several copyright exceptions and contract was revisited following the 2014 amendments to the CDPA[72] and, as a result, several uncertainties exist: whether the exceptions without an express provision dealing with the relationship to contract can be overridden by contract; what is the difference between the language of 'unenforceable' versus 'void' in section 296A of the CDPA, which implements the relevant provisions of the Software Directive; what 'restricting the doing of any act' means; and whether choice of law contracts could circumvent these provisions.

The previous discussion illustrates that at EU and national (in this case, UK) level, assessing the imperative nature of a copyright exception can be a complex exercise. As such, we need to approach carefully the issue of whether international copyright law, in fact, mandates – in the imperative sense – the right of quotation in Article 10(1) Berne. The better view, we think, is that the language of Article 10(1) Berne and indeed the remainder of Berne does not address the issue of whether Berne Union Members should treat the quotation exception as imperative such that it cannot be overridden by contract or other private ordering. However, Article 10(1) in no way *precludes* Union Members from adopting such a position and the mandatory language in the provision in fact could justify a Union Member treating the quotation exception as imperative. Thus, while the EU is not a Berne Union Member, the impact of Article 17(7) of the Digital Single Market Directive[73] on Member States (who are Members of Berne) would be consistent with Article 10(1) Berne. Specifically, Article 17(7) of the Digital Single Market Directive provides:

> 17(7). The cooperation between online content-sharing service providers and right-holders shall not result in the prevention of the availability of works or other subject matter uploaded by users, which do not infringe copyright and related rights, including where such works or other subject matter are covered by an exception or limitation.
>
> Member States shall ensure that users in each Member State are able to rely on any of the following existing exceptions or limitations when uploading and making available content generated by users on online content-sharing services:

---

[71] See section 30A(2) CDPA.

[72] Adrian Aronsson-Storrier, 'Copyright Exceptions and Contract in the UK: The Impact of Recent Amendments' (2016) 6 *Queen Mary Journal of Intellectual Property* 111.

[73] Directive (EU) 2019/790 of the European Parliament and of the Council of 17 April 2019 on Copyright and Related Rights in the Digital Single Market and amending Directives 96/9EC and 2001/29/EC OJ L 130, 17.5.2019, p. 92–125 ('Digital Single Market Directive').

(a) quotation, criticism, review;
(b) use for the purpose of caricature, parody or pastiche.

Article 17 of the Digital Single Market Directive radically overhauls the relationship between content-hosting intermediaries and rightholders and, through requiring Member States to treat online content-sharing service providers as communicating to the public where they give the public 'access to copyright-protected works or other protected subject matter uploaded by its users', the hope is to facilitate licensing agreements. The concern that is sought to be addressed in Article 17(7) Digital Single Market Directive is that, either as a result of entering into licensing agreements or because of the need to show 'best efforts' to ensure the unavailability of works, platforms might use filters or other technical measures that impede the ability of internet users to rely on certain copyright exceptions. As a result, Member States are obliged to ensure that users on online content-sharing services can rely on certain exceptions, in particular quotation and parody,[74] although how they are to ensure this is unclear.

Support for the position that Article 10(1) Berne does not require Union Members to treat the quotation exception as imperative but also does not preclude them from doing so can also be drawn from the Marrakesh Treaty and the subsequent implementation of its obligations by the EU in the Marrakesh Directive.[75] As discussed previously, the Marrakesh Treaty mandates contracting parties to provide for exceptions for and cross-border exchange of accessible format copies of copyright works for the visually impaired. In addition, Article 7 of the Marrakesh Treaty states: 'Contracting Parties shall take appropriate measures, as necessary, to ensure that when they provide adequate legal protection and effective legal remedies against the circumvention of effective technological measures, this legal protection does not prevent beneficiary persons from enjoying the limitations and exceptions provided for in this Treaty.' This provision would seem to indicate that vis-à-vis technological protection measures, the Marrakesh Treaty exceptions take priority and cannot be overridden. However, this seems to be undermined by the Agreed Statement accompanying Article 7, which states, 'It is understood that authorized entities, in

---

[74] J Quintais, G Frosio, S van Gompel, PB Hugenholtz, M Husovec, BJ Jütte, MRF Senftleben, 'Safeguarding User Freedoms in Implementing Article 17 of the Copyright in the Digital Single Market Directive: Recommendations from European Academics' (2020) 10 *Journal of Intellectual Property, Information Technology and Electronic Commerce Law* 277, describe the exceptions and limitations in Article 17(7) as '*user rights or freedoms*' and indicate that 'national lawmakers and courts must ensure that [these exceptions] remain fully operative despite licensing arrangements... and preventative obligations under Article 17(4)(b) and (c) that are likely to make inroads into this area of freedom of EU citizens'. For a general discussion of Article 17 of the Digital Single Market see Ben Allgrove and John Groom, 'Enforcement in a Digital Context: Intermediary Liability' in T Aplin (ed.), *Research Handbook on IP and Digital Technologies* (Edward Elgar 2020), ch. 25, 506–30, 527–9.

[75] Directive (EU) 2017/1564 of the European Parliament and of the Council of 13 September 2017 on Certain Permitted Uses of Certain Works and Other Subject Matter Protected by Copyright and Related Rights for the Benefit of Persons Who Are Blind, Visually Impaired or Otherwise Print-Disabled and Amending Directive 2001/29/EC on the Harmonisation of Certain Aspects of Copyright and Related Rights in the Information Society OJ L 242, 20.9.2017, pp. 6–13 ('Marrakesh Directive').

various circumstances, choose to apply technological measures in the making, distribution and making available of accessible format copies and nothing herein disturbs such practices when in accordance with national law.' In addition, the Marrakesh Treaty is silent on the relationship of its mandated exceptions to contract.

When we look to implementation at EU level, in the form of the Marrakesh Directive, we see that the position vis-à-vis contract *is* dealt with. Recital 9 and Article 3(5) state, respectively:

> Recital 9 . . . Accessible format copies should only be made of works or other subject matter to which beneficiary persons or authorized entities have lawful access. Member States should ensure that any contractual provision which seeks to prevent or limit the application of the exception in any way is void of legal effect.
>
> Article 3(5): Member States shall ensure that the exception provided for in paragraph 1 [permitting accessible format copies by a beneficiary person or authorised entity] cannot be overridden by contract.

The relationship between the exception and technological protection measures, as contained in Article 7 of the Marrakesh Treaty, is arguably dealt with by Article 8 of the Marrakesh Directive. This provision stipulates that Article 5(3)(b) of the Information Society Directive will be replaced by new wording – namely, 'uses, for the benefit of people with a disability, which are directly related to the disability and of a noncommercial nature, to the extent required by the specific disability, without prejudice to the obligations of Member States under [the Marrakesh Directive]'.

Given that Article 6(4) paragraph 1 of the Information Society Directive (discussed previously) applies to Article 5(3)(b), we could infer that not only should appropriate measures be taken to ensure the beneficiaries of this exception are not compromised by technological protection measures, but, in addition, the exceptions for disabilities in Marrakesh should also not be affected. This position, however, is less clear-cut than the Marrakesh Directive's position on contract and the visually impaired exceptions. Nevertheless, the point is that the EU's position is in no way inconsistent with the Marrakesh Treaty.

Therefore, in conclusion, we argue that while the language of Article 10(1) Berne is mandatory, such that Union Members *must* introduce this exception, this does not equate to the exception being imperative, in the sense that it cannot be overridden by contract or other private ordering. However, Article 10(1) Berne does not preclude Berne Union Members from treating the quotation exception as imperative.

II TYPES OF WORKS THAT ARE SUBJECT TO ARTICLE 10(1) BERNE

According to Advocate General Szpunar, giving an Opinion in the *Pelham* case, '[t]he quotation exception has its origin and is mainly used in literary works'.[76] In Case

---

[76] Case C-476/17 *Pelham GmbH v. Hütter* EU:C:2018:1002 (Advocate General's Opinion), [62]. Indeed, in the Belgian law of 1886, the quotation exception in Article 13 was in the part dealing with 'literary

C-516/17, *Spiegel Online*, he suggests that the exception for quotations 'has long been regarded as applying only to literary works', though he adds that 'at the present time, it does not seem inconceivable that the exception for quotations may also apply to other categories of work, in particular musical and cinematographic works, as well as works of visual art'.[77] This section explores how far the exception in Article 10(1) applies to non-literary works. As we will see, its application is broad, encompassing all Berne works, but there is no parallel obligation on countries that are party to the Rome Convention or TRIPs to recognise a quotation right in relation to non-authorial subject matters (such as sound recordings or broadcasts). In order to maintain the coherence of their legal systems, however, many countries choose to extend the quotation right to such subject matters.

A Berne Works

The Berne Convention applies to 'literary and artistic works', and Article 2(1) defines these to include 'every production in the literary, scientific and artistic domain' and goes on to give illustrative examples. It is clear from Article 2(6) of Berne that the works listed in Article 2(1), along with those mentioned in Article 2(3) ('translations, adaptations, arrangements of music and other alterations of a literary and artistic work') and Article 2(5) ('collections of literary or artistic works'), are to be protected under the Convention by Union Members. Although the enumeration in Article 2(1) is illustrative, and other categories of works may be recognised as 'literary and artistic works', history shows that the list has steadily expanded over time and that 'there has usually been a prolonged struggle which has preceded the admission of a new category of work to the list'.[78] This is because enumeration in Article 2(1) of Berne is the only mechanism to ensure a consistent approach among Union Members concerning what is included within the notion of 'literary and artistic works'.[79] Thus, Members must protect all of the illustrative categories of works specified in Article 2(1), even though they may go beyond this list.[80]

On its face the mandatory quotation exception applies to *all* types of Berne works. We should acknowledge that the *travaux*, however, reveal that this

---

works': as a result, the Supreme Court held in December 1952 that the exception could not be relied upon by a newspaper to justify publication of a photograph of a painting by Rodolphe Strebelle to illustrate a review of an ongoing exhibition: see Maurice Casteels, 'Works of Art and the Right of Quotation', (1954) 11 *RIDA* 81–97.

[77] Case C-516/17 *Spiegel Online GmbH v. Volker Beck*, EU:C:2019:16 (Advocate General's Opinion), [41]–[42].

[78] Ricketson and Ginsburg (2006), [8.09].

[79] Ricketson and Ginsburg (2006), [8.11].

[80] See D Vaver, 'The National Treatment Requirements of the Berne and Universal Copyright Conventions' (1986) 17 *IIC* 577, 596–602, who argues that even with this flexibility, there is still a bounded definition of 'works' that cannot be stretched to include anything; hence the exclusion of performances, sound recordings and broadcasts.

proposition was not shared by all participants in the reform process. Given its origins,[81] Article 10(1) was initially assumed by some to relate only to printed matter,[82] and a number of others seem to have assumed that the term 'quotation' simply could not be applied to works of art or architecture.[83] Indeed, all the examples that appear in the Study Group's 1963 discussion about extending the quotation right refer to text,[84] whereas its discussion of the 'reporting current events' exception in Article 10*bis* specifically differentiates the treatment of different types of work (so as to preclude the possibility of a report on an art exhibition including 'a large number of exposed works').[85] Perhaps, it might be argued, the term 'works' in Article 10(1) was meant to refer to something narrower than 'literary or artistic works', the phrase used elsewhere in the Convention to refer to the totality of works covered by the Convention.[86]

Nevertheless, we think the structure and purpose of the text, the unqualified reference to 'works', and the ordinary meaning of the concept of quotation in fact point irresistibly towards the conclusion that the quotation exception is intended to apply to *all* works protected under the Convention. There are indications, too, from the *travaux*, that this was the understanding of most involved, at least by the time of the adoption of the Treaty.[87] Commenting on the Study Group's 1964 proposal, the CCA said it was 'disquieted by the considerable extension' to be effected by the proposed Article 10(1), which it noted covered all categories of works.[88] It suggested that this introduced 'with dangerous possibilities, allowable quotation in the domain

---

[81] In the Brussels text, Article 10(1) only applied to quotations from 'newspaper articles or periodicals'.

[82] BIRPI: DA/22/9, p. 7 (where the International Federation of Journalists sought to clarify the notion of quotation by reference to the dictionary *Grand Larousse*, according to which (the IFJ stated) 'a quotation means a "brief" statement, the repetition of a passage from a longer text').

[83] Recht (1965), 85 ('[T]here cannot in any case be a quotation in the artistic field, the word "quotation" being applicable to excerpts from a literary work, but never to the total or partial reproduction of a plastic work. In this case it can only be a question of excerpts'). Recht refers to his own article 'La pseudo-citation dans le domaine des arts plastiques et figuratifs' (1957) 17 *RIDA* 85–119. See also a letter from the British Joint Copyright Council to the Board of Trade, 27 September 1963, where it is said that the BJCC would like to see proposed Article 10(1) specify which works were covered, objecting to inclusion of musical works, and stating that 'architectural works and artistic works cannot by their nature be quoted from': BT 209/903. But see Chapter 5, Section II, Part A, pp. 90–101, where we discuss whether the term 'quotation' is limited to textual quotation.

[84] All the examples offered in 1963 by the Study Group to support the extension were textual: BIRPI: DA/20/2, p. 45.

[85] BIRPI: DA/20/2, p. 48.

[86] Article 1, 2, 8, 9(1), 10(2), 10*bis*(2), 11*bis*(1). But note Article 12, 14, Art 15 ('literary or artistic works') and Article 16, 18 ('work', 'all works').

[87] In fact, as should be clear from Chapter 2, pp. 10–15, anyone with an appreciation of the earlier conferences would have been aware that many countries regarded quotation as extending beyond printed texts. While the Rome proposal had been limited to 'analyses or short textual quotations of published literary works', the French delegation proposed this be expanded to cover quotations of 'any literary, scientific or artistic production' and the Swiss to takings from 'literary or musical work' and 'published works of figurative art or photography'. As we also note, p. 9, n. 13, above, the French Supreme Court had on 10 March 1926 admitted the possibility of quotation of works of art through photographic reproduction.

[88] BIRPI: DA/22/7, p. 9.

of musical works'.[89] Likewise, INTERGU recognised that the quotation exception would appear to apply to music, and argued that in the case of musical works, quotation 'should be permissible only in writings'.[90] The Swiss delegation suggested limitations to the right, in part because it understood the proposal as recognising a 'right to make quotations *from all works*' (emphasis added).[91] The Report of the Committee of Government Experts, which met in Geneva in 1965, records that those opposed to limiting the purposes of quotation highlighted that the proposals of Switzerland and France did not cover a number of purposes for which quotation should be permitted, including 'aesthetic purposes (quotation from one musical work in another musical work)', and thus demonstrate that they were working on the premise that the term 'works' was unlimited.[92] Most importantly, the Minutes of Committee I indicate that it was widely understood that the quotation exception would apply to artistic works. This understanding is implicit in the arguments successfully made against the reinsertion into the text of a requirement that quotations only be permitted if they are 'short'. A key reason for rejecting any such condition was that it would raise particular problems in relation to the quotation of artistic works because moral rights would be implicated if only part was used.[93] Any such point would have lacked force, had the delegates assumed that quotation could only be literary.

An example of the quotation exception being applied to any type of work exists in Spain, in Article 32(1) of the Law on Intellectual Property,[94] which allows the inclusion in a work 'fragments ["fragmentos"] of the work of others, whether of written, sound or audiovisual character', as well as 'isolated works ["obras aisladas"] of figurative sculpture or photography ["de carácter plástico o fotográfico figurative"]'.[95] Bercovitz and Bercovitz describe this as 'perhaps the broadest exception' to authors' rights recognised in Spanish copyright law.[96] It is also clear from the

---

[89]   The British Joint Copyright Council ('BJCC') stated, in a letter to William Wallace of the British Board of Trade, dated 27 September 1963, that 'the word "work" in the proposed Article 10 would include a musical work, and this would open a very wide door'. See TNA: BT 209/903. The BJCC was based in Copyright House, Berners Street, London, the home of the Performing Right Society, and the Secretary to the BJCC who signed the letter was Royce Whale, the General Manager of the PRS. Whale was also one of the CISAC representatives in the CCA.

[90]   Pierre Recht, President of the Belgian Copyright Commission and a Member of the Legislative Committee of CISAC, notes that Schulze had made this point in a letter to the Authors' Consultative Committee, and indicates his agreement with the point: Pierre Recht, 'Should the Berne Convention include a Definition of the Right of Reproduction?' (1965) *Copyright* 82–9, 85.

[91]   BIRPI: DA/22/17.

[92]   BIRPI: DA/22/33 p. 10.

[93]   George Straschnov, in Minutes, [769], in *Records*, 861.

[94]   Consolidated Text of the law on Intellectual Property, regularizing, clarifying and harmonizing the Applicable Statutory Provisions (approved by Royal Legislative Decree No. 1/1996 of 12 April 1996).

[95]   A. Bercovitz and G. Bercovitz, 'Spain,' in L Bently (ed.), *International Copyright Law and Practice* (LexisNexis 2019), § 8[2][a].

[96]   A. Bercovitz and G. Bercovitz, 'Spain,' in L Bently, *ICLP*, § 8[2][a] cites Commercial Court (no. 6) Madrid, Jan. 13, 2010, Westlaw Jurisprudencia 2010, no. 149960 (permitting brief quotation of sounds in another musical work).

recent *Pelham* decision that the CJEU regards the quotation exception in Article 5(3)(d) of the Information Society Directive as applicable to all works. The Court noted that the wording of Article 5(3)(d) relates to 'a work or other subject matter', and inferred that the limitation 'may apply to the use of a protected musical work'.[97] Indeed, in the earlier *Painer* decision, the CJEU proceeded on the basis that the exception would be applicable to a (portrait) photograph.[98]

B Post-Berne Works

This next section considers whether the quotation right applies to (i) works: not protected under Berne, but protected by copyright in accordance with TRIPS or the WCT (most obviously, for computer programs and databases); (ii) performances, phonograms or broadcasts protected by neighbouring rights under the Rome Convention[99] or the WPPT;[100] (iii) related rights recognised in national law, for example, in published editions or 'edition princeps', non-original photographs, fixations on film, or *sui generis* rights granted in relation to databases. We consider each in turn, suggesting that the quotation right is applicable to the first category, but not necessarily to categories (ii) and (iii).

1 Computer Programs and Databases

Article 10(1) Berne applies equally to computer programs. This will be the case as between Berne Members if the country of protection treats computer programs as Berne works. However, Berne Members are not explicitly obliged to do so under Article 2 of Berne. Obligations to protect computer programs are, however, explicitly recognised in TRIPS and the WCT. Article 10(1) of TRIPS states that '[c]omputer programs, whether in source or object code, shall be protected as literary works under the Berne Convention (1971)'. Article 4 of the WCT specifies: 'Computer programs are protected as literary works within the meaning of Article 2 of the Berne Convention. Such protection applies to computer programs, whatever may be the mode or form of their expression.' An Agreed Statement to the WCT indicates that 'the scope of protection' is 'consistent with Article 2 of the Berne Convention and on a par with the relevant provisions of the TRIPS Agreement'.

The relationship between copyright in computer programs under TRIPS and the WCT and Berne works has been the subject of thoughtful examination by leading

---

[97] Case C-476/17 *Pelham GmbH* v. *Hütter* EU:C:2019:624 (CJEU, Grand Chamber), [68].

[98] Case C-145/10 *Painer* v. *Standard Verlags GmbH* EU:C:2011:798, [2012] ECDR 6 (CJEU, 3rd Chamber), [122], [123].

[99] International Convention for the Protection of Performers, Producers of Phonograms and Broadcasting Organizations, adopted at Rome on 26 October 1961 ('Rome Convention').

[100] WIPO Performances and Phonograms Treaty 1996 ('WPPT').

commentator Professor Sam Ricketson.[101] He puts the question in terms of whether Article 4 WCT and Article 10(1) TRIPS are 'constitutive' or 'declarative', arguing, in particular, that they may amount to relevant state practice (for the purposes of Article 31(3)(b) of the Vienna Convention). Unfortunately, having set out the possibilities, Ricketson does not argue convincingly for any preferred outcome. However, elsewhere he suggests that if a Berne Member did not regard computer programs as Berne works, and so only protected them under the TRIPS Agreement, then they would not be bound by the limitations – or obligations – in the menu of exceptions to Berne. Although he does not state this, it seems clear that his view is that the quotation exception would not necessarily apply to such a situation.[102]

In contrast, Professors von Lewinski and Reinbothe are significantly less circumspect about the content of the obligations applicable in relation to computer programs. Writing both about TRIPS and the WCT, they say that computer programs 'must be given the same protection as is given to other literary works listed in Article 2(1) Berne Convention'.[103] This is a view with which we agree. Under both TRIPS and the WCT, computer programs are treated 'as if' protected under Berne and thus subject to the same rights and limitations. This is supported by the *travaux* to the WCT, which indicates that Article 4 WCT 'is of a declaratory nature, and it explicitly codifies the established interpretation of Article 2 of Berne'.[104] Similarly, TRIPS was seen as incorporating the standards of Berne.[105] The effect appears to be that under TRIPS and the WCT, the mandatory quotation exception in Article 10(1) of Berne applies to computer programs, as it necessarily also does to any Berne party that treats computer programs as works. As we explain as follows, this is irrespective of whether the quotation right passes the 'three-step test'.[106]

---

[101]   Sam Ricketson, 'The Berne Convention: The Continued Relevance of an Ancient Text' in D Vaver and L Bently (eds.), *Intellectual Property in the New Millennium: Essays in Honour of William R. Cornish* (Cambridge University Press 2004) ch. 15, 230–3.

[102]   Ricketson and Ginsburg (2006), 851, [13.99].

[103]   J Reinbothe and S von Lewinski, *The WIPO Treaties 1996* (Butterworths 2002), 68–9.

[104]   Memorandum Prepared by the Chairman of the Committee of Experts, Basic Proposal for the Substantive Provisions of the Treaty on Certain Questions Concerning the Protection of Literary and Artistic Works to Be Considered by the Diplomatic Conference, CRNR/DC/4, 30 August 1996, in WIPO, *Records of the Diplomatic Conference on Certain Copyright and Neighbouring Rights Questions, Geneva 1996* (WIPO 1999), vol. 1, 161 ff., at 182 [4.01]. See also comment of Jukka Liedes, Chair of Main Committee I, 6 December 1996, in *Records of the Diplomatic Conference on Certain Copyright and Neighbouring Rights Questions, Geneva 1996* (WIPO 1999), vol. 2, 646, [82]. ('Both Articles 4 and 5 were intended to be declaratory, and what they stated was already the fair interpretation of the relevant clauses in the Berne Convention.')

[105]   MTN.GNG/NG11/4, 17 November 1987, discussing US proposal (MTN.GNG/NG11/W/14), the US representative explained, 'The annex on copyright essentially incorporated the standards provided in the Berne Convention for the Protection of Literary and Artistic Works and attempted to clarify certain aspects, for example the applicability of copyright protection to forms of expression such as computer programmes and data bases.'

[106]   Cf. F Klopmeier and K Arend in P T Stoll, J Busche and K Arend (eds.), *WTO-Trade Related Aspects of Intellectual Property Rights* (Martinus Nijhoff 2009), 258–9 (ambiguously stating that 'computer programs may be exempt from protection within the limits of Article 13 TRIPS *and under the Berne*

Article 10(2) of TRIPS and Article 5 of the WCT make similar provision in relation to compilations of data (Berne itself having dealt in express terms only with compilations of works).[107] However, here the language is noticeably different, in so far as the provisions do not refer explicitly to Article 2 of the Berne Convention. On one reading, TRIPS imposes an independent obligation to protect compilations of data, and does not require that they be protected within Berne. According to Professors Ricketson and Ginsburg, this 'appears to be a free-standing TRIPS-only obligation'.[108] The effect of this might then be that databases must be protected 'as such', but that any exception may be imposed that complies with the three-step test articulated in Article 13 of TRIPS, which might include a right of quotation but need not do so.[109] Thus, countries that are parties to Berne and TRIPS which treat databases as Berne works must subject them to the quotation exception (even if this would not comply with the three-step test, which is inapplicable), but such countries *may* treat databases as other than works, outside Berne subject matter. For those countries, as well as countries that are only in TRIPS, databases *may* be subject to a quotation exception, but only if it complies with the three-step test.

Nevertheless, the view has been expressed that Article 10(2) of TRIPS itself requires that databases be protected as 'works'. In a WIPO-prepared commentary on TRIPS, the point is made that Article 10(2) appears in the part of the agreement dealing with copyright works and has a close linguistic affinity with Article 2(5) of the Berne Convention.[110] In effect, it is understood as 'declaratory', articulating a common understanding as to the scope of Berne. This seems to be the view of Professor Neil Netanel, who describes Article 10(2) as 'declarative of the meaning of provisions in Berne'.[111] It might also be said that Article 9(1) TRIPS is to operate as an uber-principle, and that the protection that must be afforded must be that given to other works under Berne.

Convention'). For the view that none of the exceptions in Berne 'if correctly applied' conflict with steps 2 and 3 of Article 13, see WIPO, *Implications of the TRIPs Agreement for Treaties Implemented by WIPO* (WIPO 1996) 22, [52]–[53] (concluding that 'generally and normally, there is no conflict between the Berne Convention and the TRIPs Agreement as far as exceptions and limitations to the exclusive rights are concerned'), available at www.wipo.int/edocs/pubdocs/en/intproperty/464/wipo_pub_464.pdf (accessed 28 January 2020).

[107] Article 5 WCT is in slightly different terms. 'Compilations of data or other material, in any form, which by reason of the selection or arrangement of their contents constitute intellectual creations, are protected as such.'

[108] Ricketson and Ginsburg (2006), [13.100], 851.

[109] Carlos M Correa, *Trade Related Aspects of Intellectual Property Rights: A Commentary on the TRIPs Agreement* (Oxford University Press 2007), 126 (stating that this 'leaves Members freedom to determine the level of protection as they see fit.')

[110] WIPO, *Implications of the TRIPs Agreement for Treaties Implemented by WIPO* (WIPO 1996) 17, [34]–[37] ('since the provision appears in that part of the TRIPS Agreement which deals with copyright (rather than related rights)' and because of the parallel language to Article 2(5) of Berne), available at www.wipo.int/edocs/pubdocs/en/intproperty/464/wipo_pub_464.pdf (accessed 28 January 2020).

[111] N Netanel, 'The Next Round: The Impact of the WIPO Copyright Treaty on TRIPS Dispute Settlement' (1997) 37 *Va J Intl L* 441, 464.

In relation to the WCT, the situation is clearer. The Agreed Statement to Article 5 WCT seems to indicate that databases should be protected within Article 2 of Berne,[112] and given that Article 1(4) of the WCT requires parties to implement Articles 1–21 of Berne,[113] the overall effect seems to be to subject copyright in databases to the quotation right. Moreover, the preparatory documents relating to the WCT are clear in confirming the position that Article 5 declares what is already understood about the scope of Article 2 of Berne.[114] The effect is that members of Berne who are also members of the WCT, and members of the WCT who are not members of Berne must apply the quotation exception to databases. Moreover, members of Berne and/or TRIPS that join the WCT are obliged then to operate a quotation exception.

2 Rome Convention Subject Matter (Performances, Phonograms and Broadcasts)

In contrast with Berne, Member States may, but need not, offer a quotation exception under the Rome Convention. Article 15 permits (rather than requires) contracting parties to create exceptions, including 'the same kinds of limitations with regard to the protection of performers, producers of phonograms and broadcasting organisations, as it provides for, in its domestic laws and regulations, in connection with the protection of copyright in literary and artistic works'.[115] This paragraph was adopted in 1961, 2 years before the Stockholm Study Group had

---

[112]   'Agreed statements concerning Article 5: The scope of protection for compilations of data (databases) under Article 5 of this Treaty, read with Article 2, is consistent with Article 2 of the Berne Convention and on a par with the relevant provisions of the TRIPS Agreement.'

[113]   'Contracting Parties shall comply with Articles 1 to 21 and the Appendix of the Berne Convention.'

[114]   Article 5 of the WCT 'confirms what is already covered by the Berne Convention': Memorandum Prepared by the Chairman of the Committee of Experts, Basic Proposal for the Substantive Provisions of the Treaty on Certain Questions Concerning the Protection of Literary and Artistic Works to be considered by the Diplomatic Conference, CRNR/DC/4, 30 August 1996 in WIPO, *Records of the Diplomatic Conference on Certain Copyright and Neighboring Rights Questions, Geneva 1996* (WIPO 1999), vol. 1, 161 ff, at 184, [5.02]. Note also Comment of Jukka Liedes, Chair of Main Committee I, 6 December 1996, in *Records of the Diplomatic Conference on Certain Copyright and Neighboring Rights Questions, Geneva 1996* (WIPO 1999), vol. 2, 646, [82]. ('Both Articles 4 and 5 were intended to be declaratory, and what they stated was already the fair interpretation of the relevant clauses in the Berne Convention.')

[115]   Earlier drafts did not go so far: Draft International Convention concerning the Protection of Performers, Makers of Phonograms and Broadcasters (as approved unanimously by the Committee of Experts), Article 14 in (1960) *Droit D'Auteur* 162, (setting out exhaustively four optional exceptions); Report of William Wallace, Committee of Experts on the Protection of Performers, Producers of Phonograms and Broadcasters, Meeting at Hague, 9–20 May 1960, [26], in (1960) *Droit D'Auteur* 161, 173 (at Torwald Hesser's suggestion, adding a fourth exception to the Monaco draft). Two prior drafts, known as the ILO and Monaco drafts, had separate exceptions provisions for performers, record producers and broadcasters: Article 4(7), 6(4), 7(4) of the ILO draft; Article 2(6), 3(6), 5(4) of the Monaco Draft: (1960) *Droit D'Auteur* 109, 137. These were circulated in 1957, and the Finnish delegation had commented that these limitations seemed too restrictive and that there should be correspondence with exceptions to copyright: (1960) *Droit D'Auteur* 139, 144, 154.

decided to create a general mandatory right to quote.[116] Thus, parties to Rome can extend the quotation exception to these neighbouring rights but need not do so.[117]

This conclusion is reinforced by the relationship between Berne and Rome as articulated in Article 1 of Rome. This provision states that '[p]rotection granted under this Convention shall leave intact and shall in no way affect the protection of copyright in literary and artistic works. Consequently, no provision of this Convention may be interpreted as prejudicing such protection.' In so far as Article 1 Rome preserves 'the protection of copyright', this clause does not seem to treat the 'right of quotation' as part of that protection. This view is confirmed by the *travaux*,[118] as well as commentaries. The WIPO *Guide*, for example, states that Article 1 'is limited to safeguarding copyright. It does not proclaim its superiority by laying down that neighboring rights may never be stronger in content or scope than those enjoyed by authors. Indeed there are a number of examples showing that neighboring rights are not necessarily inferior."[119]

Importantly, therefore, contracting parties to Rome are not obliged to recognise a quotation exception for rights in performances, phonograms or broadcasts. Neither does TRIPS nor the WPPT create a mandatory exception for this type of subject matter. According to Article 14(6) TRIPS, 'Any Member may, in relation to the rights conferred under paragraphs 1, 2 and 3 [of Article 14], provide for conditions, limitations, exceptions and reservations to the extent permitted by the Rome Convention.' As has been discussed previously, Rome permits but does not mandate a quotation exception; therefore, a TRIPS Member would also have the option of introducing a quotation exception for performances, phonographs or broadcasts. If this were to be done, it seems that Article 13 TRIPS (i.e. the three-step test) would be inapplicable. This is for the reasons expressed by Dworkin, namely:

> Although the Article refers to the 'rightholder' rather than 'author', it is arguable that it applies only to authors' works: Article 13 refers to 'works' not to 'works and related rights'; it appears after three Articles dealing with copyright, but before Article 14, which

[116] Report of Abraham L Kaminstein on the Diplomatic Conference on the International Protection of Performers, Phonogram Producers and Broadcasting Organisations, Rome, 10–26 October 1961, in (1962) *Droit D'Auteur* 226, 237 (French) Eng sup 157, 167 (The German Proposal was doc. 100).

[117] Claude Masouyé, *Guide to the Rome Convention and Phonograms Convention* (WIPO 1981) 59, [15.9], This is merely an option given to member countries: they are under no obligation to create an exact equivalent. They might for example feel that there was no need to allow the copying of phonograms simply for the purposes of criticism. But the paragraph was intended to act as a hint to the Member States that they should in principle consider treating both copyright and neighboring rights equally in this respect. The model law on neighbouring rights, after setting out specific exceptions, has a general provision based on the thinking behind this paragraph. But it suggests in its commentary that States might preferably consider instead listing each exception separately').

[118] Report of William Wallace, Committee of Experts on the Protection of Performers, Producers of Phonograms and Broadcasters, Meeting at Hague, 9–20 May 1960, [17], in (1960) *Droit D'Auteur* 161, 170 (majority of experts opposed clause stating that the protection of the rights of performers, phonogram producers and broadcasting organisations should not be greater in content or extent than that accorded to authors).

[119] Claude Masouyé, *Guide to the Rome Convention and Phonograms Convention* (WIPO 1981), 17, [1.10].

deals separately with related rights; and Article 14(6) expressly provides for related rights: the rights provided for in that Article can be subjected to 'conditions, limitations, exceptions and reservations to the extent provided by the Rome Convention.'

When it comes to WPPT Members, Article 16 of the WPPT indicates:

> (1) Contracting Parties may, in their national legislation, provide for the same kinds of limitations or exceptions with regard to the protection of performers and producers of phonograms as they provide for, in their national legislation, in connection with the protection of copyright in literary and artistic works.

This provision clearly also allows, but does not require, contracting parties to introduce a quotation exception for performances and phonograms.[120] However, unlike TRIPS, Article 16(2) WPPT makes clear that such exceptions would be subject to the three-step test.[121] At the same time, Article 1(3) emphasises that '[t]his Treaty shall not have any connection with, nor shall it prejudice any rights and obligations under, any other treaties'. Thus, it would in no way undermine the mandatory status of Article 10(1) Berne in relation to Berne works, along with computer programs and databases, nor the fact that (as discussed in Section IV, below), the three-step test is inapplicable where Article 10(1) applies.

Many countries do, in fact, extend the quotation right to the field of related rights. Most obviously, under EU law, Article 5(3)(d) of the Information Society Directive applies to the reproduction and communication rights pertaining both to authorial works and the subject matter of related rights. Indeed, in the *Pelham* case, which concerned the extracting and reuse of a two-second sample from a sound recording by the avant-garde group of electronic musicians Kraftwerk, the question of what constituted quotation from a 'phonogram' was directly in issue. The CJEU clearly regarded the exception as applicable in principle, even if it rather carelessly referred to the acts as 'use of a protected musical work'.[122]

---

[120]   See also Article 6 of the Geneva Convention for the Protection of Producers of Phonograms against Unauthorised Duplication of Their Phonograms 1971: 'Any Contracting State which affords protection by means of copyright or other specific right, or protection by means of penal sanctions, may in its domestic law provide, with regard to the protection of producers of phonograms, the same kinds of limitations as are permitted with respect to the protection of authors of literary and artistic works.' The protection under Berne is not undermined: see Article 7(1). And, in relation to audiovisual performances, see Article 13 of Beijing Treaty on Audiovisual Performances 2012, which states, '(1) Contracting Parties may, in their national legislation, provide for the same kinds of limitations or exceptions with regard to the protection of performers as they provide for, in their national legislation, in connection with the protection of copyright in literary and artistic works.' In Article 13(2), it states that these limitations or exceptions are subject to the three-step test.

[121]   Article 16(2): 'Contracting Parties shall confine any limitations of or exceptions to rights provided for in this Treaty to certain special cases which do not conflict with a normal exploitation of the performance or phonogram and do not unreasonably prejudice the legitimate interests of the performer or of the producer of the phonogram.'

[122]   Case C-476/17 *Pelham GmbH* v. *Hütter* EU:C:2019:624 (CJEU, Grand Chamber), [68]. For further discussion, see Chapter 7, section III, pp. 211–214, below.

3 Miscellaneous Subject Matter

The Berne Convention notion of 'works' does not extend to databases protected by the *sui generis* right that exists in the EU,[123] nor does it encompass published editions,[124] non-original photographs[125] or fixations (i.e. recordings) of films[126] that are protected by related rights. Although Article 2 of Berne refers to photographic and cinematographic works, this does not extend to non-original photographs or film fixations. In both cases, this is because they are not intellectual creations (i.e. they lack originality), a requirement that is inherent in the notion of 'literary and artistic work' and articulated expressly (in relation to compilations) in Article 2(5).[127] Likewise, databases that are the result of investment in collecting, verifying or presenting data do not satisfy the requirement of originality to be a Berne work,[128] and published editions are not literary works but rather fixations of literary works. Moreover, there are no other international conventions regulating these miscellaneous types of subject matter. As such, it is a matter for national laws and, where relevant, EU law, as to whether the quotation exception applies. As it happens, many national laws do extend the quotation exception to these related rights[129] and, as mentioned previously, EU legislation allows Member States the discretion to implement the quotation exception for related rights.[130]

C *Quotation and the Intersection of Authorial Works and Related Rights*

It is clear, then, that the Berne obligation applies only to authorial works; there is no internationally mandated quotation right in relation to 'related rights' or 'entrepreneurial works'. However, in many situations, the form in which a Berne Convention work is made available will attract other rights. For example, a cinematographic film protected under Berne will be issued in an embodiment, such as a DVD, which is also a 'fixation' that is protected by a national related right. The question arises as to whether, in such circumstances, the mandatory rule under Berne carries with it an ancillary obligation for the holder of such a related right to permit quotation.

The answer to this question must be that in any situation where a quotation of an underlying work cannot be effected without involving the related or other right, the

---

[123] Directive 96/9/EC on the Legal Protection of Databases, [1996] OJ L77/20 and see in particular Article 11, which does not apply the principle of national treatment. This has been criticised by Mark Davison, *The Legal Protection of Databases* (Cambridge University Press 2003), 223–4, who argues that the *sui generis* database right in effect offers the equivalent to copyright protection.

[124] E.g. see UK Copyright Designs and Patents Act 1988, Section 8 and German Authors' Rights Law 1965, Article 70.

[125] E.g. see German Authors' Rights Law 1965, Article 72.

[126] For example, see French Intellectual Property Code 1992, Article L215–1; and Directive 2006/116/EC on the Term of Protection of Copyright and Certain Related Rights (codified version) OJ L372, 27.12.2006, pp. 12–18, Article 3(3).

[127] Ricketson and Ginsburg (2006), [8.03], 402–3.

[128] Davison (2003), 219.

[129] For example, see French Intellectual Property Code 1992, Article L211–3(3).

[130] See Article 5(3)(d) Information Society Directive.

Member State is obliged to ensure that the related right does not restrict or inhibit the ability to exercise the quotation right. The freedom granted by Article 10(1) Berne is preemptive. In some circumstances, quotation of an underlying work will be perfectly feasible without infringing a related right: for example, a person can quote from a book without replicating the typographical arrangement and may be able to quote from music without using the sound recording.[131] Matters are, however, more complex in relation to film, where the cinematographic work is often inseparable from the fixation. In so far as the protected cinematographic work encompasses the way in which the film has been edited,[132] quotation of a cinematographic work may necessarily involve quotation of the film fixation. In our understanding of the Berne right of quotation, national rights in the film as a fixation should not be capable of being invoked to impede the exercise of the quotation right.

One matter of particular interest is whether the quotation exception is applicable to the new right granted by the EU to 'press publishers'. Under Article 15 of the Digital Single Market Directive,[133] 'Member States shall provide publishers of press publications established in a Member State with the rights provided for in Article 2 and Article 3(2) of Directive 2001/29/EC for the online use of their press publications by information society service providers.' In other words, press publishers are to be recognised as having the right to reproduce a press publication and the right to make it available to the public. According to Article 15(3) of the Digital Single Market Directive, 'Articles 5 to 8 of Directive 2001/29/EC, . . . shall apply *mutatis mutandis* in respect of the rights provided for in paragraph 1 of this Article.' While, in terms, this means that Member States *may* apply Article 5(3) (d) of the Information Society Directive and permit quotations from such press publications, the question arises as to whether Member States 'must' in practice recognise such an exception for press publications. As noted elsewhere,[134] the answer might be that it is necessary as part of the fair balance recognised between the rights of press publishers and the fundamental right of freedom of expression of a user. However, we think it entirely arguable that the exception is obligatory for a distinct reason: to allow for the exercise of the mandatory freedom to

---

[131]   In this respect, it might be important to ascertain how far elements of performance can also be regarded as part of the 'musical work' and, indeed, how far choices made in relation to a particular recording can be regarded as 'musical' in nature. As Richard Arnold has observed, 'it will often be the case that a recorded piece of music created through performance is sufficiently original over any antecedent musical work to attract copyright': 'Reflections on The Triumph of Music: Copyrights and Performers' Rights in Music', 13, available at www.law.ox.ac.uk/sites/files/oxlaw/mr_justice_ar nolds_paper.pdf (accessed 21 January 2020).

[132]   *Norowzian v. Arks (No. 2)* [2000] FSR 363, 367 (EWCA Civ) (film using jump-cutting technique treated as authorial work – specifically a dramatic work – under UK law, as well as a 'film' under CDPA Section 5B).

[133]   Directive (EU) 2019/790 of the European Parliament and of the Council of 17 April 2019 on Copyright and Related Rights in the Digital Single Market and amending Directives 96/9EC and 2001/29/EC OJ L 130, 17.5.2019, p. 92–125 ('Digital Single Market Directive').

[134]   Chapter 7, section III, p. 211. See also p. 163, below.

quote works under the Berne Convention. In other words, in any situation where a person proposes to quote from a published authorial work such as a newspaper article, cartoon or photograph, the press publishers' right may not be invoked to restrict or prevent such lawful quotation. Were it to do so, there would be a breach of Article 10(1) Berne. This may have been implicitly recognised by recital 57 of the Digital Single Market Directive, which states:

> The rights granted to publishers of press publications under this Directive should also be subject to the same provisions on exceptions and limitations as those applicable to the rights provided for in Directive 2001/29/EC, including the exception in the case of quotations for purposes such as criticism or review provided for in Article 5(3)(d) of that Directive.

The specific referencing of the 'quotation' right here seems to be something more than a suggestion to Member States, but rather implying that they must extend to the new right the 'same provisions' as the Member State provides in relation to the quotation of authorial works.

III TYPES OF RIGHTS THAT ARE SUBJECT TO ARTICLE 10(1) BERNE

A *Economic Rights*

1 Under Berne

As far as Berne is concerned, the quotation right appears applicable to all economic rights in the Convention. In contrast to Article 9(2), for example, there is no restriction of Article 10(1) to the reproduction right. Since Article 10(1) declares that 'it shall be permissible' and does not restrict quotation to particular rights, then all economic rights are implicated. This is also supported by the fact that quotation may occur by way of reproduction, translation, public performance or other forms of exploitation.

2 Post-Berne

Both the TRIPS Agreement and WCT require parties to recognise economic rights not explicitly mentioned in Berne. The TRIPS Agreement, Article 11, requires recognition, for at least computer programs and cinematographic works, of rights to control 'commercial rental to the public'. The WCT, Article 7, requires a right of commercial rental to the public for authors of computer programs, cinematographic works and also works embodied in phonograms. Further, Article 6 WCT stipulates that authors of literary and artistic works shall have a right of distribution.[135] Finally,

---

[135] '[T]he exclusive right of authorizing the making available to the public of the original and copies of their works through sale or other transfer of ownership' and the Agreed Statement clarifies that this refers to 'fixed copies that can be put into circulation as tangible objects'.

Article 8 WCT states that authors of literary and artistic works shall enjoy the right of communication to the public, *including* the 'making available' right.[136]

Does the quotation exception also apply, with mandatory force, to the new rights added by the TRIPS Agreement, and particularly those in the WCT? If not, then 'quotation' is an optional exception for these rights and (confusingly) would be subject to the three-step test under Article 10(1) of the WCT.[137] This would make life very complicated for countries bound by both Berne and the WCT,[138] particularly given that the mandatory quotation exception in Article 10(1) goes beyond what could be permitted under the 'three-step test'.[139] The effect would be that country A *must permit* quotation in relation to certain acts such as reproduction, but then not in relation to critical acts of dissemination – making available, distribution and commercial rental. Although this is a surprisingly troublesome question, we think the answer is that the quotation exception in Article 10 Berne is mandatory for TRIPS and WCT Members, even with respect to the 'new' rights.

The right of commercial rental in TRIPS and the rights of commercial rental and distribution in the WCT are clearly 'new' economic rights, additional to those available in Berne.[140] However, in relation to the right of making available to the public in Article 8 WCT, there is a question about whether this clarifies the scope of the rights of communication to the public in Berne or enlarges those rights.[141] Whether Article 8 WCT is a clarification or enlargement of the Berne provisions does not matter in the end as to whether the mandatory quotation exception is applicable. It is likewise the case for the 'new' rights of distribution and commercial rental. This is because Article 10(1) Berne is, as described previously, agnostic about

---

[136] 'The making available to the public of their works in such a way that members of the public may access these works from a place and at a time individually chosen by them.'

[137] Article 10(1) WCT: 'Contracting Parties may, in their national legislation, provide for limitations of or exceptions to the rights granted to authors of literary and artistic works under this Treaty in certain special cases that do not conflict with a normal exploitation of the work and do not unreasonably prejudice the legitimate interests of the author.'

[138] As of 5 June 2020, the WCT has 105 contracting parties, whereas the 1971 Paris Act of Berne has 188 and TRIPS has 164. A total of 101 countries are in all 3, including the United Kingdom, China, the United States, Russia, the Ukraine and all the Member States of the European Union. But there are 16 countries that are just in Berne (e.g. Lebanon, Libya, the Sudan and the Holy See); 15 just in TRIPS (e.g. Pakistan and Uganda); 8 in both Berne and the WCT but not TRIPS (e.g. Belarus, Bosnia and Serbia); 46 in Berne and TRIPS but not the WCT (e.g. Brazil, Norway and Thailand) and 2 in the WCT and TRIPS but not Berne, Berne accession, as opposed to WIPO membership, not being a prerequisite for accession to the WCT (the European Union, which is not eligible to join Berne, and Madagascar). Countries that are not in any of the three agreements include Iran and Iraq.

[139] See Chapter 7, section I, pp. 190–201.

[140] Ricketson and Ginsburg (2006), [4.23]–[4.24], 151–152; [4.36], 159.

[141] Professors Ricketson and Ginsburg have noted that the question of reaffirmation versus enlargement would affect the possibility of applying compulsory licences to the 'making available' right in accordance with Article 11bis(2) of Berne. They argue that the making available right, which targets 'on-demand' transmissions (whether by wire or wireless means) is not mandated by Berne, but neither does the concept of 'communication to the public' in Berne preclude it; see Ricketson and Ginsburg (2006), [12.62], 748–9.

the economic rights to which it applies and is not limited (unlike Article 9(2) Berne) to the reproduction right. Instead, the mandatory quotation exception is tied to Berne *works* (i.e. those works within Article 2 Berne).[142] Given that the 'new' economic rights in WCT and TRIPS apply to Berne works, so too would the quotation exception. Of course, this raises the important question of the relationship between the quotation exception and the three-step test, which we address in Section IV below. Before doing so, we consider the applicability of the quotation exception to moral rights.

B *Moral Rights*

Is Article 10(1) an exception not only to economic rights but also to an author's moral rights? Moral rights of attribution and integrity are, of course, required to be recognised under Article 6*bis* of Berne.[143] The mandatory form of the exception in Article 10(1) would suggest that it is also applicable to moral rights. This view might be regarded as confirmed by Article 10(3), which, by requiring that the source be indicated, seems to expressly indicate the moral right of attribution survives. By implication, it seems that Article 10(1) qualifies at least the right of integrity. Moreover, in Article 11*bis*(2) of Berne, which specifically permits countries of the Union to determine 'the conditions under which' communication rights specified in Art 11*bis*(1) 'may be exercised', it is specified that the conditions 'shall not in any circumstances be prejudicial to the moral rights of the author'. One might infer from this, and the absence of such a qualification in Article 10(1), that moral rights are subject to the right of quotation – although a severe or disproportionate prejudicing of such rights might also render the quotation inconsistent with 'fair practice'. While this is a possible interpretation, it probably places too much emphasis on the conception of Berne as a systematically organised code, whereas in truth it is a palimpsest of provisions, accretions and additions being made at successive diplomatic conferences with precious little consideration of structure, organisation and formal systematisation. In fact, the better view is that, despite its form, the quotation right is *not* a limitation on the moral rights recognised under Article 6*bis* of Berne. This is for several reasons.

The first is that Article 10(3) (i.e. the requirement that the source be indicated) does not seem sensibly capable of interpretation as a 'without prejudice clause'. In other words, it cannot be understood as a provision stating that Article 10(1) is without prejudice *only* to the attribution right (and not the integrity right). If that was intended, then it would have been simpler to include more express language, such as 'shall not in any circumstances be prejudicial to the attribution right of the author'. Indeed, as already observed, in Article 11*bis*(2), such express language is used.[144] Moreover, the

---

[142] See pp. 44–47, above.
[143] For a discussion, see Ricketson and Ginsburg (2006), ch. 10.
[144] Ricketson and Ginsburg (2006), [10.46], 619, stating that Article 11*bis*(2) moral rights are derived from Article 6*bis* 'to which they appear to refer, and with which they are contemporaneous'.

term of moral rights was in fact only extended to correspond to the term of protection for economic rights in 1967,[145] and even then was hotly contested[146] and, as adopted, significantly qualified.[147] In the period prior to this, the attribution conditions on Article 10(1) and (2) (in the Brussels Act) operated throughout the copyright term, even though there was no obligation to recognise moral rights.

The second is that the *travaux* support this view.[148] In Bergström's report on the conclusions of the Main Committee I of the Stockholm conference, it is recorded that 'here too, as in the case of all uses of the work, the rights granted to the author under Article 6*bis* (moral rights) are reserved'.[149] Further, there are indirect indications in the *travaux* that the integrity right applies. For example, one response to the suggestion that quotations should be 'short' was to highlight that sometimes it might be necessary to take large amounts out of respect for the integrity of an author's argument or expression.[150] While in one respect this merely sought to show that it might be more author-friendly to allow longer quotations,[151] the other implication is that a requirement of shortness might undermine the effectiveness of the defence. If shortness inevitably meant breaching the author's right of integrity, but shortness was a condition of licit quotation right, the exception could be rendered ineffective.

Third, it would be strange if the Berne Convention imposed any mandatory limitation on moral rights, given that it was accepted that protection of moral rights need not be effected through 'copyright law'.[152] Article 6*bis*(3) indicates that 'the means of redress for safeguarding the rights granted by this article shall be governed by the legislation of the country where protection is claimed'. The United States, for example, purported to offer equivalent protection through a melange of civil law actions under federal law (including section 43(a) of the Lanham Act) and state law (including laws relating to defamation, privacy, publicity, unfair competition, and misrepresentation).[153] It would seem odd if Berne purported to create mandatory limitations on the operation of such regimes.

---

[145]   Article 6*bis*(2): 'The rights granted to the author in accordance with the preceding paragraph shall. After his death, be maintained, at least until the expiry of the economic rights.'

[146]   Ricketson and Ginsburg (2006), [10.12], 596–7.

[147]   Article 6*bis*(2) adds: 'However, those countries whose legislation, at the moment of their ratification or accession to this Act, does not provide for the protection after the death of the author of all the rights set out in the preceding paragraph may provide that some of these rights may, after his death, cease to be maintained.'

[148]   See also Ricketson and Ginsburg (2006), [13.46], 795–6.

[149]   Report, [205], in *Records*, 1165.

[150]   George Straschnov, in Minutes, [769], in *Records*, 861 (discussed herein at p. 27, above).

[151]   And thus, perhaps, consistent with the terms of revision laid down in Article 24 of Brussels.

[152]   Ricketson and Ginsburg (2006), [10.36], 613–14.

[153]   'Not necessarily be protected by rules within the domain of copyright': Report, [170], in *Records*, 1159. See also US Congress expressing the view, when implementing the Berne Convention via the Berne Convention Implementation Act of 1988, that a composite of US laws already gave the kind of protection required by Article 6*bis* Berne: H.R. Rep. No. 609, 100th Cong., 2d Sess. 32-34 (1988). See generally G Dworkin, 'The Moral Right of the Author: Moral Rights and the Common Law

Fourth, the view that Article 10(1) does not apply to moral rights is consistent with accounts of moral rights as part of the international human rights regime. Article 27(1) of the Universal Declaration of Human Rights (1948) provides that '[e]veryone has the right to the protection of the moral and material interests resulting from any scientific, literary, or artistic production of which he is the author'. In addition, Article 15(1)(c) on the International Covenant on Economic, Social and Cultural Rights (1966) provides for a right in similar terms: the right for everyone 'to benefit from the protection of the moral and material interests resulting from any scientific, literary or artistic production of which he is the author'. In its 2005 General Comment No. 17, the Committee on Economic, Social and Cultural Rights considers that 'moral interests' include 'the right of authors to be recognised as the creators of their scientific, literary and artistic productions and to object to any distortion, mutilation or other modification of, or other derogatory action in relation to, such productions, which would be prejudicial to their honour and reputation' and, further, that moral rights form part of the core obligations of article 15(1)(c).[154] The General Comment also observes that while this right must be balanced against other rights and freedoms, 'limitations must be compatible with the very nature of the rights protected in article 15, paragraph 1(c), which lies in the protection of the personal link between the author and his/her creation and of the means which are necessary to enable authors to enjoy an adequate standard of living'.[155]

But if moral rights under Article 6*bis* Berne are not limited by Article 10(1), how can we make sense of the attribution requirement in Article 10(3)? If Article 6*bis* survives, why have the additional obligation in Article 10(3)?[156] The answer is that Article 10(3) is a distinct requirement to attribution in Article 6*bis* because it requires attribution of the 'source'.[157] This clearly requires citation of additional information

---

Countries' (1995) 19 *Columbia-VLA Journal of Law and the Arts* 229 discussing the pre-existing laws that common law countries relied upon to show they complied with Article 6*bis* Berne.

[154] CESCR General Comment No 17, [13] and [39]

[155] CESCR General Comment No 17, [23]. Discussed in H Grosse Ruse-Khan, *The Protection of Intellectual Property in International Law* (Oxford University Press 2016) [8.17]–[8.20], 219–22.

[156] It is notable, too, that similar requirements can be found in Article 10*bis* (1), though here in quite different terms: '[T]he source must always be clearly indicated; the legal consequences of a breach of this obligation shall be determined by the legislation of the country where protection is claimed.'

[157] For the view that the attribution requirement in Article 10(1) is distinct from Article 6*bis*, see Jane C Ginsburg, 'The Most Moral of Rights: The Right to Be Recognized as the Author of One's Work' (2016) 8 *Geo Mason J Int'l Com L* 44, 51–2, arguing that Article 10(3) is a condition rather than an affirmative right (unlike Article 6*bis*) and that Article 10(3) was introduced as part of the 1948 Brussels Revision of Berne, whereas Article 6*bis* was introduced at the Rome Conference of 1928 – if the requirements were the same then Article 10(3) would have been 'superfluous'. See also Ricketson and Ginsburg (2006), [10.46], 619. The significance of Article 10(3) being a distinct requirement is that failure to comply with it may be the subject to a TRIPS dispute resolution procedure, unlike failure to comply with Article 6*bis* Berne.

such as the title of the journal or book,[158] and this would justify its inclusion in Article 10, even though the attribution right was maintained.[159]

A separate issue is whether, if the quotation right is not an exception to moral rights, these rights may stymie the operation of the exception? Or, put more neutrally, how would a conflict between the quotation exception and moral rights protection be resolved?[160] We argue that the likelihood of conflict between the quotation exception and moral rights protection is reduced given the scope of the former. In particular, Article 10(3), although not equivalent to the attribution right in Article 6*bis* Berne, will encourage the identification of the author of the work quoted. Further, the requirement in Article 10(1) Berne that the work must be already lawfully made available to the public means that any right of divulgation (which is not mandated by Berne but is recognised in many national laws) is unlikely to be infringed. When it comes to the right of integrity, the opportunity to weigh non-economic harm when assessing whether a use is in accordance with 'fair practice', as is discussed in Chapter 6, will be helpful in ensuring that conflicting outcomes do not occur.

IV NON-APPLICABILITY OF THE THREE-STEP TEST TO THE MANDATORY QUOTATION RIGHT

Another important preliminary consideration is whether the three-step test embodied in Article 9(2) of Berne, Article 13 of the TRIPS Agreement and Article 10(2) of the WIPO Copyright Treaty applies to Article 10(1) of Berne. It is our argument that it does not. As such, when it comes to national implementation of Article 10(1), countries do *not* have the additional burden of considering compliance with the three-step test.[161]

---

[158]   Proposals of ALAI, Lucerne, 5–9 May 1948 regarding 'emprunts licites' suggested that in the case of extracts from a journal or periodical review, attribution of source requires reference to the title of the journal or review, name of the author of the article; in other cases, to the title of the work, name of author and publisher.

[159]   Oliver Brand in P T Stoll, J Busche and K Arend (eds.), *WTO-Trade Related Aspects of Intellectual Property Rights* (Martinus Nijhoff 2009), 249 (considering the impact of TRIPS Article 9(1) on Article 10(3) Berne, and noting that it is 'not a mere manifestation' of the attribution right. Ricketson and Ginsburg (2006), [13.110], 858.

[160]   In relation to the parody exception and moral rights, Sabine Jacques, *The Parody Exception in Copyright Law* (Oxford University Press 2019), ch. 6 argues that national parody exceptions are likely to ensure respect for authors' moral rights – or at the very least reduce conflict with them – if the requirements of the parody exception are (i) intent to conjure up the other work; (ii) intent to be humorous; and (iii) lack of confusion between the original work and its parody use.

[161]   This also makes the approach of Advocate General Szpunar in C-516/17 *Spiegel Online v. Beck* EU: C:2019:16, [50] problematic.

A *Article 9(2) Berne*

To begin, it is straightforward to dismiss the relevance of the three-step test, as contained in Article 9(2) of Berne, to Article 10(1) Berne. This is because Article 9(2) Berne reflects a residual discretion on Berne Members to create exceptions to the reproduction right.[162] By contrast, it has often been assumed that all the exceptions permitted in the Berne Convention are subject to the three-step test embodied in Article 13 of TRIPS and Article 10(2) of the WCT.[163] As a result, it has come to be regarded as the only norm that matters when considering national freedom to define

---

[162] Ricketson and Ginsburg (2006), [13.10], 763. See also J Hughes, 'Fair Use and Its Politics – At Home and Abroad' in Ruth L Okediji (ed.), *Copyright Law in an Age of Exceptions and Limitations* (Cambridge University Press 2017), ch. 8, 234–74, 241, noting that the three-step test in Art. 9(2) Berne 'might have remained an obscure component of Berne' if not for TRIPS.

[163] G B Dinwoodie and R C Dreyfuss, *A NeoFederalist Vision of TRIPS: The Resilience of the International Intellectual Property Regime* (Oxford University Press 2012), 185 ('TRIPS negotiators adapted [Article 9(2) of Berne] to create exceptions tests that apply to all uses of copyrighted works'); G B Dinwoodie, 'The Development and Incorporation of International Norms in the Formation of Copyright Law' (2001) 62 *Ohio St L J* 733, 769 ('article 13 of TRIPS elevated [art 9(2) Berne] to a general test of permissible exceptions (including exceptions to performance rights)'; Margot E Kaminski and Dr Shlomit Yanisky-Ravid, 'The Marrakesh Treaty for Visually Impaired Persons: Why a Treaty was Preferable to Soft Law' (2014) 75 *U Pitt L Rev* 255, 266 ('Countries' systems for limitations and exceptions must fit within the three-step test'); Daniel J Gervais, 'Making Copyright Whole: A Principled Approach to Copyright Exceptions and Limitations' (2008) 5 *U Ottawa L & Tech J* 1, 4 (the three-step test has become the single sieve through which all, or almost all, exceptions to exclusive copyright rights must pass to be compatible with the TRIPS Agreement'). Gervais further states at 9 that it has 'become the cornerstone of exceptions to all copyright rights', but notes at 32 that '[i]t would seem unnecessary to apply the three-step test as a further barrier to validity because, as a matter of treaty interpretation, exceptions such as articles 10(1) and 10(2) of the Convention include a different test, namely the reference to compatibility with fair practice'. See also Michael Landau, 'Fitting United States Copyright Law into the International Scheme: Foreign and Domestic Challenges to Recent Legislation' (2007) 23 *Ga St U L Rev* 847, 855 ('Originally applicable to only the exclusive right of reproduction under Article 9(2) of the Berne Convention, the "three step test" has been expanded under Article 13 of TRIPS to apply to all of the exclusive rights'); Rochelle Cooper Dreyfuss and Andreas F Lowenfeld, 'Two Achievements of the Uruguay Round: Putting TRIPS and Dispute Settlement Together' (1997) 37 *Va J Int'l L* 275, 306 ('The TRIPS Agreement countenances exceptions to protection, *but only for* 'special cases which do not conflict with a normal exploitation of the work and do not unreasonably prejudice the legitimate interests of the right holder') (emphasis added); Lawrence R Helfer, 'World Music on a U.S. Stage: A Berne/TRIPS and Economic Analysis of the Fairness in Music Licensing Act' (2000) 80 *BU L Rev* 93, 147 ('Unlike Berne, which attaches different exceptions and limitations to each exclusive right enjoyed by copyright owners, TRIPs article 13 contains a single standard for measuring *all such restrictions*' [emphasis added]); G Dworkin, 'Exceptions to Copyright Exclusivity: Is Fair Use Consistent with Article 9.2 Berne and the New International Order' in Hugh Hansen (ed.), *International Intellectual Property Law and Policy: Volume 4* (Juris 2000), ch. 66, 66–13 ('One reading of Article 13 of TRIPS suggests that ... any exceptions under Berne are now subject to Article 9.2 safeguards and controls'); and Graham Greenleaf and David Lindsay, *Public Rights: Copyright's Public Domain* (Cambridge University Press 2018), 131–2 (suggesting that an express exception under Berne and Article 13 TRIPS should be applied cumulatively, although not such as to extend the specific exceptions in Berne).

exceptions. For example, explaining the effect of adherence to TRIPS on US law, the US President stated:

> Article 9:2 of the Berne Convention now bans the imposition of limitations on, or exceptions to, the reproduction right ... [unless] such limits or exceptions do not conflict with a normal exploitation of the work and do not unreasonably prejudice the legitimate interests of the right holder. Article 13 of the Agreement on TRIPS widens the scope of this provision to all exclusive rights in copyright and related rights, thus narrowly circumscribing the limitations and exceptions that WTO Members may impose. This approach is consistent with section 107 of the Copyright Act (17 USC 107) relating to fair use of copyrighted works.[164]

The same question was asked of the US Government within the framework of the TRIPS Council, and the US response argued that the fair use doctrine 'embodies essentially the same goals as Article 13 of TRIPS, and is applied and interpreted in a way *entirely congruent* with the standards set forth in that Article'.[165]

Likewise, some of the most respected of US legal academics have assumed that Article 13 of TRIPS constitutes a critical constraint on national law-making, casting a cloud over the legitimacy of fair use.[166] The proposition seems to have started life with Professor Paul Geller's early discussion of TRIPS drafts,[167] but was picked up and reiterated by leading commentators such as David Nimmer,[168] as well as academics such as Professors Jerome Reichman,[169] Rochelle Dreyfuss,[170] Jane

---

[164] Message from the President of the United States Transmitting the Uruguay Trade Agreements, Implementing Bill, Statement of Administrative Action, and Required Supporting Statements, H.R. Doc. No. 316, 103d Cong., 2d Sess. (1994) p. 314. The original text of this quotation incorrectly says "when" rather than "unless".

[165] Review of Legislation on Copyright and Related Rights, WTO Doc. IP/Q/USA/1.

[166] But cf. Graeme B Dinwoodie and Rochelle C Dreyfuss, *A Neo-Federalist Vision*, 186 (appearing to argue that fair use 'illustrates how extensive' the freedom remains), and Australian Law Reform Commission, *Copyright and the Digital Economy* (Report No 122) (Sydney, ALRC, 2013), 116–22 (concluding that fair use is compliant with the three-step test).

[167] Paul Geller, 'Can the GATT Incorporate Berne Whole?' (1990) 12 *EIPR* 423, 425 (raising questions of compatibility of US fair use doctrine with various proposals for TRIPS including Article 9(2) Berne).

[168] Melville B Nimmer and David Nimmer, *Nimmer on Copyright* (1996): 'a future WTO panel could conclude, for example, that the free-wheeling fair use doctrine applied by US courts ... violates Article 9(2) of the Berne Convention and hence is impermissible under TRIPS' (quoted in Dworkin).

[169] J H Reichman, 'Universal Minimum Standards of Intellectual Property Protection under the TRIPS Component of the WTO Agreement' (1995) 29 *Int'l Law* 345, 368. ('This double-barreled filter, though subject to state practice, is potentially more restrictive than the broad fair-use doctrine fashionable in the United States.')

[170] See Rochelle C Dreyfuss and Andreas F Lowenfeld, 'Two Achievements of the Uruguay Round: Putting TRIPS and Dispute Settlement Together' (1997) 37 *Va J Int'l L* 275, 306:
> 'The TRIPS Agreement countenances exceptions to protection, but only for "special cases" which do not conflict with a normal exploitation of the work and do not unreasonably prejudice the legitimate interests of the right holder. Whether these provisions are consistent with one another is not at all clear (citing Reichman, "Minimum Standards", at 368). Yet, it seems to us that panels ought to tread lightly in this area. Indeed, member states ought to resist pressures from their constituents to bring complaints involving such issues to the WTO. The extent to which fair use is considered

Ginsburg,[171] Pamela Samuelson,[172] Justin Hughes,[173] Ruth Okediji[174] and Mary Wong.[175] Professor Larry Helfer, for example, argued that the United States' 'open-textured fair use doctrine is suspect under the three-step test and ripe for WTO challenge'.[176] Likewise, Professor Gerald Dworkin suggested that '[a] generous application of the fair use defense, however justified in social terms, does raise the question whether its application always falls within the terms of Article 9.2 of the Berne Convention'.[177]

B Article 13 TRIPS

We turn first to examine how Article 13 TRIPS affects Article 10(1) Berne. Article 13 TRIPS states: 'Members shall confine limitations or exceptions to exclusive rights to certain special cases which do not conflict with a normal exploitation of the work and do not unreasonably prejudice the legitimate interests of the right holder.'

It has been queried whether Article 13 TRIPS applies only to the additional rights recognised under TRIPS. The EU mounted this argument in the so-called 'Fairness

---

necessary depends on fundamental national values, such as the importance and extent of free speech, on artistic traditions and on aesthetic sensibilities. Setting a worldwide standard on this issue would, therefore, reduce flexibility and produce a kind of cultural homogenization that might either induce noncompliance or turn the world into a much less stimulating environment.'

[171] J Ginsburg, 'Exclusive Rights, Exceptions, and Uncertain Compliance with International Norms' (2014) 242 *RIDA* 175 (arguing that the recent extension of US fair use case law and the absence of a compulsory licence feature creates an incompatibility with the three-step test).

[172] Pam Samuelson, 'Possible Futures of Fair Use' (2015) 90 *Wash L Rev* 815, 850–3, rebuts arguments that the US fair use doctrine is contrary to the three-step test in Berne and TRIPS and suggests they are correlative tests. See also Pam Samuelson, 'Unbundling Fair Uses' (2009) 77 *Fordham L Rev* 2537, 2544, n 38, observing that 'unbundling fair uses makes it easier to argue that fair use accommodates a number of "certain special cases" and that the four factors ensure that this exception does not interfere with a normal exploitation of the work or with other legitimate interests of rights holders'.

[173] J Hughes, 'Fair Use and Its Politics – at Home and Abroad' in Ruth L Okediji (ed.), *Copyright Law in an Age of Exceptions and Limitations* (Cambridge University Press 2017), ch. 8, 234–74, 247 ('to my mind whether section 107 fair use in domestic American law passes the three step test remains principally a theoretical question' and suggesting that it probably complies).

[174] Ruth L Okediji, 'Towards an International Fair Use Doctrine' (2000) 39 *Colum J Transnat'l L* 75, arguing at 126 et seq. that the US conception of fair use is not reflected in international copyright law and that fair use could violate Article 9(2) Berne and Article 13 TRIPS because of its breadth and indeterminacy.

[175] Mary W S Wong, 'Transformative User-Generated Content in Copyright Law: Infringing Derivative Works or Fair Use' (2009) 11 *Vanderbilt Journal of Entertainment and Technology Law* 1075, 1102. See also Marshall Leaffer, 'The Uncertain Future of Fair Use in a Global Information Marketplace' (2001) 62 *Ohio State Law Journal* 849, 861 (stating that serious reservations have been raised about the conformity of U.S. fair use law with the "three-part test", especially where the doctrine is applied to new technologies.')

[176] Lawrence R Helfer, 'World Music on a U.S. Stage: A Berne/TRIPS and Economic Analysis of the Fairness in Music Licensing Act' (2000) 80 *BU L Rev* 93, 184.

[177] Gerald Dworkin, 'Exceptions to Copyright Exclusivity: Is Fair Use Consistent with Article 9(2) Berne and the New International Order?' in Hugh Hansen (ed.), *International Intellectual Property Law and Policy* vol. 4 (Juris 2000), ch. 66, [66–9].

in Music Licensing case',[178] and it has some academic support.[179] However, the Dispute Resolution Body of the World Trade Organization in the 'Fairness in Music Licensing case' rejected this argument. There the Panel took the view that the 'minor exceptions' doctrine, according to which Members of the Berne Union could operate certain minor derogations from the public performance right, was to be interpreted in line with Article 13 of the TRIPS Agreement.[180] Professor Sam Ricketson also shares the view that Article 13 TRIPS is not restricted to additional rights because otherwise it would have a 'very limited sphere of application, as the only non-Berne exclusive right required to be protected under TRIPS is the rental right'. He adds that 'as Article 9(1) of TRIPS requires members to comply with Article 1 to 21 of Berne (other than Article 6*bis*), the better view must be that Article 13 applies to all the exclusive rights listed in Berne, including that of reproduction, as well as the rental right in TRIPS'.[181] Thus, it might be suggested that Article 10(1) Berne must likewise be interpreted consistently with Article 13 TRIPS.[182]

---

[178] WTO Panel Report, United States – Section 110(5) of the Copyright Act 1976, (15 June 2000), WT/DS/160/R, [6.34]:

'The principal EC argument concerning Article 13 is that it only applies to exclusive rights newly introduced under the TRIPS Agreement and that the rights conferred under Articles 1–21 of the Berne Convention (1971) as incorporated into the TRIPS Agreement can be derogated from only on the grounds of pre-existing exceptions applicable under the Berne Convention (1971). In the EC view, its position is supported by Article 2.2 of the TRIPS Agreement and Article 20 of the Berne Convention (1971), which it interprets as a prohibition on any derogation from existing standards of protection under the Berne Convention (1971).'

[179] See C Geiger, D Gervais and M Senftleben, 'The Three Step Test Revisited: How to Use the Test's Flexibility in National Copyright Law' (2014) 29 *Am U Intl L Rev* 581, 588: 'the system of exceptions and limitations as it exists in Berne was not modified by TRIPS' and as such 'need not pass the test as an additional condition'. According to them Article 13 TRIPS applies to new rights and 'rights for which no specific exception and limitation is provided in the Convention, such as the so-called small exceptions'. See also D Brennan, 'The Three Step Test Frenzy – Why the TRIPS Panel Decision Might Be Considered *Per Incuriam*' (2002) IPQ 212, 219–20, 223–4, criticising the Panel for dismissing the relevance of Art 11*bis*(2) to the dispute and suggesting that the TRIPS negotiating history does not support the conclusion that Art 13 TRIPS applies to all exceptions under Berne.

[180] WT/DS/160/R: [6.63]:

'Thus we conclude that, in the absence of any express exclusion in Article 9.1 of the TRIPS Agreement, the incorporation of Articles 11 and 11*bis* of the Berne Convention (1971) into the Agreement includes the entire *acquis* of these provisions, including the possibility of providing minor exceptions to the respective exclusive rights.'

[6.80] 'In our view, neither the express wording nor the context of Article 13 or any other provision of the TRIPS Agreement supports the interpretation that the scope of application of Article 13 is limited to the exclusive rights newly introduced under the TRIPS Agreement.'

[181] See Ricketson, SCCR/9/7, 47. However, at 49, he argues that in light of Article 2(2) TRIPS and Article 20 Berne, 'it does not seem possible to argue for any wider application of the three-step test under Article 13 of TRIPS than would otherwise be allowed under the Berne Convention'. See also Annette Kur, 'Of Oceans, Islands, and Inland Water – How Much Room for Exceptions and Limitations under the Three-Step Test?' (2009) 8 *Rich J Global L & Bus* 287, 310.

[182] See N Netanel, 'The Next Round: The Impact of the WIPO Copyright Treaty on TRIPS Dispute Settlement' (1997) 37 *Va J Intl L* 441, 459–60, arguing that Article 13 TRIPS imposes 'some constraint

The first objection to this construction is that the WTO Panel decision did *not* address the relationship between Article 13 TRIPS and Article 10(1) Berne, but rather only commented on the applicability of Article 13 TRIPS to the minor exceptions doctrine.[183] Therefore, the question of whether the mandatory quotation exception in Article 10(1) Berne must be interpreted according to the three-step test in Article 13 TRIPS remains open.[184]

A second argument is that Article 10(1) of Berne is an *obligation* on Berne Union Members and the same obligation is imposed on TRIPS Members via Article 9(1) TRIPS. It would be odd to require compliance with an obligation and yet at the same time constrain such compliance. Further, while Article 13 TRIPS might restrict the operation of an *optional* provision, Article 2(2) TRIPS specifically indicates that nothing in Article 13 derogates from *any obligation* between the parties.[185] Effectively, Article 13 TRIPS does not purport to change Article 10(1) Berne and the relevant conditions for the quotation exception are those stipulated within Article 10.

C *Article 10 WIPO Copyright Treaty 1996*

We turn next to assess the applicability of Article 10(2) of the WCT to Article 10(1) Berne. As between countries that are parties to the WCT (which as of June 2020 number 105), Article 10(2) WCT requires that '[c]ontracting Parties shall, *when applying the Berne Convention*, confine any limitations of or exceptions to rights provided for therein to certain special cases that do not conflict with a normal exploitation of the work and do not unreasonably prejudice the legitimate interests of the author' (emphasis added).

On the face of it, this provision would seem to require WCT contracting parties to apply the three-step test to the quotation exception in Article 10(1) Berne.[186] Upon

---

on the limitations and exceptions to copyright owner rights that would otherwise be permissible under Berne'.

[183] WT/DS/160/R, [6.81]. J Oliver, 'Copyright in the WTO: The Panel Decision on the Three Step Test' (2002) 25 *Colum J L & Arts* 119, 147: the 'question left open by the panel decision is whether, under TRIPS, an express Berne exception relating to free use is also subject to Article 13'.

[184] Cf. M Senftleben, 'Quotation, Parody and Fair Use' in B Hugenholtz, A Quaedvlieg and D Visser (eds.), *1912–2012: A Century of Dutch Copyright* (DeLex 2012), 354–5 (stating that 'the international three-step test is nowadays applicable to all Berne limitations by virtue of Article 13 TRIPS and Article 10(2) WCT', but then going on to add this qualification: 'Given the mandatory nature of Article 10(1) BC, the right of quotation may alternatively be seen as a right of use (of authors wishing to build upon pre-existing material) that does not fall within the scope of the three-step test').

[185] TRIPS, Article 2(2) ('*Nothing* in Parts I to IV of this Agreement *shall derogate from existing obligations that Members may have to each other under* the Paris Convention, *the Berne Convention*, the Rome Convention and the Treaty on Intellectual Property in Respect of Integrated Circuits') (emphasis added).

[186] Pam Samuelson, 'The US Digital Agenda at WIPO' (1997) 37 *Virginia Journal of International Law* 369, fn. 188, raised the question whether the predecessor to Article 10(2) WCT – namely, Article 12 in the draft WCT – would override the right of fair quotation under Article 10(1) Berne.

closer analysis, however, this turns out not to be the case for two reasons. The first is that Article 10(1) of Berne is an *obligation* on Members of the Convention and the WCT imposes that same obligation on their respective parties via Article 1(4), which states, 'Contracting Parties shall comply with Articles 1 to 21 and the Appendix of the Berne Convention.' As was just argued in relation to Article 13 TRIPS, it would be strange to require compliance with an obligation (i.e. the quotation exception in Article 10(1) Berne with the conditions specified in Article 10) and simultaneously to prohibit such compliance by imposing additional conditions (i.e. the three-step test). More significantly, while Article 10(2) of the WCT might constrain the operation of an *optional* provision, Article 1(2) specifically indicates that nothing in the treaty derogates from *any obligation* between the parties.[187] Effectively, then, the WCT does not purport to change Article 10(1) Berne, including the obligation to allow quotation – whatever the purpose – if it meets the other conditions of Article 10.

The second reason relates to the Agreed Statement to Article 10(2) of the WCT, which states: 'It is also understood that Article 10(2) *neither reduces nor extends* the scope of applicability of the limitations and exceptions permitted by the Berne Convention' (emphasis added). As Professor Sam Ricketson explains, the fact that the Agreed Statement was adopted by consensus means that it can 'be regarded as part of the context of the WCT for the purposes of Article 31(2)(a) of the Vienna Convention'.[188] As such, the effect of the Agreed Statement is as follows:

> Accordingly, WCT members are not required to modify limitations and exceptions that are consistent with the present Berne text, even if these would not pass the three-step test in Article 10(2). There will, of course, be room for argument as to whether any of the existing Berne exceptions and limitations, including the minor reservations doctrine, do, in fact, go beyond the limits of the three-step test, but, to the extent that this is so, it seems clear that the three-step test cannot "trump" these existing limitations and exceptions.[189]

Therefore, it seems clear that contracting parties to the WCT must provide for a quotation exception in relation to the exclusive rights granted by Berne and that this is not subject to the three-step requirement as well. But what, then, is the role of Article 10(2) WCT? Also, what about the exclusive rights granted by the WCT in Articles 6, 7 and 8 and the effect of Article 10(1) WCT? Does the quotation exception apply to these rights, and if so, is the three-step test also applicable?

---

[187]   WCT, Article 1(2) ('Nothing in this Treaty shall derogate from existing obligations that Contracting Parties have to each other under the Berne Convention for the Protection of Literary and Artistic Works').

[188]   S Ricketson, *WIPO Study on Limitations and Exceptions of Copyright and Related Rights in the Digital Environment* (2003) SCCR 9/7, 62.

[189]   Ricketson, SCCR/9/7, 63.

Article 10(1) WCT[190] suggests that the three-step test (as opposed to the quotation exception) would be applicable to the 'new' economic rights contained in the WCT – namely, the rights of rental, distribution and making available to the public, in Articles 6, 7 and 8 respectively.[191] Nonetheless, we argue that, in fact, the quotation exception *does* apply to the 'new' WCT economic rights as well as those contained in Berne.

Our argument relies on the impact of Article 20 Berne, which provides that special agreements can be entered into by Berne Union Members 'in so far as such agreements grant to authors more extensive rights than those granted by the Convention, or contain provisions not contrary to the Convention'. The WCT grants authors more extensive rights – in the form of the making available rental and distributions rights – but must also not be contrary to Berne. Arguably, Article 10(1) WCT requiring the application of the three-step test for economic rights granted under the WCT would be contrary to Berne insofar as it ousted Article 10(1) Berne, a mandatory exception that is not explicitly tied to any particular economic rights, but rather Berne 'works'.[192] Moreover, as already mentioned, Article 1(4) WCT emphasises the requirement for contracting parties to comply with Articles 1–21 and the Appendix of Berne. It would not be possible for contracting parties to comply with the obligation in Article 10(1) Berne, which is not tied to particular economic rights but to Berne works, *unless* they were able to provide for a quotation exception in relation to the 'new' economic rights in the WCT. Finally, as noted previously, Article 1(2) WCT reiterates that nothing in the WCT 'shall derogate from existing obligations that Contracting Parties have to each other under the Berne Convention' and the obligation to provide for a quotation exception contained in Article 10(1) Berne is not limited to particular exclusive rights but relates to Berne works. Therefore, the quotation exception ought to apply to *all* economic rights in the WCT *and* Berne.

But what role does this leave for the three-step test in Article 10 WCT? We have argued that the three-step test in Article 10 WCT does not displace the quotation exception in Berne, but it cannot be the case that there is no role at all; otherwise there would have been little point in including Article 10 WCT. In relation to Berne economic rights, while the three-step test in Article 10(2) WCT does not apply to the mandatory quotation exception, it *might* constrain the operation of an optional exception, such as Article 10(2) or 10*bis* of Berne. As such, there remains a role for

---

[190] '(1) Contracting Parties may, in their national legislation, provide for limitations of or exceptions to the rights granted to authors of literary and artistic works under this Treaty in certain special cases that do not conflict with a normal exploitation of the work and do not unreasonably prejudice the legitimate interests of the author.'

[191] Cf. Ricketson in SCCR9/7, 60–1, where he says that Article 10(1) WCT applies to the rights accorded under the WCT.

[192] Article 10(1) Berne states: 'It shall be permissible to make quotations from *a work*' (emphasis added). See Chapter 3, Section III, Part A, above.

Article 10(2) WCT.[193] Alternatively, the three-step test in Article 10(2) WCT could operate in relation to purposes or uses *not* covered by the specific exception provisions in Berne, such as Article 10 and 10*bis*. Thus, where exceptions are *not* dealing with quotation, illustration for teaching purposes or reporting current events, but deal with uses that fall within Article 9(2) Berne, such as private use or judicial and administrative uses, and which are not simply reproductions but cover broadcasting, performance or translation, then Article 10(2) WCT would be applicable.[194]

In relation to the 'new' WCT economic rights, we have argued that the mandatory quotation exception in Article 10(1) Berne must apply to these. What role, therefore, is left for Article 10(1) WCT? We suggest there is still a considerable role for this provision; in particular, for uses *other* than quotation that involve making available to the public, distribution and rental, the three-step test as contained in Article 10(1) WCT will apply and arguably constrain the optional exceptions in Berne, such as Article 10(2) and 10*bis*.

---

[193] The WTO Panel in WT/DS/160/R ruled at [6.69] that Article 10(2) WCT applies the three-step test to the minor exceptions doctrine relevant to Articles 11 and 11*bis* Berne.

[194] The relationship between Article 10(1) WCT and Article 11*bis*(2) Berne differs. See Ricketson, SCCR/ 9/7, 62:

'WCT signatories are required to apply Articles 1–21 of Berne and there should be no possibility of Article 10(1) of the WCT permitting free uses to the rights specified in Article 11*bis*(1) of Berne in cases where equitable remuneration would be required under Article 11*bis*(2). This would leave open the application of free use exceptions to Article 8 WCT rights that go beyond those specified in Article 11*bis*(2) of Berne. An example would be webcasting, which would not usually be broadcasting (by wireless means) within the meaning of Article 11*bis*(1)(i).'

4

Article 10(1) Berne: Requirements

I NO LIMITATION BY PURPOSE

Importantly, and in contrast with Article 10(2) and Article 10*bis*(2),[1] the language of Article 10(1) Berne is not limited by purpose. It simply states 'it shall be permissible to make quotations'. There is no limitation, even illustrative, such as 'for purposes such as criticism or review'. Given that the provision is mandatory, it would thus be inappropriate for a Member to introduce any limiting purpose (or at least one which operates inflexibly). Quotation is permitted, if it complies with the remaining conditions, whatever its purpose.

The Stockholm *travaux* clarify that no such limitation was regarded as appropriate or acceptable.[2] The Stockholm *travaux* can be divided into two stages, the preparation of the proposal for the new treaty and the discussions at the intergovernmental conference.[3] At each stage, the idea was mooted of limiting the purposes for which a defence of quotation would apply. On each occasion, that idea was rejected.

The Study Group proposed to broaden the Brussels quotation exception from quotations of newspaper articles and periodicals to quotations in general. The Committee of Non-official Experts thought this too broad and that quotation should be limited to 'scientific, cultural, informatory or education' purposes.[4] The Study Group considered the suggested limitation but rejected it, on the basis that it would not encompass 'artistic purposes'. The issue was again raised by the Committee of Government Experts. Here, the limitation was rejected as it would exclude from legitimate quotation, citation for judicial purposes, political purposes, aesthetic purposes and the purposes of entertainment.[5]

---

[1]   Article 10(2) permits exceptions 'by way of illustration in publications, broadcasts or sound or visual recordings for teaching' while Article 10*bis*(2) permits Members of the Union operate an exception 'for the purpose of reporting current events'.

[2]   As we explained in Chapter 2, Section II, pp. 8–11, above, an initial proposal made at Rome and limited to quotation for 'critical, polemical or educational purposes' was regarded as too narrow and ultimately had to be abandoned.

[3]   For more detail, see Chapter 2, Section IV, pp. 16–28, above.

[4]   A Tournier, 'Le Comité d'experts de Genève' (1964) 42 *RIDA* 27, 40, 42. See above, pp. 21–22.

[5]   BIRPI: DA/22/33, p.10. See above, p. 22.

The second stage at which consideration of the desirability of a limitation by purpose occurred was at the diplomatic conference itself. The Swiss delegation proposed a limitation 'to the extent that they serve as an explanation, reference or illustration in the context in which they are used'. The matter was discussed in the Main Committee, before being put to a vote. The Swiss amendment garnered some support but was ultimately defeated 27–10. Among those who voted against were the Swedish. Torwald Hesser, a Justice of the Swedish Supreme Court, stated that the Swiss proposal 'did not enumerate sufficient purposes'.[6]

Thus the *travaux* support the conclusion that Article 10(1) is not limited by purpose, which is a position also supported by commentators.[7] Hence the view taken by the CJEU in C-476/17 *Pelham v. Hütter*[8] that quotation must be intended to enter into 'dialogue' with the work quoted is plainly not required, nor is it permitted, by Article 10(1) Berne on which the provision at issue in the case – Article 5(3)(d) of Information Society Directive – is based.[9] Indeed, it was precisely this sort of limitation that the Swiss had sought, unsuccessfully, to introduce.[10]

However, there is a qualification to the proposition that the quotation may be for any purpose. This is that purposes which are covered by other special provisions in Berne fall to be treated in accordance with those provisions. Thus, a use for illustration of a book intended for use in teaching falls under Article 10(2), and as a special provision outside the more general 'quotation' exception, an exception defined by manner of use rather than purpose. The question of the relationship between the various exceptions was raised on a number of occasions before and during the Conference. Concern was prompted both by the newly proposed

---

[6] Summary Minutes, [767], in *Records*, 861, discussed in Chapter 2, above, at pp. 27–28.

[7] Raquel Xalabarder, *Study on Copyright Limitations and Exceptions for Educational Activities in North America, Europe, Caucasus, Central Asia and Israel* (WIPO, 5 November 2009), SCCR/19/8, 18, explaining that Article 10(1) Berne is 'not restricted to any specific uses' and M Senftleben, 'Internet Search Results – A Permissible Quotation?' (2013) 235 *RIDA* 3, 15 (explaining that there is no purpose requirement in Article 10(1)). For a contrary view, in the context of the quotation exception in EU copyright law, see Jane Parkin, 'The Copyright Quotation Exception: *Not* Fair Use by Another Name' (2019) 19 *OUCLJ* 55.

[8] Case C-476/17 *Pelham GmbH v. Hütter* EU:C:2019:624 (CJEU, Grand Chamber); EU:C:2018:1002 (AG Szpunar). At a workshop in Luxembourg on 7 November 2019, the Advocate General indicated that he had not been made aware of the position in the *travaux*. The Advocate General at [64] had defined 'dialogue' broadly as including 'in confrontation, as a tribute, or in any other way', but while this might thus be thought a rather vacuous condition, he deduced from it the significantly limiting requirements that the extracted work be unmodified, that it be incorporated in a quoting work and that it may be 'easily distinguished as a foreign element'. In contrast, the Court had a more exacting notion of 'dialogue' ('as for the purpose of illustrating an assertion, of defending an opinion or of allowing an intellectual comparison' [71]) but inferred only one condition from it – namely that the extract be identifiable. See Chapter 7, Section III, especially at pp. 211–2.

[9] For a contrary but unconvincing view, see Parkin (2019).

[10] For further elaboration, see Chapter 2, Section IV, pp. 27–28, above and Chapter 5, Section IV, Part B, pp. 131–136, below.

flexible exceptions clause to the reproduction right (what ultimately became Article 9(2)).[11]

A second qualification may also be regarded as implicit. There might be some purposes, which in their nature are inconsistent with 'fair practice'. For example, if a person purports to quote a whole work in order to 'compete commercially' with the copyright owner, one can see that such use might be proportionate but could never conceivably be in accordance with 'fair practice'. The same might be said of a person who records the performance of a song (musical and literary works) for commercial sale: the amount used may indeed be proportionate, but the use could not conceivably accord with 'fair practice'. Some might say, then, that the quotation exception is not completely open-ended.[12] We would agree as a matter of substance, but we think the preferable way of conceptualising this is through the 'fairness' requirement (which we discuss in detail in Chapter 6), as opposed to through restricting the purposes of quotation.

II ARTICLE 10(1) BERNE: WORK ALREADY LAWFULLY MADE AVAILABLE TO THE PUBLIC

This requirement in Article 10(1) Berne is not featured in other limitations in Berne.[13] The provision stipulates that the mandatory quotation exception applies only to those works that have 'already been lawfully made available to the public'. It stands to reason that if the work itself has been unlawfully released to the public, the copyright holder should not be impeded from preventing further circulation by users claiming that they have a right to quote from the work. However, this requirement has been treated by some courts and commentators as indirectly protecting an author's right of disclosure (despite the fact that no such moral right of divulgation is expressly recognised in the Berne Convention).[14] How much light this understanding could cast on the concept may be questioned, given the variations in the

---

[11]   BIRPI: DA. 22/2, p. 48, where the Study Group proposed that the freedom to create exceptions to the new reproduction right be subject to a requirement to have 'regard to the provisions of [the] Convention' (i.e. the specific limitations permitted, or required, elsewhere). The conditions of those provisions 'must always be respected'. DA 22/2, p. 48: 'This implies that the provisions already existing for certain special provisions (Articles 10, 10*bis* and 11*bis*, para 3) must be regarded as rules exercising limits on the questions with which they deal. Thus, the special conditions, whose presence these exceptions imply, must always be respected.' Monaco S/66. Gérard de San, [1069.1], in *Records*, 885; Straschnov [1071], in *Records*, 885.

[12]   BIRPI: DA 22/2, p. 53 ('It may be observed that the proposed provision is not to the effect that any type of use should be accepted as permissible: it is essential for it to be "fair practice"'). Note also Lionel Bochumberg, *Le Droit de Citation* (Masson 1994) 23, [26] ('The notion of fair practice. . . incorporates the teleological aspect of the quotation').

[13]   Note that Articles 9(2), 10(2) 10*bis* or 11*bis*(2) Berne do not feature this limitation. But it is featured in Article 7(3), dealing with duration of anonymous and pseudonymous works.

[14]   Case C-516/17 *Spiegel Online GmbH* v. *Volker Beck*, EU:C:2019:16 (Advocate General's Opinion), [55] (AG Szpunar); Ricketson and Ginsburg (2006), [10.37], 614 citing C Masouyé, *Guide to the Berne Convention for the Protection of Literary and Artistic Works* (1978), 58 and at [10.44], 618; Bochumberg,

scope of the 'droit de divulgation' in national law,[15] as well as the complexities of ownership of any such right where the author is deceased.[16] The Study Group, which first proposed this as a condition,[17] explained it without invoking or mentioning moral rights: 'manuscripts or works printed for the use of a private circle', it said,[18] should not be subject to the exception.

The first element[19] that the work has been 'already' made available seems to preclude any attempt to justify disclosure of a work by invoking the quotation exception itself: if material is only disclosed as a result of quotation, it follows it had not 'already' been made available. Thus, were a newspaper to wish to quote from hitherto undisclosed memoirs held by a politician,[20] it would not be able to invoke Article 10(1) Berne to do so. Flexibility in national law to ensure the lawfulness of revelation of matters of public interest contained in unreleased works must be justified through other provisions in the Berne Convention: Article 9(2), 10*bis*(2) or 17. In contrast, where a work was once made available, the right to quote should be available even if the work has subsequently be withdrawn from circulation.[21]

The second element is that the work has been 'made available', language which is also used in Article 7(3) Berne, relating to the calculation of the term of protection for anonymous and pseudonymous works. This language should be contrasted with the notion of 'publication' that is stipulated under Article 3(3) of Berne:

> The expression 'published works' means works published with the consent of their authors, whatever may be the means of manufacture of the copies, provided that the availability of such copies has been such as to satisfy the reasonable requirements of the public, having regard to the nature of the work. The performance of a dramatic, dramatico-musical, cinematographic or musical work, the public recitation of a literary work, the communication by wire or the broadcasting of literary or artistic

---

Le Droit de Citation, ch 7. A proposal to include such a right was rejected at Rome in 1928: Adeney, [6.34], 115.

[15] E Adeney, *The Moral Rights of Authors and Performers* (Oxford University Press 2006), 44–6. A longstanding dispute over whether the divulgation right recognised under French law is 'exhausted' was only resolved in 2013 when the Cour de Cassation ruled that articles first published in legal journals had been made available so that the author's moral right was not implicated when they were later placed on the Internet: Cass. civ. I, 11 Dec. 2013, Com. com. électr. 2014, comm. no. 15, note Caron, P. I. 2014, no. 50, 65, obs. Lucas.

[16] Provisions of French law elaborate in some detail who is entitled to the right: Article L121-2 of the IP Code.

[17] It had not been a requirement under Article 10(1) of the Brussels Act. On the Study Group, see Chapter 2, Section IV, esp. pp. 16–21. The only change to this part of the proposal between 1963 and 1967 was the substitution of the word 'accessible' with 'available': Report of the Authors Consultative Committee, BIRPI: DA/22/7, p. 7 and p. 10 (suggesting the change for both Article 7(3) and 10).

[18] See S/1, p. 47 in *Records*, 117.

[19] The term already was in the Study Group's initial proposal in 1963 and received no comment, either by way of explanation or criticism, at any point between then and its adoption.

[20] For example, *Ashdown v. Telegraph Group Ltd.* [2001] EWCA Civ 1142, [2002] RPC 235.

[21] *Time Warner v. Channel 4* [1994] EMLR 1 (EWCA) (use of excerpts from a film, *A Clockwork Orange*, permitted even though it had been withdrawn from circulation in the UK).

works, the exhibition of a work of art and the construction of a work of architecture shall not constitute publication.[22]

The key distinction between 'making available' under Article 10(1) and Article 7(3) and 'publication' under Article 3(3) is that making available is a broader concept. Article 10(1) Berne operates where a work has been made available 'by any means, not simply through the making available of copies of the work' and thus would include the situation where a work was made available through public performance, exhibition or communication to the public.[23] Thus, if an academic privately circulates the manuscript of a paper which they then orally present in public, another scholar may quote from the paper (at least those parts presented, though 'unpublished'), for example, in order to take issue with the arguments contained therein.[24]

The third element is that the work has been 'lawfully' made available to the public. This term also appears in Article 7(3) Berne, relating to the term of protection, and can be contrasted with the language of Article 3(3) Berne, which refers to publication 'with the consent of the author'. The choice between the two terms was carefully considered at the Stockholm Conference where, for Article 3(3), the Conference specifically chose the criterion 'with the consent of the author' (in place of 'lawfully' in the proposal),[25] while rejecting such a change for the other two articles.[26] It is clear

---

[22] For a discussion of the history and scope of this requirement, see Ricketson and Ginsburg (2006), [6.22]–[6.52], 255–78.

[23] S/1, p. 47, in *Records*, 117 ('every form of publication of the work' including by radio-diffusion); S/1, p. 37, in *Records*, 107 (in context of Article 7(3), *making available* implies making available by 'every means'); Report of the Study Group, BIRPI: DA/20/2, pp. 26–7, 38–9, 46 (located, inter alia, at TNA: BT209/1244, item 11); Ricketson and Ginsburg (2006), [13.41], 785.

[24] See A Bercovitz and G Bercovitz, 'Spain,' in L Bently, *ICLP*, § 8[2][a], who cite Audiencia Provincial (Court of Appeal) Madrid (Section 28), 21 June 2012, Aranzadi Civil 2012, no. 1345 (finding that a PhD thesis had been disclosed, and thus lawful quotations could be made, once the thesis had been deposited in a university library). Contrast German law, which distinguishes between *Veröffentlichung* (making available) and *Erscheinen* (publication) in different applications of the quotation right. Article 51(1), which permits the quotation *in extenso* of single works by scholarly or scientific works, and Article 51(3), which permits the quotation of single passages from musical works in independent musical works, only apply where the work quoted has been published; in contrast, Article 51(2) applies where a work has been made accessible. Interpreting Article 51(1), the KG (Court of Appeals) Berlin held that it was unlawful for the defendant to reproduce a letter by Strittmatter, because the letter had not been previously 'published' with the consent of the author or his heirs: 10 June 2015, *Strittmatter Brief* (Strittmatter Letter), 2015 WRP 1537, cited by M Gruenberger, 'Germany', in L Bently (ed.), *International Copyright Law and Practice* (LexisNexis 2019), [GER-110].

[25] Report of the Main Committee I, [49] in *Records*, 1139; Proposal in *Records*, 96–7 (explaining that Working Group had preferred 'with the consent of the author' but that the Committee of Government Experts favoured 'lawfully' and thus the latter term appeared in the proposal); Views of delegations in *Records*, 630 and 668 (views of UK that publication should not include publication under compulsory licence); S/42 in *Records*, 687 (proposed amendment of Article 4(5)); Summary Minutes of Main Committee I, [528]–[533], in *Records*, 845 (adopting amendment from 'lawfully' in proposal to 'with the consent of the author' in the text as approved).

[26] Main Committee I, [90], in *Records*, 1147 (in relation to Article 10(1)) and Summary Minutes, Main Committee I, [768] and [771] in *Records*, 861 (Mr Gerbrandy, Netherlands and Mr Wallace, United Kingdom). See also Ricketson and Ginsburg (2006), [6.28], 259; Proposal in *Records*, 107 (favouring

from those discussions that 'lawfully' was selected to encompass situations where works were made available under statutory provisions.[27] Indeed, consistently with the Committee discussions,[28] the Chair of the Committee indicated that 'lawfully' would include making a work available under a compulsory licence.[29] A good example might be the situation where a manuscript held by a public archive is placed online under so-called orphan works provisions: it would be strange if readers of the manuscript were not permitted to quote from it because such access, while facilitated by a lawful making available, was impermissible because its author had not expressly consented. Another situation might be where a moral right of divulgation exists, but disclosure of the work has been ordered by a court contrary to the wishes of an entitled heir (e.g. because refusal to disclose amounted to an abuse of the moral right). The reason why lawfulness rather than authorial consent is to be regarded as the appropriate standard for Article 10(1) is to be found in the fact that it is difficult for the person quoting to ascertain the precise conditions under which the work was made accessible.[30]

Perhaps ignorant of the history, there has been some debate as to whether 'lawfully' in Article 5(3)(d) of the EU Information Society Directive includes other situations where the author's consent has not been obtained but there is legitimate use, namely, where exceptions are applicable. In C-516/17 *Spiegel Online v. Beck.*, Advocate General Szpunar indicated that 'lawfully' in the context of Article 5(3)(d) of Information Society Directive means with the consent of the author or by virtue of a licence, but not according to copyright exceptions.[31] This interpretation might make sense were the purpose of the requirement to protect an author's right to divulge the work (as he supposed). The Court, however, seems to have taken a broader view, namely that a work is lawfully made available where it is 'with the authorisation of the copyright holder or in accordance with a non-contractual licence or a statutory authorisation'.[32] Although the precise scope of the term 'statutory authorisation' here is far from certain, this broader view aligns better with the *travaux* for the Stockholm Revision Conference of Berne.

'lawfully made available' in place of 'publication' for Article 7(3)); Views of delegates in *Records*, 668 (views of UK); Proposed Amendment S/42 (proposed amendment to 'with consent of author') Main Committee I, [181]–[183], in *Records* 1161 (in relation to Article 7(3), where the Committee initially preferred the language of consent and only finally reverted to the term lawfully).

[27] The Conference specifically mentioned Article 15(4), which enables designated competent authorities to represent an author of an unpublished work where their identity is unknown. A country may only do so where it is reasonable to assume the author is a national thereof.

[28] See also Main Committee I Report, [90] in *Records*, 1147, and Summary Minutes, Main Committee I, [768], [771], in *Records*, 861 (Mr Gerbrandy, Netherlands and Mr Wallace, United Kingdom). See also Ricketson and Ginsburg (2006), [6.28], 259.

[29] Summary Minutes, [528] in *Records*, 842 (rejecting 'lawfully' as the criterion for determining whether a work has been published).

[30] See Summary Minutes, Main Committee I, [771], in *Records*, 861 (Mr Wallace, United Kingdom).

[31] Case C-516/17 *Spiegel Online GmbH* v. *Volker Beck*, EU:C:2019:16 (Advocate General's Opinion), [55]–[58].

[32] Case C-516/17 *Spiegel Online GmbH* v. *Volker Beck* EU:C:2019:625 (CJEU, Grand Chamber), [89].

The facts of *Spiegel Online* highlight another important aspect of the condition that the work has been lawfully made available to the public – namely, the 'specific form' of such making available. In that case, the author, who is a politician, sought to prevent Spiegel making available the copy of an article (first published in a collection of essays in 1988) on the basis that the manuscript on which the article was based had been modified by the publisher prior to publication.[33] The Court indicated that such an article would not have been lawfully made available in that specific form unless the author had granted the publisher the right to make such editorial amendments.[34] In addition, the author himself had made available both the original manuscript and article, each accompanied by a disclaimer to the effect that he 'dissociated' himself from the paper. The Court seemed to suggest that this act by the author did not mean that a copy of the manuscript that Spiegel placed online had already been made available to the public: 'the documents were lawfully made available to the public only in so far as they were accompanied by those statements of dissociation'.[35] This rather surprising proposition seems to suggest that where a work is published only with a disclaimer, any quotation from that work must carry that disclaimer, or else will not be from a work that has been lawfully made available to the public. The effect is to convert a condition for the availability of a defence into a power to control the manner in which a work is quoted.

On its face, such a conclusion is in tension with the proposition, outlined in Chapter 3, that Article 10(1) is not merely an exception to the reproduction right but also the translation and adaptation rights.[36] If a work was lawfully made available in Russian, it could not be quoted in a French work in French, because it had not been lawfully made available in French. Such a rule is inconsistent with the intent of those involved in adopting Article 10 and national practice.[37] If the conclusion in *Spiegel Online* is regarded as desirable to protect the specific author, one might wonder whether it might not be better justified as an aspect of the application of the 'fair practice' condition.[38]

---

[33] The publisher amended the title of the manuscript, and one of its sentences was shortened. The author protested to the publisher but to no effect: [12].

[34] [92]. Most publishing contracts contain such clauses.

[35] [93]. In contrast, Advocate General Szpunar seemed to suggest republication without a disclaimer would be a question of infringement of the moral right of integrity under national law: EU: C:2019:16, [57].

[36] Chapter 3, Section 3, Part A, p. 55, above.

[37] See p. 28, above and e.g. *Jirinovski v. Daeninckx et autres*, TGI Paris, 3e Ch, 10 May 1996, in (1996) 170 *RIDA* 315; note Kerever (use of *The Last Break Southward* by Russian nationalist politician Vladimir Zhirinovsky, in Daeninckx and Drachline's *Jirinovski: The Russian Who Made the World Tremble*).

[38] As the Court in Case C-516/17 *Spiegel Online GmbH v. Volker Beck* EU:C:2019:625 (CJEU, Grand Chamber), [94], seems to suggest would be appropriate: '[I]t is for the referring court to ascertain whether the original versions of the manuscript and of the article published in the book in question, without Mr Beck's statements of dissociation from the content of those documents, were published in accordance with fair practice and to the extent required by the specific purpose of the quotation in question.'

Although seemingly the 'most straightforward' of the conditions to Article 10(1), the requirement that a work has lawfully been made available to the public does raise some intriguing issues of private international law. This is because whether a work is to be regarded as having been 'lawfully' made available will vary from jurisdiction to jurisdiction. In countries that operate a 'divulgation right', in most (if not all) situations, a work will only have been made available 'lawfully' where the author has consented. In other countries, especially those without such a moral right, a work (or part thereof) may have been lawfully made available whether the copyright owner has consented, or where the making available is under a defence or compulsory licence. Inevitably, conflicts might arise where a work has been made available lawfully in one jurisdiction in circumstances where it would not be regarded as having been so made available in another jurisdiction. For example, where a manuscript is uploaded to the Internet in the UK under the reporting current events exception,[39] or with the copyright holder's consent (where the work was created in the course of employment),[40] but without its author's consent, neither form of making available might be regarded as having been lawful under, for example, German law.[41] Similarly, though a work by a creator who is a national of the United States might be regarded as having been made available with its author's consent where the creator's employer agreed to its publication,[42] though its creator did not, such a work would not be regarded under French law as having been made available with the consent of its author. Given these divergences, the logical question then follows: if a person in Germany or France seeks to quote from the work, which law is to apply to the question of whether the making available was lawful – that of the place where the work was first made available, that of the territory of which the author is a national (so-called *lex originis*) or that in which protection is sought (so-called *lex protectionis*)? Most jurisdictions resolve these sort of conundrums by applying the law of the country in which protection is claimed: this would mean that a person in Germany could not rely on the quotation exception to quote material that had been lawfully made available only in the United Kingdom, nor could a person in France invoke the quotation exception in relation to the work made available lawfully only in the United States. However, it might be suggested that a different solution is appropriate, given that Article 10(1) recognises a 'right to quote' and the term 'lawfully' was specifically adopted to reduce the burdens on the

---

[39]   CDPA, Section 30(2): 'Fair dealing with a work (other than a photograph) for the purpose of reporting current events does not infringe any copyright in the work provided that (subject to subsection (3)) it is accompanied by a sufficient acknowledgement.'

[40]   CDPA, Section 11(2).

[41]   Copyright Act (Germany), Article 12(1) (which empowers the author 'to determine whether and how his work shall be published'). See M Gruenberger, 'Germany', in L Bently (ed.), *International Copyright Law and Practice* (LexisNexis 2019), [GER-129]–[GER-130]: 'The right to control disclosure has been enforced even in the face of competing basic rights or policies.'

[42]   See works-made-for-hire discussed in sections 101 and 201(b) US Copyright Act 1976.

person quoting.[43] If the work was made available lawfully according to the law of the country where that act (making available) occurred, it could be said that the work has been lawfully made available for the purposes of the right recognised in Article 10(1).

III ARTICLE 10(3) BERNE: ATTRIBUTION REQUIREMENT

Article 10(3) Berne states: 'Where use is made of works in accordance with the preceding paragraphs of this Article, *mention shall be made of the source, and* of the name of *the author if* it appears thereon' (emphasis added).[44] As was discussed earlier,[45] the quotation exception only applies to economic rights and does not apply to the moral rights specified in Article 6*bis*. As such, what is the purpose of the requirement in Article 10(3)? As was argued previously, it seems that Article 10(3) is a condition distinct from the attribution right in Article 6*bis* Berne.[46] This is the case even though the *travaux* to the Rome and Brussels Revision Conferences indicate that an indication of the source was linked to the moral rights of the author.[47]

Unlike Article 6*bis*, which creates an affirmative right of attribution ('le droit de revendiquer la paternité de l'œuvre'), Article 10(3) is a condition of relying on the quotation exception.[48] The key reason why Article 10(3) is not correlative with Article 6*bis* is important differences in terminology. Article 10(3) states that 'mention shall be made' of the 'source' and the 'author', which is different to language of 'right to claim authorship' in Article 6*bis*. If it had been intended to insert a requirement of attribution in accordance with Article 6*bis* in Article 10(3), then one would have expected the precise language of Article 6*bis* to be used or at least an explicit reference to moral rights, as is the case in Article 11*bis*(2) Berne. Article 11*bis*(2) stipulates that the conditions under which the rights mentioned in Article 11*bis*(1) may be exercised 'shall not in any circumstances be prejudicial to the *moral rights* of the author'.[49] Another key difference in language is that Article 10(3) refers to the 'source', whereas Article 6*bis* refers to the right to claim authorship of the *work*. Again, if it was intended to insert the right of attribution as reflected in Article 6*bis* as a condition of Article 10(1), then why is the language of 'source' rather than 'work'

---

[43] See Summary Minutes, Main Committee I, [771], in *Records*, 861 (Mr Wallace, United Kingdom).

[44] In the French text, 'faire mention de la source et du nom de l'auteur, si ce nom figure dans la source'.

[45] Chapter 3, Section III, Part B, pp. 57–58, above.

[46] Chapter 3, Section III, Part B, pp. 59–60, above.

[47] See Chapter 2, pp. 7–8 (Rome) and 13–16 (Brussels). Indeed, the Hungarian formulation that was adopted at Brussels explicitly refers to the moral right of attribution: *Documents* (1951) 247. See Chapter 2, Section III, p. 16, above.

[48] For this view, see Jane C Ginsburg, 'The Most Moral of Rights: The Right to Be Recognized as the Author of One's Work' (2016) 8 *Geo Mason J Int'l Com L* 44, 51–2.

[49] See S Ricketson, *WIPO Study on Limitations and Exceptions of Copyright and Related Rights in the Digital Environment* (2003) SCCR 9/7 at 52: 'No reference is made to "moral rights" in Article 10(3) (by contrast with Article 11*bis*(2)), and this appears to stand as a separate requirement, quite apart from Article 6*bis*. Furthermore, the requirement to identify the source of the work is distinct from that of identifying the author.'

used in Article 10(3)? The term 'source' suggests identifying from where the quotation originated,[50] but that does not necessarily have to equate to a 'work'. For example, the quotation could be a single line of poetry or a sentence from a newspaper article, and the source could be the poetry book (as opposed to the poem itself) or the newspaper (as opposed to the particular article). Indeed in the French Proposal prior to the Brussels Revision Conference, it was suggested that indication of source for extracts from newspapers or periodicals would be the name of the newspaper or periodical and the author of the article.[51] Finally, Article 10(3) only requires mention of the author *if* the name of the author appears on the work that is being quoted.[52]

Thus the attribution condition contained in Article 10(3) differs from the right of attribution in relation to 'the work' as required by Article *6bis* Berne. As a result, it can and should be viewed more flexibly.[53] 'Mention' of the author and the source could encompass attributions in abbreviated form, ones that indirectly accompany the use of the quotation (e.g. in a list of credits or acknowledgments) or which are implicit (because of the recognisability of the work/source from which the quotation is taken) or which may easily be identified via a straightforward search. In applying this standard, an important consideration could be how different cultural fields – such as the film, music, art or publishing industries – usually acknowledge other authors.

IV ARTICLE 10(1) BERNE: THE REQUIREMENT OF PROPORTIONALITY

A *The Interrelationship between Proportionality and Fair Practice*

Article 10(1) Berne stipulates that quotations must be proportionate (i.e. 'their extent does not exceed that justified by the purpose') and compatible with 'fair practice'. The next two chapters examine these requirements. At this point, we deal with some initial queries about the relationship between the two requirements. An overarching query that must be addressed is whether fair practice and proportionality are distinct requirements. Further, if they are distinct requirements, to what extent, if any, do they overlap?

It is our position that proportionality and fair practice are, in fact, distinct conditions, rather than proportionality being an elaboration or subset of 'fair practice'. There is no indication in the language of Article 10(1) that proportionality is a subset of fair practice. Instead, Article 10(1) Berne clearly states that fair practice *and*

---

[50] See Oxford English Dictionary definition – 'A place, person, or thing from which something originates or can be obtained'.

[51] *Documents* (1951), 246–7. See p. 14, above.

[52] This is adopted from the Hungarian suggestion at the Brussels Conference: Chapter 2, Section III, p. 16.

[53] Although it is interesting to note that sometimes national courts have viewed attribution under the right of attribution quite flexibly: see *Douces Transes* Cass., 12 January 1988, (1988) 137 *RIDA* 98 (as cited in Jacques (2019), 178, fn. 101).

proportionality are conditions. Similarly, in Article 10(2), the conditions appear to be treated distinctly, and in Article 10*bis*(2), proportionality is treated as a free-standing condition.[54] Further, although the *travaux* to Article 10(1) Berne reveal that concerns about removing the restriction of 'short' quotations would be dealt with by fair practice and proportionality, this does not mean they are interchangeable require-ments. This is because the *travaux* also shows that 'fair practice' was seen as the main safeguard for authors.[55]

Given the conditions of proportionality and fair practice are distinct, do they also cover distinct (and not overlapping) matters? One view is that proportionality focuses on the 'content' (i.e. the nature and purpose of the quoted use) and fair practice focuses on 'procedure' (i.e. how the quotation is presented). More specifi-cally, proportionality would interrogate the purpose of the quotation and take into account the normative value of the quotation according to freedom of expression interests or possibly distributive justice concerns. Meanwhile, fair practice would focus on the practice or conventions of quotation in relation to the genre of the source work, ensure that any quotation does not conflict with the integrity of the source work and take into account consumer interests (e.g. ensuring that the quota-tion was not misleading or discriminatory).

While this division between the requirements of proportionality and fair practice has some appeal, we argue that it should not be adopted because of two difficulties associated with this approach. The first is that the language of proportionality ('does not exceed that justified by the purpose') does not seem to embrace a normative enquiry about the purpose of quotation. Instead, it focuses on the *length/quantity* of the quoted material, and this is consistent with the *travaux*, which reveals it would be a mechanism for counterbalancing the removal of 'short' from the language of Article 10(1). A second difficulty with this approach is that the economic harm to the owner of the source work is not obviously taken into account, and it would seem odd to omit this consideration from the overall analysis.

Therefore, the preferred approach to these requirements is to see them as distinct, but with proportionality operating as an initial, logically prior assessment to that of fair practice. Proportionality, under this approach, would be concerned with whether the size of the quotation is justifiable according to its purpose. This view is supported both by the language used in Article 10(1) and the *travaux*. Thus, the proportionality condition would involve asking whether a less extensive quotation could have achieved the same purpose in effect, minimising the intrusion on the author's rights. Fair practice, on the other hand, would refer to a notion of 'fairness', and this would operate as the main normative tool for the quotation exception.

---

[54] In relation to Art 10*bis*, the Committee of Non-Official Experts recommended replacing a condition that the act relate to 'short extracts' with a condition that the act be only to 'the extent justified by the informatory purpose' (Preparatory Documents, S/1, in *Records*, 119).

[55] Main Committee I, Summary Minutes, in *Records*, 860–1. See p. 27, above.

B *The Proportionality Enquiry*

Article 10(1) Berne stipulates that quotations shall be permissible 'provided that . . . their extent does not exceed that justified by the purpose' – this is referred to here as the *proportionality requirement*. It is important to note that we use the word *proportionality* in a specific sense to refer to this requirement of Article 10(1) Berne, although we appreciate that there are constitutional, EU and human rights law principles of 'proportionality'.[56]

We have argued that quotation is not limited by purpose but is open-ended. Nonetheless, a purpose of some kind will need to be identified not least because the extent of the quotation relevant to this purpose must be assessed. However, we should remain flexible about the sorts of purposes that may be considered for this condition. The discussions in the Main Committee I at Stockholm rejected the idea of limiting quotation to certain purposes[57] and also envisaged quotation for 'scientific, critical, informatory or educational' and 'artistic' purposes. These examples demonstrate that we need not adopt a narrow approach to 'purpose' at this stage or indeed to limit the purposes that are considered when judging proportionality.[58]

The 'extent' of the quotation refers to the amount of the quotation. It is useful to remember here that 'short' was deleted from Article 10(1) Berne because quotations need not be short and, if they are to be effective, may need to be sizeable.[59] Also, as the *travaux* highlights, it could be in the author's interests if the reproduction is more

---

[56] For a discussion of those constitutional, EU and human rights law principles of 'proportionality', see Michael Fordham and Thomas de la Mare, 'Identifying the Principles of Proportionality' in Jeffrey Jowell and Jonathan Cooper (eds.), *Understanding Human Rights Principles* (Hart 2001), 27–90; Tor-Inge Harbo, 'The Function of the Proportionality Principles in EU Law' (2010) 16 *European Law Journal* 158; and Sauter Wolf, 'Proportionality in EU Law: A Balancing Act' (2012–2013) 15 *Cambridge Yearbook of European Legal Studies* 439. For a critique of proportionality, see Francisco J Urbina, *A Critique of Proportionality and Balancing* (Cambridge University Press 2017), and Stavros Tsakyrakis, 'Proportionality: An Assault on Human Rights?' (2009) 7 *Int'l J. Const. L.* 468. Common critiques are that proportionality *stricto sensu* does not recognise the incommensurability of human rights or allow space for moral reasoning. Again, we reiterate that we are not using the concept of proportionality *stricto sensu* when describing Article 10(1) Berne of quotations being 'proportionate' to their purpose.

[57] Main Committee I, in *Records*, 860–1; Minutes and Preparatory Documents, S/1, in *Records*, 116–17. See pp. 27–28, above.

[58] Contrast Spain, where Article 32(1) of the Law on Intellectual Property requires that works may be quoted only 'for analysis, comment, or critical assessment' or 'for teaching or research purposes', but in any event only 'to the extent justified by the purpose of the inclusion'. Two judicial decisions have held that the exception was unavailable where clips from one television programme were included in programmes offered by competitor channels, mostly for their comical effect: in other words the extent of use was not justified by the purpose because the purpose itself was not permitted. See A Bercovitz and G Bercovitz, 'Spain', in L Bently, *ICLP*, § 8[2][a], citing Audiencia Provincial (Court of Appeal) Barcelona (Section 15), 3 May 2010, Westlaw Jurisprudencia 2010, no. 162897; Commercial Court (no. 9) Madrid, April 19, 2010, Westlaw Jurisprudencia 2010, no. 163042. We would argue against this interpretation of 'purpose' and 'proportionality' and instead leave the purpose of the quotation to be considered as part of 'fair practice'.

[59] See Preparatory Documents, S/1, in *Records*, 116.

rather than less extensive, 'when this is necessary to ensure that his opinions are reported in a proper and accurate manner'.[60] The *travaux* go on to note: 'In other cases, a fairly extensive quotation may be necessary as the point of departure for a reply. A satisfactory delimitation could be achieved by ... emphasizing the principle that the right of quotation can only be exercised to the extent defined by its purpose.'[61] Thus, the proportionality requirement was a way of counterbalancing the removal of the restriction of 'short' quotations[62] (as was the requirement of 'compatible with fair practice').[63] As such, this condition does not preclude extensive quotations – it only requires them to be justified.

How, then, does one *justify* the extent of the quotation? One possible interpretation is that the amount of quotation must be *necessary* for achieving the stated purpose.[64] This interpretation would impose a rather strict standard, whereby the existence of alternative means of achieving the intended purpose could exclude the extent of the quotation. This interpretation would also seem to favour quotations that are used for very specifically articulated purposes and, as has been argued previously, the *travaux* envisaged the quotation exception not being limited in this way. Finally, this sort of strict interpretation would likely deny a role for assessing the quotation according to 'fair practice', and yet it is clear from the *travaux* that this was an important aspect of the quotation right.

Another possible interpretation can be constructed by borrowing from Strasbourg jurisprudence,[65] in particular by adapting the suitability and necessity[66] tests. We could start by asking whether the quotation is capable of achieving the purpose that is claimed. In other words, is there a plausible, causal link between the quotation

---

[60]   See Preparatory Documents, S/1, in *Records*, 116.

[61]   See Preparatory Documents, S/1, in *Records*, 116.

[62]   This is also seen in relation to Art 10*bis*(2): the 1963 Committee of Non-official Experts recommended that the freedom created by removing 'short extracts' could be limited through the requirement that use be only to 'the extent justified by the informatory purpose' (Preparatory Documents, S/1, in *Records*, 119).

[63]   See Main Committee I, Summary Minutes, in *Records*, 860–1.

[64]   This was the interpretation adopted by Aldous LJ in *Hyde Park Residence* v. *Yelland* [2001] Ch. 143, [37]: '[I]t is appropriate to take into account ... the extent and purpose of the use, and whether that extent was necessary for the purpose ... '. Note that Aldous LJ went on to find at [40] 'the extent of the use was excessive' because it was not necessary in order to convey the time of arrival and departure, to show photographs – a simple description in the article of having seen the photographs would have sufficed (see, in agreement, Mance LJ at [78]).

[65]   The broad proportionality test used by the Strasbourg court usually involves asking (1) whether the restriction is suitable for achieving a legitimate general aim (suitability); (2) whether the restriction/act is the least intrusive way of achieving this aim (but with similar efficacy) (necessity) and then (3) a type of cost–benefit analysis that asks whether there is a net gain when the reduction in enjoyment of rights is weighed against the achievement of the aim (fair balance or proportionality in the narrow sense). See Jonas Christoffersen, 'Straight Human Rights Talk – Why Proportionality Does (Not) Matter' (2010) 55 *Scandinavian Stud L.* 11 and Juan Cianciardo, 'The Principle of Proportionality: The Challenges of Human Rights' (2010) 3 *J. Civ. L. Stud.* 177.

[66]   See Christoffersen (2010) 22–4 – noting that the test of strict necessity has been rejected because the proportionality test is inherently flexible; the need for a margin of appreciation; a prima facie less onerous measure might in fact have repercussions on other legally relevant interests and the minimum nature of the ECHR.

and the purpose for which it is being used? We would then move on to ask whether a shorter quotation would be as effective in achieving the purpose and less restrictive of the author's rights.[67] This inevitably involves looking at both the size of the quotation and the potential impact of this on the author. As such, there will be some overlap with fair practice because 'fairness' also involves looking at the impact on the author. However, it must be remembered that the focus of the proportionality condition is assessing the 'extent', whereas the fair practice assessment weighs several different criteria that take account of author, user and public interests. As such, it is proposed that proportionality is an important, preliminary enquiry, but not one that should replace the 'fair practice' assessment. This means that the proportionality enquiry for the quotation exception should not get bogged down in evaluating the impact of the extent of the quotation on the author. This impact, along with several other considerations, is best left to the 'fair practice' assessment, to which we return in Chapter 6. Before doing so, we need to consider the core question: what is a 'quotation'?.

---

[67] This sort of approach was arguably demonstrated by Arnold J (as he then was) in *EWCB Ltd* v. *Tixdaq Ltd* [2016] EWHC 575 (Ch), [2016] RPC 21, in the context of applying the domesticated version of Art 10*bis* Berne (fair dealing for the purpose of reporting current events). In this case, the defendant created software (an 'App'), which allowed users to capture clips of broadcast footage of sporting events and upload and share these. In considering whether this was fair dealing for the purpose of reporting events, Arnold J at [149] concluded that the use was disproportionate because 'each user could upload an unlimited number of clips from each match and there was no restriction of the amount of clips that each user could upload'. It is not clear, however, whether the use was disproportionate because it exceeded what was necessary to report on current events or because of the economic harm it would have caused the rights holder or both.

5

Article 10(1) Berne: The Meaning of Quotation

I INTRODUCTION

We turn now to the important question of what constitutes a 'quotation'. Clearly, the breadth of the concept of 'quotation' will affect the scope of any quotation exception and so it is vital to identify what can be characterised as quotation. Our central argument in this chapter is that the concept of 'quotation' in Article 10(1) is far wider than the 'typical' case of textual quotation and that the attributes of 'typical' quotation must not be elevated to conditions for the availability of the exception.

What, then, is the typical example of quotation? This is where a person excerpts a portion of text from another work, places the excerpted text in quotation marks,[1] and in surrounding text authored by the 'quoter', where that surrounding text relies on the quoted material to support or critique an argument contained in the quoted text, or comments on the quoted text. In this typical example, a 'quotation' has several features, which can be conceptualised according to (i) the source material, (ii) the destination material and (iii) the relationship between the source and destination material. In relation to the source material, this typical example is a short passage from a longer text from another author. In relation to the destination material, it is an unaltered, distinct, short passage that is recognisably used in another work. Finally, the relationship between the source and destination material reflects a deliberate act of taking from one work to place in another, in order to advance an argument.

However, the paradigmatic example does not define the limits of the notion of 'quotation'. We can imagine a whole myriad of situations where one or more of the elements described above is missing, but the use of the material may nevertheless count as 'quotation'. This is particularly the case once we venture outside the realm of printed text, with its now well-established rituals of 'quotation marks', 'insetting', footnote or endnote citation.

In this chapter, we examine the features of a 'typical' quotation in order to assess whether any of these are a necessary component of the legal concept of quotation.

---

[1] Also referred to as 'speech marks' or 'inverted commas'.

We argue that it is difficult to point to any necessary features of quotation but that, even if one had to do so, the concept of quotation is much broader than has previously been appreciated.

Before we begin, it is worth noting the range of possible sources from which we can answer the question of whether particular examples of reuse of material are, in legal terms, 'quotations'.[2] According to Article 31(1) of the Vienna Convention on the Law of Treaties, 'A treaty shall be interpreted in good faith in accordance with the ordinary meaning to be given to the terms of the treaty in their context and in the light of its object and purpose'.[3] But how is ordinary meaning to be ascertained? Rather surprisingly, given its central importance to legal interpretation, 'ordinary meaning' has been rather neglected (at least in comparison to the role of legislative history) as a topic of legal analysis.[4] While judges sometimes refer to the dictionary definitions to determine 'ordinary meaning',[5] including of treaty

[2]   Our approach is in stark contrast with that taken by Lionel Bochumberg, *Le Droit de Citation* (Masson 1994), who considers the right of quotation from the perspective of comparative law with a view to identifying a 'universal legal definition' of the right. While we also refer at various points to the practice of individual states, our goal is to understand the scope of the obligation imposed by Article 10(1) (treated by Bochumberg only at 23–24, [26]), and we are conscious that national practice might in fact be inconsistent with this obligation. See Chapter 7, Section II, pp. 204–209. As explained herein, in Chapter 5, Section II, Part A, pp. 90–101, Article 10 should not be understood solely in the light of the literary/print paradigm of quotation. In contrast, Bochumberg himself notes that his 'universal definition' of quotation corresponds exactly with the notion of literary quotation and matters become more complex and nuanced when one considers quotation of and in artistic works, music and film; ibid., 128, [200].

[3]   Emphasis added. For a discussion of 'ordinary meaning' in the Vienna Convention, see Richard Gardiner, *Treaty Interpretation* (2nd ed, Oxford University Press 2015), 181 *et seq*. Appeals to 'ordinary' meaning is common in national and regional law, despite having been widely critiqued by academic writing in the United States. For an explanation of the advantages of plain meaning as a presumptive starting point, see Fred Schauer, 'Statutory Construction and the Coordinating Function of Plain Meaning' [1990] *Sup Ct Rev* 231 (reviewing the increased reliance of the Supreme Court of the US on 'plain meaning' and, given the virtually unanimous criticism of academics to that approach, seeking to develop an explanation based on the idea that 'reliance on plain meaning may be a hardly novel sub-optimizing second-best solution' for reaching agreement); David Strauss, 'Why Plain Meaning?' (1997) 72 *Notre Dame LR* 1565 (reviewing other arguments for plain meaning and, finding each problematic, arguing that Schauer's explanation is the most plausible and has broader applicability than just the Supreme Court).

[4]   Brian G Slocum, *Ordinary Meaning: A Theory of the Most Fundamental Principle of Legal Interpretation* (University of Chicago Press 2013), 27 ('Despite being a fundamental aspect of legal interpretation that is relevant to nearly all interpretations of legal texts, the ordinary meaning doctrine has not been extensively examined by courts or scholars'), 30 ('the ordinary meaning doctrine is greatly undertheorized'). See also Gardiner, *Treaty Interpretation*, 181 *et seq*.

[5]   For examples where dictionaries are referred to by the UK Supreme Court, see *Yemshaw v. London Borough of Hounslow* [2011] UKSC 3, [19] (Baroness Hale) (defining 'violence' and referring to *Shorter OED*); *HMRC v. The Rank Group Ltd* [2015] UKSC 48, [25] (per Lord Carnwath) (referring to *Concise OED* in defining 'gaming machine'); but cf. *Stocker v. Stocker* [2019] UKSC 17 (criticising use of dictionaries to determine the 'single meaning' of statements at issue in defamation cases, with Lord Kerr, at [25], explaining that 'meaning is to be determined according to how it would be understood by the ordinary reasonable reader. It is not fixed by technical, linguistically precise dictionary definitions, divorced from the context in which the statement was made'). On the increased use of dictionaries by

language,[6] this practice raises its own problems, which have been identified by a number of scholars.[7] To begin with, dictionaries may or may not see themselves as repositories of the 'ordinary meaning' of words, but as policemen of correct meaning – as prescriptive rather than descriptive.[8] There seems no reason to believe that a lexicographer's idea of a correct meaning corresponds to that envisaged by the legislature, or, in international treaty-making, the signatories. Even if a dictionary is 'descriptive', it is necessarily constrained and therefore selective in its prioritisation of particular uses from the so-called linguistic 'corpus'.[9] Furthermore, while (historically) dictionaries may have sought to define

the Supreme Court of the United States, see Samuel A Thumma and Jeffrey L Kirchmeier, 'The Lexicon Has Become a Fortress: The United States Supreme Court's Use of Dictionaries' (1999) 47 *Buff LR* 227; Jeffrey L Kirchmeier and Samuel A Thumma, 'Scaling the Lexicon Fortress: The United States Supreme Court's Use of Dictionaries in the Twenty-First Century' (2010) 94 *Marq. LR* 77; James Brudney and Lawrence Baum, 'Oasis or Mirage: The Supreme Court's Thirst for Dictionaries in the Rehnquist and Roberts Eras' (2013) 55 *William & Mary LR* 483. For an example of the CJEU in the copyright context, see C-210/13 *Deckmyn* v. *Vandersteen* EU:C:2014:2132 (CJEU, Grand Chamber), [2014] ECDR 21, [20], referring to the 'usual meaning of the term "parody" in everyday language' and the Opinion of the Advocate General Cruz Villalón delivered on 22 May 2014, where he derives the meaning from dictionary definitions in different languages [47] *et seq*. For an example of reliance on dictionaries specifically to define quotation, see Jane Parkin, 'The Copyright Quotation Exception: *Not* Fair Use by Another Name' (2019) 19 *Oxford University Commonwealth Law Journal* 55, 67 ff. (purporting to follow Advocate General Cruz Villalón's 'definitional approach'). It is notable, if regrettable, that in Case C-476/17 *Pelham GmbH* v. *Hütter* EU:C:2019:624, [71], the CJEU identified the ordinary meaning by mere intuition, referring only to the Opinion of Advocate General Szpunar, at EU:C:2018:1002, who inferred the meaning of 'quotation' from the additional words 'for purposes such as criticism or review' in Article 5(3)(d) of Directive 2001/29/EC.

6   Gardiner, *Treaty Interpretation*, 186–9. For examples in the WTO, see WTO Appellate Body Report, United States – Measures Affecting the Cross-Border Supply of Gambling and Betting Services (20 April 2005) WT/DS285/AB/R, [164]–[167] (discussing the meaning of the word 'sporting', the Appellate Body accepted that '[i]n order to identify the ordinary meaning, a Panel may start with the dictionary definitions of the terms to be interpreted'.)

7   Cunningham et al., 'Plain Meaning and Hard Cases' (1993) 103 *Yale LJ* 1561, 1614–16; Frank H Easterbrook, 'Text, History, and Structure in Statutory Interpretation' (1994) 17 *Harv. J.L. & Pub. Pol'y* 61, 67 ('[T]he choice among meanings must have a footing more solid that a dictionary – which is a museum of words, an historical catalog rather than a means to decode the work of legislatures.')

8   Patrick Hanks, 'Definition' in Philip Durkin (ed.), *The Oxford Handbook of Lexicography* (Oxford University Press 2016), 95 (describing the efforts of lexicographers to satisfy the 'folk belief' that words can be defined by way of necessary and sufficient conditions); Thumma and Kirchmeier, 'The Lexicon' (describing the historical battle between prescriptive and descriptive approaches to definition). Tribunals rarely examine the goals of dictionaries and frequently make erroneous assumptions: WTO Appellate Body Report, United States – Measures Affecting the Cross-Border Supply of Gambling and Betting Services (20 April 2005) WT/DS285/AB/R, [164]. ('[D]ictionaries ... typically aim to catalogue all meanings of words – be those meanings common or rare, universal or specialized.')

9   Sidney I Landau, *Dictionaries: The Art and Craft of Lexicography* (2nd ed., Cambridge University Press 2001), ch. 4, in particular 154 ('[The space allotted to each definition must be severely limited, else the total number of terms must be reduced'); 182 ('All definitions of things are compromises between specific accuracy and breadth of inclusiveness. ... [N]o definition can take in all of the particular things referred to by the word defined'); 204 (on the commercial pressures to include new words rather than to pay attention to 'older established words and meanings it has omitted to make

words by reference to necessary and sufficient conditions, theories of language have highlighted the futility of this aspiration and lexicographers who are conscious of this have warned that definitions should not be understood as 'implying boundaries ... the boundaries are inevitably vague and fuzzy and should be acknowledged as such'.[10] Moreover, definitions necessarily depend on other words, sometimes presenting a problem that these words need further definition.[11] Finally, even if dictionaries do purport to describe usage, dictionaries are not identical, and many offer up multiple definitions, leaving the court with the difficult question of which to choose. Indeed, evidence from the US Supreme Court suggests that dictionary definitions are selected in a conclusory fashion – that judges simply reinforce their preferred interpretation by reference to particular dictionaries that offer similar definitions.[12]

All these problems seem, if anything, to be exacerbated in an international context,[13] with multiple language versions of treaties,[14] and as consequent

room for' a practice that 'mischievously exaggerates the importance of neologisms in lexicography... to the detriment of a better understanding of the qualities that make for a good dictionary'). Many dictionaries identify meaning from a 'linguistic corpus' and utilise criteria of 'frequency' and 'predictability': as Adam Kilgarriff notes, '[C]learly, different dictionaries have different thresholds of frequency and predictability': 'I Don't Believe in Word Senses' in Thierry Fontenelle (ed.), *Practical Lexicography: A Reader* (Oxford University Press 2008), ch. 9, 135–51, 145.

[10] Patrick Hanks, 'Definition' in Philip Durkin (ed.), *The Oxford Handbook of Lexicography* (Oxford University Press 2016), 95, 115; Thierry Fontenelle, 'Introduction' in Thierry Fontanelle (ed.), *Practical Lexicography: A Reader* (Oxford University Press 2008), 1–15, 5 ('Dictionaries are based on a huge oversimplification which posits that words have enumerable, listable meanings which are divisible into discrete units').

[11] (Judge) A Raymond Randolph, 'Dictionaries, Plain Meaning, and Context in Statutory Interpretation' (1994) 17 *Harv JL & Pub Poly* 71, 72. ('[C]iting to dictionaries creates a sort of optical illusion, conveying the existence of certainty – or "plainness" – when appearance may be all there is. Lexicographers define words with words. Words in the definition are defined by more words, as are those words. The trail may be endless; sometimes, it is circular. Using a dictionary definition simply pushes the problem back.')

[12] Brudney and Baum, 'Oasis or Mirage', 49 ('seeking out definitions that fit a Justice's conception of what a word should mean rather than using dictionaries to determine that meaning'); Ellen P Aprill, 'The Law of the Word: Dictionary Shopping in the Supreme Court' (1998) 30 *Ariz St LJ* 275, 321 (suggesting Justice Scalia used dictionaries in this way). Slocum, *Ordinary Meaning*, at 34 and 215, makes a different criticism: 'acontextual dictionary definitions ... often favor inappropriately broad meanings that capture "possible" rather than "ordinary" meanings'.

[13] For discussion of the extent of the practice, as well as the desirability of principles to guide the use of dictionaries in international law, see Chang-Fa Lo, 'Good Faith Use of Dictionary in the Search of Ordinary Meaning under the WTO Dispute Settlement Understanding' (2010) 1 *Journal of International Dispute Settlement* 431, 431–2 (emphasising the frequency of resort to dictionaries and proposing guidance); Isabelle Van Damme, 'On Good Faith Use of Dictionary in the Search of Ordinary Meaning under the WTO Dispute Settlement Understanding – A Reply to Professor Chang-Fa Lo' (2011) 2 *Journal of International Dispute Settlement* 231–9 (acknowledging that during the first few years of WTO tribunals resorted extensively to dictionary definitions, but doubting the value of a set of principles); David Pavot, 'The Use of Dictionary by the WTO Appellate Body: Beyond the Search of Ordinary Meaning' (2010) 4(1) *Journal of International Dispute Settlement* 29–46.

[14] Although the Berne Convention has official texts in English, French and Spanish, where the texts vary, the French text is said to be authoritative: Berne, Art. 37.

proliferation of dictionary sources (and approaches).[15] Moreover, comparative lex-icography demonstrates that different traditions exist with respect to different lan-guage dictionaries. For example, English dictionaries are more likely to include a variety of usage than French ones. As an expert commentary notes:

> French dictionaries, such as *Larousse* or *Le Petit Robert*, and in particular the *Dictionnaire de l'Academie francaise* (DAF), are considered as reference works whose purpose is to 'inform usage'. They are the product of an exclusionary rather than inclusionary approach to language. . . . French dictionaries, whether commer-cial such as the *Larousse* or *Robert*, or government-sponsored such as the DAF, have always limited the scope of what to include. The OED project, by contrast, operated with a very different approach to inclusivity.[16]

It seems unlikely that these different approaches are recognised as and when legal tribunals are referred to or consult dictionaries, or even among commentators.[17]

Recognising the limitations of dictionary meaning, we go well beyond mere resort to dictionary sources when it comes to ascertaining the ordinary meaning of 'quotation'.[18] In addition to examining dictionaries, the works of linguists and philosophers,[19] as well as cultural theorists,[20] we draw on a broad range of sources in which the term quotation is not defined or analysed but rather is *used*.[21] That is, we try to shed further light on the

[15] See also Gardiner, *Treaty Interpretation*, 189: 'That there are so many dictionary meanings makes almost inevitable immediate recourse to context and the other aids prescribed by the rules for selection of the appropriate ordinary meaning.'

[16] D Estival and A Pennycook, 'L'Académie Française and Anglophone Language Ideologies' (2011) 10 *Language Policy* 325–41, 331, 337.

[17] WTO Panel Report, United States – Section 110(5) of the Copyright Act 1976, (15 June 2000), WT/DS/160/R, [6.108]–[6.110] (defining 'certain', 'special' and 'cases' by referring to *The New Shorter Oxford English Dictionary* (Oxford 1993), [6.164]–[6.165] (ditto for 'normal' and 'exploitation'); WTO Appellate Body Report, United States – Section 211 Omnibus Appropriations Act of 1998 (2 January 2002), WT/DS176/AB/R, [137] (referring to *Le Robert*).

[18] Parkin (2019), 65, attacks our methodology on the basis that our examples 'provide singular instances of use of the term "quotation", in the often-specialised vocabulary of particular fields'. While she agrees our examples 'represent evidence of the kind that might form part of a lexicographer's corpus', it is not at all obvious that they should be disregarded in favour, exclusively, of reliance on dictionaries, as she proposes. As Slocum, *Ordinary Meaning*, explains, at 243–4, 'even a flawed prototype analysis is typically superior, at least as a matter of ordinary meaning determination, to the practice of relying on a dictionary definition and treating it as though it sets forth necessary and sufficient conditions for category membership'.

[19] For an overview of the vast literature on quotation in the philosophy of language, see Paul Saka, 'Quotation' (2013) 8 *Philosophy Compass* 935–49. For an influential discussion of the application of the concept of quotation to the visual arts, see Nelson Goodman, 'Some Questions Concerning Quotation' (April 1974) 58(2) *The Monist* 294–306.

[20] These include Richard Dyer, *Pastiche* (Routledge 2007); Finnegan, *Why Do We Quote? The Culture and History of Quotation* (Open Book Publishers 2011); Ingeborg Hoesterey, *Pastiche: Cultural Memory in Art, Film, Literature* (Indiana University Press 2001); David Metzer, *Quotation and Cultural Meaning in Twentieth Century Music* (Cambridge University Press 2003).

[21] Cp. Phillip A Rubin, 'War of the Words: How Courts Can Use Dictionaries in Accordance with Textualist Principles' (2010) 60 *Duke LJ* 167, 205–6 (describing how in US cases involving interpreta-tion of the US Constitution, *amicus* briefs have occasionally been submitted by Professors of

meaning of quotation empirically by examining how the term 'quotation' is used in a variety of cultural contexts, contexts which range well beyond the reuse of printed text.[22] These sources are valuable and important because of the *legal* framing of the question: the question of interpretation posed by Article 10(1) is what is the ordinary understanding of quotation across the cultural fields to which that provision applies. These fields include art, film, music and architecture. As a result, the views of commentators and scholars operating in those fields seem especially relevant.[23] The way they use the term quotation then offers special assistance to the task of ascertaining the meaning of the term 'quotation' and thus the scope of the exception.

While ordinary meaning is the prescribed starting point for interpretation of Article 10(1), it is clear that ordinary meaning is not determinative of *legal* meaning.[24] Most obviously, this would be the case if the term were defined in Article 10 of the Berne Convention (though it is not). Nevertheless, there may be inferences as to its legal meaning that we can draw from the structure of legal texts (e.g. as already noted, the field in which the exception operates, as well as the formulation of other exceptions),[25] as well as from national case law interpreting these instruments.[26] There are certain

Linguistics, History and English with a view to elucidating contemporary usage of terms and thus to assist the 'textual originalist' members of the US Supreme Court).

[22] We do not claim that the meaning of 'quotation' varies from context to context. As a legal term, there is only one legal meaning, and this must be equally applicable in relation to all Berne works. What we say is that this meaning must be ascertained from the use of the term 'quotation' across those contexts (rather than solely deduced from the world of printed text). This is different from interpreting the ordinary meaning of 'quotation' *in light of* the context of the treaty – that is, the grammatical construction of the provision, punctuation, the title, headings and chapeaux, the preamble or use of the same term in other parts of the treaty. See Gardiner, *Treaty Interpretation*, 199–210.

[23] In this respect, it might be said that we do not focus on the 'usual meaning in *everyday* language', – which is said by the CJEU to be the appropriate approach: *Pelham*, [70], [71] (on quotation); an approach that can be traced at least as far back as Case C-349/85 *Denmark* v. *Commission* EU: C:1988:34, [9] (interpreting terms 'meat' and 'fat'). However, it is clear from the case law of the CJEU that 'everyday' does not imply use by the general public: see, e.g., Case C-443/17 *Abraxis Bioscience LLC* C:2019:238, [25] (defining meaning of 'active ingredient' in 'everyday language' by reference to meaning in pharmacology). We therefore do not see the sources we use as in any way inconsistent with the task of seeking the 'ordinary' or 'everyday' meaning.

[24] Vienna Convention, Article 31(4) ('A special meaning shall be given to a term if it is established that the parties so intended'). Slocum, *Ordinary Meaning*, 29 ('Ordinary meaning is the default meaning of a legal text, cancellable (often implicitly) for various reasons, including because the author(s) intended some other meaning'). We see the process of determining legal meaning as involving a necessary blending of ordinary meaning and legal inference, often carried out intuitively and through iterative processes rather than a two-stage one (as Slocum's comment might suggest). In the case of 'quotation', there are initial contextual cues from the Convention generally, and the structure of Article 10(1), that exclude certain (dictionary) meanings of quotation, and then certain other cues than enable a tribunal to select between different plausible interpretations. Cf. Fred Schauer, 'Is Law a Technical Language? (2015) 52 *San Diego L Rev* 501 (raising questions about the commonplace distinction between ordinary meaning and technical meaning in law, and the distinction between interpretation and construction, and implying that all legal texts might have technical meaning).

[25] Article 10(2) and Article 10*bis*(2), Berne.

[26] Martin Senftleben, 'Internet Search Results – A Permissible Quotation?' (2013) 235 *RIDA* 3 (exploring Dutch, German, Spanish and French cases).

'legal logics', too, that underpin legal interpretation of terms – for example, where a use is subject to an open-textured 'fairness' analysis, even if the 'ordinary meaning' suggested similar factors might be relevant to assessing whether the act counted as 'quotation', it would seem unnecessary and potentially duplicative for similar considerations to inform a threshold analysis of whether an activity fell within that concept.[27] Rather, for legal purposes, the threshold concept should be formulated in a free and open-ended manner. Moreover, when interpreting a legal concept that permits a particular activity (such as 'quotation'), even if ordinary use of the term suggested otherwise, policy logic implies that the interpretation of the concept should be broad enough to encompass *less* intrusive or *less* egregious acts of reuse.

Some guidance may also be gained from the preparatory documents (so-called *travaux*).[28] Article 32 of the Vienna Convention allows for the possibility of referring to a Treaty's *travaux préparatoires* to confirm the meaning of a term or to determine that meaning when an interpretation based on the ordinary meaning of a provision, in the light of its object and purpose, would leave the meaning of that term ambiguous or obscure or lead to a result which is manifestly absurd or unreasonable.[29]

We must also pay attention to the importance of 'quotation' as the legal concept that, in the context of copyright law, operates to facilitate *fundamental* freedoms, recognised in international conventions,[30] such as freedom of expression and freedom of art. Even if ordinary usage pointed away from certain acts being regarded as 'quotation', it might be the case that because a particular activity implicates freedom of expression and art, and cannot otherwise be accommodated within copyright's structure, a harmonious interpretation of international law[31] requires that the notion of quotation be understood more broadly than its ordinary usage to encompass such an activity.[32] (Reconciliation of the right of freedom of expression with the rights of

---

[27] For example, ordinary use might suggest that a 'misquotation' was not a quotation at all, but because the question of whether something is 'misquotation' might involve difficult questions of interpretation, legal considerations might imply that the matter is best considered under the rubric of 'fairness': misquotation might make a quotation unfair, rather than excluding it from the benefit of the defence as a matter of threshold analysis. See p. 125, below and Chapter 6, Section III, pp. 157–159.

[28] See Chapter 2.

[29] For discussion, see Gardiner, *Treaty Interpretation*, ch. 8.

[30] Universal Declaration of Human Rights, Article 19 ('Everyone has the right to freedom of opinion and expression; this right includes freedom to hold opinions without interference and to seek, receive and impart information and ideas through any media and regardless of frontiers'). Article 27(2) also recognises 'the right to the protection of the moral and material interests resulting from any scientific, literary or artistic production of which he is the author'.

[31] For a discussion, see Henning Grosse Ruse-Khan, *The Protection of Intellectual Property in International Law* (Oxford University Press 2016), [3.08], p. 34. See also *Magyar Helsinki Bizottság v. Hungary*, App No 18030/11, (ECHR, Gr Ch, Nov 8, 2016), [123].

[32] See below, pp. 159, fn. 106 and 160, fn. 107 (emphasising link between quotation right and freedom of speech); Bochumberg (1994), 31 ('Quotations must at the same time ensure educational and scientific progress, freedom of expression and freedom of information').

authors and copyright owners can be calibrated, as we will see, through the application of the 'fair practice' condition.)[33]

II CHARACTERISTICS OF QUOTATION IN RELATION TO THE SOURCE MATERIAL

A *Is Quotation Inherently Limited to Literary Works or Text?*

We have already observed (in Chapter 3, Section II) that Article 10(1) is not limited in its application to a subset of works protected under the Berne Convention: in principle, it applies to all works (including original computer programs and databases). Nevertheless, the paradigm example of a 'quotation', with many associated conditions, is of text. Indeed, etymologically, there is some basis for the view that the English 'quotation' and French 'citation' were initially terms used in the printing trade.[34] Might it be argued, then, that while formally applicable to all Berne works, 'quotation' is necessarily textual (i.e. of text and in text)? Some French scholars have, in fact, taken this position,[35] while it is perhaps implicit in some countries' laws which define quotation as involving 'transcribing',[36] or specify a maximum number of lines

---

[33] See Chapter 6, Section III, Part B, pp. 159–163, below.

[34] Edmund King, '"Small Scale Copyrights?" Quotation Marks in Theory and Practice' (March 2004) 98 (1) *The Papers of the Bibliographical Society of America* 39–53 (response to De Grazia); Case C-476/17 *Pelham GmbH* v. *Hütter*, EU:C:2018:1002 (Advocate General's Opinion), [62] ('The quotation exception has its origin and is mainly used in literary works') (AG Szpunar).

[35] André Françon, *Cours de Propriété Littéraire, Artistique et Industriel* (Litec 1999), 244 (legislation seems to have been drafted with reference to quotation from literary works so that it is difficult to imagine as lawful quotation for a musical work or work in the plastic arts); Nicolas Bouche, *Intellectual Property Law in France* (2nd ed., Kluwer 2014), 85, [235] ('This exception has been obviously intended to apply to literary works'); Henri Desbois, *Le Droit d'Auteur en France* (Dalloz 1978), 315–16, [249] (suggesting that the reference to 'short' in Article 41-3 of the French Law of 1957 would prevent artistic quotation, adding a further reason that the quoted work and borrowing work should be of the same nature); 317, [250] (arguing too that quotation is 'absolutely impossible' in music because one musical work cannot discuss another); Claude Colombet, *Propriété Littéraire et artistique et droits voisins* (9th ed., Dalloz 1999). Very occasionally, French courts have taken the same position: *Le Mauvais ceil*, 13 Oct 1959, TGI Seine, (April 1961) 31 *RIDA* 93 (refusing to use quotation exception to use of image of an eye taken from a painting); *Edgar Rice Burrough Inc.* v. *Sté Anagramme Editions H. Veyrier et al* TGI Paris, 30 September 1983, D. 1984 S.C. 289, Colombet obs. (refusing in principle to accept that a work of visual art could be quoted), both cited in Y Gaubiac, 'Freedom to Quote from an Intellectual Work' (1997) 171 *RIDA* 2, 72, fns. 66 and 67. Note also Maurice Casteels, 'Works of Art and the Right of Quotation', (1954) 11 *RIDA* 81–97 (explaining that the quotation exception in the Belgian law of 1886 was only applicable to literary works, as confirmed in a Belgian Supreme Court decision of 1952).

[36] This is the case with some states in Central and South America: Colombia, Law No. 23 of 28 January 1982 on Copyright, Article 31 ('It shall be permissible to quote an author by transcribing the necessary passages . . . '); Costa Rica, Law No. 6683 of 14 October 1982 on Copyright and Related Rights (as amended up to Law No. 8834 of 3 May 2010), Article 70; Dominican Republic, Law No. 65-00 on Copyright, Article 35; Guinea-Bissau, Copyright Code (approved by Decree-Law No. 46.980 of 28 March 1972), Article 185 ('Authors of any text shall have the right to transcribe or summarize').

or words[37] or paragraphs.[38] If quotation is so limited, the effect is, in substance, to render the exception in Article 10(1) inapplicable to painting, music, architecture, film and photography.

It is central to our argument that the term 'quotation' in Article 10(1) is not so limited, and thus that the conditions that are associated with the textual paradigm should not be regarded as necessary legal conditions for the existence of quotation. Rather the meaning of the term 'quotation' in this context must be understood to accommodate ideas of what counts as quotation in music, film and the visual arts.

To begin, it is worth noting that many dictionary definitions accept that quotation extends beyond the act of reproducing words. The *Oxford English Dictionary* (*OED*), for example, defines quotation to include '[a] short passage or tune taken from one piece of music to another or quoted elsewhere'.[39] The *Shorter OED* mentions not just music but visual art: defining a quotation as '[a] quoted passage or remark; transf. a short passage or tune taken from one piece of music and quoted in another; a visual image taken from one work of art and used in another'.[40] In her review of dictionary definitions of 'quotation' in other European languages ('citazione' in Italian, 'citation' in French and 'zitat' in German), Jane Parkin helpfully identifies a number of further examples from Italian dictionaries: *Sabatini/Colleti* defines the term in reference to architecture and the figurative arts, while *Treccani* refers to the use of preceding works in musical and dramatic works, in films or figurative artworks.[41] As we shall now show, discussions by musicologists, film experts and architectural experts regularly acknowledge the practice of quotation in these fields.

---

[37] Argentina, Law No. 26.570 of 25 November 2009, amending Law No. 11.723 of 28 September 1993 on Legal Intellectual Property Regime, Article 10 (specifying 1,000 words or 8 bars or 'the parts of the text essential for that purpose'); Eritrea, Civil Code 1993, Article 1661 (40 lines of poetry or 10,000 characters).

[38] Jordan, Law No. 22 of 1992 on Copyright and its Amendments up to 2005, Article 17(d) ('Quoting paragraphs from the work in another work') (emphasis added).

[39] J A Simpson and E S C Weiner (eds.), *The Oxford English Dictionary* (Clarendon 1989), vol. 13, 52.

[40] *Shorter Oxford English Dictionary on Historical Principles*, vol. 2 (6th ed., Oxford University Press 2007), 4a.

[41] Parkin (2019), 68, fn 100. See also Tullio de Mauro, *Grande Dizionario Italiano dell'uso* (Torino, 1999), 92 (defining quotation as including shooting and echoing of preceding work in later literary, musical or film work and giving example 'la scena finale è una [citazione] da un film de Fellini'); cf. Nicola Zingarelli, *Lo Zingarelli 1994: vocabolario della lingua italiana* (Zanichelli 1993) 375 (defining citàre as 'textual reference to passages of others in support of their own reasoning') and Pasquale Stoppelli, *Il Grande Dizionario Garzanti dell Lingua Italiana* (1993) 386 (referring to citation of passages in a text or speech). In understanding the 'textuallist' orientation of French commentators, it is notable how frequently they rely on dictionaries. For example, the influential treatise A Lucas, H-J Lucas and A Lucas-Schloetter, *Traité de la Propriété Littéraire et Artistique* (4th ed, LexisNexis 2012), 390, [426], refers to the definition in *Le Petit Robert*, ('passage cité d'un auteur'). Yves Gaubiac, 'Freedom to Quote from an Intellectual Work' (1997) 171 *RIDA* 2, 58, fn. 8 and 72, fn. 63, also cites French dictionary definitions, noting that they refer to literary sphere, but contrasts this with the fact that most of the French case law accepts potential application of quotation right to other material.

1 Music

Discussion of reuse of music as 'quotation' is very common.[42] Sometimes the term is used to describe reuse of melody (e.g. in the work of Charles Ives, Louis Armstrong or Michael Nyman)[43] or incorporation of literary material, but it is also used to refer to the reuse of recordings of music, such as Vladimir Ussachevsky's reuse of a recording of a 1951 performance of Wagner's *Parsifal* in his avant-garde *Wireless Fantasy*,[44] a 1960 sound collage combining the performance with the sounds of Morse-code signals being tapped out.[45] In line with this, most commentators characterise digital sound sampling, which first emerged in the mid-1980s and became widely associated with hip-hop music, as a form of quotation.[46] For example, John Oswald, composer and music Professor at York University, who described his use of sampling as 'plunderphonics', in turn explained that '[a] plunderphone is

[42]   See, for example, the special issue, (2014) 33(2) *Contemporary Music Review* on music borrowing and quotation; Bochumberg, *Droit de Citation*, 154, [234] (describing quotation of one musical work in another as 'a widespread phenomenon').

[43]   Christopher Ballantine, *Music and Its Social Meanings* (Gordon and Breach 1984), ch. 4 (discussing Charles Ives's use of musical quotation); J Peter Burkholder, *All Made of Tunes: Charles Ives and the Uses of Musical Borrowing* (Yale University Press 1995), 1 ('Musical quotation is one of the most characteristic facets of Charles Ives' music. ... The music Ives uses includes hymn tunes, patriotic songs, marches, bugle calls, drum patterns, popular songs, fiddle tunes, college songs and cheers, and classical pieces by composers from Bach to Debussy'); Jorge Daniel Veneciano, 'Louis Armstrong, Bricolage and the Aesthetics of Swing' in Robert G O'Meally, Brent Hayes Edwards and Farah Jasmine Griffin (eds.), *Uptown Conversation: The New Jazz Studies* (Columbia University Press 2004), 256–78, 269–70 (drawing on Armstrong's hobby of creating collages of photographs to cast light in his music, and linking it to Armstrong's use of musical quotation, perhaps most famously of Gershwin's *Rhapsody in Blue* on his 1929 solo of *Ain't Misbehavin*, as well as Armstrong's frequent quotation of advertising jingles). For more on Armstrong, see Krin Gabbard, 'The Quoter and his Culture' in Reginald Buckner and Steven Wieland (eds.), *Jazz in Mind: Essays on the History and Meaning of Jazz* (Wayne State University Press 1991). Robert Worby, 'Foreword', to P Ap Siôn, *The Music of Michael Nyman: Texts, Contexts and Intertexts* (Ashgate 2007), xi, xii ('Composers had always appropriated folk tunes or politely quoted fragments from other composers').

[44]   Available via You Tube: https://www.youtube.com/watch?v=bEShy2QIj4U (accessed 31 January 2020).

[45]   Richard Beaudoin, 'Counterpoint and Quotation in Ussachevsky's *Wireless Fantasy*' (2007) 12(2) *Organised Sound* 143–51, esp. 147–9.

[46]   David Sanjek, 'Don't Have to DJ No More: Sampling and the "Autonomous Creator"' (1992) 10 *Card Arts & Ent LJ* 607, 612, 613, 614 (describing various forms of sampling as quotation). Cf. Aram Sinnreich, *Mashed Up: Music, Technology and the Rise of Configurable Culture* (University of Massachusetts Press 2010), 124 (suggesting that sampling is 'not "quoting" because (a) it's the mediated expression itself, not merely the idea behind it, that's being used, and (b) the output often bears little or no resemblance to the input'. Quite where Sinnreich gained his 'definition' for the concept of quotation is never explained. Certainly, it was not from the manner in which his interviewees use the term quotation. On the very next page, Sinnreich quotes from an interview with Matt Wand, a UK-based composer from (Stock, Hausen and Walkman), asking, in relation to musical reuse, 'How far can you go with quotation?'). Note also Johnson Okpaluba, 'Digital Sampling and Music Industry Practices, Re-Spun' in K Bowrey and M Handler (eds.), *Copyright Law in the Age of the Entertainment Franchise* (Cambridge University Press 2014), ch. 4, 75–100, 81 ('Digital sampling ... can therefore be seen to be related to other practices of music quotation ... ', citing J P Burkholder, 'The Uses of Existing Music: Musical Borrowing as a Field' (1994) 50 *Notes* 851).

a recognisable *sonic quote*, using the actual sound of something familiar which has already been recorded'. Mark Katz, similarly, refers to sampling as 'performative quotation', as it reutilises the timbre of a unique sound event.[47] Tellef Kvifte used the term 'audio quotation'.[48] Kevin Holm-Hudson used a different term, 'timbral quotation'.[49] Serge Lacasse developed a related distinction, that between autosonic and allosonic quotation,[50] where sampling is a type of 'autosonic quotation' whereas imitation of a sound and its re-recording – a sound-alike – is 'allosonic quotation', which has been picked up and deployed in subsequent studies.[51] Although these commentators often seek to draw distinctions between sampling, a form of musical borrowing, and other forms of quotation in music generally, so as to highlight that sampling has certain special qualities, it is notable that for most the practice is treated unquestioningly as 'quotation'. Not surprisingly, therefore, in *Pelham v. Hütter*, the CJEU recognised the possibility that a sample from the recordings of avant-garde electronic artists Kraftwerk might qualify as quotations of the musical works the samples embodied.[52]

2 Film

Use of the term 'quotation' in film studies and film commentary is also very common indeed.[53] Sometimes the term refers to quotation from literary material, or the replication of film within films. A good example of the latter occurs in the comedy

---

[47] M Katz, *Capturing Sound: How Technology Has Changed Music* (University California Press 2010), 140–1 ('quotation that recreates all the details of timbre and timing that evoke and identify a unique sound event').

[48] Tellef Kvifte, 'Digital Sampling and Analogue Aesthetics' in A Melberg (ed.), *Aesthetics at Work* (Unipub 2007), 193 ('the digital sampler has always been a compositional tool. It is not only a looping device for audio quotation, ... even though this has dominated the production of hip-hop and the study of sampling'), cited by Paul Harkins, 'Microsampling: From Akufen's Microhouse to Todd Edwards and the Sound of UK Garage' in Anne Danielsen (ed.), *Musical Rhythm in the Age of Digital Reproduction* (Ashgate 2010) 177, 180 (discussing Tellef Kvifte's four meanings of sampling, explaining the third as 'that of integrating existing recordings into a new recording as a recognizable sonic quotation').

[49] K Holm-Hudson, 'Quotation and Context: Sampling and John Oswald's Plunderphonics' (1997) 7 *Leonardo Music Journal* 17–25, 17 [abstract] ('Although the music industry ... insisted that digital sampling is 'theft', it is perhaps better viewed in historical and theoretical context as timbral quotation. Often the sample functions as a quote that is recontextualized but that nevertheless bears the weight of its original context').

[50] Serge Lacasse, 'Intertextuality and Hypertextuality in Recorded Popular Music' in Michael Talbot (ed.), *The Musical Work: Reality or Invention?* (Liverpool University Press 2000), ch. 2.

[51] See e.g. Dr Justin Williams's doctoral thesis at Nottingham, 'Musical Borrowing in Hip-Hop Music' (2010), published as *Rhymin' and Stealin'* (Michigan University Press 2014).

[52] Case C-476/17 *Pelham GmbH v. Huetter* EU:C:2019:624 (CJEU, Grand Chamber), [68], [72].

[53] See L Bently, 'Copyright and Quotation in Film and TV,' CREATe Working Paper (June 2020). We are grateful to Dr Claudy Op den Kamp for sharing multiple other examples of expressive re-use of, and in, film which are described as quotation, and look forward to her forthcoming multimedia exploration: Dr Op den Kamp *Turning Your Film into Mine*; *Cultural Practices in Filmmaking and Copyright Exceptions* (forthcoming).

slasher film *Scream* (1996, dir. Wes Craven), where key characters are observed watching an earlier horror film, *Halloween* (1978, dir. John Carpenter).[54] Occasionally, the term is used to describe the referencing of works of art in film scenes, as, for example, with Derek Jarman's reference in his film *Caravaggio* (1986) to Jacques-Louis David's painting *Death of Marat* (1793). In this painting, the radical journalist Jean-Paul Marat is shown lying dead in his bath, after being murdered by Charlotte Corday. In Jarman's film *Caravaggio*, he features a scene where the storyteller is in the bath, head wrapped in a towel, writing on a typewriter and then slouched back in the tub, one arm extended outside it.[55] According to one commentator, this is in turn quoted in the television mini-series *Painted Lady* (1997, dir. Julian Jarrold), starring Helen Mirren.[56]

However, perhaps the most prevalent use of the term 'quotation' in film commentary is to describe references made in one film to scenes in another. In fact, the 'quotation' is widely deployed to describe aspects of the films of a host of other filmmakers, including Jean-Luc Godard,[57] Ridley Scott[58] and Quentin Tarantino. Indeed, Tarantino has been associated with a particular cinematographic practice, so-called 'hyperquotational cinema'.[59]

---

[54] Yvonne Sarah Morris, 'The Legal Implications Surrounding the Practice of Video Sampling in the Digital Age' in S Greenfield and G Osborn (eds.), *Readings in Law and Popular Culture* (Routledge 2008), 274–309, 286 (describing this as the quotation of *Halloween* in *Scream*).

[55] Ingeborg Hoesterey, *Pastiche: Cultural Memory in Art, Film, Literature* (Indiana University Press 2001), 67 (describes this as 'a full-fledged pictorial quotation with high recognition value').

[56] Hoesterey, *Pastiche*, 124, fn. 10 ('citing both David's painting and Jarman's quotation in *Caravaggio*').

[57] James F Austin, *Proust, Pastiche and the Postmodern or Why Style Matters* (Bucknell University Press 2013), 186 ('Godard's work in particular is known for the practice of quoting'). Mikhail Iampolski, *The Memory of Tiresias: Intertextuality and Film* (trans. Harsha Ram) (University of California Press 1998), 31. ('Jean-Luc Godard is well known as one of the most intertextually oriented of film directors. Several of his films are practically collages of quotes. Godard reveals his passion for the quotation in his very first film, *Breathless* (*A bout de souffle*). . . . *Breathless* is riddled with all sorts of quotes. The source of the widest layer of quotes in the film was American film noir.') Iampolski also quotes Godard, *Jean-Luc Godard par Jean-Luc Godard* (Cahiers du cinema 1985), 216–18, who explained, 'You have to put the blame on my taste for quoting, a taste I have always kept. But why blame me for it? In life people quote the things they like. We have a right to quote whatever we like.'

[58] Hoesterey, *Pastiche*, 47–52 (referring, for example, to 'a number of quotations from *Metropolis* that Ridley Scott pastiches in Blade Runner') (49). Giuliana Bruno, 'Ramble City: Postmodernism and Bladerunner' (1987) 41 *October* 61–74, 62: 'Pastiche is intended as aesthetics of quotations pushed to the limit: It is an incorporation of forms, an imitation of dead styles deprived of any satirical impulse' (a paraphrase of Frederic Jameson); Jack Boozer Jr, 'Crashing the Gates of Insight' in Judith B Kerman (ed.), *Retrofitting Blade Runner* (Bowling Green University Popular Press 1991), 212–28; Mike Wilmington, 'The Rain People' (January–February 1992) 28(1) *Film Comment* 17–18.

[59] Mikhail Iampolski, *The Memory of Tiresias*, esp. at 35 (explaining the notion of the 'hyperquote'); Asbjørn Grønstad, *Transfigurations: Violence, Death and Masculinity in American Cinema* (Amsterdam University Press 2008), 144, 159 (Tarantino's 'fetischistic quotationism'), 160 (Tarantino's 'aesthetics of quotation'), 162 ('hyper-quotational cinema'), 164 (referring to the 'quotational promiscuity of *Reservoir Dogs*'), 167 ('the hypermodern film aesthetic of unconstrained quotationality').

3 Architecture

Although some philosophers of language have doubted whether one architectural work can 'quote' another,[60] the term 'quotation' is also widely deployed by commentators on architecture to refer to modes of reuse of particular architectural forms.[61] Such descriptions became more widespread once the view that buildings were functional gave way to the view that buildings, like novels, tell stories.[62] Seen in this way, buildings (or at least architects) are part of a dialogue, and the audience recognises the represented form as derived from elsewhere and understand it as quotation. According to one commentator, 'quotation . . . became the very medium of architectural conception'.[63] Common examples of architects who openly acknowledged quoting include Phillip Johnson (1906–2005) and James Stirling (1926–92).

Johnson, described in his time as 'the reigning dean of American architecture',[64] famously shifted from functionalism and internationalism to a style often described

---

[60] Remei Capdevila-Werning, 'Can Buildings Quote?' (2011) 69 *Jo Aesthetics and Art Criticism* 115–24 (applying Nelson Goodman's work on quotation to architecture). Interestingly, Capdevila-Werning starts with a number of examples of use of the term 'quotation' in art.

[61] The term is also used in design. See, for example, Brenda Schmahmann, 'Intertextual Textiles: Parodies and Quotations in Cloth', (2017) 15(4) *Textile: The Journal of Cloth and Culture* 336–43 (introduction to a special issue) ('Strategies such as quotation and parody have also been deployed in numerous works made from textiles or incorporating textile elements'). In fact, the EU Design Regulation, Council Regulation (EC) No 6/2002 of 12 December 2001, Art 20(1)(c) gives an exception to 'acts of reproduction for the purpose of making citations'. In its English-language version, this seems as an explicit acknowledgement that, in law (as well as ordinary language), one can quote a design. The same inference can be drawn from the Spanish- and Italian-language versions, which refer, respectively, to 'los actos de reproducción realizados con fines de cita' and 'atti di riproduzione a fini didattici o di citazione'. It is, however, notable that in the French-language version of the Regulation, the exception is worded differently: '[D]'actes de reproduction à des fins d'illustration'. In Cases C-24/16 and C-25/16, *Nintendo Co Ltd v. Big Ben Interactive GmbH*, EU:C:2017:724, the CJEU offered a 'purposive' interpretation of 'citation' to ensure that design rights did not discourage innovation. It therefore held, at [76]–[77], that 'citation' included advertising of a lawful product that included an image of a protected design in order to demonstrate the joint use of both products.

[62] Stephen Barthelmess, 'Richard Meier's Stadthaus Project at Ulm' (1990) (Spr) 44(3) *Jo Architectural Education* 2–19, 12 (relating emergence of historical quotation in architecture to the turn away from abstract functionalism); Cynthia Davidson (ed.), *Robert A M Stern: Tradition and Invention in Architecture: Conversations and Essays* (Yale University Press 2011), 5 ('Architecture is a narrative art, and architectural style is analogous to poetic diction. Simple writing may communicate on a basic level but it does not give much pleasure. Since the time of ancient Greece, storytellers have embroidered their tales with references to and quotations from works of the past, thereby linking with tradition and perpetuating age-old tales. The complexity of narrative – its allusiveness, its resonance, its aggrandizement of the reader's own experience – raises the statement of a simple theme, whether literary or architectural, to the realm of art'); Hoesterey, *Pastiche*, 33 ('The 'textuality' of architecture, to be deciphered like a text, became a central topos in the discourse of architectural form and ornament').

[63] Barthelmess, 'Richard Meier's Stadthaus', 12. See also Mary MacLeod, 'Architecture and Practice in the Reagan Era' (February 1989) 8 *Assemblage* 22–59, 34.

[64] Marvin Trachtenberg and Isabelle Hyman, *Architecture: From Prehistory to Postmodernism* (2nd ed., Pearson 2001), 573.

as postmodernism or modern classicism.[65] One building that symbolised this shift was built to house the headquarters of the US communications giant AT&T at 550 Madison Avenue in New York,[66] which one commentator called 'a granite-clad, goldleafed, postmodern masterwork'.[67] Colloquially known as the 'Chippendale' building,[68] because it was thought to look 'like a colossal Chippendale highboy cabinet',[69] the 647-feet, 36-storey skyscraper is a mix of styles.[70] One online commentary by David Landon[71] describes the top as the

> single most important architectural detail of the last fifty years. Emerging bravely from the glassy sea of Madison Avenue skyscrapers in midtown Manhattan, the open pediment atop [the] 1984 AT&T Building ... singlehandedly turned the architectural world on its head. *This playful deployment of historical quotation* explicitly contradicted modernist imperatives and heralded the mainstream arrival of an approach to design defined instead by a search for architectural meaning.[72]

Similarly, well-known art critic Craig Owens called the AT&T building 'a compendium of legible historical references and quotations'.[73] Although it is widely acknowledged that the building contains a number of quotations, there is less

[65] Frank Schulze, *Philip Johnson: Life and Work* (Alfred Knopf 1994), 333 ('Postmodernist architecture . . . .as it developed in the 1970s and 1980s, treated the history of building as one immense source book'); Hoesterey, *Pastiche* ('For two decades architects practiced the evolving aesthetics of quotation and incorporation of past forms and styles with a vengeance'). At 34, Hoesterey offers the example of Charles Moore's Piazza d'Italia (New Orleans) and mentions his 'quotation style'.

[66] For an image, see www.archdaily.com/611169/ad-classics-at-and-t-building-philip-johnson-and-john-burgee (accessed 3 July 2020). When AT&T went into financial decline, Sony bought the building and occupied it until 2013. Apparently, it is now owned by Olayan and Chelsfield and is empty, apart from a ground-floor restaurant.

[67] 'Preface' by John O'Connor in Hilary Lewis and John O'Connor, *Philip Johnson: The Architect in his Own Words* (Rizzoli 1994), 8 (stating that 'Johnson references the gamut'); Hilary Lewis, 'No Rules, Just Art' in *The Architecture of Philip Johnson* (Bullfinch Press 2002), 3–4, 4 ('Johnson at his most postmodern'). However, contrast the views of Charles Jencks, who called the AT&T Building 'the reverse of postmodernism': Charles Jencks, 'Contextual Counterpoint in Architecture' (2012) 24 *Log* 71–80, 73.

[68] Paul Goldberger, 'Philip Johnson Is Dead at 98: Architecture's Restless Intellect', *New York Times* (New York, 27 January 2005) ('Chippendale skyscraper').

[69] Trachtenberg & Hyman, 574. The eighteenth-century English cabinet maker Thomas Chippendale's works were widely copied for the US market.

[70] Leland M Roth, *Understanding Architecture: Its Elements, History, Meaning* (The Herbert Press 1993/1994), ch. 21, 'Late Twentieth-Century Architecture: A Question of Meaning) 506 ('whose classical loggia base and so-called Chippendale top made clear allusions to such New York skyscrapers of the 1920s as Warren and Wetmore's New York Central Building (Helmsley Building) of 1929'); Stanley Abercrombie, 'A Few Good Buildings: Reading the Obituaries of Philip Johnson' (2005) 74 (2) *The American Scholar* 117–20.

[71] 'AD Classics: AT&T Building' (20 March 2015), at www.archdaily.com/611169/ad-classics-at-and-t-building-philip-johnson-and-john-burgee (accessed 2 February 2020).

[72] Emphasis added.

[73] Craig Owens, 'Philip Johnson: History, Genealogy, Historicism' in Kenneth Frampton, *Philip Johnson: Processes. The Glass House, 1949 and The AT&T Corporate Headquarters*, 1978 (Inst for Arch & Urban Studies NY 1978), 3. See also Robert Stern, *Modern Classicism* (T&H) 84–6 ('One can pick out the references').

agreement as to which prior works were being quoted by the architect.[74] Although Johnson is generally said to have been willing to acknowledge his sources,[75] with respect to the AT&T, he was rather coy when asked about the topic. He denied the top came from a Chippendale clock, though hinted that the inspiration for the base was the Pazzi Chapel in Florence (a work commonly attributed to Brunelleschi).[76] Others have found the source much closer to home: from 558 Madison Avenue.[77]

The technique of James Stirling,[78] who Ada Louse Huxtable described as a 'creative genius',[79] has likewise been described as 'quotational'.[80] One famous example is his Leicester University Engineering building,[81] the lecture theatres for

[74] Though Johnson's critics, preferred other terms, such as pastiche: Ada Louise Huxtable, architecture columnist for the New York Times, called it 'a pastiche of historical references' ('Johnson's Latest – Clever Tricks or True Art?' *New York Times* (New York, 16 April 1978), 26, quoted in Schulze, *Philip Johnson*, at 351). Elsewhere she referred to it as 'pedestrian pastiche' (Architecture View: '"Towering" Achievements of '78', *New York Times*, 31 December 1978, D21) and Johnson's work generally as 'clever cannibalism' (Huxtable, 'The Troubled State of Architecture', *New York Review of Books*, 1 May 1980, 22–9, cited in Schulze, *Philip Johnson*, at 366). Johnson said he had no objection to describing his work as pastiche.

[75] Hilary Lewis and John O'Connor, *Philip Johnson: The Architect in His Own Words* (Rizzoli 1994), 14. Many of Johnson's other works, and probably most notoriously the Hines College of Architecture, University of Houston (1983), clearly adapted from the work of French architect Claude Nicolas Ledoux, have been described in similar terms: Schulze, *Philip Johnson*, 334 (describing Johnsons chapel in Thanksgiving Square, Dallas, which was based on the ninth-century mosque at Samarra as 'candidly mimicking the conventional look ... of the minaret that crowned the Samarra mosque'); Charles Jencks, 'Philip Johnson and the Smile of Medusa' in Emmanuel Petit (ed.), *Philip Johnson: The Constancy of Change* (Yale University Press 2009), 136, 146 (stating that for the Glass House in New Canaan, Johnson 'cast about in a veritable snake pit of historical references').

[76] Christian Bjone, *Philip Johnson and his Mischief: Appropriation in Art and Architecture* (Images Publishing Group 2014), 31 (quoting Johnson as saying that base was designed 'rather like the Pazzi Chapel in Florence (Brunelleschi), the middle to copy the Chicago Tribune middle and the top – well, I'm not sure, but it did not come from a Chippendale clock').

[77] C Bjone, *Philip Johnson*, 32 and fn. 15 (based on an interview with Renny Booth in 2013).

[78] For a gossip-filled biographical account, see Mark Girouard, *Big Jim* (Pimlico 2000).

[79] Ada Louise Huxtable, 'Architecture: Bigger – And May Be Better: The Outlook in Architecture' *New York Times* (26 August 1978), 83 ('one of the few authentic creative geniuses of our time').

[80] Francesco Dal Co refers to Stirling's 'quotational tendency': 'The Melancholy Experience of Contemporaneity' (1993) 2 (Sept/Oct) ANY (*Architecture New York*) 26–9, 27 (special issue on Stirling). Vittorio Pizzigoni, an architect and researcher who teaches architectural design at the University of Genoa, has published an analysis of Stirling's Florey Building in Oxford, noting the 'never-ending quotation process through which Stirling reuses any piece of the architecture of the past in his projects untroubled by their origin' and observing that 'Stirling preferred to choose cryptic and difficult rather than predictable and explicit quotations ... one can easily find formal echoes with the work of Le Corbusier, Aalto or Melnikov, but it's much more difficult to find a single specific quotation'. www.gizmoweb.org/2009/12/the-florey-building-a-key-project-of-stirlings-work/ (accessed 2 February 2020). See also Claire Zimmerman, 'Stirling Reassembled' (2007) 56 AA Files 30–41, 34 (explaining that Stirling 'combined dense architectural quotation with postwar ambivalence. ... Stirling copied, repeated and recombined motifs ... ' and describing Stirling as a montagist); Manfredo Tafuri, 'L'Architecture dans le Boudoir: The Language of Criticism and the Criticism of Language' in K Michael Hays (ed.), *Architecture Theory Since 1968* (MIT Press 1998), 146–73, 149 ('the difficult task of determining the meaning of Stirling's enigmatic and ironic use of the "quotation"').

[81] www2.le.ac.uk/departments/engineering/about/building (accessed 3 July 2020).

which are trapezoidal forms protruding from the main building.[82] For many commentators, these are quotations from the constructivist work of Konstantin Melnikov (1890–1974)[83] – in particular, his Rusakov Club in Moscow.[84] Although Mark Crinson has cast doubt on whether Stirling knew of Melnikov's works at the relevant time,[85] those who believed this to be the source of the form of the lecture theatres in the Leicester Engineering Building have rarely hesitated to use the language of 'quotation' to describe Stirling's practice. Amanda Reese-Lawrence, for example, in an important study of Stirling's practice, which she describes as 're-visioning', proclaims that the Leicester project 'openly referenced a much broader range of recognizable and specific quotations – most famously the Rusakov Workers' Club'.[86] The same is true of Stirling's Stuttgart museum, which Barthelmess called 'an initial testing ground for the project of quotation from the history of architecture',[87] while the German newspaper *Die Zeit* identified so many quotations that it dubbed the building 'Das zitatenmuseum'.[88] Moreover, Amanda Reese-Lawrence has explored a further dimension of Stirling's work, his 'self-quotation' in architecture, focusing on Stirling's proposal to reuse thirty of his own earlier projects, sometimes in the

[82] Kenneth Frampton, 'Leicester University Engineering Laboratory' (1964) 34(2) *Architectural Design* 61; John McKean, *Leicester University Engineering Building: James Stirling and James Gowan* (Phaidon 1994).

[83] Owen Hatherley, 'Konstantin Melnikov's Legacy' *Architectural Review* (28 August 2015).

[84] For an image, see www.archdaily.com/155470/ad-classics-rusakov-workers-club-konstantin-melnikov.

[85] Mark Crinson, 'Melnikov in Leicester – A Mythology' (2013) 4 *Leuchtturmprojekte* 48–63; Mark Crinson, *Stirling and Gowan: Architecture from Austerity to Affluence* (Yale University Press 2012), 78 ('given the obscurity of Melnikov's work at this time this seems unlikely'); 240 ('the question of how Stirling and Gowan might have seen Melnikov's design is not easily resolved'). Cf. Amanda Reese-Lawrence, *James Stirling: Revisionary Modernists* (Yale University Press 2012), 112 ('Melnikov's influence is unquestionable though perhaps overemphasized and oversimplified'), and Mark Girouard, *Big Jim* (Pimlico 2000), 77 ('The idea of showing the shape of the lecture theatres [in Sheffield University design of 1953] externally comes without doubt from the Constructivist architect Melnikov's Workers' Clubhouse in Moscow (1926). Jim certainly knew of this at this date, although there were occasions when he claimed that he did not'); Owen Hatherley, 'Whose Modernist Icon Is It Anyway?' (2010) (April 23) *Building Design* 9 (Stirling 'borrowed' from Melnikov's design); 'Actually Existing Social Condensers: On the Mundanity of Soviet Modernism' (2017) 22(3) *Journal of Architecture* 512, 518 (saying Melnikov was 'widely plagiarized', including by Stirling).

[86] *James Stirling: Revisionary Modernists* (Yale University Press 2012), 84. At 106 she refers to 'the numerous historical quotations' and at 112 describes the over-hanging lecture theatres as 'the most accessible and certainly the most discussed "quotation" in the building'. Here she uses inverted commas, probably to emphasise that Stirling's work is more than simply quotation. As she argues, at 3, 'Stirling didn't simply string together a series of direct quotations: he interrogated precedent based on a discovered or desired connection between the original and his own project, often citing a continued functional or programmatic use.'

[87] Barthelmess, 'Richard Meier's Stadthaus', 13. See also Robert Campbell, 'Architect James Stirling: Controversial, Daring, Amazing', *The Boston Globe* (30 June 1992) ('Stuttgart is an anthology of private jokes, of bits and pieces quoted from the work of other architects and other styles').

[88] Manfred Sack, *Die Zeit*, 9 March 1984, at www.zeit.de/1984/11/das-zitatenmuseum/seite-4 (accessed 3 July 2020); Kenneth Frampton, 'James Stirling: A Premature Critique' (1993) 26 *AA Files* 3–6, 6 ('the historical quotation is a grotesque parody'); Emilio Ambasz, 'Popular Pantheon' (December 1984) *Architectural Review* 35 ('a work full of parodies').

entirety.[89] Reese-Lawrence suggests that it is Stirling's 'forays into self-quotation' that define his 'entire oeuvre'.[90]

Quotation, then, does not seem to be an intrinsically textual concept. Recognition of this, rather than some peculiar adherence to formalism, almost certainly informed the Study Group's decision to extend the quotation exception to all works.[91] In turn, importantly, we can infer that the meaning of quotation was not to be interpreted by reference only to its 'textual' conception. The notion of quotation in the Convention must be understood in a manner that enables it to be applied to all Berne works. Importantly this means that a rather liberal approach should be taken when determining which, and how many, of the 'typical' features associated with the proto-typical – text – notion of quotation must be present to render a particular practice 'quotation'.

Although courts have (as yet) to draw on these sorts of sources, they have rarely hesitated to extend quotation and related exceptions to music, painting, photography and film. The CJEU in *Pelham* treats quotation as including reuse not only of text but also of music (embodied in a sound recording);[92] and in *Painer*, as extending to the use of a photograph;[93] while in *Spiegel Online*, AG Szpunar also recognises that quotation might involve artworks or film.[94] National courts have taken a similar position: the English Court of Appeal applied the 'fair dealing for criticism or review' exception to significant portions of the film *A Clockwork Orange* in a broadcast documentary reviewing the decision to withdraw the film from circulation in the United Kingdom,[95] while the German *Bundesgerichtshof* permitted the insertion of two film excerpts, in total about five minutes, inside a documentary film, with a length of forty-three minutes.[96] According to Yves Gaubiac, much French case law recognises that

[89] Amanda Reese-Lawrence 'The Return of the Dead: Stirling's Self-Revision at Roma Interotta' (2011) 22 *Log* 22–31. (With respect to Stuttgart, *De Zeit* adds, 'Of course, Stirling also quotes Stirling, but that is not bad at all; every architect is in love with some of his former inventions.')

[90] See also Amanda Reese-Lawrence, *James Stirling*, 79 (referring to Stirling's 'strategy of self-quotation'). On self-quotation as 'quotation' for Article 10, see pp. 109–11, below.

[91] See Chapter 2, Section IV, Part A, pp. 19–22.

[92] Case C-476/17 *Pelham GmbH* v. *Hütter* EU:C:2019:624 (CJEU, Grand Chamber), [72]; EU: C:2018:1002 (Advocate General's Opinion), [62], [64].

[93] Case C-145/10 *Painer* v. *Standard Verlags GmbH* EU:C:2011:798, [2012] ECDR 6 (CJEU, 3rd Chamber), [122]–[123].

[94] Case C-516/17 *Spiegel Online GmbH* v. *Volker Beck*, EU:C:2019:16 (Advocate General's Opinion), [42].

[95] *Time Warner* v. *Channel 4* [1994] EMLR 1; Miguel Emery, 'Argentina' in L. Bently (ed.), *International Copyright Law and Practice* (LexisNexis 2019) ARG-49, refers to a case where it was accepted that the exception applied to use of an audiovisual work in a television programme, but the court rejected the defence on the facts because the quotation amounted to seventy-six minutes from the film and so did not meet the condition of fair practice: C.N. Crim. & Correc., Sala II, Aug. 25, 1978, E.D. 81–87.

[96] BGH (Federal Court of Justice), Dec. 4, 1986 – *Filmzitat* (Film Quote), 1987 GRUR 362, as explained by Michael Gruenberger, 'Germany' in L Bently (ed.), *International Copyright Law and Practice* (LexisNexis 2019), GER-189.

in principle the exception can apply to quotation from artistic works, video games and films,[97] while the Court of Appeal in Paris even admitted the possibility of the quotation of sports events.[98] As a result, French scholars have declared that the strict confinement of the exception to text is no longer defended.[99]

Moreover, legal application of quotation exceptions to non-textual material is not new: the historical records reveal a host of cases applying quotation exceptions in national law to non-textual works, including musical and artistic material. A Belgian case from 1895 considered the quotation of music;[100] a German case involved reuse of a motif from Richard Strauss by Heinrich Gottlieb Noren (in his *Kaleidoskop*);[101] the French court, having at the turn of the nineteenth century denied the possibility of quotation of drawings (in a case concerning the works of Henri Gabriel Ibels),[102] two decades later reversed its position and recognised the quotation of artistic works (in a case concerning use of photographs of works of Corot and Rodin in a history of France);[103] and of music in another musical work in the 1930s.[104] Some national legislation applied the term quotation specifically to re-use of musical works, highlighting that there is nothing intrinsically 'literary' to the legal concept of quotation.[105]

Finally, there is plenty of evidence that those involved in negotiating the revision of Berne well understood that the French term 'citation' and English 'quotation' were not intrinsically limited to uses of, or indeed in, text. Speaking at the Thirty-Fifth Congress of the ALAI in Warsaw in September 1926, its President, Georges Maillard, explained that photographic reductions of paintings could constitute

---

[97] Y Gaubiac, 'Freedom to Quote from an Intellectual Work' (1997) 171 *RIDA* 2, 46, citing *Sté MH Films et autres v. Sté Dima Films et autres*, TGI, 14 Sept 1994, (1995) (Apr.) 164 *RIDA* 407 (film); *Fabris v. Loudmer* Cass. 1st Civ. 22 January 1991 (visual art); *Sotheby's v. Fabris* Cass. 1st Civ 22 January 1991 (visual art); *Tardy v. Libraire Larousse* Cass. 1st Civ. 13 April 1988 (visual art); 22 Sept 1988, CA Paris, D. 1988 IR 258, JCP 1990, II 265 (videogame). See Nicolas Bouche, *Intellectual Property Law in France* (2nd ed., Kluwer 2014), 85, [235] ('case-law applies it even to pictorial, graphical and sculptural works').

[98] *TFI v. Antenne 2*, 15 June 1989, as explained by Y Gaubiac, 'Freedom to Quote from an Intellectual Work' (1997) 171 *RIDA* 2, 72, fn. 73.

[99] Marie Cornu and Nathalie Mallet-Poujol, 'Le droit de Citation Audiovisuelle: Légitimer la Culture par L'image' [1998] *Legicom* 119–45 ('Le strict cantonnement de l'exception au domaine littéraire n'est plus guère défendu'). Belgian law explicitly abandoned the limitation of the quotation exception to short quotation and, as a result, 'quotation in Belgium is no longer interpreted as limited to literary works and it is now assumed that the exception is extended to works of all kinds': J Cabay and M Lambrecht, 'Remix Prohibited: How Rigid EU Copyright Laws Inhibit Creativity' (2015) 10(5) *Journal of Intellectual Property Law & Practice* 359, 370.

[100] P Wauwermans, 'Lettre de Belgique' (June 1895) *Le Droit D'Auteur* 75–8. See further Edouard Fueter, 'Musikalische Zitate', *Schweizerisch Musikzeitung*, 27 January 1923.

[101] *Lauterbach & Kuhn v. Leuckart* reported in (March 1910) *Le Droit D'Auteur* 37.

[102] *Ibels v. Grand Carteret*, Tribunal de la Seine, in (February 1901) *Le Droit D'Auteur* 18.

[103] *Chamouillet et autres v. Librairie Hachette*, (1924) *Le Droit D'Auteur* 48 (Tribunal Correctionel de La Seine); Albert Vaunois, 'Letter of France' (March 1925) *Le Droit D'Auteur* 29–32.

[104] *Société Raoul Breton v. Choudens*, Gazette de Palais, 26 October 1934, discussed in (July 1935) *Le Droit D'Auteur* 81 (also referring to an article by Fançois Hepp that 'admettre la licéité de la citation musicale textuelle d'asprit parodique').

[105] For example, the Austrian Copyright Law of 1920, Article 43.

'quotations': 'un reproduction de ce genre est une citation artistique'.[106] Two years before then, a study by the Berne Bureau had proposed an article for the Convention in which Members recognised the right to quote in terms of 'analyses et courtes citations textuelles' – the adjective 'textuelle' itself implicitly recognising the linguistic possibility, even in French, of non-textual quotation (whatever a few late-twentieth-century Francophone commentators might assert).[107] Likewise, as we explained in Chapter 2, Section II, in a proposal for the Rome Revision Conference in 1928, it was explicitly suggested that the Convention exempt 'textual' quotations. That qualification again recognises the possibility of non-textual quotation, and its absence from later texts implies that precisely such a broader conception of quotation was intended. Moreover, in the proceedings in 1948, the Director-General of the Bureau, Bénigne Mentha, observed (contrasting Article 10 with that of Article 9) that the reproduction of artistic works 'could be considered as a quotation'.[108]

It is reasonable to assume that the Study Group for the Stockholm revision was fully cognisant of this background. The proposal appeared to view the 'universal application' of the quotation exception as implicit but in need of *expressis verbis*. However, it also acknowledged this was an enlargement and thus recommended the condition that the work quoted had been lawfully made available to the public.[109] In response to the Study Group's second Report (1964), the Authors' Consultative Committee (CCA), set up by BIRPI, said it was 'disquieted by the considerable extension' to be effected by the proposed Article 10(1), which it noted covered all categories of works.[110] However, the Swiss proposal to the Committee of Government Experts to limit the quotation right, given that in its proposed form it applied to all works,[111] was rejected. As such, there is nothing in the history of Article 10(1) Berne to suggest that 'quotation' was conceived as being only possible with, or in, text. The absence of any express limit, in fact, confirms precisely the opposite.

B *Is a Quotation Inherently Short?*

In the paradigm textual example, a quotation is a short passage selected from a longer text, and the passage quoted is incorporated by the quoter in a longer text. Although, unsurprisingly, several dictionary definitions define quotation in terms of 'shortness',[112] we suggest that there is no such quantitative limit *intrinsic* to the concept of quotation, either as a matter of common understanding of the concept

---

[106] (November 1926) *Le Droit D'Auteur* 128.
[107] 'Les Emprunts Licite', (1924) *Le Droit D'Auteur* 87, 97.
[108] *Documents* (1951), 249
[109] BIRPI: DA/20/2, p. 46. See Chapter 2, Section IV, pp. 19–20, above.
[110] BIRPI: DA/22/7, p. 9. See pp. 22–23, above.
[111] BIRPI: DA/22/17. See p. 25, above.
[112] See eg J A Simpson and E S C Weiner (eds.), *The Oxford English Dictionary* (Clarendon 1989), vol. XIII, 52, 3c: 'A *short* passage or tune taken from one piece of music to another or quoted elsewhere' (emphasis added).

of 'quotation', or as a matter of law (though we recognise that the amount of material used is a very significant factor in assessing whether a use is proportionate and compatible with 'fair practice').

The ordinary use of the term 'quotation' would certainly seem to encompass instances of sizeable reproductions. Indeed, it is common to talk of 'lengthy quotations', or 'quoting extensively', and it is frequently recognised that this may be necessary and desirable to represent or 'do justice' to the author and their argument. For example, in the preface of a dictionary of philosophical quotations,[113] Jane O'Grady describes the dilemmas facing a compiler of such a work: 'To reproduce too many long closely argued passages runs the risk of boring the reader; to produce only the conclusions to such arguments would be baffling and frustrating; and it is often misleading, distorting or impossible to convey an argument in small chunks or in passages full of ellipses.' What is interesting here is, once again, less what O'Grady states than what she takes for granted. She states the problem of taking closely argued passages as that of 'boring the reader'; she does not suggest that such passages would not qualify as 'quotations'. To the contrary, she takes for granted that a dictionary of 'quotations' *could* include such material.

Outside of the literary context, 'shortness' seems particularly irrelevant.[114] In an important study entitled *Quotation and Cultural Meaning in Twentieth Century Music*, the musicologist David Metzer discusses Douglas Gordon's *24 Hour Psycho* (1993), which is an art piece comprising a slowed down (and mute) rendering of Hitchcock's famous film to two frames per minute.[115] Metzer recognises that the change creates a new experience[116] and that each viewer will, in fact, only watch for a segment of the full twenty-four-hour rendering. Although Metzer is uncomfortable with describing this as quotation, he also articulates the position that Gordon's work is at the 'outer limit' of quotation and that, in the late twentieth century, the concept of quotation can include transformative uses of 'entire or nearly entire pieces'.[117] Thus, Metzer implies that the term 'quotation' is flexible as to extent: quotations can be short or long.

In the context of the visual arts of painting, drawing, sculpture, engraving or architecture, the idea that 'quotation' is necessarily 'short' is problematic, since these cultural forms are not conceived in terms of 'length'. Some commentators and courts have inferred from this that the quotation exception cannot apply to such works.[118]

---

[113] J O'Grady, 'Introduction' in A J Ayer and J O'Grady (eds.), *A Dictionary of Philosophical Quotations* (Blackwell 1992), vii.

[114] Indeed, as already noted, French commentators have often treated the quotation right in France as limited to text precisely because the domestic legislation uses the term 'short' ('courtes').

[115] D Metzer, *Quotation and Cultural Meaning in Twentieth Century Music* (Cambridge University Press 2003). Metzer is Professor of Musicology at the University of British Columbia.

[116] Metzer, *Quotation and Cultural Meaning*, 214.

[117] Metzer, *Quotation and Cultural Meaning*, 217.

[118] Pierre Recht, 'Pseudo-Quotation in the Field of the Plastic and figurative Arts' (1957) 17 *RIDA* 84, 104 ('We think, as a matter of fact, that the word "quotation" can only apply to quotations of a written phrase or a musical phrase, in a literary work, but never to a total or fragmentary reproduction of

However, as we will see, this is to analyse the matter in the wrong order. Indeed, the legal sources indicate that 'shortness' was explicitly rejected as a condition for the application of the quotation exception in the Berne Convention, in part because it was recognised that such a qualification could not sensibly be applied to artistic works. To reimport a condition of shortness, and then to infer that the exception cannot apply to artistic works, is to reverse the logic that informed the removal of the condition.

It will be recalled that in its 1948 Brussels version, the Berne Convention permitted the use of 'small quotations' (from journals and newspapers), but when the BIRPI/ Swedish Study Group drafted a text for the Stockholm revision, the term 'short' was specifically abandoned. The Study Group reported that while a quotation normally should be short 'this principle does not have absolute universal validity'.[119] When the French delegation sought to reintroduce such a requirement,[120] it was discussed in the Main Committee, with the British and German delegates speaking against such a limitation. The British delegate William Wallace pointed out that a quotation that was not short could nevertheless be regarded as in accordance with fair practice.[121] Dietrich Reimer, the German delegate, stated that 'cases occurred in which quotations were permissible even though they were not short', referring to provisions in the then recently adopted German Act, which, he explained, placed no quantitative restriction on what may be a legitimate quotation.[122] The Swedish delegate and member of the Study Group, Torwald Hesser, a Justice of the Supreme Court, offered his support for the British view that 'long quotations' might be justified and that the real limitation was to be found in the 'fair practice' condition.[123] The Monaco delegate, Georges Straschnov, who was also legal director of the European Broadcasting Union, drew attention to the fact that the adjective short would raise particular problems in relation to the quotation of artistic works, where moral rights would be implicated if only part was used. The effect, he said, of its introduction would be to prevent the exception applying to the showing of a picture in a television programme. The condition was thus not desirable.[124] While the French delegate indicated that he approved of this effect, the Conference rejected the proposal. As a result, there is evidently no condition of shortness, and the quotation right must be applicable to use of artistic works. The legal commentaries also support this view.[125]

---

a plastic work'; also citing other authors such as Francois Hepp, 'The International Protection of the Plastic Arts' (1957) *Le Droit D'Auteur* 144).

[119] Preparatory Documents S/1, p 46 in *Records*, vol. I, 116. See further Chapter 2, Section IV, pp. 19–20.

[120] 'Texts of Documents S/13 to S/302', in *Records*, vol. I, 615. The French delegate sought explicit reference to such a condition precisely because in its view the notion of 'quotation' did not of itself 'involve the idea of brevity': Robert Touzery, Main Committee, [762], in *Records*, vol. II, 860.

[121] Main Committee, [764] in *Records*, vol. II, 860. See pp. 26–28, above.

[122] Main Committee, [765] in *Records*, vol. II, 860.

[123] Main Committee, [767] in *Records*, vol. II, 861.

[124] George Straschnov, in Minutes, [769], *Records*, vol. II, 861.

[125] Claude Masouyé, *Guide to the Berne Convention* (WIPO 1978), 59, and Paul Goldstein, *International Copyright: Principles, Law, Practice* (Oxford University Press 2001), 304.

In addition, the idea that a 'quotation' must in itself be short seems incompatible with another condition placed on the quotation exception in Article 10 of the Berne Convention: the requirement of 'proportionality' to purpose. We discuss this in more detail in Chapter 4,[126] but for the moment, it is sufficient to note that Article 10(1) places a limit on the extent of permissible quotation – namely that 'their extent does not exceed that justified by the purpose'. Such a condition would be strange if 'quotation' itself implied a *small* taking – not least because the extent required by the purpose might be quantitatively substantial. Imagine, for example, that one wanted to present evidence in a manner that clearly included the context of particular statements so that there could be no misunderstanding (or accusation of selective quotation or quotation out of context), or where a person wishes to compare two texts to identify and discuss differences, or where the text being referred to is not otherwise easily accessible.[127] In these cases, long extracts might be justified to achieve the purpose.

C Is It Possible to Quote an Entire Work?

In the typical situation, a 'quotation' involves use of 'a part' of the quoted work.[128] Indeed, especially when focusing on textual reuse, dictionaries very frequently define 'quotation' as 'a passage'. One legal commentator seeks to define the legal concept as 'an excerpt from a larger work'.[129] If a person reproduced the entirety of a novel, we simply would struggle to call that a quotation. But must a quotation always be a small proportion of the work from which the quotation derives? Could it even involve reuse of the whole?

Some legal systems appear to have rejected the possibility that there can be a quotation if the whole of a work is reproduced. For example, in France, the exception is limited to analyses and 'short quotations',[130] and while it is not clear from that whether 'short' refers to an intrinsic characteristic, or is to be viewed from the perspective of the source from which the quotation is taken, one court has stated that 'the complete reproduction of a work of art, whatever its format, cannot in any

---

[126] Chapter 4, Section IV, Part B, pp. 80–82.

[127] Stephen O Murray and Will Roscoe, *Islamic Homosexualities: Culture, History, and Literature* (New York University Press 1997), 10 ('lengthy quotations are meant to minimise distortion of what earlier writers wrote. . . . There has been so much misrepresentation . . . that lengthy quotations . . . are invaluable').

[128] Kevin Holm-Hudson, 'Quotation and Context: Sampling and John Oswald's Plunderphonics' (1997) 7 *Leonardo Music Journal* 17–25, 17. 'The act of quotation in music (here defined as reproducing a melodic, stylistic or timbral *excerpt of* a pre-existing musical work in the new context of another musical work)' (emphasis added). Metzer, *Quotation and Cultural Meaning*, 4: 'The practice, as defined here, refers to the placement of *parts of* a preexistent piece in a new composition or performance' (emphasis added).

[129] Jørgen Blomqvist, *Primer on International Copyright and Related Rights* (Edward Elgar 2014), 161.

[130] Article L122–5(3)(a) of the IP Code exempts 'analyses and brief quotations justified on the grounds of the critical, polemic, educational, scientific, or informative character of the work in which they are incorporated'. For a list of countries that follow the French, see Bochumberg, *Le Droit de Citation*, 65, [114].

case be deemed to be brief quotation'.[131] Likewise, Spanish law refers to 'fragments of the works of others'.[132] Moreover, Ricketson and Ginsburg refer to quotation in the context of Article 10 of Berne as 'the taking of some part of a greater whole'.[133] The notion of taking 'part' of the work rather than the whole is implicit also in the Advocate General's Opinion in C-476/17 *Pelham v. Hütter*.[134]

We think this is incorrect both as a matter of 'ordinary meaning' and as a necessary consequence of the state of the law. After all, the phrase 'quote in full' is regularly used to describe an act of quotation that reproduces the totality of a work. A good example of reproduction of the whole of a work in another work is provided by the field of painting, where artists sometimes create works that include in the subject matter preexisting works. Take, for example, Cézanne's *Compotier, verre et pommes* (trans. *Fruit Bowl, Glass and Apples*),[135] which he painted in 1878–9, and which for the next decade or two was owned by Paul Gauguin.[136] Gauguin featured it as a backdrop to his 1890 painting *Portrait de femme à la nature morte de Cézanne*.[137]

---

[131] *Fabris v. Guy Loudmer*, Cass., Ass. plen., 5 Nov. 1993, (1994) 159 *RIDA* 320 (in relation to catalogues of works of Maurice Utrillo); *Antenne 2 v. Spadem*, Cass 1 ère Ch Civ, 4 July 1995, (1996) 167 *RIDA* 262 (reproduction of murals by Edouard Vuillard, which adorn walls of theatre bar, in a broadcast about new dramatic productions at the theatre could not be justified as 'courtes citations' because the murals were reproduced in full if only for a short time); *Mr X, Promocom, FNAC v. Moulinsart*, Cass. civ. I, 26 May 2011, (2011) 229 *RIDA* 468 (not allowing reproductions of full images of the character 'Tintin' from a comic book in an educational book). Martin Senftleben, 'Internet Search Results – A Permissible Quotation?' (2013) 235 *RIDA* 3, 71–3 (discussing how this operated to exclude search results in the form of thumbnails from the French conception of 'quotation'). See also Maurice Casteels, 'Works of Art and the Right of Quotation' (January 1954) 11 *RIDA* 81–97 (representative of AAPB, a society representing professional artists, discussing the quotation exception in the Belgian law of 1886, which was only applicable to literary works, but arguing that were it regarded as applicable to works of art, it could not justify publishing the whole of such a work).

[132] Consolidated Text of the Law on Intellectual Property, regularizing, clarifying and harmonizing the Applicable Statutory Provisions (approved by Royal Legislative Decree No. 1/1996 of April 12, 1996), Art. 32(1); the reproduction of the whole of a short story in a collection is not a 'fragment': Audiencia Provincial Madrid (Section 28) July 25, 2019, Aranzadi Civil 2019, no. 1413. See also Greek Copyright Law No 2121/1993, Article 19, 'Quotation of short extracts of a lawfully published work . . . shall be permissible' (WIPO translation).

[133] S Ricketson and J Ginsburg, *The Berne Convention and Beyond* (Oxford University Press 2006), 788, [13.40]; Claude Masouyé, *Guide to the Berne Convention* (WIPO 1978) 59 (stating that the dictionary meaning involves an 'extract'). But cf. J C Ginsburg, 'Copyright without Walls? Speculations on Literary Property in the Library of the Future' (1993) 42 *Representations* 53, 53: 'Where collecting quotations from printed sources today requires transcription or photocopying, in the library of the future it may be possible to download and print out excerpts, or even the entire work, through the user's personal computer.'

[134] EU:C:2018:1002, [65], in stating that 'the *extract* quoted must be incorporated in the quoting work' (emphasis added).

[135] An image of the painting can be viewed on the Museum of Modern Art's website: www.moma.org /collection/works/78670 (accessed 3 July 2020).

[136] Anne Distel, Michel Hoog and Charles S. Moffett, *Impressionism: A Centenary Exhibition* (New York: Metropolitan Museum of Art 1974), 56 (available at www.metmuseum.org/art/metpubli cations/impressionism_a_centenary_exhibition#) (accessed 2 February 2020).

[137] The image can be seen on the website of its holder, the Art Institute of Chicago: www.artic.edu /artworks/16648/woman-in-front-of-a-still-life-by-cezanne. For Gauguin's ownership of the Cézanne, see Merete Bodelsen, 'Gauguin's Cézannes' (1962) 104 *Burlington Magazine* 204, 208 (identifying

Cézanne's painting is also featured in Maurice Denis's *Homage to Cézanne* (1900),[138] a work that depicts the various members of the 'Nabis' group of painters (Odilon Redon, Édouard Vuillard, André Mellerio, Ambroise Vollard, Maurice Denis, Paul Sérusier, Paul Ranson, Ker-Xavier Roussel, Pierre Bonnard and Madame Maurice Denis) 'gazing, like spellbound disciples, at one of the Master's paintings'.[139]

Is the depiction of Cézanne's painting a 'quotation'? Certainly, art historians seem happy to use the word to describe the practice. In a lengthy comment on the painting, Katherine Kuenzli refers to the three pictures in the background, noting that 'Hanging along the back wall are examples of paintings by Gauguin, Renoir and Vuillard. Denis paints recognizable types of their works *rather than quoting specific canvases.'*[140] In contrast, Denis is clearly regarded as quoting Cézanne's painting.

Although one might observe that Denis does not reproduce the whole Cézanne, as Serusier's hand blocks the view of a part of the picture, the idea that this might be regarded as 'quotation' but a version that had been slightly differently composed would not do so seems wholly unattractive: the canvas depicted would function in precisely the same way in both instances. Similarly, one could suggest that Denis does not quote the 'whole' because the representation within the picture is smaller and necessarily different (painted by Denis) than in the Cézanne version. That might imply that reductions and perhaps lower-resolution versions of images could be 'quotations', as well as photographs (or films) of paintings could be quotation,[141] but full versions in the same form (e.g. photographs of photographs) would not be.

Compotier, verre et pommes as one of Cézanne's paintings that Gauguin owned in the late 1880s, and noting that Gauguin 'includes [it] in the background of his portrait'); Donatien Grau, 'Theoretical Brutality: Cézanne and Gauguin', *Brooklyn Rail* (February 2014), at https://brooklynrail.org/2014/02/criticspage/theoretical-brutality-czanne-and-gaugui. The Cézanne is also said to have inspired Gauguin's 'Bowl of Fruit and Tankard before a Window' (1890), which can be seen at www.nationalgallery.org.uk/paintings/paul-gauguin-bowl-of-fruit-and-tankard-before-a-window.

138   The work is owned by the Musée d'Orsay, Paris, and can be viewed on the Museum's website: www.musee-orsay.fr/en/collections/works-in-focus/painting.html?no_cache=1&zoom=1&tx_dam zoom_pi1%5BshowUid%5D=2312 (accessed 3 July 2020).

139   Richard Cork, 'A Master of Mind and Matter', *The Times*, 10 October 1995, 34. Apparently, Cézanne wrote to Denis expressing his gratitude: Carolyn Lanchner, *Paul Cézanne* (Museum of Modern Art, 2011), 8. Denis would in 1914 again reprise Cézanne's *Compotier, verre et pommes* as a lithograph for a deluxe folio album published by the Bernheim brothers to raise money for Maillol's sculptural monument to Cézanne.

140   Katherine Marie Kuenzli, 'Aesthetics and Cultural Politics in the Age of Dreyfus: Maurice Denis's *Homage To Cézanne*' (2007) 30 *Art History* 683 (emphasis added).

141   Iampolski, *The Memory of Tiresias*, 38 (describing the shots of Picasso's painting in Jean-Luc Godard's *Breathless* as 'quotations from Picasso' and explain that, reaffirming the dialogue, 'the quotes here function much like a teacher's comments in red ink'). For a useful account of the making of films about painters and painting, especially those of Alain Resnais, see Steven Jacobs, *Framing Pictures: Film and the Visual Arts* (Edinburgh University Press 2011), ch. 1 (suggesting, at 30, that such filmmakers had a duty to show the whole picture). For discussion of a film about the artist Francis Bacon, *Love Is the Devil: Study for a Portrait of Francis Bacon* (1998; director John Maybury), which featured no images of his paintings because Bacon's estate refused permission, see Bently, 'Copyright and Quotation in Film and TV'.

Again, attempting to exclude from quotation replication of 'the whole' seems to require some arbitrary and thus unattractive distinctions.

Our view that 'quotation' might include reproducing the whole of the work also seems correct as a matter of specifically legal interpretation. However odd it might be as a matter of 'ordinary use', the evolution in the scope of protection by copyright means that the legal meaning of 'quotation' must include reproduction of the whole. There are many circumstances in which the work that is protected is much less extensive than a novel. In such cases, a requirement that a quotation be a proportionately small fragment from the source work has the potential to render the quotation exception meaningless. Consider, for example, the example of a title, a slogan, epigram or a very short poem (a haiku). Jurisprudence in many countries, including now the United Kingdom, suggests that there are circumstances in which such small works might be protected as original literary works.[142] Partial reproduction of such small works would in many, if not all, cases be completely meaningless. It seems therefore that 'quotation' must extend to reproduction of the whole.

Our view gains some support from the Berne legislative history (though there is no indication that the various participants had in mind the possible protection of trivial works). The Swedish/BIRPI Study Group, focusing on press reuse of material relating to politics, economics, religion and culture, noted that 'sufficient direction' might not be provided unless it was permissible to reproduce 'in some cases, fairly considerable portions of articles constituting the contributions of others to public discussions'.[143] The Study Group rejected any *a priori* standard, preferring to emphasise the principle of proportionality. As we argued in Section I, Part B (discussing whether a quotation must be 'short'), there may be cases where a person's aim can only be achieved by reproducing the whole – for example, when discussing the compositional structure of a painting (as opposed to some detail therein). This suggests that the notion of 'quotation' should not be limited to cases of partial reproduction.

Many national laws, implementing the Convention, recognise that use of the whole work is permissible in certain cases. In particular, acknowledging that it might be inconsistent with an author's moral right of integrity (recognised under Article 6*bis*) to reproduce only a part, certain laws specify that quotation of the whole might be necessary. For example, the copyright legislation of Bosnia and Herzogovina,[144]

---

[142] Case C-5/08 *Infopaq Int v. Danske Dagblades Forening* [2009] ECR-I 6569 (4th Ch), [45]–[48] (indicating that work is protected if it is 'author's own intellectual creation' and leaving it to national court to determine whether 11-word extract reached this standard); Parkin, 'Copyright Quotation Exception' (2019), 62 (agreeing that, in light of *Infopaq*, quotation could be of material that could be regarded in itself as an original work).

[143] General Report of the Swedish/BIRPI Study Group, established June 1, 1963, BIRPI: DA/20/2, p. 45; S/1, p. 46 in *Records*, vol. I, 116. See, herein, pp. 19–20, above.

[144] Bosnia and Herzogovina, Law of July 13, 2010, Article 47. ('It shall be permitted to literally quote passages and quotations from a disclosed work or individual disclosed works of photography, fine art, architecture, applied art and industrial and graphic design.')

Brazil[145] and Ecuador[146] each allows for quotation of 'individual works' from the visual arts. Moreover, explicitly recognising that 'small works' might be original, the statutory rules operating in the Czech Republic specifically permits uses of 'excerpts from a work, or small works in their entirety'.[147]

Case law and commentary also accept the possibility that it might be a justifiable quotation to reproduce the whole of a work.[148] The CJEU in *Pelham* v. *Hütter* defined 'quotation' as 'the use, by a user . . . of a work or, more generally, of an extract from a work' – the qualification 'or more generally' acknowledging explicitly the possibility, if appropriate, of quotation of a whole work.[149] Von Lewinski argues that while the Berne language 'from a work' ('les citations tirées d'une œuvre') suggests that only parts may be quoted, 'it should also cover quotations of entire works, where this is the only way to reach the purpose of quotation, as in the case of a photograph, drawing, or other art-work'.[150] Walter and von Lewinski, who generally adopt a broad reading of copyright's prohibitions, when discussing Article 5(3)(d) of the Information Society Directive, state that 'where excerpting is not possible' then quotation might cover reuse of 'the entire work (such as a photograph or short poem)'.[151] Even the French courts have acknowledged, through some contorted reasoning, that reproduction of the whole of a work might be warranted in certain situations.[152]

---

[145] Brazil, Law No. 9.610 of February 19, 1998 on Copyright and Neighboring Rights, Article 46(VIII) ('the reproduction in any work of short extracts from existing works, regardless of their nature, or of the whole work in the case of a work of three-dimensional art').

[146] Ecuador, Intellectual Property Law (Consolidation No. 2006-13), Article 83a ('the inclusion in a given work of fragments of other works by other people in written, aural or audiovisual form, and also that of individual three dimensional, photographic, figurative or analogous works, provided that the works concerned have already been disclosed and that the inclusion thereof is by way of quotation').

[147] Czech Republic, Consolidated Version of Act No. 121/2000 Coll., on Copyright and Rights Related to Copyright and on Amendment to Certain Acts (the Copyright Act, as amended by Act No. 81/2005 Coll., Act No. 61/2006 Coll. and Act No. 216/2006 Coll.), Article 31(1)(b).

[148] *Fraser-Woodward* v. *BBC* [2005] FSR 762 (inclusion of copyright photographs in broadcast was fair, taking into account the brief time for which the images were shown); *Hubbard* v. *Vosper* [1972] 2 QB 84, 94–5, 98 (Megaw LJ) (example of a parishioner quoting an epitaph on a tombstone in the churchyard); *Sillitoe* v. *McGraw Hill* [1983] FSR 545; *Associated Newspapers Group* v. *News Group Newspapers* [1986] RPC 515, 520; cf. *Zamacois* v. *Douville* [1943] 2 DLR 257, where the Canadian Exchequer Court suggested that the copying of an entire work cannot qualify as fair dealing. See also the Opinion of the Advocate General Trstenjak in Case C-145/10 *Painer* v. *Standard Verlags GmbH*, EU:C:2011:239, [212] and Opinion of Advocate General Szpunar in Case C-516/17 *Spiegel Online GmbH* v. *Volker Beck*, EU:C:2019:16, [45], which envisage circumstances in which quotation of the full work might be permitted.

[149] Case C-476/17 *Pelham GmbH v. Huetter* EU:C:2019:624 (CJEU, Grand Chamber), [71].

[150] Silke von Lewinski, *International Copyright Law and Policy* (Oxford University Press 2008), 156–7, [5.164].

[151] M M Walter and Silke von Lewinski, *European Copyright Law: A Commentary* (Oxford University Press 2010), 1050, [11.5.58].

[152] Pascal Kamina, 'France', in L. Bently (ed.), *International Copyright Law and Practice* (2019), FRA-135, refers to a decision of Paris, 14th ch, 12 October 2007, P.I. 2008, no. 27, 219, obs. A. Lucas (applying the quotation exception to the reproduction of one photograph to illustrate an article in a magazine, though referring to Article 5(3)(c) of Directive 2001/29/EC).

D *Must the Quotation Be Taken from Another Author?*

Returning to the typical situation, the text that is reproduced will normally be the text of another author, and this is reflected expressly in the terms of some national laws. For example, Spanish law states that it shall be lawful 'to include in one's own work fragments of the works *of others*'.[153] However, we suggest that normal use of the term 'quotation' includes 'self-quotation'. Indeed, the literature that deals with what is referred to as academic 'self-plagiarism' seems to assume that 'self-quotation' is legitimate, as long as it complies with certain rituals associated with quotation of others. As we will suggest, there certainly seems no good normative reason to limit the concept of 'quotation' in Article 10(1) Berne to quotation of works other than those of the quoting author.

The reuse by creators of their own material has been very common historically. Writing in 1960, Winton Dean observed that 'many, perhaps most, composers of the past have borrowed from their own earlier work'.[154] The same seems true of artists, who have frequently returned to subjects and utilised images and motifs repeatedly.[155] Such re-use is often called 'self-quotation'. Certainly, historians of music have used the term in this way when describing the practice of 'self-borrowing' that was prevalent among many of those who have received the imprimatur of the critics and entered into the musical canon and which 'can be regarded as normal compositional procedure'.[156] While music scholars frequently refer to these practices as 'self-borrowing', they regularly also talk about 'quotation'. For example, discussing French baroque composer Rameau, one commentator notes that 'some listeners might hear as *self-quotation* which I would regard as mere chance resemblance'.[157] Similarly, when cataloguing self-borrowing by the twentieth-century composer Charles Ives (1874–1954), Clayton Henderson observes, 'Ives often borrowed from himself. While this can be termed *self-quotation*, the manner in which he used his own material differs significantly from the way he quoted from the music of others."[158] Likewise, David Metzer treats self-borrowing as quotation, referring to Schoenberg's self-borrowing from his own *Am Wegrand* in the closing scene of *Erwartung* as 'quotation'.[159] And Pwyll Ap Siôn describes as 'self-quotations' Michael Nyman's reuse of his own material, such as the

---

[153] Consolidated Text of the law on Intellectual Property, regularizing, clarifying and harmonizing the Applicable Statutory Provisions (approved by Royal Legislative Decree No. 1/1996 of April 12, 1996), Article 32(1) (emphasis added).

[154] Winton Dean, 'Bizet's Self-Borrowings' (1960) 41(3) *Music and Letters* 238–44, 238.

[155] Eliza E Rathbone, William H Robinson, Elizabeth Steele and Marcia Steele, *Van Gogh Repetitions* (Yale University Press 2013). Another example would be Matisse's use of his 'bilboquets' in multiple compositions. On architectural self-quotation, see p. 99, above.

[156] Benoît Gibson, *The Instrumental Music of Iannis Xenakis: Theory, Practice, Self-Borrowing* (Pendragon Press 2011), xix.

[157] G Sadler, 'A Re-examination of Rameau's Self-Borrowings' in J H Heyer (ed.), *Jean-Baptiste Lully and the French Baroque: Essays in Honor of James R. Anthony* (Cambridge University Press 1989), 259, 260.

[158] Clayton W. Henderson, *The Charles Ives Tunebook* (2nd ed., Indiana University Press 2008), 7–8.

[159] Metzer, *Quotation and Cultural Meaning*, 7. See also ch. 3, esp. 79–83.

use in *Concerto for Harpsichord* of elements from *Tango for Tim* (1994) that themselves appeared in the soundtrack for A *La Folie*.[160]

If the 'normal use' of 'quotation' includes 'self-quotation', as we suggest, is there any reason why international copyright law should have a narrower understanding? In normative terms, it seems unnecessary to exclude authorial 'self-copying' from the notion of quotation: it makes little sense to allow any third party to use material but not allow the author to do so. In fact, in cases where an author has assigned copyright (for example, to a publisher), the availability of a 'quotation' exception may offer important freedom to the author to refer to and reuse their own work. It is perhaps notable that no provision is made in Article 5 of the Information Society Directive for an exception covering authorial self-copying, so that any such exceptions in national law (such as that contained in section 64 of the CDPA) would fall to be justified – almost certainly – by reference to Article 5(3)(d) of that Directive (i.e. as 'quotations'). Indeed, this exception is justified under Article 10(1) Berne, the limitation to not copying 'the main design' being best seen as legislative indications of a key factor in a 'fair practice' analysis.[161]

III CHARACTERISTICS OF QUOTATION IN RELATION TO THE DESTINATION MATERIAL

A *Must the Quotation Be Used in Another 'Work'?*

In order for an excerpt from a work to be recognised as a 'quotation', does the destination material in which the quote is incorporated have to be a 'work'? Certainly not in the narrow sense of another printed work – words, for example, can be quoted in a visual work, sound recording, film or broadcast, and, of course, in unrecorded expression, such as recitation or performance (which might not implicate the reproduction right conferred by copyright, so much as the public performance right or the right of communication to the public).[162]

This may appear uncontroversial, but curiously some national laws seem to have been formulated in a way that would preclude the operation of the 'quotation', exception in the absence of something that meets the legal definition of a 'work'. For example, Article L. 122–5(3)(a) of the French IP Code exempts 'analyses and brief quotations justified on the grounds of the critical, polemic, educational, scientific,

---

[160]   P Ap Siôn, *The Music of Michael Nyman: Texts, Contexts and Intertexts* (Ashgate 2007), 70. The author is a composer and musicologist, Professor of Music at Bangor University.

[161]   The formal devices of the use of quotation marks and attribution may operate to indicate that a self-quotation is something one has said before, and thus provide valuable information to some readers. Insofar as the attribution requirement is understood as a more flexible variant of the authors' moral right (see pp. 77–78, above), it is probably unobjectionable for such a condition to be waived in a case of self-copying. More problematic, however, is that exceptions such as those in Copyright Designs and Patents Act 1988 ('CDPA'), section 64, also extend to works that have not been 'made available'.

[162]   Ricketson and Ginsburg (2006), [13.42], 788.

or informative character of *the work in which they are incorporated*' (emphasis added). German law likewise purports to limit the quotation exception in Article 51 of the Copyright Act 1965 to cases of reproduction in 'an independent scientific work', 'an independent work of language' or 'an independent musical work'.[163]

This may be viewed as consistent with the claim that the right to quote is itself 'an author's right', which has been offered as an explanation for why Article 10(1) is included in a convention devoted to the protection of authors' rights,[164] and how the formal expansion of the right in the Stockholm Revision can be regarded as consistent with the fundamental premise of Berne that it gradually extends the rights of authors.[165] It is also consistent with the theoretical claim, developed from Kantian premises, that the right to quote lies at the point where the claims of an earlier author runs up against those of a later author; 'authors have exclusive rights in respect of their works only where such rights are consistent with everyone else's equal authorship'.[166] This conceptualisation is perhaps expressed most vividly in the legislation of Guinea-Bissau,[167] which frames the right to quote as an author's right, but limited to the authors of 'a text': 'Authors of any text shall have the right . . . '.

Nevertheless, the idea that there must be a 'work' into which the quoted material is incorporated seems strange as a matter of both ordinary language and legal policy. With respect to ordinary language, consider the example of a selected fragment of text placed on a building. Texts that are regarded as having particularly poignancy or relevance are frequently placed on or near buildings (or other spaces open to the public), such as courts, law schools,[168] libraries and even sports stadia.[169] These inscriptions typically signal, exhort or promote the values that those learning, working or playing inside the building should possess. Consider, for example, the lines taken from John Milton's *Areopagitica* that '[a] good book is the precious life-blood of a master spirit, embalmed and treasured up on purpose to a life beyond life'. This much-beloved statement appears on a number of libraries in the United States including the New York Public Library, Indiana University Library (now Franklin

---

[163] Lionel Bochumberg, *Le Droit de Citation*, 50 (describing incorporation requirement as 'a notion universally recognised').

[164] Berne, Article 1 ('The countries to which this Convention applies constitute a Union for the protection of *the rights of authors* in their literary and artistic works'); Preamble ('The countries of the Union, being equally animated by the desire to protect, in as effective and uniform a manner as possible, *the rights of authors* in their literary and artistic works') (emphasis added).

[165] See Chapter 3, Section I, Part A.

[166] Abraham Drassinower, *What's Wrong with Copying* (Harvard University Press 2015), 56. Framing this idea, Drassinower refers, at 55, to the public domain as 'an irreducible condition of the audience's entitlement to respond to and participate in the ongoing conversation of which the author is but a part'. For further discussion, see Section IV, Part B, pp. 131–136, below.

[167] Guinea-Bissau, Copyright Code (approved by Decree-Law No. 46.980 of March 28, 1972), Article 185.

[168] For an example of an exhibition of quotations about justice in Harvard Law School, see 'Words of Justice', at http://library.law.harvard.edu/justicequotes/ (accessed 2 February 2020).

[169] Lines from Rudyard Kipling's poem *If* appear above the entrance to the Centre Court at Wimbledon.

Hall), Chicago Cultural Center, and Cardinal Cushing Library at Emmanuel College, Boston. The inscription recognises the importance of books and therefore the value of libraries as repositories and providers of access. Of course, such inscriptions can be controversial, particularly in so far as they suggest a religious affiliation. Our interest, however, is much more mundane. There can be little doubt that such reuse of material is commonly referred to as quotation. For example, the Langdell room at Harvard Law School includes a series of inscriptions from Cicero, Justinian, Psalms, Ecclesiasticus and Sir Edward Coke. A guide identifying these is entitled 'Quotations in the Langdell Reading Room'.[170] Likewise, the Library of Congress publishes a guide to the building called 'On these Walls: Inscriptions and Quotations in the Buildings of the Library of Congress'.[171] We do not want to belabour the point. It should be clear that the ordinary use of the word 'quotation' includes many situations where material, particularly words, are merely taken and placed in a new context. The context may sometimes be a copyright work itself – a compilation (as in a dictionary of quotations) or an architectural work – but this is absolutely irrelevant to the characterisation of the reuse of the material as a quotation.[172]

Equally, consider statements on the back cover of a book recommending it (or statements from newspaper reviews on the sign boards outside a theatre). Or the statements made by Andy Warhol, such as 'Pop Art is for everyone', featured on the back of Campbell's soup cans in the company's 2012 limited edition?[173] Wouldn't we happily refer to these as 'quotations'? We think so. Of course, we could argue that the recommendation on the back cover is part of a compilation (along with the work itself and all the remaining 'front matter' and 'back matter'). But such an argument feels so strained (like that in relation to inscriptions on buildings) that it really clarifies that a freestanding replication of material can, in fact, ordinarily be called a 'quotation'.

There is no basis in the specific law and history of the Berne Convention for eschewing the ordinary meaning of quotation and adding a condition of incorporation into another work. Nor is there a basis in state practice.[174] Indeed, given our

---

[170]   http://hls.harvard.edu/library/about-the-library/history-of-the-harvard-law-school-library/quotations-in-the-langdell-reading-room (accessed 2 February 2020).

[171]   www.loc.gov/loc/walls/jeffi.html (accessed 2 February 2020).

[172]   In certain circumstances, courts have treated the combination of words, representation and placement as a work: Cour de Cassation, No 06-19021, 2008, translated by Jane Ginsburg in Jane Ginsburg and Edouard Treppoz, *International Copyright Law: US and EU Perspectives, Text and Cases* (Edward Elgar 2015), 289 (stencil of word PARADISE in gold over door of dilapidated building regarded as a 'personal creation').

[173]   Chris Michaud, 'Life imitating art? Warhol-inspired soup for sale', *Reuters, Arts*, 11 September 2012, at www.reuters.com/article/us-art-warhol-soup/life-imitating-art-warhol-inspired-soup-for-sale-idUSBRE88A0VE20120911 (accessed 9 June 2020).

[174]   Cf. Lionel Bochumberg, *Le Droit de Citation*, ch. 3 (insisting on incorporation in a second work as 'universally recognised').

argument that the quotation limitation is a mandatory exception,[175] such a condition is probably contrary to the Convention.

B *Must the Quotation Be Proportionately Short?*

Must the 'quoting' text in which a segment of an earlier work appears be longer than the 'quoted text'? One of the leading commentaries on the EU Information Society Directive, Walter and von Lewinski, suggest this must be so, or at least that the quoted text must be ancillary. There is also a requirement of this sort in French case law, where it has been suggested that the 'quoting text' must be able to operate effectively without the 'quoted text'.[176]

Once again, we suggest there is no such requirement. After all, we have just argued that there need not be a 'quoting text'. Of course, there will very often be a work (or other material) in which a quotation is incorporated. Even then, however, we see nothing intrinsic in the concept of 'quotation' to suggest that the quoting context must be in some sense 'larger' than the quoted material.

To require that the 'quoting text' be more substantial than the 'quoted elements' would raise practical and theoretical questions about how to appraise different contributions. First, one would be required to identify precisely the quoting 'text': in some cases, of course, this will be straightforward – it will be the article or chapter or book in which the quoted material is included; or the image that is depicted within the frame; or the film that is presented to an audience for viewing in a single session. But in the online environment these traditional frames are often less clear: web pages and websites being often amalgamations of materials derived from different sources and having diverse character. A 'snippet', returned in response to a search, sits amid an array of different possible works.

Even where it is possible to identify the 'quoting text', there arises the question of 'evaluation'. How is one to decide whether the 'quoting' text is significant compared with the 'quoted text'? Is this a quantitative matter? Consider, for example, a film being quoted in a painting;[177] or a painting in a photograph;[178] or a textual caption

---

[175]   Chapter 3, Section I, pp. 29–38.

[176]   *Editions Musicales AB et Lucky Imprimerie* v. *Editions Durand*, Cour d'Appel Paris, 4th ch, 22 May 2002, (2002) 194 *RIDA* 320, 323 (in relation to books for teaching musical theory, finding no quotation where the books could not 'survive withdrawal' of the quoted material ['ne peut survivre à leur retrait, qu'il n'y a donc pas incorporation des citations dans une oeuvre seconde']).

[177]   In Chapter 5, Section III, Part C, pp. 118–120, below, we give the example of the schoolmistress/nurse in *The Battleship Potemkin* being quoted by Francis Bacon.

[178]   For example, Victor Burgin's quotation of Edward Hopper's *Office by Night* (1940) in Burgin's 1986 series of photographs of the same name. See Jan Estep, 'Victor Burgin', in Lynne Warren (ed), *Encyclopaedia of Twentieth Century Photography* (Routledge 2006), vol. 1, 179. Burgin himself describes his 'direct quotation of Hopper's painted secretary and boss' in some of his images: Victor Burgin, 'The Separateness of Things' at www.tate.org.uk/research/publications/tate-papers /03/the-separateness-of-things-victor-burgin. See also Filip Lipinski, 'The Elusive Everyday and the "Life" of Edward Hopper's Paintings', *Textes and Contextes*, https://preo.u-bourgogne.fr/textesetcon

added to an image of a painting in a manner that radically re-shapes the meaning of the painting.[179] In these examples of trans-media quotation, the whole idea that the quoting work must, in some sense, be greater than the quoted would require the comparison of expressive material from distinct genres that are simply incommensurable. Nor is the challenge of incommensurability resolved by asking questions about the relative proportion of creative effort. To start to investigate the creative effort that particular creators have embodied in specific works would necessarily open a pandora's box.

Of course, it must be right that the smaller the contribution from the quoter, the more likely the re-use is to appear as mere reproduction whose only function is to harm the market for the work reproduced. But the numerous counter examples, such as those in the previous part of this chapter, imply that these sorts of evaluations are not relevant to determining whether there is a 'quotation', as such; rather they relate to whether the quotation is in accordance with fair practice.[180]

C Must the Quotation Be Unaltered?

In the typical printed-text situation, the quoted text is kept distinct from the quoting text, and its integrity is intact. Is this latter feature part of the definition of when something is a quotation? The *Collins Pocket Dictionary of the English Language* offers some basis for such a suggestion, defining a quotation as 'a written or spoken passage repeated *exactly* in a later work, speech or conversation, usually with an acknowledgment of its source'.[181]

Some national legal systems have treated the maintenance of textual integrity as a condition for the operation of the quotation exception. Indeed, Advocate General Trstenjak seemed to suggest such a condition for the operation of the European quotation exception.[182] Some commentators support this narrow view, in particular by arguing that a summary is not a quotation.[183]

---

textes/index.php?id=2517#bodyftn3 (referring to the 'frequent quotations' of Hopper's images in art and visual culture) (accessed 3 July 2020).

[179] For example, Barbara Kruger's body of work where found images, usually pre-existing and wholly unremarkable stock commercial photographs, are reproduced in black and white with terse captions in red-and-white superimposed, the brief text demanding that the viewer interrogate and understand the image in a particular way. Famous examples are Untitled ('Your Body Is a Battleground') (1989) and Untitled ('I Shop, Therefore I Am') (1987).

[180] See Chapter 6, Section III, Part A, esp. pp. 155, 185, below.

[181] *Collins Pocket Dictionary of the English Language* (1989) 691 (emphasis added).

[182] Case C-145/10 *Painer* v. *Standard Verlags GmbH*, EU:C:2011:239 (Advocate General's Opinion), [210] (Advocate General Trstenjak): 'In natural language usage, it is extremely important for a quotation that third-party intellectual property is reproduced without modification in identifiable form.'

[183] Ricketson and Ginsburg (2006), 787, [13.41] ('the making of a summary is not the same thing as the making of a quotation'); Silke von Lewinski, *International Copyright Law and Policy* (Oxford University Press 2008), 157–8, [5.16] ('summaries of texts do not constitute quotations'); Mihály Ficsor, *Guide to the Copyright and Related Rights Treaties Administered by WIPO*

Again, we suggest this is incorrect. Maintenance of the absolute identity of the quoted material is not consistent with many ordinary usages of the term 'quotation' and makes little sense as a matter of law or policy. Indeed, even the narrowest conceptions of literary quotation provide for standardised ways in which what is quoted in print may be altered: sections may be omitted by using ' ... ', and new matter can be inserted for explanatory purposes, conventionally in square brackets. We suggest that the term 'quotation' is even broader and might, for example, include summary or paraphrase of text, the incorporation of a phrase of music in a composition and its elaboration, or a transformative use of an artwork in a later artwork or film.

In the context of textual reuse, philosophers of language have explored this question of transformative use, denominating these different types of 'quotation' as 'direct' and 'indirect'. According to Nelson Goodman,[184] direct and indirect quotation are possible, but share two necessary conditions: '(a) *containment* of some paraphrase of what is quoted, and (b) *reference* to what is quoted, either by naming or predication'.[185] For direct quotation, there needs to be 'syntactic identity' between what is quoted and what is contained; whereas, for indirect quotation, there needs to be 'semantic paraphrasis' – that is, 'some sort of equivalent of reference or meaning'.[186] While Goodman's attempts to define the conditions of quotation may be queried, not least because they do not easily encompass pictorial or musical quotation, it is encouraging to see that his definition (which operates effectively in literary quotation) includes a notion of paraphrase.

Outside the field of text, 'reuse' of derived material is frequently described as 'quotation', irrespective of the fact that the material is re-worked, altered or adapted. Certainly this is the view of musicology professor David Metzer. In his book *Quotation and Cultural Meaning in Twentieth Century Music*,[187] Metzer reviews quotation practices in music during the last century, highlighting the role of quotation as a cultural agent. For Metzer, a key aspect of quotation is that it stands out in the text in which it is deployed, but it is also transformed. Mark Katz also emphasises the necessary transformation.[188] Most digital sampling involves some level of

---

(Geneva: WIPO 2003), 62. ('A "summary" itself is obviously not a quotation, since the faithful repetition of a part of the quoted text is an indispensable element of the concept of quotation. Instead of a possible self-contradictory interpretation according to which a quotation could take the form of summaries, here again, another more reasonable interpretation offers itself; namely that, in this case, quotations – in harmony with the above-mentioned justified purposes of quotations – may be parts of such summaries (rather than being summaries themselves).')

[184] Nelson Goodman, *Ways of Worldmaking* (Hackett 1978), ch. 3, 'Some Questions Concerning Quotation'. See also Edward Said, *Beginnings: Intention and Method* (Columbia University Press 1985), 22 (referring to quotation as taking the form of paraphrase and allusion).

[185] Goodman, *Ways of Worldmaking*, 43.

[186] Goodman, *Ways of Worldmaking*, 43.

[187] Metzer, *Quotation and Cultural Meaning*.

[188] M Katz, *Capturing Sound: How Technology Has Changed Music* (University California Press 2010), 156.

transformation, but it nevertheless is, as already explained, commonly described as 'quotation'.

Beyond the views of commentators turning their minds to what constitutes quotation, we can see a wide array of uses of the term 'quotation' to describe transformative use of material from earlier works. This is especially relevant in relation to the use of material other than printed text. Indeed, perhaps the most widely discussed example of 'quotation' among art historians concerns just such a case of adaptation (as opposed to replication). Edouard Manet (1832–3), the great 'pre-impressionist',[189] was involved in 'overt citation of a whole host of canonical old masters',[190] including in his, most famous work *Le Déjeuner sur l'herbe* (Lunch on the Grass, 1862–3).[191] Comprising an image of two bearded men picnicking with a naked woman, while in the middle distance another woman appears to be washing her feet in a pond, this painting is usually honoured for Manet's superb handling of paint and stark objectivity'.[192] The painting also generates a level of discomfort in the viewer: 'the nude looks at us too intently; the conversational partners appear to ignore one another; and a distant, wading figure refuses to keep her distance and threatens to make a quarter of the foreground trio, whose existence she nevertheless seems to ignore.'[193]

The painting is also widely acknowledged to have been based upon a detail from a Marcantonio Raimondi engraving of Raphael's *Judgment of Paris*.[194] The three

[189] David Carrier, 'Manet and His Interpreters' (1985) 8(3) *Art History* 320 calls Manet 'the first modernist and/or the last old master', before interrogating whether his work might be regarded as 'postmodern'; Michael Fried, *Manet's Modernism: or, The Face of Painting in the 1860s* (University of Chicago Press 1996), 1 ('by common agreement the pivotal figure in the modern history of painting').

[190] Eik Kahng, (ed.), *The Repeating Image: Multiples in French Painting from David to Matisse* (Yale University Press 2007), 16. According to Michael Fried, *Manet's Modernism*, 23, it is an 'extraordinary fact' that '[m]ost of the important pictures of the 1860s depend either wholly or in part on works of Velásquez, Goya, Rubens, Van Dyck, Raphael, Titian, Giorgione, Veronese, Le Nain, Watteau, Chardin, Corbet'. Fried's interest is to explain 'the most remarkable aspect of Manet's borrowings, the literalness and obviousness with which he often quoted earlier paintings' (24). Others describe Manet's practice as quotation: David Carrier, 'Manet and His Interpreters' (1985) 8(3) *Art History* 320 (describing how *Olympia* has been interpreted as 'a Titian-quotation' and that critics have referred to the 'erudition manifested in Manet's quotations'), 332 ('the notion of image-appropriation does not distinguish Manet from Rubens, whose art is filled with quotations').

[191] Fried, *Manet's Modernism*, 57 ('his sheerest, most intractable masterpiece'); Farwell (1981), 1 ('among the most famous paintings executed in France in the 19th century'). The painting is housed in the Musée d'Orsay in Paris and can be viewed here: https://m.musee-orsay.fr/en/works/commentaire_id/luncheon-on-the-grass-7123.html (accessed 9 June 2020).

[192] George L Mauner, *Manet, Peintre-Philosophe: A Study of the Painter's Themes* (Pennsylvania State University Press 1975), 6.

[193] Mauner, *Manet, peintre-philosophe*, 6.

[194] The work can be seen at www.metmuseum.org/art/collection/search/337058 (accessed 9 June 2020). According to Fried, *Manet's Modernism*, there are also references in *Le Déjeuner* to Titian's *Concert champêtre* [Pastoral Concert] (1508), Courbet's *Young Woman on the Banks of the Seine* (1856–7) (as regards subject matter, and via the inclusion of the rowing boat).

figures in Raphael are 'two river gods and a water nymph sitting by the marshes' but, in Manet, become 'two Parisian men about town and their naked female companion'.[195] Tucker notes: 'While retaining the general disposition of the classical figures, Manet not only altered their identities and poses but he also changed their trappings, attitudes, setting, and relationships, giving them greater individuality and presence than they possessed in the original."[196]

Michael Fried has made much of what he refers to as Manet's 'strategy of more or less conspicuous allusion to or citation of particular "sources"'[197] to establish his Frenchness and his connection to European painting. Manet was engaging, as his contemporaries did 'in some version of citing or conspicuously adapting the art of the past'[198] actively and explicitly with the art of the past.[199] Here, we note Fried's commentary for the more pedestrian purpose of establishing that Manet's practice, as with that of many other great artists, is today commonly described as 'quotation'. Fried[200] calls *Le Déjeuner* 'perhaps the most notorious instance of quotation from the Old Masters in Manet's oeuvre'.[201] Fried explains 'the three foregrounded figures in Manet's painting are a direct quotation from Marcantonio Raimondi's engraving'.[202] Fried is not alone in describing the use as quotation: Beatrice Farwell, answering her question 'Why did he [Manet] need Raphael', explains that in doing so Manet was invoking the ideal, and that it 'is this and not "weakness of imagination" that lay behind Manet's quotations of the old masters'.[203] Likewise, Professor of Art History Carol Armstrong calls it 'perhaps the most concentrated exercise in eclectic quotation since *The Old Musician* of 1860'.[204]

---

[195] Paul Hayes Tucker, *Manet's Le déjeuner sur L'herbe* (Cambridge University Press 1998), 19.

[196] Tucker, *Manet's Le déjeuner*, 20.

[197] Fried, *Manet's Modernism*, 4.

[198] Fried, *Manet's Modernism*, 13.

[199] Fried, *Manet's Modernism*, 10–13.

[200] Fried, *Manet's Modernism*, 150.

[201] E H Gombrich, *The Ideas of Progress and their Impact on Art* (Cooper Union 1971), 76 ('a simple transposition of a detail from a composition by Raphael').

[202] Fried, *Manet's Modernism*, 56 and 152. Fried sees in Manet not just the emergence of modernist painting but 'a particular moment in the history of quotation in art' (183). See also *Manet's Modernism*, at 24, 28, 29 (referring to 'the obviously deliberate quotations of specific paintings by previous masters that one finds in [Old Musician (1862)]'); 30 ('the apparent gratuitousness of the almost literal quotations from [Velasquez's] the Drinkers'); 37 (stating that in contrast Manet's use of Watteau 'rarely entailed direct quotation of specific works'); 37 ('Bazin has shown [La Pêche] contains quotations from two paintings by Rubens'); 68; 136 ('Manet's practice of quotation and allusion'); 138 ('Manet's practice of quotation').

[203] Beatrice Farwell, *Manet and the Nude: A Study in Iconography in the Second Empire* (Garland 1981), 255.

[204] Carol Armstrong, 'To Paint, To Point, To Pose: Manet's *Le déjeuner sur L'herbe*' in P H Tucker (ed.), *Manet's Le déjeuner sur L'herbe* (Cambridge University Press 1998), ch. 4 (90–118), 94. See also Jean Clay, 'Ointments, Makeup, Pollen' (trans John Shepley), (1983) 27 *October* 4–5 ('It is precisely because he quotes – and by his mode of quotation – that Manet breaks with the fiction of an art history always already grounded in precedent'); Theodore Reff, *Manet, Olympia* (Allen Lane 1976), 59–60 (discussing 'allusion, parody and quotation').

Other examples of practices that are regarded as examples of 'quotation' include uses of film and photographic subjects in painting[205] and, of course, in other film. Here, we want to draw attention to a couple of examples involving the use of material from Sergei Eisenstein's classic black-and-white movie *The Battleship Potemkin* (1925),[206] a film of a similar iconic stature to Manet's *Le Déjeuner*.[207] As is well known, the film was set in tsarist Russia, and the subject of the film is a mutiny in 1905 by the starving and ill-treated sailors who man the battleship *Potemkin* when it is touring the Black Sea. When the ship docks at the port of Odessa, the local residents show support for the sailors, and in the most famous sequence, set on the enormous set of sandstone stairs leading down from the town to the harbour, many are massacred by the Tsar's artillery.[208] In the face of the panicking stampede of citizens, running amok among the injured and dead, an old woman wearing a white head-scarf (said to be a schoolmistress or nurse) and round, pince-nez spectacles proposes that they 'go and talk them [the militia] out of it', but the firing continues. A woman picks up and carries her injured son and pleads with the militia ('My boy is very ill. . . . Don't shoot'), only to be mercilessly shot down. A fleeing woman pushing a child in a pram reaches the top of the stairs and turns. The pram teeters on the edge and, as the mother is shot and falls, begins its descent down the stairs, miraculously staying upright as it speeds from one flight to the next. The scene culminates as the pram collapses at the bottom, and the schoolmistress/nurse, who had proposed negotiation moments earlier, is savagely and repeatedly struck by the sword of a Cossack soldier; her glasses are smashed, and she is bleeding from her right eye.

Not surprisingly, given its status, much has been written about the film and particularly the Richelieu (known as the 'Potemkin') steps scene – especially in relation to Eisenstein's technique of montage and the way in which the film cuts repeatedly between a number of scenes with ever-increasing speed and intensity. In addition, the film has proved remarkably influential on subsequent artists and

[205] Van Deren Coke, *The Painter and the Photograph from Delacroix to Warhol* (University of New Mexico Press 1964), 208, describes André Derain's *Bal des Soldats à Suresnes/At the Suresnes Ball* (1903), as 'a quotation from a snapshot of soldiers off duty' from a photograph, 'Soldiers Off Duty', in (1903).

[206] Eisenstein is himself said to quote Disney's *Snow White* in *Ivan the Terrible*: Anne Nesbet, 'Inanimations: Snow White and Ivan the Terrible' (1997) 50(4) *Film Quarterly* 20, 29, fn. 6. ('Not only does the latter film provide *a visual quotation* (Ivan's men digging are framed by their cavern just as the dwarfs are framed by theirs), but it also plays this scene as a musical number, the dwarfs' work song transformed into a minor-key (but equally rhythmic) meditation on war preparation' (emphasis added).)

[207] James M Brandon, 'Battleship Potemkin' in Philip C Di Mare (ed.), *Movies in American History: An Encyclopaedia*, vol. 1 (ABC-CLIO 2011), 27 ('worthy of consideration as one of the greatest films of all time').

[208] Richard Taylor, *The Battleship Potemkin: The Film Companion* (I. B. Tauris 2000), 35. ('The pivotal Odessa Steps sequence of *The Battleship Potemkin* may well lay claim to being the most famous single sequence of images in the history of world cinema.') The sequence can be viewed online. For a brief written description, see James Goodwin, *Eisenstein, Cinema, and History* (University of Illinois Press 1993), 67–9; Robert P Kolker, *Film, Form, and Culture* (4th ed., Routledge 2016), 105ff.

filmmakers. It has been said to have been 'almost as widely quoted and parodied as the "Mona Lisa"'.[209] For example, the British painter Francis Bacon drew on the scene for a range of images of screaming figures (including his well-known image of Pope Innocent).[210] Various stills of the schoolmistress were found in Bacon's studio,[211] and the capturing in a silent movie of her 'scream' must have offered a key aid to Bacon's aspiration 'to make the best painting of the human cry'.[212] The reference is explicit in the 1957 painting 'Study for the Nurse from the Battleship Potemkin'.[213]

Writing of this, the English art critic Lawrence Alloway chose to describe Bacon's use of the image as a 'quotation':

> He used, in screaming heads that he painted at this time, a still from an old movie, *The Battleship Potemkin*. This image, of the nurse wounded in the eye in the Odessa-steps sequence, though mixed with other elements, of course, was central to the meaning of the work . . . *The difference between Bacon's use of quotations from the mass media and other, earlier uses is this: recognition of the photographic origin of a part of his image is central to his intention.*[214]

Similarly Rachel Tant refers to Bacon's 'quotation of the screaming nurse',[215] while Roy Behrens having described the scene observes that it 'was "quoted" (just as

[209] Ian Christie, 'Introduction: Rediscovering Eisenstein' in Ian Christie and Richard Taylor (eds.), *Eisenstein Rediscovered* (Routledge 1993), 1, 1.

[210] It is cited as an influence for *Study for a Portrait* (1949) and *Untitled (Study after Velasquez)* (1950) in Anthony Bond (ed.), *Francis Bacon: Five Decades* (Thames and Hudson 2013), 100, 108, as well as Head VI (1949) in Paul Joannides, 'Bacon, Michelangelo and the Classical Tradition' in P Joannides, A Geitner, and T Morel (eds.), *Francis Bacon and the Masters* (Fontanka Publications 2015), 26, 35; David Syvester, 'Un Parcours', 13–32, 17, while Dawn Ades sees the gaze of the schoolmistress 'echoed' in Head III (1949): Dawn Ades, 'Web of Images', in Dawn Ades et al., *Francis Bacon* (The Tate Gallery in association with Thames and Hudson 1985), 15. Bacon has been described as 'an eclectic modernist, who took what he needed from the art of the past to make the art of the present'. Paul Greenhalgh in *Francis Bacon and the Masters* (Fontanka Publications 2015), 12.

[211] For the most well-known image, see this still on the website of the Museum of Modern Art in New York: www.moma.org/collection/works/89286 (accessed 9 June 2020).

[212] David Sylvester, *Interviews with Francis Bacon* (3rd ed., Thames and Hudson 1987), 34 (discussing *The Battleship Potemkin* and saying that 'I was not able to do it and it's much better in the Eisenstein and there it is').

[213] For this work, see https://sammlung.staedelmuseum.de/en/work/study-for-the-nurse-in-the-film-battleship-potemkin-by-eisen (accessed 9 June 2020) (the accompanying text explains 'Francis Bacon has locked a naked, screaming woman into a confined space. . . . He quoted the image from a scene in Sergei Eisenstein's "Battleship Potemkin"' (accessed 16 February 2020).

[214] Lawrence Alloway, '"Pop Art" Since 1949' *The Listener* (London, 27 December 1962), reprinted Richard Kalina (ed.), *Imagining the Present: Essays by Lawrence Alloway* (Routledge 2006), 81 (emphasis added). Victoria Walsh, 'Real Imagination in Technical Imagination' in Matthew Gale and Chris Stephens (eds.), *Francis Bacon* (Tate Publishing 2008), 74, 76, describes the practice as 'borrowing'.

[215] Rachel Tant, 'Archive' in Matthew Gale and Chris Stephens (eds.), *Francis Bacon* (Tate Publishing 2008), 165–8, 165 (citing Robert Melville, 'Francis Bacon', (December 1949–January 1950) 20(120–1) *Horizon* 419–23).

famously) 25 years later by British painter Francis Bacon in his portraits of pontiffs in boxes'.[216] One critic regards these pictures as not among Bacon's best because they 'rely too much on direct quotations'.[217]

Perhaps the most widely acknowledged revisitation of the 'Odessa Steps' sequence is in Brian De Palma's 1987 film *The Untouchables*.[218] The film is set in 1930s United States and concerns a very different subject – the the US Treasury's pursuit (led by Eliot Ness) of the gangster Al Capone. One scene is clearly influenced by *The Battleship Potemkin*.[219] The scene is set on the steps of a railway station (Union Station, Chicago), and when the two sides, government officers and Capone's mob, confront one another, Ness lets go of a pram containing a baby, and the pram begins tumbling down the steps.[220] Ness, played by Kevin Costner, pursues the pram, as the child's mother screams inaudibly 'My baby!' As in *Potemkin*, the film is cut so as to repeatedly revisit the pram, but in contrast with the silent film, the wheels of the pram make a rhythmic thud as they traverse each step. Ultimately the pram is stopped at the bottom of the stairs by a brave official, George Stone (played by Andy Garcia), who dives underneath it. Meanwhile, one of the mobsters grabs Walter Payne, Capone's chief bookmaker, and puts a gun to his head. In an image reminiscent of the schoolmistress (or nurse) in *Potemkin*, the bookmaker, wearing round spectacles and a hat, screams.[221]

This sort of 'borrowing' was nothing new to De Palma, whose earlier films often reproduced scenes from Hitchcock movies.[222] While the reuse of Eisenstein is sometimes described in terms such as 'sampling', 'mimickery' or 'parody',[223] film scholars have not hesitated to describe it as an example of 'quotation' in film. For

---

[216]   Roy Behrens, Review of 'Eisenstein: The Master's House' (2004) 37(3) *Leonardo* 252.

[217]   John Russell, *Francis Bacon* (Thames and Hudson 1993), reviewed by Andres Zervigón, 'Remaking Bacon' (1995) 54(2) *Art Journal* 87, 88.

[218]   Beverly Heisner, *Production Design in the Contemporary American Film: A Critical Study of 23 Movies and their Designers* (McFarland & Co 2004), 77. The two scenes have been excerpted on this YouTube video: www.youtube.com/watch?v=QR-U6WXnoMo (accessed 9 June 2020).

[219]   John Biguenet, 'Double Takes: The Role of Allusion in Cinema' in Andrew Horton, Stuart Y McDougal (eds.), *Play It Again, Sam: Retakes on Remakes* (University of California Press 1998), 138 (highlighting that while the position of the state differs (oppressor in *Potemkin*, liberator in *The Untouchables*), both films depict the Tsar and Capone as similarly savage).

[220]   Although De Palma is reputedly a 'master of suspense', the scene in fact begins tediously with Costner waiting for Capone's mob, scrutinising various members of the public as they traverse the terminal, and eventually deciding to help a mother who was struggling to get her child and pram up the stairs.

[221]   Bruce Weber, 'Cool Head, Hot Images' in Laurence Knapp (ed.), *Brian De Palma – Interviews* (University Press of Mississippi 2003), 108–19, at 112–13 (describing scene and discussion with De Palma).

[222]   Michael Bliss, *Brian De Palma* (Scarecrow Press 1983) xii–xiii (discussing 'film homages' to Hitchcock and giving an example of the recreation of the shower scene – 'down to every angle and cut' – from *Psycho* in *Phantom of the Paradise*).

[223]   John Biguenet, 'Double Takes' 138 ('homage'); James M Brandon, 'Battleship Potemkin', in Philip C Di Mare (ed.), *Movies in American History: An Encyclopaedia*, vol. 1 (ABC-CLIO 2011), 29 (sample); Robert Edgar, John Marland, Steven Rawle, *The Language of Film* (2nd ed., Bloomsbury 2015), 196 (mimick).

example, Laurence Knapp (who did his doctoral thesis on De Palma) explains 'De Palma *quotes openly, and unapologetically, from other films* ... Sergei Eisenstein's *The Battleship Potemkin* for *The Untouchables*'.[224] American Film critic and NYU Professor Emanuel Levy says that De Palma's 'use of film quotation' is here 'marked by pastiche'.[225]

The use of the term 'quotation' to describe De Palma's refiguring of Eisenstein's scene is by no means unusual in film scholarship. To reiterate, we are not concerned with the possibility that such uses infringe copyright (arguably in many of the instances described as quotation what is reused is merely the idea, something unprotected by copyright). Rather, we are merely concerned with the characteristics of the usage. For our purposes, the significance of the usage implies that 'quotation' is not limited to reuse of material in exactly the same form, as in all situations the filmmaker remakes the shot. In other words, the ordinary use of 'quotation' in this context does not imply as a necessary condition that the quoted material remain distinct in the quoting text. Without wanting to belabour the point, similar usage of the term quotation can be seen in music scholarship.

The normal use of the term 'quotation' thus seems to encompass a broad range of 'uses' of existing materials. Is there any reason why the legal meaning should not follow this ordinary usage of the word *quotation*? We think the language and structure of Berne as well as good policy, in fact, confirm that 'quotation' encompasses reuse of material that has been altered, for example, by way of paraphrase or summary.

With respect to language, it is notable that Article 10(1) of Berne explicitly includes within the concept of 'quotation' so-called 'press summaries'. On its face this would seem conclusively to indicate that 'quotation' is not limited to verbatim reproduction or replication. This is probably the correct inference; nevertheless, we should note that at least two commentators consider this to be a misinterpretation. Both Ricketson and Ginsburg and von Lewinski argue that 'press summaries' does not refer to 'summaries', but rather *reviews* by replication of news items.[226] The basis for so saying is the French-language version of the Berne text,[227] which in the case of differences is to be regarded as 'authoritative' (Article 37(3) Berne) and which refers to 'revues de presse'. This would, they say, include the presentation of a number of news stories from different sources in a form that is identical to that in which they first appeared.[228] If that is right, they say, no inference can be drawn from the

---

[224] Laurence F Knapp (ed.), *Brian De Palma: Interviews* (University Press of Mississippi 2003), 11 (emphasis added).
[225] Emanuel Levy, *Cinema of Outsiders: The Rise of American Independent Film* (New York University Press 1999), 56.
[226] Ricketson and Ginsburg (2006), [13.41], 787; Silke von Lewinski, *International Copyright Law and Policy* (Oxford University Press 2008), 158, [5.167].
[227] The Spanish version also refers to 'revistas de prensa' (press reviews). On this, see J Marín López, 'Derecho de Autor, Revistas de Prensa y Press Clipping' (2008) 215 *RIDA* pp. 2–101, 15.
[228] Ricketson and Ginsburg (2006), [13.41], 787, 'a collection of quotations from a range of newspapers and periodicals, all concerning a single topic, with the purpose of illustrating how different

reference to press reviews that 'quotation' covers non-identical uses. However, just because 'press reviews' include identical uses does not mean that they do not also include summaries. The reference to press reviews was thought to be a useful clarification, and the proposal to delete it at Stockholm (made by the Japanese delegation) was rejected.[229] We think that the significance of retaining the reference was that it was thought to assist in defining the scope of the notion of quotation: to include *both* extracts without commentary *and* summaries. The English-language version helps clarify the latter aspect.[230]

This view is reinforced by the structure of the Stockholm and Paris Revision of the Berne Convention. Various rights that Union Members must recognise for Berne works are set out – without particular logic – in a number of articles: Article 8 concerns the 'right of translation'; Article 9 the 'right of reproduction'; Article 11, 11*bis*(1) and 11*ter* with various rights to control public performance, communication to the public and broadcasting; and Article 12 the 'right of adaptation'. The provisions concerning exceptions are also located in different places, sometimes as applicable only in relation to a specific right (as with Article 9(2) with respect to the reproduction right and Article 13 as regards recording of musical works). Others, such as Article 10*bis*(2), specify acts that are permitted for particular purposes. In contrast, the two exceptions – one mandatory, the other optional – in Article 10 are not limited by reference to any particular right. The implication is that a person may quote a work in a text, artwork, film, sound recording (a reproduction) or by way of performance (e.g. reciting a poem), communication to the public or broadcast or translation or adaptation. The structure of the Convention then implies that quotation might be a limitation on any right recognised by the Treaty. In turn, this implies that quotation includes translation and adaptation.

The third reason that we think the legal concept of 'quotation' includes adapted versions such as summaries, paraphrased and transformed versions (such as De Palma's quotation of Eisenstein or Manet's of Raphael) is that there seems no good policy reason for limiting 'quotation' to replication. Indeed, because the user has to expend their own effort and skill to produce a paraphrase, summary or adaptation, such a reuse is to be regarded as less intrusive on the copyright owner's rights than replication. It is less intrusive because it reproduces primarily the unprotected elements – facts, ideas, style – rather than the (protected) choices as to how these are expressed. (It is a distinct question of whether a quotation of this sort might violate an author's right of integrity.) It does not make sense for Article 10 of Berne to require the more

---

publications report on, or express opinions about, the same issue. In consequence, the genre of "*revue de presse*" necessarily includes quotations'.

[229] Note 'Texts of Documents S/13 to S/302', in *Records*, vol. I, 624 (Japanese proposal to delete this as duplicative was rejected).

[230] Indeed, the Spanish implementation states 'Periodical compilations made in the form of *press summaries or press reviews shall be treated as quotations*' (emphasis added).

intrusive act, quotation-by-replication, to be allowed but to require parties to prohibit a less intrusive act, such as quotation-by-summary or paraphrase.

A fourth reason to think that quotation in Article 10(1) includes modified forms relates to the history. As explained in Chapter 2, in 1928, a quotation exception was included in the conference programme at Rome but rejected.[231] The proposal explicitly required that the quotation (and other borrowings) '*doivent être conformes au texte original*', and explained this implied that any borrower should 'not alter the text of the original', given that an alteration of his work is capable of damaging (an author's) reputation as a writer.[232] However, the deliberations of the Rome Conference made clear that various countries wanted the freedom to allow such changes to be made where they were deemed necessary, given the purpose of the publication. No provision on 'conformity' exists in Article 10 as adopted in 1967, the moral interests of authors being secured through Article 6*bis* and the concept of 'fair practice'.

One objection to legal recognition of a broad notion of 'quotation' that extends beyond literal reproduction is the overlap that this would create with other exceptions, such as that relating to 'parody, caricature and pastiche' in Article 5(3)(k) of the EU Information Society Directive (and in UK law, CDPA s 30A(1)).[233] As is well known, many countries subject such an exception to specific limitations, for example, that the parodic use accords with the 'rules of the genre' and/or does not produce any confusion as to the origin of the parody.[234] In the EU, the Court of Justice has said that a 'parody' must 'evoke' the parodied work and be intended to be humorous.[235] If 'quotation' in Article 10(1) Berne and Article 5(3)(d) of the Information Society Directive covers adaptations and other versions of the quoted work, could quotation not include parody?

Cultural theorist Richard Dyer, in his exploration of 'pastiche', distinguishes quotation from pastiche.[236] Dyer argues that a distinctive attribute of pastiche is 'imitation', which he says is distinct from 'unmediated reproduction'. He offers an example from Robbie Williams's 1998 work 'Millennium', which reuses 'the repeated lush string cadence' of the James Bond theme "You Only Live Twice" (1967). Whether this was done by orchestra or by sampling, Dyer argues, does not matter, because Williams 'was not trying to be like it but was reproducing it'. Dyer contrasts this with Williams's *Swing When You're Winning* (2001), where he imitates Frank Sinatra. This, for Dyer, is pastiche or homage. Dyer seeks to develop the distinction:

---

[231] Chapter 2, Section II, pp. 8–10.

[232] Union Internationale pour La Protection des Oeuvres Littéraire et Artistique, *Actes de la Conférence Réunie A Rome Du 7 Mai au 2 Juin 1928* (Berne: Bureau de L'Union, 1929), 74–75. See Chapter 2, herein, pp. 8–9. For opposition to such a limitation, see p. 9, fn. 12.

[233] CDPA, section 30A(1) ('Fair dealing with a work for the purposes of caricature, parody or pastiche does not infringe copyright in the work').

[234] See further Chapter 7, Section IV, pp. 216–222.

[235] Case C-210/13 *Deckmyn v. Vandersteen* EU:C:2014:2132 (CJEU, Grand Chamber), [2014] ECDR 21, [20] ('the essential characteristics of parody are, first, to evoke an existing work while being noticeably different from it, and, secondly, to constitute an expression of humour or mockery').

[236] R Dyer, *Pastiche* (Routledge 2007), 23.

'An imitated work is like or similar to another, but does not replicate it; reproduction, on the other hand, actually as far as possible, does.' We struggle with Dyer's attempted distinction. Much of what is ordinarily described as 'quotation' cannot easily be called replication and involves transformation;[237] as a result, it comes very close to 'imitation'. As a consequence, we think it is better to acknowledge that 'pastiche' is a subgenre of quotation: pastiche involves quotation,[238] but not all quotation is pastiche.

Would this not undermine the aims of the limitations on the availability of the parody defence in national or EU law? Our view is that this does not come close to being a fatal objection to the broad notion of quotation that we have recognised. This is for two reasons. The first is that (formally at least) the EU and national elaborations of the circumstances in which parody is permissible do not merely add conditions: they also clarify that parody is permissible *even in the absence of attribution.* This implies that there might be situations in which the quotation exception will not exempt a reuse that would be permissible under the parody defence. In other words, that defence is not rendered redundant. The second reason is that we think the parody exceptions in national and EU law ought, in fact, to be thought of as a sub-set of particular cases that do fall within the quotation right. That is, we think parody is precisely an example of a practice that is ordinarily described as 'quotation'.[239] There is no other place in the Berne Convention for such an exception. (Article 9(2) offering only freedom to create exceptions as regards 'certain special cases' to the 'reproduction right', though parodies often-times implicate rather the adaptation right.) Freedom to create parodies, like freedom to quote, is underpinned by the internationally recognised fundamental right of free expression.[240] In effect, we suggest that Article 10 itself requires recognition of freedom to parody. Of course, it would need to be in accordance with fair practice, proportionate and appropriately attributed. National and regional elaborations of a specific parody exception represent national understandings of fair practice and clarify that formal attribution is in practice unnecessary in the cases of parody, caricature and pastiche.

---

[237]   Dyer recognises this, at least in part, at 49, fn. 24 ('In so far as quotation, citation and sampling both deform the selected element (by taking it out of context, deracinating it) and transform it (putting it in a new context, rooting it in new connections), they do some of the things that imitation and, a fortiori, signalled, evaluative imitation, including pastiche, do').

[238]   Contrast Emily Hudson, 'The Pastiche Exception in Copyright Law: A Case of Mashed-Up Drafting?' [2017] *IPQ* 346, 362, who argues for a broad interpretation of 'pastiche', which draws on its ordinary meaning as 'imitation of style of pre-existing works, the incorporation of parts of earlier works into new works, and the production of medleys' (362). While Hudson considers the relationship of pastiche to parody, she does not consider its relationship to quotation.

[239]   As we saw at p. 121, above, with Emanuel Levy's description of De Palma's *The Untouchables* as 'quotation by pastiche'.

[240]   G Dinwoodie and R Dreyfuss, A *Neo-federalist Vision of TRIPS* (Oxford University Press 2012), 187 (differentiating between purposes of 'quotation' and 'parody' exceptions, the former important to the cumulative nature of knowledge production, the latter to do with creativity).

Another possible objection to treating quotation as including the modification of parts of preexisting works is that it implies 'quotation' includes 'misquotation'. We accept that this is so and do not see it as an objection with any merit. Misquotation is simply a form of quotation. This does not mean that it will be impossible for an author to oppose misquotation. If the alteration, whether intentional or not, distorts the quotation, the use might still be opposed under moral rights. Moreover, as we explain in Chapter 6, prejudice to such moral interests might also render a use incompatible with fair practice.[241]

One important consequence of this aspect of the ordinary (and thus legal) meaning of quotation is that quotation of another's work is – like translation – not inconsistent with the authorship of the quoting work.[242] A summary of the writing of another, or a compilation, may well have its own originality as a summary, so that it is the intellectual creation of the summariser or compiler, as well as a reproduction or adaptation of the text that is summarised or collected. Copyright lawyers are at ease with this kind of layering of works and rights, though there can be little doubt that such layering adds complexities to other features of 'quotation' (such as the need to acknowledge that the text is, in fact, an expression of another).

D Must the Quotation Be Identifiable?

In the 'typical' situation, one which involves printed text, a 'quotation' is placed in quotation marks (in French 'guillemets' or angle quotes – «»), perhaps set in from the surrounding text, in such a way that it is kept distinct.[243] Is the maintenance of the

---

[241] Chapter 3, Section III, Part B, pp. 57–60 (moral rights); Chapter 6, Section III, Part A, pp. 157–159.

[242] Some might suggest that 'quotation' is *necessarily* authorship. Consider Ralph Waldo Emerson's contention that '[w]e are as much informed of a writer's genius by what he selects as by what he originates. We read the quotation with his eyes, and find a new and fervent sense; as a passage from one of the poets, well recited, borrows new interest from the rendering.' ('Quotation and Originality' in R W Emerson, *Letters and Social Aims* (Houghton Mifflin 1875), 194.) Leo Steinberg, 'The Glorious Company' in Jean Lipman and Richard Marshall, *Art about Art* (Whitney Museum 1978), 8–31, 25 ('there is as much unpredictable originality in quoting, imitating, transposing, and echoing, as there is in inventing').

[243] These rituals are relatively recent in historical terms. Indeed, quotation marks once operated as suggestions to readers as to what should be quoted from a text. See Douglas C McMurtrie, *Concerning Quotation Marks* (New York: 1934) (at http://media.aphelis.net/wp-content/uploads/2012/12/McMURTRIE_1933_Quotation_Mark_light.pdf) (accessed 9 June 2020); Marjorie Garber, *Quotation Marks* (Routledge 2003), 13ff.; Keith Houston, *Shady Characters: The Secret Life of Punctuation, Symbols, and Other Typographical Marks* (Norton & Co 2013); Ruth Finnegan, *Why Do We Quote? The Culture and History of Quotation* (Open Book Publishers 2011), https://doi.org/10.11647/OBP.0012, ch. 4; Margreta de Grazia, 'Sanctioning Voice: Quotation Marks, the Abolition of Torture, and the Fifth Amendment' in M Woodmansee and P Jaszi (eds.), *The Construction of Authorship: Textual Appropriation in Law and Literature* (Duke University Press 1994), 281–302, 287–90; Margreta de Grazia, 'Shakespeare in Quotation Marks' in Jean I Marsden (ed.), *The Appropriation of Shakespeare: Post-Renaissance Reconstructions of the Works and the Myth* (St Martin's Press 1992), 57–71; Kevin Petersen, 'Shakespeare and Sententiae: The Use of Quotation in Lucrece' in Julie Maxwell and Kate Rumbold (eds.), *Shakespeare and Quotation* (Cambridge University Press 2018), ch. 2. But cf. Edmund King, 'Small Scale Copyrights' (questioning the historical accuracy of some of De Grazia's claims).

quoted text (image, sound, etc.) as 'distinct', or even just 'identifiable', merely a characteristic of the typical case of textual quotation or a condition that must be met before any reuse of other creative material can be described as 'quotation'?[244] Some academic commentators see this as a characteristic of quotation. For example, Canadian philosopher of music Dr Jeanette Bicknell described a musical quotation as 'one intended to be heard as a reference to other music, and that succeeds, minimally, in being so heard, at least by its intended audience'. Noting the absence of anything akin to quotation marks, Bicknell states that 'the composer has to rely on recognition, which in turn requires, if not direct familiarity, then some degree of musical literacy'.[245] She asserts that 'a quotation that is not recognised as such is not aesthetically effective as a quotation'.[246] In some national laws, this requirement is made explicit.[247] Indeed, in the *Pelham* v. *Hütter* decision, the CJEU specifically held that in order to fall within the quotation exception in Article 5(3)(d) of the Information Society Directive, the quoted material must be 'identifiable' in any quoting work: 'the concept of "quotations", referred to in that provision, does not extend to a situation in which it is not possible to identify the work concerned by the quotation in question'.[248]

We suggest 'distinctness' is not required – either as a matter of ordinary usage, nor as a matter of law (while we acknowledge that a failure to indicate clearly where a quote begins and ends may be relevant when assessing fair practice in some genres). We have already considered a number of examples of practices that have been described as quotation: Denis's representation of Cézanne's still life, Manet's reuse of the three figures from Raphael, and Bacon's and De Palma's use of images and sequences from Eisenstein's *The Battleship Potemkin*. Each of these were described as 'quotation', but only in Denis's *Homage* is the quoted work distinguished – there by the frame that surrounds the still life. Rather, a 'quotation' may become evident from all sorts of triggers that allow the connection to be made between works. Richard Dyer, in his work on *Pastiche*, identifies 'textually signalling' as an important characteristic of parody, pastiche and homage.[249] Picking up on this cue, Justin Williams explores

---

[244] See Nelson Goodman, *Ways of Worldmaking* (Hackett 1978), ch. 3, requiring that the quoting text 'refer to' the quoted text and discussing how this requirement could be met across the cultural field, for example, in music, painting or architecture.

[245] J Bicknell, 'The Problem of Reference in Musical Quotation: A Phenomenological Approach' (2001) 59 *Journal of Aesthetics and Art Criticism* 185, 190–1.

[246] Bicknell, 'The Problem of Reference in Musical Quotation', 190.

[247] For example, Guinea-Bissau, Copyright Code (approved by Decree-Law No. 46.980 of March 28, 1972), Article 185 (allowing quotation 'as long as such extracts are distinguished from their own text').

[248] Case C-476/17 *Pelham GmbH v. Huetter* EU:C:2019:624 (CJEU, Grand Chamber), [74]. See *Metall auf Metall IV* (BGH), Case No I ZR 115/16 (30 April 2020) (finding no quotation "because there is no indication that the listeners ... could assume that the [sample] was taken from another work or sound recording").

[249] R Dyer, *Pastiche* (Routledge 2007), 24. Dyer argues that 'pastiche intends that it is understood as pastiche by those who read, see or hear it' (3). The case 'for any given work being considered pastiche has to be made through a combination of contextual and paratextual indications, textual markers and aesthetic judgment'.

'signals' in hip-hop music that indicate quotation, highlighting that there is a very wide range of such signals, from including the 'hiss' of vinyl, the timbre of television or radio, material obviously from different genres, to a simple aesthetic sense that the quoted material 'does not fit'. He says that recognition of these signals depends on the 'imagined community' of hip-hop.[250]

It seems, then, that the ordinary use of the term 'quotation' outside the sphere of text does not require that the quoted material remain clearly distinguished from that which the quoter adds. However, the grammatical signals – such as quotation marks, 'air-quotes' in oral presentations, frames around pictures and so forth – do achieve a function over and above marking the distinctness of the quoted text, image or other material: they signal the fact that a quotation exists and thereby facilitate its recognition. This may suggest that a defining feature of quotation is the very *recognisability* of material as having been quoted. There is support for this view from Metzer. He states:

> [E]lectronic idioms have pushed quotation to extremes. Studio technologies have allowed musicians to transform borrowed sounds to the brink of unrecognizability. Many musicians have been drawn to that point and some have travelled beyond it. These far-reaching sonic alterations threaten to collapse quotation. For, as asked above, if the original is not recognized at all, is there a quotation?[251]

Metzer's apparent support for recognisability is because he is interested in quotation as a vehicle for 'cultural exchange', and this

> can start only if the listener can recognize the quotation. As described above, quotations are displayed more markedly than other types of borrowing, but that prominence does not ensure that the listener will be able to identify the particular borrowing. The listener has to be able to 'name' the quotation in order to understand fully what it stands for. Recognition then forms a crux for quotation, especially in its role as a cultural agent.[252]

Nevertheless, Metzer agrees that 'some quotations can sneak by without being spotted', even though they stand out stylistically.[253] Meanwhile, McLeod and DiCola have no difficulty with the idea of an 'unrecognizable musical quotations'.[254] And Ap Siôn[255] has written about how musical quotations can be heavily integrated to produce a synthetic whole.[256]

---

[250]   J Williams, *Rhymin' and Stealin'* (University of Michigan Press 2013), 9 ff.; repeated in J Williams, 'Theoretical Approaches to Quotation in Hip-Hop Recordings' (2014) 33(2) *Contemporary Music Review* 188–209, 196.

[251]   Metzer, *Quotation and Cultural Meaning*, 11–12.

[252]   Metzer, *Quotation and Cultural Meaning*, 6.

[253]   Metzer, *Quotation and Cultural Meaning*, 7–8, mentioning Eliot's *The Waste Land* or the Ghanaian national anthem in Stockhausen's *Hymnen*.

[254]   K McLeod and P Dicola, *Creative Licence: The Law and Culture of Digital Sampling* (Duke University Press 2011), 4.

[255]   Ap Siôn, 'Hidden Discontinuities and Uncanny Meaning' (2014) 33(2) *Contemporary Music Review* 167.

[256]   Ibid. (referring to Procul Harum's 'A Whiter Shade of Pale' as incorporating 'quotations', even though they are used to produce a synthetic whole). Ap Siôn uses this as a starting point for discussion

We do think that recognisability is a feature of the kinds of practice that are, in ordinary language, described as 'quotation': material has been re-located and is capable of being recognised as deriving from a different authorship or source. However, as the examples demonstrate, 'recognisability' does not add much: the derivation might be recognised by a substantial section of the immediate audience (as might have been the case with *The Untouchables*), but – as in the case of Manet's *Le Déjeuner sur l'herbe* – might only occur much later. One critic at the time is known to have noted Manet's reference,[257] even if – according to Michael Fried – Manet's uses of quotation were themselves intended as a form of homage or 'acknowledgment'.[258] Fried argues that 'the sheer perspicuousness with which both paintings [*Le Déjeuner* and *Olympia*] refer to their Italian sources [signify] that Manet wanted to make the clearest possible – the most explicit – public acknowledgment of what was probably the most important alteration in his vision of the art of the past that he had yet experienced'.[259] If 'recognisability' only requires that experts at some time after the creation of the quoted work are able to see that parts derive from the authorship of third parties, then the requirement hardly adds much more than the requirement that material emanating from such a third party has been used.[260]

IV CHARACTERISTICS OF QUOTATION ACCORDING TO THE INTERRELATIONSHIP BETWEEN THE SOURCE AND DESTINATION MATERIAL

A *Must a Quotation Be Deliberately Used?*

In the paradigmatic example, an act of quotation is a conscious, deliberate act. Intention is also assumed to be present in many of the non-legal descriptions of quotation. This is a view expressed by a number of philosophers. For example, Jeanette Bicknell states:

---

of poly-stylistic composition and collage works, such as those of Stockhausen and Kagel and ultimately Lera Auerbach's 2008 composition 'Sogno de Stabat Mater'.

[257] Beatrice Farwell, *Manet and the Nude: A Study in Iconography in the Second Empire* (Garland 1981), 255 ('Only the sophisticated eye of Ernest Chesneau in 1863 recognized Manet's reference, but he saw no more in it than a deplorable profanation'); Theodore Reff, *Manet, Olympia* (Allen Lane 1976), 48 (noting that Chesneau noted Manet's debt to Raimondi in a footnote to his 1864 work, *L'Art et les artistes modern en France et en Angleterre* (Paris 1864), 190, fn. 1.); Michael Fried, *Manet's Modernism*, 23 (a few of Manet's 'historically aware contemporaries recognized explicit references to past art in some of his important pictures of [the 1860s]'). Cf. Tucker, 19 ('no critic noticed the now often cited appropriations that Manet had made from earlier art').

[258] Fried, *Manet's Modernism*, 37.

[259] Fried, *Manet's Modernism*, 90.

[260] Iampolski, *The Memory of Tiresias*, 31–2 (describing a 'quote' by Jean-Luc Godard from Jean-Luc Godard's Forty Guns as a 'buried quote', only discernible because Godard later referred to it, and suggesting that 'prior to Godard's commentary, this episode, paradoxically enough, was not a quote').

A musical quotation is a deliberate evocation within a composition of a different musical work. It can be distinguished from both coincidental similarities between works and plagiarism on the basis of intention: The composer does not mean for the audience to hear the quoted passage as his or her own unproblematically.[261]

Likewise Robert Sokolowski comments:

Quotation is not merely repetition, even though it involves repeating what someone else has said. Quotation is repeating something as having been stated by another. The difference is one of *presentational or intentional form*. There may be no difference in the words being repeated, but they are repeated differently: it is as though we no longer saw an object directly but now only in a mirror. To quote is to say something as said by someone else.[262]

Indeed, all the examples so far examined – Denis's use of Cézanne, Manet's use of Raphael, Bacon's and De Palma's use of Eisenstein (all of which are described as quotation) – are also recognised deliberate acts of reuse (and reference).

Nevertheless, as film theorist Richard Dyer has observed, 'intention is a notion that has made cultural theorists twitchy for at least a century'.[263] Relatedly, perhaps, there is also a growing body of scholarship that acknowledges the possibility of 'unintentional quotation'. This begins with the work of the French post-structuralists of the 1960s, such as Roland Barthes, who argued works were not to be understood by reference to the intentions of their authors, but rather, that meaning was generated by readers. Barthes rejected the idea of a chain of influence from author-to-work-to-reader, in which the reader seeks out the meaning of the work by reference to the (presumed) thought of the author, and embraced in its stead the notion of 'intertextuality' – that individuals do not 'author' works so much as serve as vehicles through which language and previous works combine, and that when readers read those works they understand them by reference to the connections to and differences from the works that precede them. Barthes thus conceived any work as a 'tissue of quotations'.[264] Others have characterised cultural productions as 'palimpsests' and postmodernism as practising the 'aesthetics of quotation'.[265]

Importantly, this characterisation does not conceive of 'quotation' as an intentional act of a conscious cultural agent. It allows for the possibility that 'quotation' might be simply a result of the operation of preexisting texts *through* an 'authorial'

---

[261] J Bicknell, 'The Problem of Reference in Musical Quotation: A Phenomenological Approach' (2001) 59 *Journal of Aesthetics and Art Criticism* 185.

[262] Robert Sokolowski, 'Quotation' (1984) 37(4) *The Review of Metaphysics* 699, 699 (emphasis added).

[263] *Pastiche* (2007), 2 (discussing whether intention is necessary for pastiche and arguing that 'it is really not extravagantly speculative to say that a work is meant to be funny or sad, in this or that genre, is or is not pastiche').

[264] Roland Barthes, *Image, Music, Text* (Fontana Press 1984), 146.

[265] M Calinescu, 'Rewriting' in Hans Bertens and Douwe W Fokkema (eds.), *International Postmodernism: Theory and Literary Practice* (J Benjamins 1997), 243–8, 246.

subject. Writing in the context of film theory, NYU Professor Robert Stam indicates such a possibility: in his description of the theory of 'intertextual dialogism', he claims that 'all texts are tissues of anonymous formulae ..., variations on those formulae, *conscious and unconscious quotations*, and conflations and inversions of other texts'.[266]

It might, we anticipate, be said that the linguistic uses of 'post-structuralists' should not count towards any consideration of 'ordinary meaning' (perhaps on the basis that this was not the 'ordinary meaning' in 1967 and 1971 – the dates of the Stockholm and Paris Revision conferences, when these movements were just taking root). We recognise the concern (even if we do not share it and certainly do not feel comfortable with it) that, given some of the starting points adopted, some such commentators might not be said to be using language 'ordinarily'. Perhaps these commentators, for whom questions involving the 'play', 'joy' or 'excess' of language are so central, cannot be taken as examples of a notion of 'ordinary use'.

There is nothing in the language of Article 10(1) of Berne that requires there to be a subjective, conscious intention to quote. Possibly the proportionality condition – namely that the extent of the quotation does not exceed that justified by the purpose – comes closest to suggesting that 'quotation' must be intentional. But a user may have a 'purpose' without having an intention to quote. Moreover, there are at least two advantages with eliminating 'intention' from any legal definition of 'quotation'. The first is that questions of subjective intention always raise problematic evidential questions, and legal regimes frequently, therefore, try to avoid such conditions. Indeed, most copyright regimes do not make infringement dependent on the intention for precisely this reason. It was also for this reason that the UK courts preferred to exclude considerations of subjective intent from the interpretation of the fair-dealing defences available under the CDPA 1988 (as enacted).[267] Second, it is not obvious why a legal system would want to privilege an intentional act over an unintentional or subconscious (albeit purposive) act. What copyright policy is served by exempting the reuse of eight notes where that use is intentional (and therefore quotation), but to regard the same act as infringing because the alleged infringer had not appreciated they were using someone else's work?

Of course, unconscious reuse may often lack other characteristics necessary to constitute an exempt quotation, in particular, attribution of the source and author.[268] But that, as we have noted, is different from excluding unintentional reuse of material from the notion of quotation.

---

[266] Robert Stam, *Film Theory: An Introduction* (Blackwell 2000), 201 (emphasis added).

[267] *Hyde Park Residence* v. *Yelland* [2000] EMLR 363, [21]: Aldous LJ indicated that 'for the purposes' of is equivalent to 'in the context of', a matter to be decided objectively. See also *Pro Sieben Media* v. *Carlton Television* [1999] FSR 610, 620, per Walker LJ indicating that deciding whether a use was 'for the purposes of criticism or review' was not to be decided by the court putting itself in the shoes of the infringer, but that 'intentions and motives of the user ... .are most highly relevant on the issue of fair dealing'.

[268] Contrast Board of Trade, *Report of the Copyright Committee* (1951–2) (Cmd. 8662), p. 16 (acknowledgment should only be required only for 'definite' and 'deliberate' quotations 'where a large part of a work is reproduced by fair dealing').

B *Must a Quotation Be Used to Further an Argument*

In the paradigm textual example, the 'quoted text' is used as part of an argument that is made by the quoting text: the quote may be used to support the argument being made, or as a starting point from which to interrogate and critique the assertions contained in the quoted text.[269] This attribute is sometimes referred to in dictionary definitions. For example, the *Collins Dictionary* defines quotation as 'a phrase or passage from a book, poem, play, etc, remembered and spoken, esp to illustrate succinctly or support a point or an argument'.[270] Indeed, the use of quotations in support of argument is widely recognised as one of the most important benefits of the practice of quoting. According to Marjorie Garber, 'no kind of utterance or reference is more powerful when accurately deployed, for ... the quotation creates authority by its very nature and form. It instates an authority elsewhere, and, at the same time, it imparts that authority, temporarily, to the speaker or the writer.'[271]

It is one thing to suggest that use of text in a particular manner (e.g. to support an argument) is an important and valuable type of quotation (as 'esp' does in the *Collins* definition), but quite another to suggest that this function is intrinsic to the very characterisation of the extract as a 'quotation'. Nevertheless, just such an understanding of quotation is embodied specifically in some laws: in Greece, a statutory quotation exception is limited to circumstances where the act of quotation is 'necessary in order to support one's own opinion, or to criticize the opinion of another'.[272] French and German courts have also embraced such a standard, though it has not been held to completely consistently. In France, the legislation itself exempts 'analysis or brief quotation' on the grounds of the nature of the 'quoting work', and this has been said to imply that the 'prior work should be used solely to illustrate the argument, theme, or tenor of the subsequent 'quoting' work'.[273] Likewise, German case law has sometimes required that there be 'some contextual

---

[269] Indeed, Samuel Johnson's *A Dictionary of the English Language* (W Strahan 1755), 1626 (reprint, New York, 1967), defines a 'quotation' as a 'Passage adduced out of an author as evidence or illustration'. Interestingly, though, Johnson's definition of the verb 'quote' is not so restricted: 'To cite an author or passage of an author; to adduce by way of authority or illustration the words of another.'

[270] HarperCollins (2008), 1363.

[271] Marjorie Garber, *Quotation Marks* (Routledge 2003), 2. See also Edward Said, *Beginnings: Intention and Method* (Columbia University Press 1985), 22: 'Quotation can serve to accommodate, to incorporate, to falsify ..., to accumulate, to defend, or to conquer.' There are many aims of quotation in music: see Bicknell (2001), 190–1. ('Quotational links between pieces of music can have many aims: homage, irony, comment, joke, technical challenge, and so on'.)

[272] Greek Copyright Act, Article 19 ('Quotation of short extracts of a lawfully published work by an author for the purpose of providing support for a case advanced by the person making the quotation or a critique of the position of the author shall be permissible') (WIPO translation).

[273] Pascal Kamina, 'France' in L. Bently (ed.), *International Copyright: Law and Practice* (Lexis-Nexis 2019) FRA-134, citing Paris, 1re ch, 10 Sept. 1996, [1997] 171 *RIDA* 3. See also *Le Monde* v. *Microfor*, Cass. civ. I, 9 Nov. 1983, [1984] ECC 271, [7] (in English); Cass., Ass. plen., 30 Oct. 1987, [1988] 135 *RIDA* 78, [1988] ECC 297 (in English) discussed in Chapter 7, Section II, p. 207, fn. 115, below.

relation with the quoting text: for example, the quotation may clarify a larger context or illustrate the quoting text'.[274] Most recently, the CJEU has indicated in relation to Article 5(3)(d) of the EU Information Society Directive that quotation is permitted 'for the purpose of illustrating an assertion, of defending an opinion or allowing an intellectual comparison between that work and the assertions of that user'.[275] These purposes the Court characterised as a requirement that the user wishing to rely on the exception must have 'the intention of entering into "dialogue" with that work'. In so doing, the Court drew on the Opinion of Advocate General Szpunar, who himself was influenced by the specific formula in Article 5(3)(d) – in particular, the illustration that quotation could be permitted 'for purposes such as criticism or review'. It was on the basis of these words that the Advocate General founded the 'dialogue limitation'. Yet, those words are not present in Article 10(1) of Berne, which the provision is intended to implement. Treated purely as an illustration, these words are, of course, unobjectionable: many, possibly most, quotations will be for such purposes. However, by understanding the examples (criticism or review) as a basis from which to generalise a restriction on the operation of the exception, the Court set itself on a course which, if followed, will place European Union law at odds with the international obligations of its Member States (and its own, under TRIPS and the WCT).

While, in identifying a dialogic limitation on the right of quotation, the Court followed the Opinion of the Advocate General, it is less clear that the Court shared the Advocate General's understanding of the concept. In one respect, the Court seems to have a narrower conception: illustration of an assertion, defence of an opinion or comparison. In contrast, the Advocate General referenced a broader array of dialogical interactions including 'confrontation, as a tribute to or in any other way, interaction between the quoting work'.[276] Whether the Court was deliberately seeking to narrow acceptable forms of 'quotation' is not clear. One matter which suggests it did not intend to do so is that the Court appeared to accept that sampling of sounds might involve the required dialogue, whereas the Advocate General went out of his way to rule out such a possibility.[277]

[274] Michael Gruenberger, 'Germany' in L. Bently (ed.), *International Copyright: Law and Practice* (LexisNexis 2019), at [GER-187]–[GER-189]. See further Chapter 7, Section II, pp. 206–208, below.

[275] Case C-476/17 *Pelham*, EU:C:2019:624 (CJEU, Grand Chamber), [71]. Similarly, when considering 'citation' exception in Council Regulation (EC) No. 6/2002, Art 20(1)(c), the CJEU's starting point was that citation involves use of a design to 'serve as a basis for the explanations or commentary': Cases C-24/16 and C-25/16, *Nintendo Co Ltd v. Big Ben Interactive GmbH*, EU:C:2017:724, [76]. As noted at p. 95, fn. 61 above, the CJEU went on to rule that 'citation' was not so limited. This conclusion was informed both by divergences in different language versions of the Regulation and in the purposive approach taken to interpretation, the latter leading the CJEU to prefer an interpretation that ensured the rights granted to design holders did not unjustifiably limit further innovation.

[276] Case C-476/17 *Pelham GmbH v. Hütter* EU:C:2018:1002 (Advocate General's Opinion), [64].

[277] Case C-476/17 *Pelham GmbH v. Hütter* EU:C:2019:624 (CJEU, Grand Chamber), [72]; EU:C:2018:1002 (Advocate General's Opinion), [64].

Some commentators have welcomed the CJEU's invocation of the concept of dialogue on the grounds that it aligns interpretation of Article 5(3)(d) with a Kantian conception of copyright,[278] perhaps similar to that developed by Canadian legal philosopher Abraham Drassinower in his book *What's Wrong with Copying?*[279] Without belabouring his elegant text with references to Kant's famous representation of copyright as protecting an author's act of communicating the work to the public, Drassinower claims that contemporary Canadian copyright law is undergirded by the idea of protecting authorial communication.[280] Importantly, in such a 'dialogic' understanding of copyright,[281] protection by copyright should give way where it conflicts with the ability of other (subsequent) authors to communicate.[282] Were it to require one author to obtain permission from another author to speak, including to respond to the first, the law would not be respecting equally the dignity of each author.[283] Drassinower thus sees the right to quote as part of the necessary limits of copyright.[284] The public domain, which would include the right to quote, is, he says, is a 'radically non-negotiable set of conditions for dialogue flowing from the very nature of copyright subject matter as communication'.[285]

Whether or not the CJEU was intending to invoke Kant's vision of copyright, it is worth noting, if only in passing, that it is not the only 'dialogic' account of copyright law. Indeed, another Canadian law professor, Carys Craig, has presented a feminist vision of copyright as communication that invokes quite a different set of philosophical starting points.[286] Rather than drawing on Kant, Craig develops the work of the early-twentieth-century Russian philosopher Mikhail Bakhtin, whose work gave

---

[278]   Alexander Peukert, keynote talk, University of Luxembourg, 7 November 2019 (complimenting the CJEU on preferring a Kantian understanding of copyright to that of Josef Kohler which, Peukert explained, had dominated German interpretation during the twentieth century).

[279]   Abraham Drassinower, *What's Wrong with Copying?* (Harvard University Press, 2015).

[280]   Ibid., 6 ('copyright law is a construal, under the rubric of right, of the communicative nexus between authors and public in respect of works of authorship'); 8 ('a work of authorship – is a communicative act . . . copyright infringement is wrongful because it is compelled speech'); 111 ('The right attendant on speaking in one's own words is thus a right to preclude others from repeating one's speech'); ch. 4 (generally).

[281]   Ibid., 11 ('"dialogue" rather than "balance," is a more appropriate metaphor to guide copyright interpretation'); 220 (referring to his 'narrative of copyright as dialogue'); 221–2, 225 (referring to the 'dialogic model' of copyright).

[282]   Ibid., 8 ('because a work is a communicative act, rights attendant on it must (a) be consistent with the communicative rights of others, especially where such rights require copying of a work for the purpose of responding to its author's communication'); 64.

[283]   Ibid., 56 ('authors have exclusive rights in respect of their works only where such rights are consistent with everyone else's equal authorship'); 222 (critiquing the so-called 'work right' under US law as inconsistent with this).

[284]   Ibid., 55 ('the audience's entitlement to respond to and participate in the ongoing conversation of which the author is but a part').

[285]   Ibid., 182.

[286]   *Copyright, Communication and Culture: Towards a Relational Theory of Copyright Law* (Edward Elgar 2011).

rise to much writing on 'dialogism'.[287] Bakhtin's conception of 'dialogue' was the inspiration for the late-twentieth-century discussion of intertextuality (and even the 'death of the author'),[288] and the implications of this conception of dialogue are very different from those of Kant. Perhaps importantly, every act of communication is said by Bakhtin to be an act of dialogue; every word is already 'inhabited by others' voices'.[289] Craig sees Bakhtin as offering a way of thinking about copyright divorced from the transcendental self that underpins romanticism (and much personalist theorising of copyright) by recognising 'speakers' as situated, using signs and symbols 'already saturated with the voices of others' and yet possessing at least some agency (that later theories of intertextuality seem to deny). Authorship, Craig concludes, involves 'interacting with the meanings and texts and discourses that are already out there . . . and adding to them something of ourselves and our (socially constructed) subjectivity'.[290] This relational theory of authorship 'must leave room for others to engage in a similar communicative process [. . .] to acknowledge, respond to, and build upon the contribution the author has made'.[291] In many ways, Craig's and Drassinower's approaches mirror one another, but given the starting point of a situated, derivative notion of authorship, it seems implicit that Craig's invocation of dialogue would generate a broader set of limitations that permit 'access to and participation in cultural dialogue'. Use privileges, such as 'quotation' rights, would not be limited to those that 'create works', at least as far as current law understands such creation.

Whatever the precise philosophical conception of dialogue, the CJEU's require-ment of an intent to enter into dialogue probably constitutes a broadening in the interpretation of the notion of quotation from that previously being deployed in the laws of some Member States of the EU. Nevertheless, in our view, it is wrong to elevate this typical characteristic as to the function of many quotations into a necessary condition for the existence of a quotation.[292] Indeed, to do so conflicts both with the ordinary meaning of 'quotation' and with the legislative history of Article 10(1).

---

[287]   Craig (2011), 38–42. For previous deployments of Bakhtin within feminist scholarship, see Dale M Bauer and S. Jaret McKinstry (eds.), *Feminism, Bakhtin and the Dialogic* (State University of New York 1991).

[288]   Graham Allen, *Intertextuality* (Routledge 2000), 14–30.

[289]   M. Bakhtin, *Problems of Dostoevsky's Poetics*, (trans, C. Emerson, University of Minnesota Press 1984) quoted in Allen (2000), 27

[290]   Craig (2011), 40.

[291]   Craig (2011), 54.

[292]   See also B Justin Jütte and João Pedro Quintais, 'Sample, Sample in My Song, Can They Tell Where You Are From?' *Kluwer Copyright Blog*, 19 November 2019, at http://copyrightblog.kluweriplaw.com/2019/11/19/sample-sample-in-my-song-can-they-tell-where-you-are-from-the-pelham-judgment-part-ii/?doing_wp_cron=1591532283.08548188820953369140625 (accessed 9 June 2020) (highlighting the potential difficulties of establishing such an intention as illustrating 'the problematic nature of this requirement').

Perhaps the most obvious common use of the term 'quotation' that does not envisage the quoted text to be situated within a discussion is that of the 'dictionary of quotations'.[293] Since the first dictionary of quotations was published in the late eighteenth century,[294] a wide range of such publications have been compiled, typified by extracts from poems, plays and novels,[295] some arranging the passages by authors[296] and some by subject.[297] Perhaps the most famous in the United Kingdom is *The Oxford Dictionary of Quotations*, which was first published in 1941, containing about 11,000 'quotations'. The latest edition (the seventh), edited by Elizabeth Knowles (2009), contains more than 20,000 'quotations'. As Ruth Finnegan (Visiting Research Professor and Emeritus Professor in the Faculty of Social Sciences at the Open University) explains:

> Here is a different strand in the treatment of others' words which complements the strategy of using quotation signs to demarcate them inside a longer text. This is not recognition in the midst of other words, but the decisive extracting of chunks of wordage, gathered in a frame of other quoted units. . . . Here we are dealing with sharply demarcated excerpts, short sayings picked out from the innumerable words of human beings to be preserved in deliberately constructed stores.[298]

The quotations are not discussed: they are collected together, ordered and categorised. There can be no doubt that as a matter of common language, these are described as 'quotations'. The same would be said of a host of other books that record

[293] In Section III, Part A, pp. 111–112, above, we discuss another obvious example: the use of inscriptions on buildings. Here there is a clear intention to use the quotation to exhort or inspire or recommend but there is no 'work' entering into dialogue with the quoted material.

[294] David Evans MacDonnel, *A Dictionary of Quotations in Most Frequent Use: Taken from the Greek, Latin, French, Spanish and Italian Languages* (3rd ed., Pr. for G.G. and J. Robinson 1799).

[295] Eugene Ehrlich and Marshall DeBruhl, *The International Thesaurus of Quotations* (Harper Perennial 1996) (16,000 quotations; does not include 'lengthy quotations'; limits to 50 words).

[296] John Bartlett (1820–1905) and Justin Kaplan, *Bartlett's Familiar Quotations* (17th ed., Little, Brown 2002) (1st ed., 1855) (arranged alphabetically by author with index by topic); Donald Fraser (ed.), *Dictionary of Quotations* (Collins 1983) (8,000 quotations from 1,300 authors arranged alphabetically by author, and within alphabetically by work); J M and M J Cohen, *The New Penguin Dictionary of Quotations* (Viking 1992); Rosalind Fergusson, *The Hamlyn Dictionary of Quotations* (Hamlyn 1989) (3,500 quotations arranged alphabetically by author); D C Browning, *Dictionary of Quotations and Proverbs* (Chancellor 1952) (just over 10,000 quotations and proverbs arranged alphabetically by author; within each author heading chronologically).

[297] James Randall (ed.), *Anthology of Quotations: Over 12,000 Quotations Arranged by Theme* (Bloomsbury 2002) (divided into 700 themes); Auriel Douglas and Michael Strumpf, *Webster's New World Dictionary of Quotations* (Macmillan 1998) (organised by topic); Dorothy Winbush Riley, *My Soul Looks Back, 'Less I Forget: A Collection of Quotations by People of Color'* (Harper Perennial 1995) (alphabetical by topic, within the topic chronologically); Robert I Fitzhenry, *Say It Again, Sam: A Book of Quotations* (Michael O'Mara 1996) (by topic); John Chapin, *The Book of Catholic Quotations* (John Calder 1957), vii (10,400 quotation arranged under subject headings and within topic in chronological order); Ian Crofton, *A Dictionary of Art Quotations* (Routledge 1988) (arranged alphabetical by topic); J L Baron, *A Treasury of Jewish Quotations* (Crown, New York 1956) (alphabetically under topics).

[298] Ruth E Finnegan, *Why Do We Quote? The Culture and History of Quotation* (Open Book Publishers 2011), ch. 5, 113–14.

examples of clever, apposite, funny or even ridiculous things people have said.[299] These are books of 'quotations', a term understood in its ordinary meaning to encompass cases of extraction and representation of texts of others, even in the absence of discussion or referencing back. This is not to say that the 'referencing back' is irrelevant to the legal assessment of the legitimacy of any given quotation: it certainly is something that could help justify the taking of sizeable passages. However, the function of an act of reuse is relevant to its proportionality and fairness, rather than the threshold requirement of whether there is quotation.

This 'ordinary language' understanding of 'quotation' was embraced by the treaty makers at the Stockholm Revision. As will be recalled, various Member States proposed revisions to the Swedish/BIRPI proposed text. Among them was a Swiss proposal to limit, inter alia, permissible quotations 'to the extent that they serve as an explanation, reference or illustration in the context in which they are used'.[300] However, the Swiss amendment was duly rejected by twenty-seven votes to ten.[301] In these circumstances, it seems particularly regrettable that some national courts, as well as the CJEU, have sought to reintroduce the very same requirement that the Conference rejected.[302]

Might it be said that such a requirement can be deduced from state practice? We have noted that a number of national laws have adopted this condition, either in legislation or jurisprudence. But it certainly cannot be said that there is unanimity. Although Dutch law once contained such a requirement, as Senftleben and others show, it was abandoned in the *Damave/Trouw* case, which concerned the inclusion of an illustration from the book *The Growing Pains of Adrian Mole* in a review of the book (a review that barely commented on the illustration).[303]

If we are correct, and 'quotation' does not require any discussion or referencing, is not the possibility raised of considerable overlap with other exceptions – for example, 'illustration' for teaching? Article 10(2) of Berne explicitly permits Members of the Union to allow the use of copyright-protected works for the purposes of illustration in education.[304] The provision envisages use not just in

---

[299]   Marjorie Garber, *Quotation Marks* (Routledge 2003), 17–19 (referring to these as 'disembodied quotations').

[300]   Preparatory Documents, S/68, in *Records*, 690. See pp. 27–28, above.

[301]   Amendment proposed by Czechoslovakia, Hungary, Poland, Preparatory Documents, S/51, in *Records*, 688; Chairman, Minutes, [780] in *Records*, 861.

[302]   At a conference of the University of Luxembourg, 'Owning Expression and Propertizing Speech', on 7 November 2019, Advocate General Szpunar acknowledged that he had been unaware of this background and, had he been, his Opinion might have been different. The conference proceedings are available at wwwfr.uni.lu/universite/presentation/galerie_de_videos (accessed 9 June 2020).

[303]   Martin Senftleben, 'Internet Search Results – A Permissible Quotation?' (2013) 235 RIDA 3, 17–19; Senftleben, *A Century*, 356–8.

[304]   '(2) It shall be a matter for legislation in the countries of the Union, and for special agreements existing or to be concluded between them, to permit the utilisation, to the extent justified by the purpose, of literary or artistic works by way of illustration in publications, broadcasts or sound or visual recordings for teaching, provided such utilisation is compatible with fair practice.' For EU countries, this possibility is recognised in Article 5(3)(a) of the EU's Information Society Directive.

the classroom but also in publications and broadcasts. If such uses were capable of being construed as 'quotation', would there be any place for the operation of Article 10(2)? The answer is that there could indeed be considerable overlap, as must have been clear from the various attempts to limit quotation to only certain purposes, which typically included education and/or instruction. Moreover, the overlap was recognised at the Stockholm Revision Conference. As we explain in chapter 2,[305] the UK delegation specifically raised the possibility that Article 10(2) might be redundant given the breadth of Article 10(1).[306] However, at that stage, the proposal relating to Article 10(2) retained a similar scope to that in the Brussels Revision, and as a result was not subject to a fair practice requirement. Once that was added during the Stockholm conference, the difference between Article 10(1) and 10(2) was very considerably diminished.[307] Nevertheless, at least at a formal level, it is possible to identify some role for Article 10(2). For example, it extends to works that have not been made available to the public, whereas Article 10(1) does not do so. More significantly, it seems likely that while the quotation exception cannot be subject to a requirement of remuneration,[308] the optional educational exception might be. As a result, where a use would be regarded as fair only if the economic harm to the right holder is avoided through some form of equitable compensation, a broader array of re-uses might be permissible under Article 10(2) than under Article 10(1).[309] A good example might be an educational course pack for use in a university in the developed world that is comprised solely of lengthy extracts (e.g. over 25%) from published works: such use might count as quotation but not be in accordance with fair practice so not be mandatorily permitted under

---

[305] S/13 in *Records*, 630. Note also the Publishers Association to William Wallace, Board of Trade, 14 October 1963, (raising issue of overlap between proposed Articles 10(1) and 10(2) in the Study Group's 1963 draft); comment of Mr R. Bowen of the Board of Trade, wondering whether Article 10(2) was 'necessary at all' in the light of the proposed Articles 10(1) and 9(2): Third Meeting of the Copyright Committee, 11 August 1966, TNA: BT 209/908. See, generally, Chapter 2, Section IV, Part E, pp. 25–26, above.

[306] One answer to this seeming conundrum was to see Article 10(2) as a 'lex specialis' and Article 10(1) as a 'lex generalis'. According to this principle, which William Wallace advocated to the Drafting Committee at the Stockholm Revision Conference, each specific exception was to operate in its own domain, and the conditions recognised were not to be undermined by other exceptions. If a use falls within Article 10(2), i.e. relates to 'utilization . . .of literary or artistic works by way of illustration in publications, broadcasts or sound or visual recordings for teaching', then its operation is covered by Article 10(2), not Article 10(1). See Bergström, *Report*, [14] in *Records*, 1134 (mentioning specifically the relationship between Article 9 and Articles 10, 10*bis*, 11*bis* and 13).

[307] On the breadth of Article 10(2) see Professor Raquel Xalabarder's Study for the World Intellectual Property Organisation's Standing Committee on Copyright and Related Rights (Nineteenth Session, Geneva, 14–18 December 2009), entitled 'Study on Copyright Limitations and Exceptions for Educational Activities in North America, Europe, Caucasus, Central Asia and Israel' (SCCR/19/8).

[308] See Chapter 6, pp. 150–151 and Chapter 7, Part I, Section F, p. 204, below.

[309] Indeed, the German delegate to the 1965 Committee of Government Experts suggested retaining Article 9(2) of Brussels, but qualifying it by an author's right to obtain equitable remuneration: BIRPI: DA/22/22. For a report of the discussion, see BIRPI: DA/22/33, [56].

Article 10(1), but at the same time might be acceptable, coupled with compensation, under Article 10(2).[310]

V CONCLUSION

This chapter extensively examined the outer limits of 'quotation' and sought to identify whether there are any necessary conditions that need to be satisfied before an act can be characterised in law as 'quotation'. Importantly, we have shown that the breadth of quotation extends well beyond the 'typical' case of textual quotation, and it is critically important that such typical features do not end up being elevated into conditions for the availability of the exception. We do not, however, suggest that the concept of quotation is limitless. Importantly, we suggest that 'quotation' refers to a range of practices that have a 'family resemblance'. Like Wittgenstein's famous example of 'games', quotation is a phenomenon characterised by 'a complicated network of similarities overlapping and criss-crossing: sometimes overall similarities, sometimes similarities of detail'.[311] Or, as Slocum explains:

> [C]ourts often choose to proceed by assuming that categories inherently possess necessary and sufficient membership criteria. Such an assumption, though, is inconsistent with research from linguists and psychologists on the prototypical structure of categories. Instead of clear criteria for membership, many categories are instead characterized by having no explicit definition, at least in terms of necessary and sufficient conditions. Similarity of features plays a significant role in category membership, with certain features being generally true of category members but not uniformly so. Many categories will thus have a graded structure in which some items are more clearly and uncontroversially members of the category than are others. The graded membership structure means that features do not involve simple binary truth values (i.e., membership vs. nonmembership). Instead, some items are members of a category to a greater extent than are other items.[312]

If it was necessary to identify any *necessary* features that render a specific act one of 'quotation', it would be that (i) the quotation involves the reuse of expressive material (ii) for its expressive qualities, where (iii) that material is recognisable, or could be recognised, as material authored by another and (iv) is used or intended to be used in an act of expression, or at least in representation, for its expressive

---

[310]   Such uses in a developing country might be regarded as permissible under Berne Art 10(2) or 9(2) even without remuneration. See *The Chancellor, Masters and Scholars of the University of Oxford v. Rameshwari* (Delhi High Court, 9 December 2016), [63] (discussing the leeway offered by Berne Article 9(2) to India's copyright law in the context of a case concerning the creation of 'course-packs' by a photocopying shop for use by students at the University of Delhi. One of the extracts was 141 pages from a book of 416 pages, i.e. 33.8 per cent; but in most the number of pages and proportions were considerably smaller).

[311]   Wittgenstein, *Philosophical Investigations* (4th rev. ed., Wiley-Blackwell 2009), [66].

[312]   Slocum, *Ordinary Meaning*, 275.

qualities. As a result, we think that, neither in ordinary use nor in legal usage, would 'quotation' encompass copying entire works at home purely so as to have a duplicate, nor creating back-up copies of software. Nor would it cover decompilation of software in order to develop connections that allow different components to 'interoperate'. Nor would it encompass mass-digitisation, such as the Google Books project, nor digitisation for non-expressive purposes.

Nevertheless, the concept of quotation is broader than has often been appreciated. Viewed in this way, the quotation defence that is required to be given effect in the laws of all Berne Union countries comes close to a 'fair use' defence. It encompasses, for example, the reuse of music and sounds as a result of digital sampling,[313] appropriation art, the creation of snippets and at least the presentation of the results of text mining. To the extent that any such practices of reuse might be regarded as infringing, it must be on the basis that other aspects of Article 10, such as sufficient acknowledgment, proportionality and compatibility with fair practice, have not been complied with. As William Wallace, the British representative at the Stockholm Revision noted, 'the real safeguard for authors' is to be found in the words 'provided they are compatible with fair practice'.[314] It is to the significance of this condition that we now turn.

---

[313]   However, it should be acknowledged that the range of uses of digital sampling makes generalisations dangerous: see Johnson Okpaluba, 'Digital Sampling and Music Industry Practices, Re-Spun' in K Bowrey and M Handler (eds.), *Copyright Law in the Age of the Entertainment Franchise* (Cambridge University Press 2014), ch. 4, 75–100, esp. 81–82; J Okpaluba, 'Digitisation, Culture and Copyright Law: Digital Sampling, A Case Study' (PhD thesis, King's College London, 2000), pp. 69–76. One problematic example might be what Okpaluba describes as the 'layering slivers of barely recognisable sound samples to create a dense aural collage': at the point it becomes impossible to identify the source of the sounds as those of another source, it might be thought, such reuse loses the quality of 'quotation'. For a focus on the problem of recognisability, see David Metzer's definition of sampling: *Quotation and Cultural Meaning*, 163. Metzer identifies two sorts of sample – building blocks; and more extended 'interlopers that stand out in the mix, creating a constant give and take between the associations of the original source and those of the new surroundings. In other words, these extended samples are quotations . . .' (163). He argues that 'if the borrowed work is transformed beyond recognition, especially if the original has never been stated, then there is no evidence of a borrowing. Once altered so severely, the dynamics between original and transformation that define quotation disappear, as all that is left is a strange new sound rather than a transformed old sound' (171–2). See pp. 127–128, above. Importantly, the CJEU resolved this conundrum in the Kraftwerk case by ruling that, in the context of artistic re-use, there would be no reproduction of 'a part' and thus no infringement if the part was no longer recognisable to the human ear: *Pelham*, [31]–[39]. On this, see James Parish, 'Sampling and Copyright – Did the CJEU Make the Right Noises?' [2020] 79 *Cambridge Law Journal* 31, 32–33.

[314]   Main Committee, 7th Meeting, 16 June 1967. See further Chapter 2, Section IV, Part G, pp. 26–28.

6

Article 10(1) Berne: Fair Practice

I INTRODUCTION

The single most important of the conditions for the availability of the exception is that the quotation be 'compatible with fair practice'. As noted in Chapter 2, it was the introduction of the concept of fair practice that enabled the parties to agree on a quotation exception. Previous attempts to reach an international consensus, which had sought to limit quotation by reference to type of work, extent of taking or purpose, had failed to provide a sufficiently flexible criterion. The concept of 'fair practice' (or 'bons usages') proved the magic solution.

Given its importance, it may be surprising that the concept, which also appears in relation to the teaching exception under Article 10(2), receives little definition in the Berne Convention. The *travaux* do not reveal a whole lot more. In the early proposals, 'fair practice' seems to have been considered as requiring a consideration of whether the practice was consistent with trade norms. For example, it was said to be understood among the press what was fair.[1] With the broadening out, to cover all types of quotation and all types of works, the concept seemed – at least to contemporaries – rather vague.[2] Some called it typically English,[3] but even the British content industry seemed uncomfortable with it. The Publishers Association, for example, complained.[4] The lawyer for the BBC, E. C. Robbins, said, 'The broadcasting authorities were regarding this article [10(1)] as their fair dealings charter to bring them in

---

[1] International Federation of Journalists, BIRPI: DA/22/9 p. 7.
[2] It was criticised as 'too vague' by Mr Touzery (France): see Main Committee I, Summary Minutes, [762] in *Records*, 860.
[3] See C Masouyé, 'Perspectives de revision de la Convention de Berne' (1964) 43 *RIDA* 5, 26 (describing 'fair practice' as 'a notion of Anglo-Saxon law which seems to some too general and too vague'). More recently, see Lionel Bochumberg, *Le Droit de Citation* (Masson, 1994) 23, [26] (describing the notion of 'bons usages' as in truth very close to the Anglo-Saxon concept of 'fair use').
[4] Ian Parsons, Chatto and Windus Ltd, to Board of Trade, 2 October 1963 (fairness criterion 'invites litigation'); Publishers Association to Wallace, 14 October 1963 (arguing that a limitation on permissible quotations through a condition that the quotation be 'short' should be retained as the proposed concepts of fair practice and proportionality are too vague): both in TNA: BT 209/903.

line with the press.'[5] Sometimes it was suggested that fair use might be a preferable term.[6] According to Ricketson and Ginsburg, in the programme for the Stockholm conference, it was stated that 'fair practice' must be determined 'after an objective appreciation'.[7] Further, the *travaux* suggest that the absence of a requirement of 'short' quotations would be counterbalanced by the fair practice criterion.[8]

Given the limited guidance in Berne and its *travaux* about the meaning of 'fair practice', a question arises about how this terminology is to be understood in the context of Article 10(1). This chapter argues that Article 10(1) reflects a pluralistic notion of fairness, one that is independent of the three-step test, and which can be conceived of in several ways: according to notions of harm (both economic and moral), freedom of expression, distributive justice and, where appropriate, industry-based norms. Based on this approach, considerations relevant to fairness would include the nature or purpose of the use, the type of expressive use, the size of the quotation and its proportion in relation to the source work, the nature of the source work, harm to the market of the source work and the integrity interests of the author of the source work.

Three other possible approaches to 'fair practice' are rejected. The first alternative approach is to accept that there is minimal guidance in the international instrument and that the notion of fair practice is thus left entirely to the discretion of Berne Union Members. This would mean that what is 'fair' would be assessed according to the national laws of each Berne Member. The second is a variation on this approach, which is to suggest that, in the absence of international standards of 'fair practice', State practice can determine what this means. In other words, we would look to factors that appear common to Berne Union Members in implementing the quotation exception in order to inform what is required by fair practice in Article 10(1).[9] A third approach is to treat fair practice as synonymous with the three-step test, in particular limbs 2 and 3 of that test.

This chapter begins by setting out the three possible approaches and the reasons why they should not be adopted. It then elaborates in detail the pluralistic notion of 'fair practice' that is supported by Article 10(1) Berne.

---

[5] Third Meeting of the Copyright Committee, 11 August 1966, TNA: BT 209/908.

[6] Letter from Bernard Alton, Secretary to the Newspaper Proprietors Association to William Wallace, Board of Trade, 10 October 1963 (suggesting 'fair use' preferable to 'fair practice') in TNA: BT 209/903; Letter from Publishers Association to William Wallace, 26 October 1965 in TNA: BT209/1247.

[7] Committee of Government Experts (1965) BIRPI: DA/22/2, 53–54; Preparatory Documents S/1 (Berne Convention), 117, cited in Rickeston and Ginsburg (2006), [13.41], 786, fn. 99.

[8] Main Committee I, Summary Minutes, *Records*, 860, per Mr Wallace from the UK and 861 per Mr Hesser (Sweden), Mr O'Hannrachain (Ireland). See Chapter 2, herein, pp. 27–28.

[9] Although Dr Bochumberg's goal in *Le Droit de Citation* (1994) is not to interpret Article 10(1) Berne, his method very much corresponds with this, in so far as he seeks inductively to generate universal standards from the study of comparative law of the quotation right.

II REJECTING THREE POSSIBLE APPROACHES TO FAIR PRACTICE

A *Fair Practice as Solely Determined by National Law*

This approach assumes that there is little or no guidance in Article 10(1) Berne about the content of 'fair practice', and as such, it is left entirely to the discretion of Berne Union Members as to how they interpret and apply this aspect of the mandatory obligation. Leading commentators, including Professors Ricketson, Ginsburg and Okediji, support such an approach.[10] Prof. Ginsburg has emphasised the autonomy allowed to states in crafting copyright exceptions and suggests that 'fair practice', in relation to quotation, should be locally determined since 'norms of fairness may differ' between States.[11]

Moreover, there is precedent for this approach in relation to other obligations (albeit minimum standards) in Berne, such as the originality requirement and duration for works of joint authorship. The requirement of originality is implicit in Berne, via Articles 1 and 2 and the notion of literary and artistic *works*. The reference to 'intellectual creations' in Article 2(5) in the context of compilations has been understood to articulate a more general premise that literary and artistic works must be intellectual creations. Yet, it is the view of leading commentators that Berne does not specify the standard of originality and, as such, this accounts for prior and existing variations in national laws,[12] with tests such as 'skill and labour',[13] 'level of creativity',[14] 'skill and judgment',[15] 'imprint of the author's personality'[16] and 'sweat of the brow'.[17] Similarly, Article 7*bis* of Berne refers to works of joint authorship in the context of

---

[10]   Sam Ricketson and Jane C Ginsburg, *International Copyright and Neighbouring Rights: The Berne Convention and Beyond* (2nd ed., Oxford University Press 2006), [13.41], 786, state that fair practice 'seems essentially a question for national tribunals to determine in each particular instance' but they go on to note that '[l]ength is certainly a matter which is relevant to the question of "fair practice", as is the purpose of the quotation'. See also R Okediji, 'Toward an International Fair Use Doctrine' (2000) 39 *Columbia Journal of Transnational Law* 75, 160.

[11]   J Ginsburg, 'International Copyright: From a "Bundle" of National Copyright Laws to a Supranational Code?' (2000) 47 *Journal of Copyright Society of the USA* 265, 267.

[12]   See Ricketson and Ginsburg (2006), [8.05], 404–5. Contrast D Gervais, 'The Compatibility of the Skill and Labour Originality Standard with the Berne Convention and TRIPS Agreement' [2004] *EIPR* 75, arguing that originality as a matter of international copyright law refers to 'creativity' and creative choices and would not countenance a test of skill and labour.

[13]   United Kingdom (prior to EU harmonisation): *Walter v. Lane* [1900] AC 539; *Ladbroke v. William Hill* [1964] 1 WLR 273; *Hyperion Records v. Sawkins* [2005] EWCA Civ 565, [2005] RPC 32.

[14]   United States: *Feist Publications v. Rural Telephone* 111 S Ct 1282 (1991); Germany: *Unauthorised Reproduction of Telephone Directories on CD-Rom* [2002] ECDR 3 (BGH).

[15]   Canada: *CCH Canadian Ltd v. Law Society of Upper Canada* [2004] 1 SCR 339.

[16]   P Kamina, 'France' in L Bently (ed.), *International Copyright Law and Practice* (Lexis, 2019, annually updated), [FRA-23]–[FRA-24].

[17]   Previously the position under US Law prior to *Feist*. See J Ginsburg, 'Creation and Commercial Value' (1990) 90 *Columbia L Rev* 1805. This was not followed in Singapore: *Global Yellow Pages Ltd v. Promedia Directories Pte Ltd* [2017] SGCA 28, [26], which has used a combined test of 'intellectual effort, creativity, or the exercise of mental labour, skill or judgment'. [24] The court sees the standards in various jurisdictions today as interchangeable [27].

assessing terms of protection, but there is no definition or understanding of the requirements for joint authorship. Hence, there are significant variations in national laws as to whether contributions must be distinct (separable) or integrated, themselves original in nature, and whether an intention of joint authorship is required.[18]

If it is assumed that Berne Union Members are at liberty to interpret 'fair practice' as they see fit, a variety of approaches in national laws becomes apparent.[19] There is the 'fair use' exception in section 107 of the US Copyright Act 1976, which codifies judge-made practice prior to the 1976 Copyright Act.[20] The US fair use provision specifies the factors to weigh in determining whether there is fair use. These include:

'(1) the purpose and character of the use, including whether such use is of a commercial nature or is for non-profit education purposes;

(2) the nature of the copyrighted work;

(3) the amount and substantiality of the portion used in relation to the copyrighted work as a whole; and

(4) the effect of the use upon the potential market for or value of the copyrighted work.'

Section 107 adds: 'The fact that a work is unpublished shall not itself bar a finding of fair use if such finding is made upon consideration of all the above factors.' The United States Supreme Court has interpreted section 107 on several occasions,[21] and commentators have examined the scope and application of fair use at length.[22]

Fair use, similar to the US notion, has been adopted in other jurisdictions, such as Sri Lanka, Singapore and Israel.[23] The Sri Lankan law, section 11 of the Intellectual

---

[18] Compare e.g. Section 10(1) CDPA 1988 (as interpreted in *Brighton* v. *Jones* [2004] EMLR 26), the definition of 'joint work' in Section 101 US Copyright Act 1976 (as interpreted in *Childress* v. *Taylor* 945 F. 2d 500 (2d Cir. 1991) and *Thomson* v. *Larsen* 147 F. 3d 195 (2d Cir. 1998)) and Article L113–2 IP Code France, referring to collaborative works.

[19] See also Graham Greenleaf and David Lindsay, *Public Rights: Copyright's Public Domain* (Cambridge University Press 2018), 357–62, discussing the diversity in the way in which Article 10(1) Berne has been implemented in national laws.

[20] William W Fisher III, 'Reconstructing the Fair Use Doctrine' (1988) 101 *Harv L Rev* 1659, 1662–3. See also Matthew Sag, 'The Prehistory of Fair Use' (2011) 76 *Brooklyn L Rev* 1371.

[21] For Supreme Court decisions, see *Sony Corporation of America* v. *Universal City Studios., Inc.*, 464 US 417 (1984); *Harper & Row* v. *Nation Enterprises* 471 US 539 (1985); *Stewart* v. *Abend* 495 US 207 (1990); *Campbell* v. *Acuff-Rose Music* 510 US 569 (1994), 114 S Ct 1164 (1994).

[22] A selection of articles from a richly populated field includes Barton Beebe, 'An Empirical Study of U.S. Copyright Fair Use Opinions, 1978–2005' (2008) 156 *U Pa L Rev* 549; J C Ginsburg, 'Fair Use for Free, or Permitted-But-Paid?' (2014) 29 *Berkeley Technology L J* 1383; Wendy J Gordon, 'Fair Use as Market Failure: A Structural and Economic Analysis of the *Betamax* Case and Its Predecessors' (1982) 82 *Colum L Rev* 1600; P Leval, 'Toward a Fair Use Standard' (1990) 103 *Harv L Rev* 1105; Matthew Sag, 'Predicting Fair Use' (2012) 73 *Ohio St L J* 47; Pam Samuelson, 'Unbundling Fair Uses' (2009) 77 *Fordham L Rev* 2537; Pam Samuelson, 'Possible Futures of Fair Use' (2015) 90 *Wash L Rev* 815; Lloyd L Weinreb, 'Fair's Fair: A Comment on the Fair Use Doctrine' (1990) 103 *Harv L Rev* 1137; Lloyd L Weinreb, 'Fair Use' (1999) 67 *Fordham L Rev* 1291.

[23] For discussion, see J Hughes, 'Fair Use and Its Politics – At Home and Abroad' in Ruth Okediji (ed.), *Copyright Law in an Age of Exceptions and Limitations* (Cambridge University Press 2017), ch. 8, 234–74; and for discussion of how fair use is being globally 'transplanted', see Peter K Yu,

Property Act No 36 of 2003, replicates the US fair use provision (including the fair use factors), except with two key differences. The first is that the rider about unpublished works contained in section 107 of the US Copyright Act is not included in the Sri Lankan provision. Second, and more significantly, section 11(3) of the 2003 Law states that the 'acts of fair use shall include the circumstances specified in section 12'. Section 12 refers to 'the private reproduction of a published work in a single copy' (albeit with certain exceptions),[24] a quotation exception, reproductions for teaching purposes and by educational institutions in certain circumstances, reproduction by libraries and archives, certain acts for reporting current events and other news purposes, copies of computer programs for use and back-up purposes, performance or display of a work by educational institutions for educational purposes and reception of a transmission on private receiving apparatus. In other words, section 12 sets out specific exceptions, with their own requirements and limitations. Two problematic features of this structure are (i) how to reconcile the specific purposes and requirements set out in section 12 with the fair use exception in section 11 and (ii) whether the exceptions stipulated in section 12 must also be subject to the fairness assessment in section 11.

Singapore added a fair dealing provision into its Copyright Act 1987,[25] which uses language similar to section 107 of the US Copyright Act. Similar to the Sri Lankan copyright law, the Singaporean amendment creates some structural difficulties in terms of the relationship between the pre-existing fair dealing provisions and the new, fair use-type provision. Section 35 of the Singapore Copyright Act provides for fair dealing with works, other than for a purpose referred to in sections 36 or 37, and states that the purposes shall include research and study. Section 36 refers to the purpose of criticism or review and section 37 refers to reporting current events. Unlike section 35, sections 36 and 37 do not refer to fairness factors, whereas section 35 refers to the same factors as in section 107 of the US Copyright Act 1977 but adds a fifth factor – namely, 'the possibility of obtaining the work or adaptation within a reasonable time at an ordinary commercial price'.[26]

On the face of it, section 35 appears to create a fair use-type exception because it refers to any purpose, including research or study.[27] However, the fact that it

---

'Customizing Fair Use Transplants' (2018) 7 *Laws* 1 and Peter K Yu, 'Fair Use and its Global Paradigm Evolution' (2019) 2019 *U Ill L Rev* 111.

[24] For works of architecture that are buildings, reprography of the whole or substantial part of a book or of a musical work in the form of notations, of the whole or substantial part of databases or computer programs or where the reproduction would conflict with 'a normal exploitation of the work or would otherwise unreasonably prejudice the legitimate interests of the owner of the copyright'.

[25] Section 35 was added in 2004, and the Singapore Copyright Act was most recently revised in 2006. See Ng-Loy Wee Loon, *Law of Intellectual Property of Singapore* (rev. ed., Sweet & Maxwell 2009) [11.3.16].

[26] Section 35(2) Singapore Copyright Act 1987. This makes the list of factors identical to those found in section 40(2) of the Australian Copyright Act 1968 (Cth).

[27] Wee Loon (2009), [11.3.20] *et seq*, suggesting that parodies and private copying such as format shifting could now be covered.

excludes certain purposes (i.e. criticism, review or reporting current events) and requires sufficient acknowledgment for fair dealing means that section 35 is not unlimited in scope. Moreover, section 35 does not appear to involve scenarios that are covered by specific exceptions, such as decompilation (section 39A). In the words of one commentator, 'absent its express preservation, section 35 cannot colonise what is already covered by another provision'.[28] When it comes to the fairness factors, the assumption is that these do not apply to sections 36 or 37.[29] However, it has been argued that the factors emerging in case law largely correspond to those set out in section 35(2) and could be considered by the courts.[30]

Israel has a fair use exception, introduced by section 19 of the Copyright Act 2007, which refers to the factors to be considered in determining whether use is fair as including:

'1) the purpose and character of the use;

2) the character of the work used;

3) the scope of the use, quantitatively and qualitatively, in relation to the work as a whole;

4) the impact of the use on the value of the work and its potential market'.

The Israeli provision reflects a simplified articulation of the US fairness factors, and Professors Elkin-Koren and Netanel have explored how Israeli courts have developed an independent jurisprudence for these factors alongside occasionally looking to US case law for guidance, such that a distinct Israeli version of fair use has been developed.[31] This includes the Israeli courts placing significant weight on the commercial nature of the use and taking into account (lack of) attribution of the author, even though this is not one of the fairness factors.[32] If we look at other jurisdictions, we see that most Caribbean countries replicate the US fairness factors, as do the Philippines, Malaysia and Uganda.[33]

Turning to examine the United Kingdom, there are no fairness factors articulated in the fair dealing exceptions contained in sections 29 and 30 of the Copyright Designs and Patents Act 1988 (CDPA), including where fair dealing is for the purposes of quotation in section 30(1ZA) CDPA. Rather, the factors have been entirely developed through case law. These factors include the extent of what has been used; the amount and importance of the work taken; and the proportion of

---

[28] Wee Loon (2009), [11.3.26].

[29] Hughes (2017), 258.

[30] Wee Loon (2009), [11.3.31].

[31] Niva Elkin-Koren and Neil W Netanel, 'Transplanting Fair Use across the Globe: A Case Study Testing the Credibility of U.S. Opposition' (May 11, 2020). *Hastings Law Journal*, forthcoming. Available at SSRN: https://ssrn.com/abstract=3598160 (accessed 9 June 2020).

[32] Elkin-Koren and Netanel (2020).

[33] See J Band and J Gerafi, *The Fair Use/Fair Dealing Handbook* (May 2013), available at http://papers .ssrn.com/sol3/papers.cfm?abstract_id=2333863 (accessed 28 January 2020).

what has been used in relation to the rest of the work or the commentary, dishonest acquisition of the work, excessive use in relation to the purpose, commercially competing with the claimant's work and the unpublished nature of the work.[34] However, not all of these factors are regularly taken into account. Moreover, factors such as the nature of the claimant's work and the subject matter of the defendant's article have not been taken into account at all.[35] Unlike the US courts, UK judges have not really considered 'transformative use'[36] or the nature of the copyright work. While there is some overlap between the UK factors and the second and fourth fair use factors in the United States, the extent to which the use impacts on the market for the work has not been explored in the same depth as it has in the United States.[37] Further, when it comes to the unpublished nature of the work, this is a precondition for certain fair dealing exceptions,[38] rather than a factor affecting the fairness balance, which is also in contrast to section 107 of the US Copyright Act 1976.

Looking at quotation exceptions in civil law jurisdictions, these do not stipulate fairness factors in the way that a fair use exception does or in the way developed by English and Commonwealth courts in relation to fair dealing. Nevertheless, it is possible to see courts taking into account some similar considerations albeit not under the explicit umbrella of 'fairness'.

For example, French authors' rights law builds into the statutory provision a consideration of the amount of the work copied/quoted, by its reference to 'short quotations'.[39] Courts have rejected the quotation of entire graphic works.[40]

---

[34] See *Hubbard* v. *Vosper* [1972] 2 QB 84; *Hyde Park Residence* v. *Yelland* [2001] Ch. 143; *Ashdown* v. *Telegraph News* [2002] Ch. 149.

[35] Much to the regret of J Griffiths, 'Copyright Law after *Ashdown*: Time to Deal Fairly with the Public' [2002] *IPQ* 240, 257–9.

[36] For a discussion of 'transformative use' under US fair use, see P Leval, 'Toward a Fair Use Standard' (1990) 103 *Harv L Rev* 1105; Lloyd L Weinreb, 'Fair's Fair: A Comment on the Fair Use Doctrine' (1990) 103 *Harv L Rev* 1137; J Ginsburg, 'Exclusive Rights, Exceptions, and Uncertain Compliance with International Norms' (2014) 242 *RIDA* 175 and Jiarui Liu, 'An Empirical Study of Transformative Use in Copyright Law' (2019) 22 *Stan Tech L Rev* 163.

[37] For example, US courts have grappled with the existence (or lack thereof) of licences to assess the impact on the market for the work: *Cambridge University Press* v. *Patton* 769 F 3d 1232 (11th Cir. 2014); *Cambridge University Press* v. *Albert* 906 F 3d 1290 (11th Cir. 2018). For a discussion of whether the approach in this litigation begs an empirical or normative approach to market harm see E Hudson, 'The Georgia State Litigation: Literal Copying in Education' (2019) 82 *MLR* 508. See generally on this issue: Wendy J Gordon, 'Fair Use Markets: On Weighing Potential License Fees' (2011) 79 *Geo Wash L Rev* 1814.

[38] Fair dealing for criticism or review and also for quotation – Section 30(1A) and Section 30(1ZA) CDPA. The work has to have been made available to the public.

[39] Article L122–5(3)(a) of the French I.P. Code 1992 exempts 'analyses and short quotations justified by the critical, polemic, educational, scientific, or informatory nature of the work in which they are incorporated'. For a comprehensive discussion, see Y Gaubiac, 'Freedom to Quote from an Intellectual Work' ('La liberté de citer une oeuvre de l'esprit') (1997) 171 *RIDA* 2.

[40] See Cass. Plen. Ass. 5 Nov. 1993, J.C.P. 1994, ed. G. II, 22201, noted in Gaubiac (1997), 60 at fn. 10.; also *Maurice Lengelle, dit Tardy* v. *Libraire Larousse et autres* Cass. (1988) 138 *RIDA* 297; *Mr X, Promocom, FNAC* v. *Moulinsart* Cass. civ. I, 26 May 2011, (2011) 229 *RIDA* 468 (not allowing reproductions of full images from a comic book in an educational book). Cf. Paris, 14e ch, 12 Oct.

However, the Court of Cassation has accepted an almost complete reproduction from a musical work because the purpose of the quotation justified this substantial extract.[41] The purpose of the quotation is a key factor as well, judged according to the quoting work, and quotation for advertising purposes has been excluded.[42] However, the interpretation of the purposes has shown some flexibility and can only act as a guide.[43] In addition, it has been suggested that the analyses of shortness of the quotation must be undertaken alongside that of the purpose of the quotation.[44] The Court of Cassation has also taken into account whether the quotation substitutes for referring to the original work or not.[45]

Article 51 of the German Authors' Rights Law 1965[46] allows quotation to the extent required by the purpose of the quotation at issue. In interpreting this exception German courts have taken into account the fact that there is competition between the quoting and quoted works[47] and whether or not the quotation enables independent artistic expression.[48]

In Italy,[49] Article 70(1) of the Law No 633 of 22 April 1941, the Protection of Copyright and Neighbouring Rights (as amended), allows the abridgment, quotation or reproduction, as well as the communication to the public, of fragments or

2007, P.I. 2008, no. 27, 219, obs. A. Lucas (permitting reproduction of a photograph to illustrate an article in a magazine).

[41] *Sté le minotaure* v. *Fauvet et Fléouter* 1st Civ. 22 May 1979, (1980) 105 *RIDA* 166.

[42] Paris TGI (1996) 170 *RIDA* 324.

[43] Gaubiac (1997), 40, 42.

[44] Gaubaic (1997), 60, fn. 22.

[45] Gaubiac (1997), 66, fn. 44. See also *Dutronc et autres* v. *Sté Musidisc* TGI Paris 10 May 1996, (1996) 170 *RIDA* 324.

[46] Article 51: 'It shall be permissible to reproduce, distribute and communicate to the public a published work for the purpose of quotation so far as such exploitation is justified to that extent by the particular purpose. This shall be permissible in particular where

    1. subsequent to publication individual works are included in an independent scientific work for the purpose of explaining the contents,

    2. subsequent to publication passages from a work are quoted in an independent work of language,

    3. individual passages from a released musical work are quoted in an independent musical work.'

[47] *Übernahme nicht genehmigter Zitate aus Tagebüchern und Briefen in eine Biografie* KG (Court of Appeal) Berlin, Dec. 21, 2001, 2002 GRUR-RR 313. For further discussion, see E Adeney, 'Appropriation in the Name of Art: Is a Quotation Exception the Answer?' (2013) 23 *AIPJ* 142, 148–54.

[48] *Germania 3* case, BVerfG, Beschluss vom 29.06.2000 – 1 BvR 825/98, discussed in Adeney (2013), 152–3.

[49] Article 70: 'The abridgment, quotation or reproduction of fragments or parts of a work for the purpose of criticism or discussion, or for instructional purposes, shall be permitted within the limits justified for such purposes, provided such acts do not conflict with the commercial exploitation of the work.

    'In anthologies for school use, reproduction shall not exceed the extent specified in the regulations, that shall also lay down the manner for determining the equitable remuneration for such reproduction.

    'The abridgment, quotation or reproduction must always be accompanied by a mention of the title of the work and of the names of the author, the publisher and, in the case of a translation, the translator, whenever such mentions appear on the work that has been reproduced.'

parts of ('di brani o di parti') a work for the purposes of criticism, discussion, education or research. According to Professor Falce, this exception is construed restrictively.[50] Article 70(1) states expressly that, in order to be exempt such use must be only to the extent justified by the relevant purpose and must not enter into commercial competition with the work. In one case, use of Irving Berlin's 'White Christmas' in a television advertisement was found to fall outside the exemption because it was a commercial use of the material.[51] The statutory exemption also specifies that use is only permitted in teaching or scientific research, where it is illustrative and non-commercial. All such uses must be accompanied by a mention of the work, the name of its author, publisher and, where it has been translated, of its translator.[52]

Thus, there are variations in how Berne Union Members approach what constitutes 'fair practice' when it comes to quotation. The difficulty with accepting national variations in the approach to fair practice is a lack of overarching consistency. It also means that, normatively speaking, international copyright law has little role to play in framing what is meant by *fair* in a copyright context. It seems doubtful that the framers of Article 10(1) Berne expected 'fair practice' to be a phrase without *any* content at all. It would be remarkably at odds with the way in which international copyright law has operated in relation to other exceptions, such as the three-step test, which has been given a normative component,[53] and also run counter to the mandatory nature of the quotation exception.

We turn next to consider whether, in fact, it is possible to point to a particular understanding of 'fair practice' among states.

B Fair Practice as a Matter of State Practice

Article 31(3)(b) of the Vienna Convention permits 'any subsequent practice in the application of the treaty which establishes the agreement of the parties regarding its interpretation' to be taken into account when interpreting Article 10(1). In other words, Article 31(3)(b) of the Vienna Convention points to the role of customary international law.

Is there evidence of subsequent practice among Berne Union Members as to the meaning of fair practice in Article 10(1) Berne? As the discussion in the previous section illustrated, while there may be some commonality between jurisdictions that

---

[50] Valeria Falce, 'Italy,' in L Bently (ed.), *International Copyright Law and Practice* (Lexis Nexis 2019, annually updated). This paragraph draws on Professor Falce's account.

[51] Court of Appeal, Milan, 28 May 1999, Diritto di Autore, 1999, 594.

[52] Tribunal, Milan, 23 January 2003, Diritto di Autore, 2004, 96 (awarding claimant damages for failure to attribute songs quoted in film about the 1960s). See also Tribunal, Milan, 8 July 2009, Diritto di Autore, 2009, 634 (finding liability in relation to quotations which, while generally meeting the conditions of Article 70(1), failed to mention the author or publisher).

[53] Articulated by the WTO Panel Report, United States – Section 110(5) of the Copyright Act 1976, (15 June 2000), WT/DS/160/R, 15 June 2000.

have adopted fair use/fair dealing exceptions that cover quotation, there are also several (civil law) jurisdictions that include specific quotation exceptions.[54] Across all of these approaches, however, there is not a single, unified approach to when quotation is consistent with 'fair practice'. Rather, there are two – somewhat loose – areas of overlap, namely, the amount or extent of the work copied and the effect of the use on the market for the copyright work.[55] Thus, relying on state practice as giving content to what is 'fair' quotation in Article 10(1) involves making modest progress. First, and perhaps most importantly, these two areas of overlap do not, in themselves, provide much guidance. When it comes to the amount of the work copied, it is unclear whether this is to be considered *distinct* from the proportionality requirement ('to the extent justified by the purpose') in Article 10(1) or whether the amount used is somehow linked to a notion of harm to the author. Further, the effect of the quotation on the market for the work could mean a variety of things. For example, it could refer to actual and/or potential harm. Or to the harm to incentives to create and disseminate the work (such as through market substitution), as opposed to harm to the full market value of the work.[56] The harm could be evaluated factually (as occurs in competition or antitrust law) or more heuristically (as in unfair competition law)[57] or from an intuitive perspective of 'reasonable exploitation'.[58]

Second, relying on state practice still leaves national laws and courts the flexibility to take account of a range of additional considerations, meaning that there will be little consistency in approach if state practice is what solely informs the notion of 'fair practice' as mandated by Article 10(1) Berne. Finally, a key disadvantage of relying on state practice is that it is – at best – normatively ambivalent and – at worst – normatively bereft in terms of how 'fair practice' should operate.[59]

As such, this chapter turns to consider the third possibility for determining the meaning of 'fair practice' – namely, that it coincides with the three-step test

---

[54]   For a discussion, see Lucie M C R Guibault, *Copyright Limitations and Contracts: An Analysis of the Contractual Overridability of Limitations on Copyright* (Kluwer 2002), 33–40; Bochumberg, (1994), 24, [27].

[55]   Cf. Bochumberg (1994), which identifies universal standards in three aspects of the quotation right, namely, 'purposes', 'materiality' and 'attribution' ('finalité, matérialité, paternité'). On the question of 'materiality', see Bochumberg, ch. 4, which differentiates between quantitative and qualitative assessments of the amount taken, the latter including uses that compete.

[56]   See G S Lunney Jr., 'A Tale of Two Copyrights' (February 26, 2020). Available at SSRN: https://ssrn .com/abstract=3544757 or http://dx.doi.org/10.2139/ssrn.3544757 (accessed 10 June 2020).

[57]   A Ohly, 'A Fairness-Based Approach to Economic Rights' in P B Hugenholtz (ed.) *Rethinking Copyright's Economic Rights in a Time of Highly Dynamic Technological and Economic Change* (Kluwer 2018), ch. 4, 83–119.

[58]   See Ole-Andreas Rognstad, 'Restructuring the Economic Rights in Copyright – Some Reflections on an Alternative Model' (2015) 62 J *Copyright Soc'y USA* 503, who proposes 'reasonable exploitation' as the overriding norm for determining the scope of copyright, in particular the economic rights.

[59]   Cf. Bochumberg (1994), 79, [142], who concludes that the appraisal of the 'universal standard' of the 'materiality' of a quotation dissolves into judicial arbitrariness, and thus becomes the 'soft underbelly' ('le ventre mou') of the definition of quotation.

articulated in Article 9(2) of Berne and replicated in later treaties, such as TRIPS and the WCT.

C Fair Practice as Synonymous with the Three-Step Test

Ricketson and Ginsburg suggest that the criteria of Article 9(2) Berne, in particular the normal exploitation of the work and unreasonable prejudice to the legitimate interests of the author, could be relevant to determining 'fair practice'.[60] This would be one means of ensuring 'fair practice' had a meaning according to international copyright law. However, it is worth noting that the Working Group on the Right of Reproduction at the Stockholm Conference, in formulating Article 9(2), preferred a general clause rather than specific exceptions to the reproduction right and that, in formulating this general clause, did not consider a 'fair practice' criterion.[61] Therefore, we should be cautious about assuming that the criteria under Article 9(2) can be imported into 'fair practice' or seeing the three-step test and the condition of 'fair practice' as synonymous.

A further distinction that has been made between Article 9(2) and Article 10(1) of Berne is that the former permits free use as well as royalty-based exceptions, whereas the latter is simply 'free use'.[62] However, this is an assumption that needs to be questioned, not least because Ricketson and Ginsburg suggest that Article 10(1), in principle, could include remunerated quotations and that this 'should more readily satisfy the requirement of compatibility with fair practice than would a free use'.[63]

It seems, however, that the better view is that Article 10(1) only covers an unremunerated or 'free use' exception. This is for a couple of reasons. First, nothing in the *travaux* suggests that the quotation exception would give rise to a royalty-based exception and subsequent state practice indicates that Berne Union Members have generally implemented Article 10(1) as an unremunerated exception. While the title to Article 10 'Certain Free Uses of Works' supports this

[60] Ricketson and Ginsburg (2006), [13.41], 786. See also D Gervais, 'Making Copyright Whole: A Principled Approach to Copyright Exceptions and Limitations' (2008) 5 *UOLTJ* 1, 33, and S Ricketson, 'The Boundaries of Copyright: Its Proper Limitations and Exceptions: International Conventions and Treaties' [1999] *IPQ* 56, 65.

[61] Summary Minutes (Main Committee I) (Stockholm) in *Records*, 857–8; 883–5.

[62] See B Hugenholtz and R L Okediji, 'Conceiving an International Instrument on Limitations and Exceptions to Copyright' *Amsterdam Law School Legal Studies Research Paper No 2012–43* at http://ssrn.com/abstract=2017629 (accessed 28 January 2020) at 51, describing quotation as an 'uncompensated limitation'; R L Okediji, 'Reframing International Copyright Limitations and Exceptions as Development Policy' in R Okediji (ed.), *Copyright Law in an Age of Limitations and Exceptions* (Cambridge University Press 2016), ch. 14, 429–95 at 454; Raquel Xalabarder, 'On-line Teaching and Copyright: Any Hopes for an EU Harmonized Playground?' in Paul Torremans (ed.), *Copyright Law: A Handbook of Contemporary Research* (Edward Elgar 2007), ch. 15, 397, 'no compensation applies', and Pascale Chapdelaine, *Copyright User Rights: Contracts and the Erosion of Property* (Oxford University Press 2017), 37, fn. 43.

[63] Ricketson and Ginsburg (2006), [13.41], 786.

position,[64] this cannot be relied upon because titles are not part of the text of the Berne Convention but are there only 'to facilitate the identification of the contents of the articles'.[65] Nevertheless, this does not detract from the fact that the *travaux* did not discuss – and Berne Union Members have not subsequently treated – Article 10(1) as supporting a remunerated exception.[66]

Second, to adopt a royalty-based approach to 'fair practice' could create difficult implementation issues for national legislatures because it would mean identifying certain categories of fair quotation deserving of remuneration from others that are simply 'free' fair quotation. This sort of ex ante specificity could be very difficult to achieve. An alternative would be, as suggested by Professor Griffiths, that courts could permit certain activities in return for appropriate remuneration.[67] In this way, the challenge of ex ante specificity is circumvented, and the matter is left to an ex post evaluation of fairness by the courts. However, while this might be a practical solution, it would operate in tension with the underpinning rationale for the quotation exception, namely, freedom of expression. If copyright law is to give proper effect to freedom of expression, then it could have a serious 'chilling effect' to countenance royalty-based quotation exceptions that are judicially determined on a case-by-case basis.[68]

Even if Article 10(1) and Article 9(2) of Berne share some similarity (and this is discussed as follows), this does not mean that 'fair practice' in Article 10(1) is synonymous with the second and third limbs of the three-step test in Article 9(2) Berne. Instead, it is possible to point to a distinct notion of fairness, given the difference in language between the two provisions. This independent, pluralistic meaning will now be explored.

III FAIR PRACTICE AS AN INDEPENDENT, PLURALISTIC NORM

The argument is that a normative meaning can and should be attributed to 'fair practice' in Article 10(1). This is contrary to the view adopted by some scholars that

---

[64] Article 31 Vienna Convention and R Gardiner, *Treaty Interpretation* (2nd ed, Oxford University Press 2017), 201, explain how titles can ordinarily be legitimately treated as part of the context for the purposes of interpretation.

[65] See M Ficsor, *Guide to the Copyright and Related Rights Treaties Administered by WIPO* (WIPO 2003), 129, fn. 12.

[66] With the highly controversial exception of the so-called 'Google tax' in Spain: Intellectual Property Law, Art. 32(2) (introduced by Act 21 of 4 November 2014); the amended law permits the aggregation of 'insignificant fragments; from periodicals on payment of 'equitable compensation'. It has been criticised precisely on the basis of conflict with the 'free use' character of the quotation right: R. Xalabarder, 'The Remunerated Statutory Limitation for News Aggregation and Search Engines Proposed by the Spanish Government; Its Compliance with International and EU Law', IN3 (Internet Interdisciplinary Institute) Working Paper, available at https://papers.ssrn.com/sol3/papers.cfm?abstract_id=2504596 (accessed 3 July 2020).

[67] J Griffiths, 'Unsticking the Centre-Piece – The Liberation of European Copyright Law?' [2010] JIPITEC 87, [35].

[68] See also M Senftleben, *Copyright, Limitations and the Three-Step Test: An Analysis of the Three-Step Test in International and EC Copyright Law* (Kluwer, 2004), 232, observing that if quotations were licensed this would 'have a corrosive effect on intellectual debate'.

suggest latitude in how international copyright obligations in Berne are to be understood. For example, in relation to the Berne Convention, Professor Dinwoodie refers to the struggle between the universalists (who wanted an international copyright code that would apply in each signatory state) and the pragmatists (who proposed the principles of national treatment and minimum standards). He explains:

> Although the universalists made periodic inroads into this model throughout the twentieth century in the form of serial upwards revision of the minimum standards, there remained significant latitude for signatory states to develop distinctive national copyright policies tailored to their own cultural or economic priorities.[69]

In other words, the Berne Convention reflects a tension between 'providing copyright protection on an international scale, and a respect for cultural and economic diversity'.[70] Professor Dinwoodie also describes how minimum standards largely reflected national standards and were 'behind the curve of social and technological developments'.[71] However, he argues that this landscape has changed in recent years. International copyright law has sought to deal with issues raised by technological advances sooner; there has been faster development of international norms and international copyright standards are now enforceable through the mechanism of the WTO Dispute Settlement System.[72] Even so, Professors Dinwoodie and Dreyfuss argue that the WTO Panel should preserve the autonomy of member states to adopt their own individual responses.[73]

Professor Ginsburg also shares the view that international copyright law provides much latitude to Berne Union Members. She sees international copyright conventions as providing a general framework and preserving 'some national autonomy regarding the content ... of copyright exceptions'. As such, the 'US fair use exception may co-exist with a more rigid continental-style closed list of specific exemptions'.[74] Further, Professor Ginsburg suggests that 'fair practice' in relation

---

[69] G Dinwoodie, 'A New Copyright Order: Why National Courts Should Create Global Norms' (2000) 149 *U Pa L Rev* 469, 491. See also G Dinwoodie, 'The Development and Incorporation of International Norms in the Formation of Copyright Law' (2001) 62 *Ohio St L J* 733, 742; J Ginsburg, 'International Copyright: From a "Bundle" of National Copyright Laws to a Supranational Code?' (2000) 47 *Journal of Copyright Society of the USA* 265, 267–8; and Ricketson and Ginsburg (2006), [2.02]–[2.04], 42–44.

[70] Dinwoodie (2001), 742.

[71] Dinwoodie (2001), 740.

[72] Dinwoodie (2001), 746. He also refers to the WTO Panel Report, United States – Section 110(5) of the Copyright Act 1976, (15 June 2000), WT/DS/160/R and says that it apparently reflects continuing deference to national autonomy but that this emanated more from a textual reading of Article 13 TRIPS rather than a 'Berne based philosophical commitment to national autonomy' (765).

[73] G B Dinwoodie and R C Dreyfuss, *A NeoFederalist Vision of TRIPS: The Resilience of the International Intellectual Property Regime* (Oxford University Press 2012).

[74] Ginsburg (2000), 287.

to quotation should be locally determined since 'norms of fairness may differ' between States.[75]

We do not share the view that Article 10(1) leaves the meaning of 'fair practice' entirely to Berne Union Members. Instead, we argue that Article 10(1), as a mandatory obligation, has a normative content that leaves limited autonomy to Berne Union countries to determine its meaning. The independent meaning of 'fair practice' is pluralistic in nature and informed by notions of economic and moral harm; freedom of expression principles; distributive justice; and, to a limited extent, custom. It requires the following considerations to be taken into account: the nature or purpose of the use (if it is expressive use of a commercial, artistic or political nature; if it is for educational or other public interest purposes); the size of the quotation and its proportion to the source work; the nature of the source work; harm to the market for the source work and the impact on the integrity interests of the author of the source work. Good or bad faith, however, should not have a role to play, and custom or industry norms should only be relevant in very limited circumstances, where those customs or norms are reliable.

These are several arguments supporting an independent, normative content to Article 10(1), despite the points made by Professors Dinwoodie and Ginsburg. The first argument is that it seems unlikely that the framers of Article 10(1) intended 'fair practice' to be without *any* content at all. This rider was seen by those participating at the Diplomatic Conference as a crucial mechanism for ensuring that the quotation exception was bounded. As such, it would seem counterintuitive that complete latitude would be allowed in determining the scope of 'fair practice'. Second, autonomy in determining the scope of the quotation exception would make no sense, given the mandatory nature of the exception. Third, and perhaps most importantly, the interpretation that is proposed here is consistent with the norms set out in the Vienna Convention – in particular, Articles 31 and 32. The ordinary meaning of 'fair practice' has to be determined according to the terms in context and in light of the treaty's object and purpose.[76] Extrinsic aids, such as the *travaux*, can be used to confirm an interpretation resulting from Article 31 or where the meaning is ambiguous or lead to a result that is unreasonable. Thus, 'harm', in an economic and moral sense, can be taken as the basis for interpreting Article 10(1) because Berne is concerned with the protection of *authors* in relation to their literary and artistic works, and the rationales for this protection are grounded in either economic or moral theory. In addition, the rationale for the quotation exception, in particular, is linked to freedom of expression. Therefore, free speech principles ought to be considered. The *travaux* to Berne also suggests that trade norms might sometimes be relevant. When it comes to equity or distributive justice concerns, these also seem to

---

[75] Ginsburg (2000), 288.
[76] We do not rely on the dictionary meaning of 'fair', for the reasons discussed in Chapter 5, Section I, pp. 84–86.

have a basis in international copyright law, by virtue of the need to ensure that public interests are taken into account.

This chapter now turns to discuss in detail the basis of the normative content of 'fair practice'.

A Fair Practice – The Role of Harm

A possible way of assessing 'fairness' is according to the relevant harm that copyright is aimed at protecting against. One type of relevant harm is economic in nature, in line with the economic or utilitarian justification that is advocated for copyright law and shared by some Berne Union Members.[77] This justification identifies the purpose of copyright as minimising free-riding by users because of the need to provide adequate incentives to create and disseminate works, in order to promote overall social welfare. As such, the role of exceptions comes into play where there are economically insignificant uses or where there are market failures in relation to certain uses.[78] Fairness assessed according to a norm of economic harm might therefore focus on the commercial nature of the use (because the commercial use might suggest this is a market that the copyright owner could have exploited), the size of the quotation and its proportion to the work from which it has been taken (because this might indicate that the defendant's use is substituting for the claimant's work), and the extent to which the use of quotation harms the market (either actual or potential) for the work, and the nature of the claimant's work.[79] This latter factor – the nature of the claimant's work – can be explained according to the incentive function of the economic rationale of copyright protection. The idea is that the copyright system should incentivise works and that there is a need to incentivise works that either require substantial investment or are particularly valuable because they are highly expressive.

---

[77] See W Landes and R Posner, 'An Economic Analysis of Copyright Law' (1989) 18 J Legal Studies 325. P Geller, 'Must Copyright Be For Ever Caught between Marketplace and Authorship Norms?' in Brad Sherman and Alain Strowel (eds.), Of Authors and Origins (Clarendon Press 1994), 159–201.

[78] See P Samuelson, 'Justifications for Copyright Limitations and Exceptions' in R Okediji (ed.), Copyright Law in an Age of Limitations and Exceptions (Cambridge University Press 2016), ch. 1, 12–59 at 37–42. Note that Wendy J Gordon, 'Fair Use as Market Failure: A Structural and Economic Analysis of the Betamax Case and its Predecessors' (1982) 82 Colum L Rev 1600 sees these factors as cumulative. She indicates that US fair use should come into play where there is (i) market failure, (ii) a public interest that is served and (iii) the incentives of the copyright owner are not substantially impaired.

[79] Gordon (1982), 1635, 1639–40. For a particularly technical assessment of fair use according to economic net efficiency, see William W Fisher III, 'Reconstructing the Fair Use Doctrine' (1988) 101 Harv L Rev 1659, 1705–18, who comments that it is 'hopelessly impractical' in the context of judicial decisions.

However, as was pointed out previously, there are different conceptions of economic harm, including whether it is confined to harm to incentives or harm to the full market value of the work.[80] Professor Bohannan[81] has argued, for example, that harm should be limited 'to foreseeable uses and other harmful uses that are likely to reduce ex ante incentives to create or distribute copyrighted works'.[82] On this approach, there is clearly harm where the alleged infringer has 'copied the work verbatim and supplanted the copyright owner's sales in the intended market'.[83] The situation is more difficult, however, when the harm alleged is a lost licensing fee,[84] and Bohannan's concern is that courts must identify *proof* of harm.[85] She argues that the general, tortious principle of foreseeability should apply so that harm is only presumed where 'the defendant's use usurps the copyright holder's most foreseeable markets, or those markets which a reasonable copyright owner would have taken into account in deciding whether to create or distribute the copyright work'.[86] In all other circumstances, Bohannan argues that 'copyright holders must be required to prove actual harm in order to establish infringement'.[87] On this harm-based approach to fairness, the key factor would be harm to the market for the work and other factors, such as the commercial nature of the use or the amount of the use, would have little weight.

Another difficulty of the above approach to determining 'fair' practice is that the economic or utilitarian justification for copyright has attracted criticism from some commentators[88] and does not align with jurisdictions that

---

[80] See G S Lunney Jr, 'A Tale of Two Copyrights' (February 26, 2020). Available at SSRN: https://ssrn .com/abstract=3544757 or http://dx.doi.org/10.2139/ssrn.3544757 (accessed 10 June 2020). See also Ohly (2018), 111–112, who argues that both harm to incentives and 'unjust enrichment' should be catered for by copyright law.

[81] C Bohannan, 'Copyright Harm, Foreseeability, and Fair Use' (2007) 85 *Washington University L Rev* 969.

[82] Bohannan (2007), 970.

[83] Bohannan (2007), 978.

[84] Bohannan (2007), 978.

[85] Bohannan (2007), 980.

[86] Bohannan (2007), 989.

[87] Bohannan (2007), 989.

[88] See e.g. L J Lacey, 'Of Bread and Roses and Copyright' [1989] *Duke L J* 1532 and P Geller, 'Copyright History and Future: What's Culture Got to Do with It?' (2000) 47 *J Copyright Society of USA* 209, 258; Alfred C Yen, 'Restoring the Natural law: Copyright as Labor and Possession' (1990) 51 *Ohio State L J* 517; N Elkin-Koren and Eli M Salzberger, *The Law and Economics of Intellectual Property in the Digital Age: The limits of analysis* (Routledge 2013), ch. 3. In addition, there is the significant body of empirical literature that suggests non-economic incentives (along with non-legal sanctions or private ordering) operate to ensure creativity and its protection in certain spheres; see the references at fn. 164 (below) and also Jessica Silbey, *The Eureka Myth: Creators, Innovators and Everyday Intellectual Property* (Stanford University Press 2015). See also E Derclaye and T Taylor, 'Happy IP: Replacing the Law and Economics Justification for Intellectual Property Rights with a Well-Being Approach' [2015] *EIPR* 197, and E Derclaye and T Taylor, 'Happy IP: Aligning Intellectual Property Rights with Well-Being' (2015) *IPQ* 1 (arguing that the 'utility' in a utilitarian justification should not be confined to wealth maximisation and should include well-being, as identified by 'markers' derived from different theories of well-being).

conceive of copyright law in terms of natural or human rights.[89] An economic rationale for copyright also ignores what commentators have articulated as the 'communicative' or 'democratic' function of copyright.[90] Also, even if one agrees with an economic or utilitarian rationale, this does not preclude notions of 'fairness' having a broader ambit. According to Professor Weinreb, in the context of US fair use, general notions of fairness should guide the analysis so that, in addition to the four statutory factors, customary practice and the prevailing understanding of fair conduct are also relevant.[91] While acknowledging the limitations of a utilitarian or economic justification for copyright, it would seem unwise to jettison economic harm considerations entirely from a notion of 'fairness'. In part, this is because it would deny the reality of copyright exploitation – economic remuneration of some kind for use of a copyright work (even if the degree can be disputed) – is an expectation of authors and owners and the public. And, as we shall see, a harm-based approach to fairness grounded in natural rights is also consistent with the creator being entitled to monetary reward.

---

[89] P Geller, 'Must Copyright Be For Ever Caught between Marketplace and Authorship Norms?' in Brad Sherman and Alain Strowel (eds.), *Of Authors and Origins* (Clarendon Press 1994), 159–201. There is an oft-cited trope that common law jurisdictions adopt a utilitarian rationale for copyright and civil law systems reflect a natural rights rationale for authors' rights. However, Professor Ginsburg argues that, historically, the differences between civilian author's rights and common law copyright jurisdictions as to the rationale for protection were 'neither as extensive nor as venerable as typically described': J Ginsburg, 'A Tale of Two Copyrights: Literary Property in Revolutionary France and America' (1990) 64 *Tul L Rev* 991, 994. Moreover, we see some common law copyright jurisdictions reflecting a natural rights basis; see Irish Copyright and Related Rights Act 2000 and Ronan Kennedy, 'Was It Author's Rights All the Time?: Copyright as a Constitutional Right in Ireland' (2011) 33 *DULJ* 253.

[90] For example, see Anne Barron, 'Kant, Copyright and Communicative Freedom' (2002) 31 *L & Phil* 1 (arguing that communicative freedom goes beyond individual agency to encompass participation in public discourse); Carys J Craig, *Copyright, Communication and Culture: Towards a Relational Theory of Copyright Law* (Edward Elgar 2011) (copyright as a 'system designed to further the public good by encouraging improved relations of communication between members of society, and maximising discursive engagement in collective conversation' (p. 3) (discussed further at pp. 133–134 above)); Abrahan Drassinower, *What's Wrong with Copying?* (Harvard University Press 2015) (arguing that a copyright work is a communicative *act* and infringement is unauthorised appropriation of another person's speech) (discussed further at p. 133 above); Séverine Dusollier, 'Realigning Economic Rights with Exploitation of Works: The Control of Authors over Circulation of Works in the Public Sphere' in P B Hugenholtz (ed.), *Copyright Reconstructed: Rethinking Copyright's Economic Rights in a Time of Highly Dynamic Technological and Economic Change* (Kluwer 2018), ch. 6 (arguing that the purpose of copyright is to enable authors to circulate their works in the public sphere and that the object of circulation is as a communicative act).

[91] Lloyd L Weinreb, 'Fair's Fair: A Comment on the Fair Use Doctrine' (1990) 103 *Harv L Rev* 1137, 1140, and Lloyd L Weinreb, 'Fair Use' (1999) 67 *Fordham L Rev* 1291, in which he argues that fair use cannot be assessed according to either utilitarian or authors' right justifications because copyright straddles these. Thus, fair use is 'uncabined and inexact' (1310).

A harm-based approach to fairness could be grounded in a natural rights justification for copyright protection.[92] This type of justification can be based on either a Lockean labour theory[93] or Kantian[94] or Hegelian[95] personality theory.

If a Lockean labour justification[96] is relied upon as a natural rights justification instead of a personality based one, how might the approach to 'fair practice' differ? A labour-based approach to copyright views intellectual labour that is mixed with something from the intellectual commons[97] and results in an intangible object as the property of the labourer. The property rights operate as a reward either for the author's intellectual labour or for the contribution that the intangible object makes to society.[98] According to Professor Drahos, it does not necessarily have to lead to strong property rights, particularly when one takes into account the sufficiency and waste provisos.[99] A Lockean approach to fair practice is more likely to focus on economic harm, rather than harm to moral rights interests, because of its focus on rewarding *labour* or the *contribution* of the intangible object. As such, we would expect to see consideration of the commercial nature of the use, the size of the quotation and its proportion to the work from which it has been taken, the nature of the claimant's copyright work and the extent to which the use of quotation harms the market (either actual or potential) for the work.

Particularly according to a personality theory of copyright, one can expect moral rights (i.e. non-economic harm) to be of at least equal importance to economic rights (i.e. economic harm). Thus, as part of a fairness assessment, harm to moral rights would

---

92   The moral justifications of copyright are different from whether the law features transparent moral principles according to Alina Ng, 'Copyright and Moral Norms' (2012–13) 14 *Loy J Pub Int L* 57. Ng argues at p. 80 that 'copyright law must be concerned with the protection of human dignity and the development of a well- functioning society'.

93   P Drahos, *A Philosophy of Intellectual Property* (Dartmouth 1996); Wendy J. Gordon, 'A Property Right in Self-Expression: Equality and Individualism in the Natural Law of Intellectual Property' (1993) 102 *Yale L J* 1533; Justin Hughes, 'The Philosophy of Intellectual Property' (1988) 77 *Georgetown L J* 287. Note that Benjamin G Damstedt, 'Limiting Lock: A Natural Law Justification for the Fair Use Doctrine' (2003) 112 *Yale L J* 1179, 1215–16, argues that US fair use would need to be more expansive in order to align with Lockean principles, in particular the waste prohibition.

94   S Strömholm, 'Droit Moral – The International and Comparative Scene from a Scandinavian Viewpoint' (1983) 14 *IIC* 1.

95   M J Radin, 'Property and Personhood' (1982) 34 *Stanford L Rev* 957.

96   For a general discussion, see R P Merges, *Justifying Intellectual Property* (Harvard University Press 2011), ch. 2, and Drahos (1996), ch. 3.

97   There are, of course, different views as to what forms part of the intellectual commons: W Fisher, 'Theories of Intellectual Property' in S Munzer (ed.), *New Essays in the Legal and Political Theory of Property* (Cambridge University Press 2001), 186.

98   Locke's theory can be used as a consequentialist justification: see Hughes (1988), 303, 305, and B Friedman, 'From Deontology to Dialogue: The Cultural Consequences of Copyright' (1995) 13 *Cardozo Arts & Ent L J* 157, 166–7. However, the standard account is as a natural rights justification: see E C Hettinger, 'Justifying Intellectual Property' (1989) 18 *Philosophy and Public Affairs* 31, 40–1, and S V Shiffrin, 'Lockean Arguments for Private Intellectual Property' in S R Munzer (ed.), *New Essays in the Legal and Political Theory of Property* (Cambridge University Press 2001), 138–67, 148.

99   Drahos (1996), 51–54.

need to feature.[100] As discussed in Chapter 3,[101] it is the case that Article 10(1) does not operate as a mandatory limitation on moral rights so that a quotation could amount to an infringement of, say, the right of integrity. As such, this might make the inclusion of the same considerations in 'fair practice' duplicative. Nevertheless, those legal systems that do not regard moral rights as separate from economic rights – so-called monistic regimes such as Germany and Austria – might not regard that duplication as unnecessary or illogical. Moreover, consideration of integrity interests as part of 'fair practice' may help ensure that conflicting outcomes (i.e. economic rights infringement being exempt under the quotation exception but at the same time infringing the right of integrity) are minimised. Further, it can be argued that moral rights interests as a matter of 'fair practice' and whether a moral right is infringed are related but different matters. When it comes to assessing the scope of an author's integrity right, Article 6*bis* Berne indicates that the minimum standard is an objective test of whether the derogatory action in relation to the work is prejudicial to an author's honour or reputation.[102] Because this is a minimum standard of protection, Union Members may stipulate that the integrity right is infringed according to a subjective test, as is the case in France.[103] Yet the possibility of using a subjective view of integrity as part of a 'fair practice' assessment seems strange for several reasons.

The first is that often a quotation defence will be raised in proceedings between the holder of the economic rights in the work, as opposed to the author of the work, and the user of the work (or defendant). Where the author and the person exercising economic rights in the work are different, it would seem difficult to build in subjective considerations of integrity into a 'fairness' assessment. In addition, if the author is, in fact, the claimant in the litigation, then it is likely the integrity interests would be properly ventilated by a claim for infringement of the integrity right, rather than raised as a factor indicating that a quotation was not fair and thus impermissible. A further reason is that there may be an inherent tension between the practice of quotation and the integrity interests of authors (as is particularly the case for parody[104]). The nature of

---

[100] Ricketson (1999), 66, indicates: 'No explicit mention is made of integrity rights, but it would hardly be consistent with "fair practice" if an author were quoted out of context, inaccurately or the extract was edited in some inappropriate way.' See also Senftleben (2004): 'The moral interests of the quoted author. . .must be strictly observed.'

[101] Chapter 3, Section III, Part B, pp. 57–60, above.

[102] See Ricketson and Ginsburg (2006), [10.23], 603, and [10.27], 606; G Davies and K Garnett (eds.), *Moral Rights* (2nd ed., Sweet and Maxwell 2016), [12-011], 373, explains that French law is far stronger than Berne because under French law 'the author only needs to show that the integrity of the work has been violated, by way of alteration in form or spirit' and there is no need to show prejudice as is the case under Art 6*bis* Berne.

[103] E Adeney, *The Moral Rights of Authors and Performers: An International and Comparative Analysis* (Oxford University Press 2006), [8.65], 182; Davies and Garnett (2010), [12-012], 374.

[104] See e.g. C-210/13 *Deckmyn v. Vandersteen* EU:C:2014:2132 (CJEU, Grand Chamber), [2014] ECDR 21. See also Sabine Jacques, *The Parody Exception in Copyright Law* (Oxford University Press 2019), ch. 6.

quotation, with its capacity to involve differing amounts (including short quotations) and reuse in other works, for a variety of purposes, means that it is likely to tread near to what authors might object to when it comes to use of their works. A means of reconciling this inherent tension between an author's right of integrity and users' ability to quote is to adopt an objective view, focusing on prejudice to the author's honour or reputation, of the impact on the integrity of the work as part of the 'fairness' assessment. Moreover, the effect on the integrity of the work should also be considered a factor relevant to 'fair practice' and not a condition of the quotation exception. Therefore, it will need to be weighed along with other relevant factors when determining 'fair practice'. And where the claimant in the litigation is the owner of economic rights (or the person exercising those economic rights), as opposed to the author of the work, it may be appropriate to give much less weight to harm to integrity interests as part of the 'fairness' assessment. This is because where the claimant is *not* the author, they have much less stake (if any) in the moral rights interests in the work.

An author's divulgation right is a moral right recognised in some Berne Union countries (such as France) but not within Article 6*bis* of the Berne Convention. Divulgation interests, however, are reflected in some of the provisions of Berne, such as in Article 10(1), where there is the condition that the work must have been lawfully made available to the public.[105] Given that divulgation interests are taken care of by this condition, it is argued that whether the work is unpublished or not should be irrelevant to fairness considerations. To consider the published or unpublished nature of a work as part of 'fair practice' would be redundant and overly restrictive. Similarly, given the express requirement in Article 10(3) that mention shall be made of the source and the name of the author, it would be duplicative and unnecessary to consider the absence or presence of attribution as part of the 'fair practice' enquiry.

Thus, in summary, a fair practice assessment in Article 10(1) Berne that took into account moral harm, in the form of protection of personality interests, would focus mainly on the integrity of the work judged according to an objective test, but this would be only a factor – and one that might be given significantly less weight, depending on whether it was the author of the work or the person exercising economic rights in the work that was the claimant.

B *Fair Practice – The Role of Freedom of Expression*

Another approach to 'fair practice' in Article 10(1) is to give content to this concept according to the rationale for the quotation exception[106] – namely that of promoting

---

[105] For a discussion, see Chapter 4, Section II, pp. 71–77, above.

[106] Guibault (2002), 103–4. Interpreting the quotation exception in the light of freedom of expression, i.e. using a fundamental or human right as part of the 'internal' regulation of copyright, does not preclude a role for an 'external' freedom of expression exception at national level: see C Geiger and E Izyumenko, 'The Constitutionalisation of Intellectual Property Law in the EU and the Funke Medien, Pelham and Spiegel Online Decisions of the CJEU: Progress, but Still Some Way to Go!' (2020) 51 *IIC* 282, describing as 'regrettable' the CJEU's 'move to categorically exclude any external

freedom of expression.[107] Freedom of expression (or speech) is recognised as a fundamental right in various instruments, including Article 19 of the International Covenant on Civil and Political Rights, Article 10 of the European Convention of Human Rights and Article 11 of the EU Charter on Fundamental Rights and Freedoms. The protection of freedom of expression springs from various rationales – the need to promote truth, to allow self-fulfilment or self-development, to ensure democratic participation and to avoid state coercion in matters of moral autonomy.[108]

A focus on freedom of expression would entail giving greater attention to the *expressive* nature of the speech involved, including whether the quotation is used as part of commercial, artistic or political expression. The European Court of Human Rights, for example, treats most kinds of speech as coming with Article 10 of the ECHR, but distinguishes between types of speech when it comes to the proportionality analysis and the margin of appreciation (i.e. deference) given to national authorities. The court may give different weight, depending on the category of expression, with political speech and debate on matters of public interest generally afforded the most weight and commercial speech the least.[109] The CJEU has also

---

FoE review of copyright norms' (302). Querying the benefit of a separate or 'external' freedom of expression defence, see P Masiyakurima, 'The Free Speech Benefits of Fair Dealing Defences' in Paul L C Torremans (ed.), *Intellectual Property and Human Rights: Enhanced Edition of Copyright and Human Rights* (Kluwer, 2008), ch. 9, 252–6. Considering how Canadian copyright law might be constitutionally challenged on the basis of the Charter right to freedom of expression, see Graham J Reynolds, 'Reconsidering Copyright's Constitutionality' (2016) 53 *Osgoode Hall Law Journal* 898.

[107]   T Dreier, 'The Wittem Project of a European Copyright Code' in Christopher Geiger (ed.) *Construction European Intellectual Property: Achievements and Perspectives* (Edward Elgar, 2013), ch. 13, 292–313, at 307 (describing the quotation exception in Article 5(3)(d) of the Information Society Directive as a use 'for the purpose of freedom of expression'); Guibault (2002), 32, describing Article 10(1) as 'the only mandatory limitation' under Berne and 'the most important limitation for the safeguard of the user's freedom of expression'; B J Jütte, *Reconstructing European Copyright Law for the Digital Single Market* (Hart/Nomos 2017), 257 (noting that the quotation exception directly implicates freedom of expression); Okediji (2000), 113; Ansgar Ohly, 'European Fundamental Rights and Intellectual Property' in A Ohly and J Pila (eds.), *The Europeanization of Intellectual Property Law: Towards a European Legal Methodology* (Oxford University Press 2013), ch. 8, 156; Senftleben (2004), 28. See also Case C-145/10 *Painer v. Standard Verlags GmbH*, EU:C:2011:239 (Advocate General's Opinion), [186], [190], [196] and [205], Advocate General Trstenjak noting that Art 5(3)(d) Information Society Directive 'serves in particular to realise freedom of opinion and freedom of the press' and Case C-145/10 *Painer v. Standard Verlags GmbH* EU:C:2011:798, [2012] ECDR 6 (CJEU, 3rd Chamber), [135].

[108]   E Barendt, *Freedom of Speech* (2nd ed., Oxford University Press 2005), 6–23. See also *Handyside v UK* (1976) 1 EHRR 737, [49]: 'Freedom of Expression Constitutes One of the Essential Foundations of a Society, One of the Basic Conditions for Its Progress and for the Development of Every Man'.

[109]   See e.g. also *Ashby Donald and others v. France* [2013] App No 36769/08, [39]; *Krone Verlag GmbH & Co KG v. Austria* No. 34315/96 (2003) 36 EHRR 57, [35]; *VgT Verein gegen Tiefabriken v. Switzerland* App No 24699/94 (2002) 34 EHRR 4, [71]; *Nilsen and Johnsen v. Norway* App No. 23118/93 (2000) 30 EHRR 878, [46]. See also A Nicol, G Millar and A Sharland, *Media Law & Human Rights*, 2nd ed (Oxford University Press, 2009), [2.46]; Maya Hertig Randall, 'Commercial Speech under the European Convention on Human Rights: Subordinate or Equal?' (2006) 6 *Human Rights L Rev* 53, although arguing that not all commercial speech should be considered of lower value that political speech; and C R Munro, 'The Value of Commercial Speech' (2003) 62 *Cambridge L J* 134, 138 *et seq.*

indicated the need for the nature of speech to be taken into account, particularly where it is political discourse.[110] Similarly, in the United States, 'core' First Amendment protection is given to political speech (i.e. it is subject to strict scrutiny), whereas commercial speech is subjected to intermediate-level scrutiny,[111] 'a test much less severe than strict scrutiny but harder to satisfy than a "reasonable basis" test. . . . [It] requires the state to show that there is a *substantial* interest to support the restriction, and further that the measure was narrowly tailored to achieve that interest, without disproportionately suppressing speech.'[112]

A 'fair practice' assessment that was attuned to freedom of expression would focus on the nature of the defendant's expression.[113] To take an example, in *Ashdown* v. *Telegraph News*,[114] while the media defendant was a commercial entity and so had commercial motivations for publishing news, the article in which the copyright expression was included (indeed quoted) was political speech, given that it related to discussions about a possible coalition government in the UK. As Professor Griffiths notes, unfortunately the Court of Appeal in *Ashdown* did not give sufficient weight, in assessing the fair dealing exceptions, to the fact that the claimant's copyright work was used as part of the defendant's political expression that had significant public interest.[115] Indeed, Professor Griffiths argues that a failure to appreciate the nature of the defendant's use meant that inappropriate weight was given to factors such as the for-profit activities of the media defendant, the commercial impact on the claimant, the amount that was published and also the unpublished status of the work.

Thus, a fairness assessment that gave prominence to freedom of expression would need to pay close attention to the expressive nature and value of defendant's speech that incorporates quotation from the claimant's work,[116] including whether it is

---

[110]   See Case C-469/17 *Funke Medien NRW GmbH* v. *Bundesrepublik Deutschland* EU:C:2019:623 (CJEU, Grand Chamber), [74]: 'As is clear from the case-law of the European Court of Human Rights, for the purpose of striking a balance between copyright and the right to freedom of expression, that court has, in particular, referred to the need to take into account the fact that the nature of the "speech" or information at issue is of particular importance, inter alia in political discourse and discourse concerning matters of the public interest.' See also Case C-516/17 *Spiegel Online GmbH* v. *Volker Beck* EU:C:2019:625 (CJEU, Grand Chamber), [58].

[111]   Commercial speech was only recognised as within the First Amendment of the US Constitution relatively late: see *Virginia State Board of Pharmacy* v. *Virginia Citizens Consumer Council, Inc*, 425 US 748 (1976). For a discussion of the contested nature of commercial speech under the First Amendment, see R C Post, 'The Constitutional Status of Commercial Speech' (2000) 48 *UCLA L Rev* 1, and David F McGowan, 'A Critical Analysis of Commercial Speech' (1990) 78 *Cal L Rev* 359. For a discussion of the ECHR and US position and the arguments for/against protecting commercial speech, see Barendt (2005), ch. XI.

[112]   Barendt (2005), 51. See also Munro (2003), 135–8.

[113]   See also Adeney (2013), 156, who suggests considering 'whether the use of the quotation furthers the community interest in free speech or the freedom of artistic expression'.

[114]   *Ashdown* v. *Telegraph News* [2002] Ch. 149.

[115]   J Griffiths, 'Copyright Law after *Ashdown* – Time to Deal Fairly with the Public' (2002) 3 *IPQ* 240, 257–8.

[116]   For a similar argument that the parody exception should include an assessment of the expressive value of the speech, see Jacques (2019), 166.

expressive at all.[117] But, here, it should be noted that (i) the different types of speech may not be straightforward to distinguish or may be hybrid[118] and (ii) the fact that commercial expression is protected by the right of free speech is seen as controversial. In relation to the first point, commentators have argued that courts have been inconsistent in how they characterise 'commercial' speech.[119] Moreover, there may be instances of hybrid speech which may make it difficult to characterise the speech interests at stake.[120] On the latter point, some commentators have queried whether the underpinning rationales for freedom of expression can extend to commercial speech, while others have pointed to justifications rooted in personal autonomy and social utility.[121] While there are these difficulties, they should not detract from the usefulness of a freedom of expression perspective as part of a 'fair practice' assessment. First, there is a significant judicial experience and scholarly commentary to draw upon, in order to understand freedom of expression/speech and the value of different types of speech.[122] Second, the fundamental-rights basis of freedom of expression and the fact that it underpins the quotation exception means that it should not be ignored. Third, it is not suggested that freedom of expression would be the sole barometer of 'fair practice'. Other factors (emerging from the harm-based discussion noted previously) would likely remain relevant, but how they are weighted may be affected by taking into account freedom of expression/speech.

Moreover, attention to the freedom of expression rationale behind the exception could necessitate the nature of the claimant's copyright work being taken into account. This is because the expressive interests of a defendant are often weighed against the countervailing interests of the copyright owner. For example, the CJEU

---

[117]   For example, see Dusollier (2018), 177–183 who argues that copyright exploitation should be redefined as using a work for its expressive content and publicly disseminating the work. She argues this from a 'communicative' justification for copyright rather than specifically a freedom of expression basis, although in describing a work as a 'public act of speech initiating a dialogue with the public' (182), this is consistent with a right to freedom of expression. Dusollier adds (at 196) that text and data mining would not infringe under her proposed model because the expressive content of the work is not used and there is no circulation of the work.

[118]   As in *Karatas v. Turkey*, App. No. 23168/94 ECHR 1999-IV, IHRL 2880 (artistic and political poem).

[119]   See Post (2000), 15–25; McGowan (1990), 382–90.

[120]   Although Randall (2006), 72, notes that hybrid cases can be problematic, she also warns against overestimating the quantity of cases in this 'grey zone'. See also Munro (2003), 148–9.

[121]   See Post (2000), 4: 'Commercial speech differs from public discourse because it is constitutionally valued merely for the information it disseminates, rather than for being itself a valuable way of participating in democratic self-determination'; and Barendt (2005), 399–406. Contrast Randall (2006), 79–80, who admits participation in democracy does not justify protection of commercial speech but argues that self-fulfillment justifies protection of political, artistic and commercial speech. See also Munro (2003), 157, arguing that commercial speech enables individuals 'to make improved economic choices' and that the making of these choices is an important part of self-fulfillment personal autonomy. Further that when 'advertising represents the artistic creations of individuals, there is also justification by the same arguments for self-expression as apply to other artistic works'.

[122]   Discussing this judicial experience in a European context, see N A Moreham and Sir M Warby, *Tugendhat and Christie: The Law of Privacy and the Media*, 3rd ed (Oxford University Press, 2016), [11.133]–[11.135]; Jacques (2019), 139–151; Nicol et al. (2009), ch. 2.

has remarked on several occasions that there must occur a 'fair balance' between the rights holder's fundamental right to intellectual property as enshrined in the EU Charter of Fundamental Rights of the European Union 2000, Article 17(2) and the user's right to freedom of expression in Article 11.[123] While this necessitates interrogating the speech interest at stake,[124] it could also entail assessing the nature of the copyright work – whether it is expressive or factual or reflects a high degree of author's intellectual creativity[125] – in order to evaluate the weight of the countervailing (intellectual) property interest.

C *Fair Practice – The Role of Distributive Justice*

The reference to *fair* practice potentially invokes notions of distributive justice – that is, the fair allocation and reallocation of resources in society. In the copyright literature, distributive justice theories have not featured significantly and have been overshadowed by utilitarian, economic and natural rights perspectives on copyright. There is, however, a small but emerging body of scholarship that engages with intellectual property, including copyright, and distributive justice. Broadly speaking, commentators have considered distributive justice theories as either a justification for copyright protection or as a tool for reshaping copyright principles. In other words, they have grappled with the question of fairness *of* copyright versus fairness *within* the institution of copyright.[126]

When it comes to assessing the fairness of copyright, commentators usually draw upon Rawls's theory of justice,[127] not least because the theory is compatible with

---

[123] Case C-476/17 *Pelham GmbH* v. *Hütter* EU:C:2019:624 (CJEU, Grand Chamber), [35]; Case C-516/17 *Spiegel Online GmbH* v. *Volker Beck* EU:C:2019:625 (CJEU, Grand Chamber), [54]; Case C-469/17 *Funke Medien NRW GmbH* v. *Bundesrepublik Deutschland* EU:C:2019:623 (CJEU, Grand Chamber), [70]–[74]. For a discussion of the significance of these rulings in relation to freedom of expression and copyright, see Geiger and Izyumenko (2020). For a more general consideration of copyright as a fundamental or human right, see Paul L C Torremans, 'Copyright (and Other Intellectual Property Rights) as a Human Right' in Paul L C Torremans (ed.) *Intellectual Property and Human Rights: Enhanced Edition of Copyright and Human Rights* (Kluwer, 2008), ch. 7, and the interaction of freedom of expression with copyright, see D Voorhoof, 'Freedom of Expression and the Right to Information: Implications for Copyright' in C Geiger (ed.) *Research Handbook on Human Rights and Intellectual Property* (Edward Elgar, 2015), ch. 17, 331–53.

[124] See Case C-469/17 *Funke Medien NRW GmbH* v. *Bundesrepublik Deutschland* EU:C:2019:623 (CJEU, Grand Chamber), [74] ('As is clear from the case-law of the European Court of Human Rights, for the purpose of striking a balance between copyright and the right to freedom of expression, that court has, in particular, referred to the need to take into account the fact that the nature of the 'speech' or information at issue is of particular importance, inter alia in political discourse and discourse concerning matters of the public interest').

[125] Arguing this in a UK context, see Griffiths (2002), 250–60.

[126] Robert P Merges, *Justifying Intellectual Property* (Harvard University Press 2011), ch. 4, 102–3.

[127] See Merges (2011); Deming Liu, 'Copyright and the Pursuit of Justice: A Rawlsian Analysis' (2012) 32 *Legal Studies* 600; Drahos (1996), ch. 8; Schlomit Yanisky-Ravid, 'The Hidden though Flourishing Justification of Intellectual Property Laws: Distributive Justice, National Versus International Approaches' (2017) 21 *Lewis & Clark L Rev* 1.

property rights.[128] Rawlsian justice refers to two key principles: the first is the liberty principle – that is, the notion that 'each person is to have an equal right to the most extensive total system of basic liberties compatible with a similar system of liberty for all'. The second is the difference principle, wherein 'social and economic inequalities are to be arranged so that they are both: (a) to the greatest benefit of the least advantaged . . . and (b) attached to offices and positions open to all under conditions of fair equality of opportunity'.[129] In relation to the first principle, Professor Merges argues that 'creative freedom and autonomy are important enough values that they should join the list of essential liberties'.[130] In addition, Professor Merges argues that intellectual property rights are justifiable forms of inequality because they provide 'significant benefits to the least advantaged'.[131] In relation to copyright, specifically, Merges, along with Professor Hughes, observes

> if copyright gives incentives for the production of music, literature, and audiovisual works that improve the lives of all or almost all (free broadcast television entertainment, free broadcast radio entertainment, libraries, etc) then even if the copyright law causes some concentration of income and wealth among creators and copyright owners, this may be justified as inequalities that make better-off the least advantaged citizens.[132]

Professors Hughes and Merges make the further claim that the copyright system provides an effective tool to allow certain disadvantaged groups, in particular African Americans, a fair equality of opportunity when it comes to accumulation of wealth.[133] Not everyone, however, agrees with a distributive justice rationale for copyright. Professor Kapczynski, for example, argues that there should be more emphasis on intellectual property alternatives, such as commons-based production and government rewards.[134] She describes the problem with intellectual property as rationing access 'via the price mechanism . . . so it distributes resources in a way that is sensitive to the background allocation of resources', which themselves may be unjust.[135] Further, any attempt to loosen exceptions leads to the paradox that while the disadvantaged might have more access, less is likely to be created.[136]

---

[128]   Merges (2011), 105; Drahos (1996), 173. Justin Hughes and Robert P Merges, 'Copyright and Distributive Justice' (2016) 92 *Notre Dame L Rev* 513.
[129]   John Rawls, *A Theory of Justice* (rev. ed., Oxford University Press 1999), 53.
[130]   Merges (2011), 112. In addition, Merges argues at 103 that the 'rules and doctrines that reflect third-party interests and general fairness in the scope and impact of particular IP rights – go a long way toward justifying IP institutions as a whole'.
[131]   Merges (2011), 117. See also Drahos (1996), 177.
[132]   Hughes and Merges (2016), 528.
[133]   Hughes and Merges (2016), 547 *et seq.*
[134]   A Kapczynski, 'The Cost of Price: Why and How to Get beyond Intellectual Property Internalism' (2012) 59 *UCLA L Rev* 970.
[135]   Kapczynski (2012), 996.
[136]   Kapczynski (2012), 997.

Another focus of the literature is fairness *within* copyright (i.e. the potential for distributive justice to influence the shape of copyright principles). Commentators have adopted both international and national perspectives in this regard. Professor Chon has written extensively about how global intellectual property law-making needs to be tied to distributive justice principles. In particular, she argues for a 'substantive equality principle ... in global IP norm-setting and norm-interpreting activities in order to facilitate access to essential information goods'.[137] In part, support for this substantive equality norm is embedded with the term 'development' referenced in the preamble to TRIPS[138] and, in turn, incorporated into domestic law.[139] This principle would lead *inter alia* to a 'heightened embrace, as opposed to suspicion, of various exceptions and limitations' expressed in international conventions and would ensure copyright norms are more responsive 'to the differently situated development concerns of various countries' in relation to educational materials.[140] This would lead to a principle of strict scrutiny of international provisions, such as TRIPS, to ensure that basic needs, such as capability for basic education, are served. Professor Yanisky-Ravid argues that international copyright law has begun to embody distributive justice principles and points to the Marrakesh Treaty[141] as such an example.[142]

At the national level, various commentators have suggested reforms to copyright laws in order to better reflect distributive justice concerns. Professor Shaver, for example, is very much troubled by the inability of the poor in developing countries to access copyright works. She argues that copyright makes cultural works more expensive and tends to serve dominant language markets.[143] As such, she proposes that copyright law should be reshaped to address this distributive concern and makes various suggestions: extending the first sale doctrine to ebooks; opposing further extensions of copyright term; and adjusting fair use to recognise the transformative nature of translations, particularly for neglected languages.[144] In the context of Australian copyright law, Professors Elmahjub and Suzor have argued that distributive justice considerations have greater potential to affect copyright at the national,

---

137 M Chon, 'Intellectual Property "from Below": Copyright and Capability for Education' (2007) 40 *UC Davis L Rev* 803, 834. See also M Chon, 'Intellectual Property and the Development Divide' (2006) *Cardozo L Rev* 2821, and M Chon, 'Intellectual Property Equality' (2010) 9 *Seattle Journal for Social Justice* 259.

138 Chon (2006), 2901.

139 Chon (2006), 2906.

140 Chon (2007), 834. For a more detailed exposition of how such a substantive equality principle would work, see Chon (2006), 2907–9.

141 Marrakesh Treaty to Facilitate Access to Published Works for Persons Who Are Blind, Visually Impaired or Otherwise Print Disabled, 27 June 2013.

142 Yanisky-Ravid (2017), 29–31. Although querying the ability of the Marrakesh Treaty to improve access to print works by visually impaired persons in developing countries in the Middle East see Rami Olwan, 'The Ratification and Implementation of the Marrakesh Treaty for Visually Impaired Persons in the Arab Gulf States' (2017) 20 *J World Intell Prop* 178.

143 L Shaver, 'Copyright and Inequality' (2014) 92 *Washington University L Rev* 117, 135–6.

144 Shaver (2014), 155 *et seq.*

rather than international, level, particularly when utilitarian logic has led to a policy or political impasse. They argue that a distributive justice perspective supports viewing copyright exceptions and limitations as positive user rights along with the introduction of fair use into Australian copyright law.[145]

Professor Van Houweling has noted the positive distributive impacts of copyright. Copyright can indirectly subsidise would-be creators; the fair use exception allows poorly financed creators to build on pre-existing works; and copyright 'has not, until recently, been enforced frequently against those infringers who are unlikely to be able to pay for their uses of copyrighted works'.[146] However, Professor van Houweling argues that technological developments have changed these distributive impacts. While new technology is 'a boon for creativity and for the broad distribution of creative opportunities' it creates 'the threat of copyright enforcement ... for a class of creators who have traditionally been spared copyright's burdens'.[147] In order to respond to these changes, Professor Van Houweling argues for changes to the fair use analysis that would see a presumption of fair use arise where a creator is reusing a copyright work without exploiting the monetary benefits of copyright,[148] which could be defeated 'where it is shown that the defendant's use competes with the plaintiff's commercial exploitation of her work and undermines her market'.[149] In addition, ability to pay would be taken into account in the fairness assessment (i.e. 'avoiding unaffordable license fees could be considered a valid "purpose" of unauthorized copying').[150]

Professors Bracha and Syed consider the normative criteria for determining which types of users warrant distributive priority.[151] They also argue that targeted measures benefiting priority groups, rather than general rules or policy, are required. In examining lower-income users, they note that a possibility is 'directly factoring in the defendant's income as relevant to fair-use analysis, not only for follow-on creative uses but also for purely private, consumptive copying'.[152] Professor Lunney meanwhile imagines what should happen in a world where machine learning and algorithmic

---

[145] E Elmahjub and N Suzor, 'Fair Use and Fairness in Copyright: A Distributive Justice Perspective on Users' Rights' (2017) 43 *Monash U L Rev* 274.

[146] Molly Shafer Van Houweling, 'Distributive Values in Copyright' (2005) 83 *Texas L Rev* 1535, 1540.

[147] Van Houweling (2005), 1564.

[148] This is a distinct definition of non-commercial use. Arguing along similar lines, see Jessica Litman, 'Lawful Personal Use' (2007) 85 *Texas L Rev* 1871.

[149] Van Houweling (2005), 1567. But a market for permission to reuse would not defeat a fair use exception. Shubha Ghosh, 'The Merits of Ownership; Or How I Learned to Stop Worrying and Love Intellectual Property. Review Essay of Lawrence Lessig, *The Future of Ideas*, and Siva Vaidhyanathan, *Copyrights and Copywrongs*' (2002) 15 *Harv J L & Tech* 453, 494, argues that, in order to account for distributive justice, a fair use claim should require a showing of actual harm to a potential market in order for it to fail.

[150] Van Houweling (2005), 1569.

[151] O Bracha and T Syed, 'Beyond Efficiency: Consequence-Sensitive Theories of Copyright' (2014) 29 *Berkeley Tech L J* 229.

[152] Bracha and Syed (2014), 308.

pricing allows for perfect price discrimination.[153] In particular, he considers whether the copyright owner should be permitted to capture the full market value of the work or only that value that represents the persuasion cost for authoring and distributing a work. He observes that while both options are neutral from an efficiency perspective and so are 'costless', the distributional impacts (whether producer or consumer surplus) do matter. He argues that the surplus should be shared amongst the many (i.e. consumers) rather than concentrated in the hands of the few (i.e. authors and producers), so that this should usually point to a regime of costless copyright minimalism – that is, allowing capture only of the incentives needed to create and disseminate the work.

Opposition to the integration of distributive justice principles within copyright law comes from Professor Benoliel, who prefers an economic approach.[154] His argument is that a more efficient form of redistribution of resources occurs through taxation and welfare law, rather than private law. Copyright law, on the other hand, only benefits 'small fractions of the population', depending on when disputes arise, and requires 'the status of parties to litigation ... to correspond to those groups that should benefit from redistribution'.[155] This, however, misses the point. As Professors Bracha and Syed argue, the distributive concerns are not general concerns but ones linked to the distributive impacts of copyright.[156] In addition, Professor Benoliel underplays the impact that litigation outcomes have on wider groups of users, namely, the fact that they can inform user behaviour.[157]

What does all this mean for *fair* practice in Article 10(1) of Berne? Distributive justice is unlikely to be the sole gauge of fairness, but an interpretation sensitive to these concerns may provide some guidance and thus should be embraced. As such, fair practice would need to take into account the distributional impacts of copyright on certain types of users. Although quotation may be for *any* purpose, it may be that fair quotation for some purposes, such as education, access to works for the visually or aurally impaired, or access to works for the illiterate, could be given more weight. Moreover, a user's ability to pay could be a relevant factor to consider, along with the non-commercial nature of the quotation.

---

[153] Lunney (2020). See also J E Cohen, 'Copyright and the Perfect Curve' (2000) 53 *Vand L Rev* 1799 (challenging the view that a move to perfect price discrimination is value-neutral).

[154] D Benoliel, 'Copyright Distributive Justice' (2007) 10 *Yale J L & Tech* 45.

[155] Benoliel (2007), 72.

[156] Bracha and Syed (2014), 289.

[157] Consider, for example, the decision in *Bridgeport Music* v. *Dimension Films* 410 F 3d 792 (6th Circuit), which found that the *de minimis* principle did not apply to samples, so that a two second sample of an arpeggiated chord played on guitar, taken from the musical composition and sound recording 'Get Off Your Ass and Jam', was held to be an infringement. McLeod and Dicola suggest that this decision contributed to the practice of licensing samples and an aversion to relying on de minimis copying or fair use. See K McLeod and P Dicola, *Creative License: The Law and Culture of Digital Sampling* (Duke University Press 2011).

D *Fair Practice – The Role of Custom*

The deliberate use of the term fair *practice*, in contrast to fair *use* or *dealing*, in Article 10(1) Berne and its initial linking to trade norms, as revealed by the *travaux*, suggest that sectoral norms or customs could be relevant when considering fairness. In addition, when looking at the French version of Article 10(1), which refers to 'bons usages', it is arguable that this is a mixture of fair and common practice.[158]

As we shall see, however, the understanding and role of custom and norms are contested and potentially problematic in this sphere. At best, customs or norms of quotation *might* be useful in determining fair practice but only *if* the basis and scope of these are interrogated fully.

Starting with custom, Professors Kadens and Young have demonstrated that 'the history of customary law indicates a longstanding struggle to find a cogent and functional definition of custom'.[159] One understanding relates to customary law or binding custom.[160] A further understanding is that of customary international law – that is, where there is a general and consistent practice of states derived from a sense of legal obligation.[161] Linked to this question of definition is whether custom may itself be considered *as* law. By way of contrast, the literature examining norms points to social norms, as distinct from law,[162] indeed substituting for law, and emphasises that social norms are enforced through social (as opposed to state or legal) sanction.[163] Scholars have also examined why social norms emerge, suggesting reputational or esteem effects, as well as repeat and coordination games.[164]

---

[158]   André R Bertrand, *Droit d'auteur* 3rd ed (Dalloz 2010).

[159]   E Kadens and E A Young, 'How Customary Is Customary International Law?' (2013) 54 *Wm & Mary L Rev* 885, 906.

[160]   Kadens and Young (2013).

[161]   Ryan M Scoville, 'Finding Customary International Law' (2016) 101 *Iowa L Rev* 1893, 1895.

[162]   Robert D Cooter, 'Three Effects of Social Norms on Law: Expression, Deterrence and Internationalisation' (2000) 79 *Oregon L Rev* 1.

[163]   Cass R Sunstein, 'Social Norms and Social Roles' (1996) 96 *Colum L Rev* 903, 915; Robert C Ellickson, 'Of Coase and Cattle: Dispute Resolution among Neighbors in Shasta County' (1985–1986) 38 *Stan. L Rev* 623; Robert C Ellickson, *Order without Law: How Neighbours Settle Disputes* (Harvard University Press 1991); Robert C Ellickson, 'The Evolution of Social Norms: A Perspective from the Legal Academy' 1 July 1999, Yale Law School Working Paper No. 230, available at https://ssrn.com/abstract=191392 or http://dx.doi.org/10.2139/ssrn.191392 (accessed 28 January 2020); Richard H McAdams, 'The Origin, Development and Regulation of Norms' (1998) 96 *Mich L R* 338, 340; Barak D Richman, 'Norms and Law: Putting the Horse before the Cart' (2012) 62 *Duke L J* 739, 745, 748–9. Richman distinguishes social norms from the 'law's shadow', which he describes as 'the broad space in which parties understand the possibility of legal coercion' (744) and where 'the state ultimately secures transactional credibility' (749).

[164]   See e.g. Eric A Posner, 'Standards, Rules, and Social Norms' (1997) 21 *Harv J L Public Pol'y* 101 (theorising that it is repeat games and signaling or coordination games); Richard H McAdams, 'The Origin, Development and Regulation of Norms' (1998) 96 *Mich L R* 338 (discussing that norms emerge because people seek the esteem of others); and Robert C Ellickson, 'Of Coase and Cattle: Dispute Resolution among Neighbors in Shasta County' (1986) 38 *Stan L Rev* 623, 628 (discussing that informal norms emerge because transaction

Therefore, it seems that the key difference between custom and norms is that the former is treated *as* law, whereas the latter operates *instead* of or alongside law.

The intellectual property literature discusses the role of both custom[165] and norms,[166] although does not always clearly distinguish between the two. For example, Professor Rothman, who was written extensively on the role of custom in copyright law, refers to 'custom' as an umbrella term including both industry practice and norms.[167] Professor Rosenblatt refers to customs and norms interchangeably.[168] By way of contrast, Professors Elkin-Koren and Fischman-Afori distinguish between norms and customs because they describe codes of 'Best Practice' in the fair use context as norms or a normative stance and are at pains to emphasise they are *not* a custom.[169] Similarly, scholars who have conducted empirical investigations of communities of creators, such as French chefs, stand-up comedians, graffiti artists and drag queens, identify their findings as social norms with social sanctions (and as part of the 'law and norms scholarships') and do not stray into the language of 'custom'.[170] Noting the differing degrees of terminological precision surrounding custom and norms in copyright law, we turn now to examine

costs are high). Cooter (2000), 21 notes that 'social norms have the advantages of flexibility and low transaction costs'. Sunstein (1996) refers to the reputational effects of complying or violating norms (915, 967). Barak D Richman, 'Norms and Law: Putting the Horse Before the Cart' (2012) 62 *Duke L J* 739, 764, refers to reputation mechanisms as a key feature of private enforcement but notes that it is only effective for those who place value in maintaining a good reputation.

[165] See e.g. J E Rothman, 'The Questionable Use of Custom in Intellectual Property' (2007) 93 *Va L Rev* 1899; J E Rothman, 'Custom, Comedy and the Value of Dissent' (2009) 95 *Va L Rev Brief* 19; J E Rothman, 'Why Custom Cannot Save Copyright's Fair Use Defense' (2007) 93 *Va L Rev Brief* 243; Richard A Epstein, 'Some Reflections on Custom in the IP Universe' (2008) 93 *Va L Rev Brief* 223; Thomas Field, 'From Custom to Law in Copyright' (2008) 49 *IDEA* 125; Stephen L Carter, 'Custom, Adjudication and Petrushevsky's Watch: Some Notes from the Intellectual Property Front' (1992) 78 *Va L Rev* 129; Harry N Rosenfield, 'Customary Use as "Fair Use" in Copyright Law' (1975) 25 *Buff L Rev* 119.

[166] D Oliar and C Sprigman, 'There's No Free Laugh (Anymore): The Emergence of Intellectual Property Norms and the Transformation of Stand-Up Comedy' (2009) 94(8) *Va L Rev* 1787; E Fauchart and E von Hippel, 'Norms-Based Intellectual Property Systems: The Case of French Chefs' (2008) 19(2) *Organization Science* 187; E L Rosenblatt, 'A Theory of IP's Negative Space' (2011) *Columbia Journal of Law and the Arts* 317.

[167] Rothman (2007), 1905–6.

[168] Rosenblatt (2011), 340.

[169] N Elkin-Koren and O Fischman-Afori, 'Taking Users' Rights to the Next Level: A Pragmatist Approach to Fair Use' (2015) 33 *Cardozo Arts & Ent L J* 1, 21.

[170] Fauchart and von Hippel (2008); Oliar and Sprigman, (2009); M Iljadica, *Copyright Beyond Law: Regulating Creativity in the Graffiti Subculture* (Hart 2016), 56 *et seq*, and E Sarid, 'Don't Be a Drag, Just Be a Queen – How Drag Queens Protect their Intellectual Property without Law' (2014) 10 *FIU L Rev* 133. Although note that Rothman describes these norms as custom – see Rothman, (2009).

the advantages and disadvantages of utilising norms or custom in a 'fair practice' analysis for Article 10(1) Berne.

Scholars have advocated the use of codes of best practice in applying or assessing fair use, in US and Israeli copyright law. Professors Aufederheide and Jaszi in their book *Reclaiming Fair Use*[171] describe best practice projects – that is, 'the creation of codes of best practice in fair use that provide consensus interpretation targeted to particular communities of practice'.[172] They utilise the 'story of how filmmakers got their code of best practice' to show 'the challenges and opportunities of this approach'[173] and detail how other communities in the United States develop codes of best practice. The book includes practical advice[174] on how to go about developing a code of best of practice and a template for such a code.[175] The authors see the benefit of developing such codes of best practice as empowering users through making fair use more usable and understandable and, in turn, combating the overprotection of copyright owners.[176] In other words, the focus of the codes is on enabling copyright users as opposed to influencing courts and lawmakers about what is 'fair' use.

Professors Dotan, Elkin-Koren, Fischman-Afori and Haramati-Alpern have published an account of how they developed a code of Fair Use Best Practices in the Higher Education sector in Israel.[177] This was in reaction to the introduction of the fair use exception in Israeli copyright law in 2007 and the high degree of uncertainty associated with this doctrine. The rationale of the project was to create a shared understanding of fair use for higher education that would create more certainty and, in turn, reduce the chilling effect on educational use.[178] The hope was that academic institutions would adopt and implement the code.[179] A further hope was that if academic institutions engaged in less risk-averse conduct (i.e. by not acquiring a licence when this was unnecessary), this practice might influence how courts perceive the impact of the use on the market.[180] Thus, in contrast to Professors Aufederheide and Jaszi, these scholars see codes of best practice as both an enabling mechanism for copyright users and a potential influence on the judiciary.

Professors Elkin-Koren and Fischman-Afori have further developed their argument that codes of best practices can and should inform courts. They argue that 'bottom-up guidelines developed by the community are a relevant factor that courts

[171] P Aufderheide and P Jaszi, *Reclaiming Fair Use: How to Put Balance Back in Copyright* (University of Chicago Press 2011) and (2nd ed., University of Chicago Press 2018).

[172] Aufderheide and Jaszi (2018), 102.

[173] Aufderheide and Jaszi (2018), 102.

[174] Aufderheide and Jaszi (2018), ch. 9.

[175] Aufderheide and Jaszi (2011), app. B.

[176] Aufderheide and Jaszi (2018), intro.

[177] A Dotan, N Elkin-Koren, O Fischman-Afori, R Haramati-Alpern, 'Fair Use Best Practices for Higher Education Institutions: The Israeli Experience' (2010) 57 *J Copyright Soc'y USA* 447.

[178] Dotan et al (2010), 454.

[179] Dotan et al (2010), 470.

[180] Dotan et al (2010), 454.

should take into account when determining the scope of fair use'.[181] More particularly, they argue that codes of fair use best practices offer

> courts several indicators for applying the multifactor analysis. They signal concrete needs of unlicensed use of copyrighted works in particular creative contexts; they inform the courts of what might be considered normative conduct under the circumstances; and finally, *they may describe the customary conduct in a particular field of practice*, thus influencing, though not dictating, the reasonable benchmark at stake.[182]

While Professors Elkin-Koren and Fischman-Afori are at pains to say that Fair Use Best Practices are *not* a custom because they 'do not reflect how users actually behave' but 'reflect a *normative stance*, how people ought to behave',[183] the previously provided quotation recognises that such codes may, in fact, describe 'customary conduct in a particular field of practice'. The authors also indicate that such codes should be relevant, but not determinative, of fair use.

By way of contrast, Professor Crews heavily criticises the use of custom to inform fair use analysis.[184] He particularly targets early fair use guidelines, such as the Classroom Guidelines, the CONTU Guidelines and the Guidelines emerging from CONFU. He classifies these into three categories: (i) privately developed guidelines that have a congressional imprimatur, (ii) guidelines developed by a governmental commission and (iii) privately developed guidelines that have the endorsement of administrative agencies.[185] In reviewing how the courts have dealt with these guidelines, Professor Crews argues that 'courts have stretched application of the guidelines not to find a foundation for a ruling, but instead to reinforce a ruling already reached'.[186] Overall, he is highly dubious about the role of fair use guidelines and observes that the guidelines are not law, reflect a minimalistic view of fair use and risk fixing understandings of fair use and undermining its flexibility.[187] Professor Crews concludes that '[t]he guidelines have become a convenient distraction from the responsibility of copyright owners, users, courts, and even Congress to work with the law itself' and that it is rights holders who have an interest in advocating the guidelines.[188] This is not to say that guidelines are necessarily useless or flawed. They can be useful if they are properly reflective of the law on fair use,

---

[181] N Elkin-Koren and O Fischman-Afori, 'Taking Users' Rights to the Next Level: A Pragmatist Approach to Fair Use' (2015) 33 *Cardozo Arts & Ent L J* 1, 22.

[182] Elkin-Koren and Fischman-Afori (2015), 29 (emphasis added).

[183] Elkin-Koren and Fischman-Afori (2015), 21 (emphasis original).

[184] K D Crews, 'The Law of Fair Use and the Illusion of Fair Use Guidelines' (2001) 62 *Ohio St L J* 599. See also Stephen L Carter, 'Custom, Adjudication and Petrushevsky's Watch: Some Notes from the Intellectual Property Front' (1992) 78 *Va L Rev* 129, 131–2, who queries whether customs are efficient and whether they can be adjudicated by courts.

[185] Crews (2001), 635–6.

[186] Crews (2001), 662, 693.

[187] Crews (2001), 692–3.

[188] Crews (2001), 694.

flexible in nature, reflect independent development and only attract the support of
government agencies where there has been an appropriate debate and transparency
in their development.[189]

Another vocal opponent of custom informing (judicial) analysis of fair use is
Professor Rothman. In her work, she examines litigation avoidance customs and
normative and aspirational customs.[190] The former are aimed at creating greater
certainty in the face of unpredictable litigation outcomes, and examples include
licensing practices (or the 'clearance culture'), agreed-upon guidelines, in-house
guidelines and best practice statements or codes.[191] The latter refer to customary
practices and norms that emerge in situations where communities believe intellectual property law has a minimal role or disavow enforcement of intellectual property. Examples include how chefs use and share recipes, social norms in cyberspace,
university IP policies and the open-source and free software movements.[192]

Professor Rothman's scholarship[193] is particularly critical of courts' use of custom to determine what is 'fair'. She points out that courts make use of custom in the
fair use analysis in different ways – 'as a proxy for market effects and the commercial or non-commercial character of a use',[194] 'to evaluate what reasonable uses or
behaviours are'[195] and to assess what is 'fair'.[196] Professor Rothman argues that
reliance on custom, in the form of licensing practices, to evaluate market harm for
the purposes of determining fair use is circular.[197] In addition, she views using
custom to evaluate 'fairness' as disadvantageous because of its tendency to be
treated as a ceiling rather than a floor, in effect narrowing fair use.[198] Further,
she expresses concern at the potential unrepresentativeness of customs in the
copyright sphere, which undermines their optimality.[199] In Professor Rothman's
view, there *can* be a role for custom to play but it must be measured against
a framework of factors: 'the certainty of the custom, the motivation for the custom,
the representativeness of the custom, how the custom is applied (both against
whom and for what proposition), and the implications of the custom's

---

[189]   Crews (2001), 698–9.
[190]   J E Rothman, 'The Questionable Use of Custom in Intellectual Property' (2007) 93 *Va L Rev* 1899,
        1905–6.
[191]   Rothman (2007), 1909–24.
[192]   Rothman (2007), 1924–30.
[193]   See also J E Rothman, 'Best Intentions: Reconsidering Best Practices Statements in the Context of
        Fair Use and Copyright Law' (2010) 57 *J Copyright Soc'y USA* 371, and J E Rothman, 'Custom,
        Comedy, and the Value of Dissent' (2009) 95 *Va L Rev Brief* 19.
[194]   Rothman (2007), 1932.
[195]   Rothman (2007), 1941.
[196]   Rothman (2007), 1937.
[197]   'The circularity concern arises because the existence of a licensing market for a work depends entirely
        on a court determination of whether a given use is fair or not. If a use is fair, there will be no licensing
        market, and if a use is not fair, a licensing market will develop': Rothman (2007), 1933–4.
[198]   Rothman (2007), 1940.
[199]   Rothman (2010), 384.

adoption'.[200] Thus, customs that are 'uniformly recognised and supported', formulated as an 'aspirational set of practices' rather than as litigation avoidance techniques, are developed 'with a diverse representation of interests' and applied to those who participated in the custom generation or were represented in that process, should be given more weight.[201]

In response to Professor Rothman's article, Professor Epstein agrees that dubious customs can unduly narrow the fair use defence. However, he disagrees with Professor Rothman insofar as he argues that there are useful customs, such as the Classroom Guidelines, which provide 'an intelligible safe harbour ... [reducing] uncertainty and [saving] administrative costs'.[202] In response, Professor Rothman challenges the potential for industry to develop optimal rules and clarifies that while copyright guidelines might be a good idea, 'such guidelines should not lead courts to bind parties who did not develop or agree to them'.[203]

The concerns that custom may inaccurately describe the legal principles or may conservatively indicate a 'floor' and, as such, constrain what is regarded as 'fair' is reflected in some of the guidelines relating to quotation. For example, the 2016 'Guidelines for Quotation and other Academic Uses of Excerpts from Journal Articles', issued by the International Association of Scientific, Technical and Medical Publishers (STM) and the Professional Scholarly & Publishing Division of the Association of American Publishers (PSP), stipulate conservative guidance about permissible quotation, frequently emphasising that only 'short' quotations in scholarship are acceptable. The Guidelines indicate that, in relation to journal articles, only use of single text extracts of less than one hundred words or a series of text extracts totalling less than three hundred words is permissible quotation where the purpose is scholarly comment, non-commercial research or educational use.[204] Individual publishers have adopted these guidelines as a framework.[205] Sometimes publishers have gone beyond the STM and PSP Guidelines, but only marginally. For example, Wiley[206] indicates that permission is 'required for single quotations over 400 words or multiple quotations from the same source that cumulatively total more than 800 words'. Similarly, the Society of Biblical Literature

[200] Rothman (2007), 1908.
[201] Rothman (2007), 1908. See also 1967 *et seq.*
[202] Richard A Epstein, 'Some Reflections on Custom in the IP Universe' (2008) 93 *Va L Rev Brief* 223, 228.
[203] J E Rothman 'Why Custom Cannot Save Copyright's Fair Use Defense' (2008) 93 *Va L Rev Brief* 243, 248.
[204] www.stm-assoc.org/2016_01_05_Guidelines_for_Quotation_From_Journal_Articles.pdf (accessed 28 January 2020).
[205] AIP Publishing, American Chemical Society, BMJ Publishing Group Ltd, Cambridge University Press, Elsevier, Institute of Physics, International Union of Crystallography, John Wiley & Sons (including Blackwell), Oxford University Press journals, Portland Press Limited, Royal Society of Chemistry, SAGE Publications, Springer Science + Business Media, Taylor & Francis.
[206] https://authorservices.wiley.com/asset/book-author-documents.html/Permissions_Guidelines_Full .pdf (accessed 28 January 2020).

recommends that in relation to prose selection from books it is permissible to use 'up to 10% or a total of 1,000 words in the aggregate, whichever is less' and for articles 'up to 10% or 250 words in the aggregate, whichever is less'.[207] CENGAGE, an education and technology company, advises its authors that '[i]f several short, non-consecutive quotations from one source add up to more than 300 words all together, you must apply for and receive written permission'.[208]

For some publishers, rather than adopt the prescriptive STM or PSP Guidelines, their guidance is open-ended and leaves the risk and judgment of obtaining permission with the user. For example, Harvard University Press indicates that permission is not required where there is fair use and provides links to generic guidance on fair use factors to help users assess whether their use falls within the scope of the exception.[209] Wolters Kluwer takes a similar approach,[210] as does Edward Elgar, which indicates that '[f]air dealing covers text reproduced for the purposes of criticism, review, non-commercial research or the reporting of current events'.[211] Meanwhile, guidance provided on UK copyright law by the UK Copyright Service,[212] the Office of Scholarly Communications, Cambridge University Libraries[213] and Joint Information Systems Committee (UK) (JISC)[214] tends to emphasise that the purpose of the use must be criticism or review, the use of the material quoted must be accompanied by actual discussion or comment, and only a portion of the work will be used. Again, such guidance does not reflect the full, potential breadth of the quotation exception. In relation to the UK Publishers Association, Professor Deazley has commented that their Permission Guidelines[215] 'interpret the existing exceptions far more narrowly than it needs to' and that authors are usually made responsible for securing the relevant permissions.[216] The way the quotation exception is depicted in their Permission Guidelines is as a new exception where the scope has not yet been interpreted by the courts and where obtaining legal advice or a licence from the rights holder is recommended.[217]

---

[207] www.sbl-site.org/publications/publishing_fairuse.aspx (accessed 28 January 2020).

[208] https://college.cengage.com/reviewers_authors/ra_author_guidelines_part03.html (accessed 9 June 2020).

[209] www.hup.harvard.edu/rights/permissions-frequently-asked-questions.html#before-applying (accessed 28 January 2020).

[210] https://lrus.wolterskluwer.com/policies/faqs-permissions-reprints-and-licensing-services/ (accessed 28 January 2020).

[211] www.e-elgar.com/resources/rights-permissions (accessed 28 January 2020).

[212] www.copyrightservice.co.uk/copyright/p27_work_of_others (accessed 28 January 2020).

[213] https://issuu.com/cambridgeosc/docs/hnd_fairdealingfactsheet_v1_2019022 (accessed 28 January 2020).

[214] www.jisc.ac.uk/guides/copyright-law/exceptions-to-infringement-of-copyright (accessed 28 January 2020).

[215] https://publishers.org.uk/resources/rights-and-contracts/, updated 10 February 2016 (accessed 28 January 2020).

[216] R Deazley and J Mathis, 'Writing about Comics and Copyright' CREATe Working Paper 2013/9 (December 2013), pp. 23–4.

[217] Organisations, such as the US Copyright Clearance Center, have instead focused their efforts on automated permissions such as RightsLink (www.copyright.com/publishers/rightslink-permissions/),

The previously noted guidelines tend to focus on books and articles. For other types of works, the view is even more risk averse. For example, Taylor & Francis indicate that while short extracts of text may be permitted on a limited basis, 'a quotation from a song lyric or a poem ... will always require written permission from a copyright holder'.[218] Oxford University Press indicates in its copyright guidelines to its authors that they should seek permission for pictures (including drawings and photographs); any extract from a journal, newspaper, magazine, poem or song lyrics; and any text extract that is 'not for the purpose of criticism, review, or reporting current events ... or that forms the main argument of the work being quoted'.[219] The Society of Biblical Literature advises that 'up to 10% or 250 words in the aggregate, whichever is less, may be used without permission' in relation to dramatic works and that, in the case of poetry and song lyrics, 'up to 10% or 10 lines, whichever is less, may be used without requesting permission' but that permission is 'required for the use of a complete literary unit (chapter, verse, or stanza) of a poem, regardless of length' and for all music.[220] In relation to musical works, the UK Music Publishers Association in its Code of Fair Practice Agreed between Composers, Publishers and Users of Printed Music[221] stipulates that when it comes to copying or arranging musical works, the fair dealing exception for quotation in UK law could be relevant. However, the Code goes on to say that '[t]he exact parameters of this new exception are yet uncertain and if in doubt, it might be prudent to obtain legal advice'.[222] In the case of musical or audiovisual works, there is a dearth of guidance and the emphasis appears to be on obtaining permission to use samples or excerpts. Indeed, when it comes to music sampling in the UK music industry, there has been an unwritten 'three-second' threshold for when permission needs to be sought,[223] and even this view has been challenged, with some guidance, including from the Mechanical-

---

rather than providing workable guidance on the fair use exception. See also the UK Publishers' Licensing Services at https://plsclear.com/ (accessed 28 January 2020).

[218] Guidelines from Taylor & Francis (http://authorservices.taylorandfrancis.com/using-third-party-material-in-your-article/) (accessed 28 January 2020). CENGAGE Publishing states the following: 'You will need permission for short excerpts from highly expressive works such as poems, songs, plays, and films, and for certain other types of materials. Examples include one or more lines of poetry; any identifiable phrase from a song; quotations from plays, movies, or television, if more than one or two lines; dictionary definitions (we recommend that you take and request permission to use definitions from *The American Heritage Dictionary*, published by Houghton Mifflin); problems, exercises, or test items; and essential matter–for example, an abstract of a research project may be only a fraction of the whole but contain its essence.' See https://college.cengage.com/reviewers_authors/ra_author_guide lines_part03.html (accessed 28 January 2020).

[219] https://global.oup.com/academic/authors/author-guidelines/copyright-permissions/?lan g=en&cc=gb (accessed 28 January 2020).

[220] The American College of Healthcare Executives and the Society of Biblical Literature: www.sbl-site.org/publications/publishing_fairuse.aspx (accessed 28 January 2020).

[221] www.mpaonline.org.uk/wp-content/uploads/2017/09/The_Code_of_Fair_Practice_Revised_Apr_2016 .pdf (accessed 28 January 2020).

[222] ibid p. 6.

[223] S Bate and L Abramson, 'To Sample or Not to Sample' [1997] *Ent L R* 193, 194.

Copyright Protection Society (UK), suggesting that *any* sample requires clearance.[224]

The provided examples demonstrate the concern that custom may reflect inaccurate or conservative views of the scope of an exception, in this case quotation.[225] Thus, to treat guidelines such as these as indicative of 'fair' practice would be problematic, at least not without interrogating the basis for these customs in the way that Professor Rothman suggests. Yet, there are likely to be real issues about the representativeness of these quotation guidelines and whether the motivation underlying them is about litigation-avoidance or optimal practices.

In conclusion, it seems that while customs surrounding quotation could in theory inform the notion of 'fair' practice, there are major challenges associated with this approach. Courts would need to scrutinise any quotation guidelines or practices carefully to ensure that they were sufficiently certain, representative and aspirational and to evaluate their impact.

E *Fair Practice – The Role of Good or Bad Faith*

To what extent can notions of good or bad faith animate an understanding of 'fair' practice in Article 10(1) Berne? This issue has arisen at the domestic level in assessments of fair dealing and fair use. For example, in the UK, courts have placed weight on how the work was obtained – surreptitiously, or without authorisation – in determining whether there has been fair dealing.[226] In a similar vein, if an alleged infringer is acting dishonestly or with 'bad faith' motives, such as being primarily motivated by financial gain, this will weigh against the dealing being fair.[227]

---

[224] *Are You Sampling Music?* (MCPS Sample Clearance Dept. 1996) (copy on file with the authors); www.sampleclearance.com/sample-clearance (accessed 12 June 2020). See also www.mondaq.com /uk/x/23823/Patent/The+Song+Remains+the+Same+Music+Sampling+in+the+Digital+Age (accessed 28 January 2020).

[225] Although, importantly, the guidelines do indicate that quotations from unpublished works should not occur – see e.g. https://global.oup.com/academic/authors/author-guidelines/copyright-permissions/?lang g=en&cc=gb (accessed 28 January 2020) and https://authorservices.wiley.com/asset/book-author-documents.html/Permissions_Guidelines_Full.pdf (accessed 28 January 2020) and that the author should be attributed https://authorservices.taylorandfrancis.com/using-third-party-material-in-your-article/ and www.stm-assoc.org/2016_01_05_Guidelines_for_Quotation_From_Journal_Articles.pdf (accessed 28 January 2020).

[226] *Beloff* v. *Pressdram* [1973] FSR 33, 63 (where an unpublished memorandum was leaked from a newspaper organisation); *HMSO* v. *Green Amps* [2007] EWHC 2755 (Ch), [24] (judging fair dealing according to how a 'fair minded and honest person would have dealt with the copyright work' and noting the 'covert manner' in which the digital maps had been downloaded by the defendant). But see contra *Time Warner Entertainment Co Ltd* v. *Channel 4 Television Corp Plc* [1994] EMLR 1 (CA), 10 Neill LJ stating that 'the method by which the copyright material had been obtained' would seldom be an unfair dealing where the work was published and that other actions, such as breach of confidence, can be utilised.

[227] *EWCB Ltd* v. *Tixdaq Ltd* [2016] EWHC 575 (Ch), [2016] RPC 21, [85]; *Hyde Park Residence* v. *Yelland* [2001] Ch. 143, [36]–[37] per Aldous LJ (referring to the motives and intention of the alleged infringer) and at [40] 'I do not believe that a fair minded and honest person would pay for the

However, when it comes to assessing whether a work (or a substantial part thereof) has been copied (i.e. infringed), the UK Court of Appeal has treated *animus furandi* as irrelevant and a 'red herring'.[228]

In the United States, the Supreme Court in *Harper & Row*[229] referred to the propriety of the defendant's conduct in assessing the purpose and character of the use under factor one of the fair use assessment in section 107 of the US Copyright Act 1976. In particular, the court referred to the trial court finding that '[t]he Nation knowingly exploited a purloined manuscript'.[230] Subsequently, in *Campbell* v. *Acuff-Rose*,[231] the Supreme Court dealt ambiguously with the issue of good faith, leaving open whether good faith was central to fair use, but finding that 'being denied permission to use a work does not weigh against a finding of fair use'.[232] However, in contradiction to this statement in *Campbell*, the Ninth Circuit of the Federal Court in *LA News Services* v. *K-Cal TV Channel*[233] found that the propriety of the defendant's conduct was 'relevant to the character of the use to the extent that it may knowingly have exploited a purloined work for free that could have been obtained for a fee'.[234] Further, in *Field* v. *Google*,[235] the US District Court for Nevada treated good faith as an additional fair use factor. In particular, the court found that Google's actions of providing cached links to web pages were in good faith because Google enabled web page owners to opt out of such links being made and took steps to ensure that users could easily access the original web page. As such, this weighed in favour of fair use.[236]

In the scholarship, it has been debated whether good or bad faith should be relevant to a fair use or fair dealing assessment. Perhaps an initial difficulty arising out of domestic cases is what precisely is encompassed by 'bad faith'. The case law ranges over factors, such as the manner in which the defendant obtained or accessed the work (was it stolen or surreptitiously acquired or used knowing it had been acquired in such a manner); the motives of the defendant (were they seeking to gain financially or somehow to harm the copyright owner) and whether the defendant had sought to

---

dishonestly taken driveway stills and publish them in a newspaper knowing that they had not been published or circulated when their only relevance'; *Pro Sieben Media* v. *Carlton Television* [1999] FSR 610, 620 per Walker LJ (referring to intentions and motives of the alleged infringer as relevant to *fair* dealing as opposed to the purpose of the dealing); *Beloff* v. *Pressdram* [1973] FSR 33, 63.

228 *Baigent* v. *Random House Group Ltd* [2007] EWCA Civ 247, [2007] FSR 24, [97] Lloyd LJ (with whom Rix and Mummery LJJ agreed).

229 *Harper & Row, Publishers Inc* v. *Nation Enterprises* 105 S Ct 2218, 2231-2. See also *Fisher* v. *Dees* 794 F. 2d 432 (9th Cir. 1986), 436-7.

230 *Harper & Row*, 2232. Note that Brennan J (White and Marshall J joining) criticised the majority, taking this factor into account since it had not been found that the manuscript had been purloined or, if it had, *The Nation* were responsible (2247).

231 *Campbell* v. *Acuff Rose Music* 510 US 569 (1994), 114 S Ct 1164 (1994).

232 *Campbell*, fn. 18. Discussed in Simon J Frankel and M Kellogg, 'Bad Faith and Fair Use' (2013) 60 J Copyright Soc'y USA 1, 13.

233 108 F. 3d 1123 (9th Cir. 1997).

234 108 F. 3d 1123 (9th Cir. 1997), 1122.

235 412 F. Supp. 2d 1106 (D. Nev. 2006).

236 412 F. Supp. 2d 1106 (D. Nev. 2006), 1122-3.

obtain permission to use the work. Professor Subotnik has argued that it is important to distinguish between these different categories, in order fully to assess whether each category is justified in being considered as part of the fair use analysis.[237] We would agree that it makes sense to unpick notions of 'bad faith', in order to assess whether that conduct may be legitimately assessed as part of a 'fairness' enquiry.

Considering the way in which the work has been obtained or accessed tends to conjure up a sense of whether the user has been acting as a good citizen or in a way that is 'moral'. Professor Weinrib has argued that 'more general considerations of fairness may come into play'[238] when assessing a 'fair' use under section 107 of the US Copyright Act 1976. As such, Weinrib argues that 'it makes a difference whether a user obtained his copy of the original work lawfully or by theft, and if lawfully, by a means that is entirely proper or in some manner underhanded'.[239] By way of contrast, several scholars have persuasively argued that this type of bad faith should be irrelevant to a fair use assessment.[240] Judge Pierre Leval, for example, argues that moral considerations are at odds with the purpose of US copyright law, which 'seeks to maximize the creation and publication of socially useful material' and is not 'a privilege reserved for the well-behaved'.[241] In addition, there are other sources of law (such as tort or criminal law) that can regulate immoral behaviour relating to unlawful acquisition of copyright works. Similarly, Professor Subotnik argues that 'there is only an attenuated nexus between an actor's general moral character and the encouragement of socially valuable fair uses'.[242] Moreover, it is usually the case that courts are one-sided in their focus, looking at 'whether bad faith should weigh against fair use, and not whether good faith should favour fair use'.[243] Finally, she suggests that such bad behavior can be regulated by different legal means, such as tort and criminal law.[244] In a UK context, David Bradshaw has applauded the fact that the Court of Appeal in *Time Warner* held that a fair dealing defence cannot be defeated by bad-faith conduct in obtaining the copyright work. In Bradshaw's view, methods of obtaining a work (and their lawfulness) should not be confused with questions of infringement of copyright.[245]

---

[237]   Eva E Subotnik, 'Intent in Fair Use' (2014) 18 *Lewis and Clark L Rev* 935. Prof. Subotnik refers at 948 to intention to be a good citizen, i.e. the intention to act 'with good moral character'; intent to communicate new meaning, i.e. intention to transform the work; and intent to comply, i.e. the user's intentions to make a lawful fair use.

[238]   Lloyd L Weinrib, 'Fair's Fair: A Comment on the Fair Use Doctrine' (1990) 103 *Harv L R* 1137, 1152.

[239]   Weinrib (1990), 1152.

[240]   P Leval, 'Toward a Fair Use Standard' (1990) 103 *Harvard L Rev* 1105, 1126–8.

[241]   Leval (1990), 1126.

[242]   Subotnik (2014), 963.

[243]   Subotnik (2014), 968.

[244]   Subotnik (2014), 969.

[245]   D Bradshaw, 'Fair Dealing and the Clockwork Orange Case: "A Thieves' Charter"?' [1994] 5 *Ent LR* 6, 7. Contrast Adeney (2013), 156, who argues that favour of good faith being a factor relevant to whether there is fair quotation.

Judge Leval explains that two misunderstandings of early US case law lead to this 'false morality factor'.[246] The first is the focus on the terminology *animus furandi* in early cases, which did not, in fact, signify a concern with the defendant's conduct.[247] The second is a mistaken assumption that fair use is a creature of equity, when in fact it is about balancing 'the social benefit of a transformative secondary use against injury to the incentives of authorship'.[248] Similarly, Professors Frankel and Kellogg[249] contend that consideration of 'bad faith' reflects a mistaken understanding of the fair use doctrine as equitable in nature[250] and does not reflect historical cases that focus on the use and not the user.

If the other 'strains' of bad faith are considered (i.e. motives of the defendant in using the copyright work or failure to seek permission to use the work), Professors Frankel and Kellogg have argued that such considerations are contrary to the utilitarian purpose of copyright, in tension with freedom of expression, and likely to increase uncertainty and costs of litigation.[251] Professor Madison similarly argues that, given the utilitarian purpose of US copyright, 'the question ought not to be whether the defendant believes that he or she was acting legitimately, but whether the outcome of the defendant's efforts was more socially valuable than the outcome produced by allowing the copyright holder to enjoin the use or obtain payment'.[252]

Professor Subotnik, however, argues to the contrary. She suggests that a user's intention to communicate new meaning may be relevant to the purpose and character of the use, but its probative value must be fully assessed.[253] Further, she argues that intent to comply (e.g. an attempt to secure a licence) should be weighed in close cases because this will positively encourage users to internalise 'fair use sensibilities'.[254]

We argue that failure to seek permission to quote from a work is irrelevant to whether the 'fair practice' criterion in Article 10(1) Berne is met. This is because the premise of the quotation exception (or indeed any exception) is that permission is not required. To then consider whether permission has been sought by the user of the work as part of assessing whether there is a 'fair' quotation seems to undermine the ability to rely on the exception. The availability of licences, if they are to be taken into account at all, would seem most relevant to assessing the extent to which there is economic harm caused by quoting the work. Further, the motive or purpose in using

---

[246] Leval (1990), 1126.
[247] Contra R Anthony Reese 'Innocent Infringement in U.S. Copyright Law: A History' (2007) 30 *Columbia Journal of Law and the Arts* 133, 168.
[248] Leval (1990), 1127.
[249] Simon J Frankel and M Kellogg, 'Bad Faith and Fair Use' (2013) 60 *J Copyright Soc'y USA* 1.
[250] See also J Dratler Jr, 'Distilling the Witches' Brew of Fair Use in Copyright Law' (1988) 43 *U Miami. L Rev* 233, 334, who argues that fair use 'has no substantial basis in commercial morality'.
[251] Frankel and Kellogg (2013).
[252] Michael J Madison, 'A Pattern-Oriented Approach to Fair Use' (2004) 45 *Wm & Mary L Rev* 1525, 1555–6.
[253] Subotnik (2014), 976–7.
[254] Subotnik (2014), 978.

the quoted work – whether to gain financially or for some other reason – should not be a 'bad faith' consideration. To the extent that the purpose of the quotation is primarily to make a profit, then this is likely to make the claim to 'fairness' less compelling because the 'profiting' *may* point to economic harm to the copyright author/owner, and there may not be any countervailing expressive, speech interest of the user or distributional impacts to consider. Thus, while the *purpose* of the quotation *is* relevant to the assessment of whether the use comports with 'fair practice', it is misleading and makes no sense to bundle this under a 'bad faith' label that risks vague and moralistic overtones.

Thus, there are sound reasons to ignore bad faith as a fairness factor, particularly in a copyright system where the purpose of protection is utilitarian in nature. Similarly, reliance on good or bad faith in assessing 'fair practice' is unjustified in traditions with a natural rights rationale for copyright/authors' right. This is because the role of exceptions in those traditions is to serve the public interest or to give effect to competing rights (such as the right to freedom of expression).[255] While the purpose of the quotation will be relevant to those public interests or fundamental rights, how a work is obtained or whether permission was sought for the use is irrelevant to whether the public interest or freedom of expression is being served. Therefore, it is argued that the absence or presence of good faith should be irrelevant to whether a quotation is consistent with fair practice in both copyright and authors' rights countries.

F *Fair Practice – A Role for Honest Commercial Practices?*

The concept of 'honest commercial practices' is one that is central to unfair competition and trade mark law. For example, Article 10*bis*(2) of the Paris Convention[256] states that '[a]ny act of competition contrary to honest practices in industrial or commercial matters constitutes an act of unfair competition'. The question, of course, is which acts are prohibited and, in turn, what is meant by 'honest [industrial or commercial] practices'. Article 10*bis*(3) of Paris goes on to illustrate which activities, in particular, shall be prohibited:

> '(i) all acts of such a nature as to create confusion by any means whatever with the establishment, the goods, or the industrial or commercial activities, of a competitor;

---

[255] Senftleben (2004), 24, '[F]reedom of expression by far is the most powerful justification of copyright limitations and at 28 noting that parody and quotation exceptions "constitute a focal point in the context of freedom of expression" and that the necessity for limitations to give effect to freedom of expression 'has been realised throughout both legal traditions of copyright law.'

[256] Paris Convention for the Protection of Industrial Property (as amended on 28 September 1979), official translation available at https://wipolex.wipo.int/en/treaties/textdetails/12633 (accessed 28 January 2020).

(ii) false allegations in the course of trade of such a nature as to discredit the establishment, the goods, or the industrial or commercial activities, of a competitor;

(iii) indications or allegations the use of which in the course of trade is liable to mislead the public as to the nature, the manufacturing process, the characteristics, the suitability for their purpose, or the quantity, of the goods.'

These examples, which were added at the Hague (1925) and Lisbon (1958) Revision Conferences as a means of strengthening the protection given by Article 10*bis*(2), indicate that false or misleading conduct in commercial activities are contrary to 'honest practices'.[257] Professor Wadlow suggests that Article 10*bis*(2) is to be understood as 'interstitial, dealing with misrepresentations in competition which are not among those listed [in Article 10*bis*(3)]'.[258] Moreover, Professor Wadlow argues that 'honest practices' are concerned with what is actually done by the generality of honest traders according to international standards.[259] Other commentators, however, suggest that Article 10*bis*(2) is not restricted to misrepresentations and could include misappropriations, such as unauthorised use of trade secrets.[260] Still others argue that the conceptual contours of 'honest practices' should be left to national legislators and courts.[261] This divergence of opinion offers limited normative guidance in a 'fairness' assessment in the context of Article 10(1) Berne. First, to the extent that 'honest practices' means commercial conduct that is not misleading or disparaging, this does not map on well to copyright, which has a focus on *authorship* rather than commercial, competitive activity. Notions of misleading or disparaging competitive activity are not what concern copyright authors and

---

[257] G H C Bodenhausen, *Guide to the Application of the Paris Convention for the Protection of Industrial Property*, WIPO Publication No. 611 (1969), 142–6. See also F Henning-Bodewig, 'International Unfair Competition Law' in in R M Hilty and F Henning-Bodewig (eds.), *Law against Unfair Competition – Towards a New Paradigm in Europe?* (Springer 2007), 53–60, 55–6.

[258] C Wadlow, *The Law of Passing Off: Unfair Competition by Misrepresentation* (5th ed., Sweet & Maxwell 2016), [2-30].

[259] C Wadlow, 'Regulatory Data Protection under TRIPS Article 39(3) and Article 10*bis* of the Paris Convention: Is There a Doctor in the House?' [2008] *IPQ* 355, 370; and Bodenhausen (1969), 144.

[260] See N P de Carvalho, *The TRIPS Regime of Antitrust and Undisclosed Information* (Kluwer 2008), 191–207. For the contrary view, see M Höpperger and M Senftleben, 'Protection against Unfair Competition at the International Level' in R M Hilty and F Henning-Bodewig (eds.), *Law against Unfair Competition – Towards a New Paradigm in Europe?* (Springer 2007), 61–76 at 67; and Wadlow (2016), [2-031].

[261] S P Ladas, *Patents, Trademarks and Related Rights* (Harvard University Press 1975), ch. 45. Contrast F Henning-Bodewig, 'International Unfair Competition Law' in R M Hilty and F Henning-Bodewig (eds.), *Law against Unfair Competition – Towards a New Paradigm in Europe?* (Springer 2007), 53–60, 57, stating that Article 10*bis* Paris should be construed 'autonomously, i.e. from within itself' but noting 'the lack of detailed analysis of the contents of Article 10*bis*'.

owners. Rather, as described previously,[262] copyright authors and owners are concerned with the economic or moral harm that arises from unauthorised use of protected expression. Second, to the extent that 'honest [commercial] practices' is a proxy for customary trading standards, this is also unhelpful in the copyright sphere, for the reasons discussed above.[263] Finally, if it is the case that Article 10*bis*(2) allows complete autonomy to Paris members about the interpretation of 'honest practices', this is unhelpful to Article 10(1) Berne, which, as has been argued earlier, as a mandatory exception, ought to be given an autonomous, normative interpretation.

There is reference to 'honest commercial practices' in other international intellectual property instruments – namely, Article 39 TRIPS. This provision, in setting out an obligation to protect trade secrets 'in the course of ensuring effective protection against unfair competition' in paragraph 1, also refers to 'honest commercial practices' in paragraph 2. Further, a note to Article 39 states that '"a manner contrary to honest commercial practices" shall mean at least practices such as breach of contract, breach of confidence and inducement to breach, and includes the acquisition of undisclosed information by third parties who knew, or were grossly negligent in failing to know, that such practices were involved in the acquisition'. It seems that the understanding of 'honest commercial practices' in this provision relates to unlawful conduct (e.g. breaches of existing contractual, tortious or equitable obligations) or acquiring undisclosed information *knowing* that such unlawful conduct had been involved. Again, it is questionable whether these concepts can be usefully transplanted to 'fair practice' in Article 10(1) Berne. For a start, if this notion were adopted, it would mean that as long as, in using the quotation, no unlawful conduct (separate from the issue of copyright infringement) was involved, it would be automatically 'fair'. Yet it is hard to imagine many situations where quoting a copyright work would involve unlawful conduct, such as breach of contract, breach of confidence or trespass. In which case, this would give very little role to the requirement of 'fair practice'.

The interpretation given to 'honest [commercial] practices' at a regional level is also of limited use in a copyright context. For example, in the EU, Article 6 of the 1988 EU Trade Marks Directive[264] stipulated that trade mark limitations were subject to the proviso that the acts were 'in accordance with honest practices in industrial or commercial matters'. Article 12 of the 2009 Community Trade Mark Regulation[265] contained a similar proviso. The most recent versions of the Trade Marks Directive[266]

---

[262]   Section III, Part A, above.
[263]   Section III, Part D, above.
[264]   First Council Directive 89/104/EEC of 21 December 1988 to approximate the laws of the Member States relating to Trade Marks OJ L 40, 11.2.1989, pp. 1–7.
[265]   Council Regulation (EC) No 207/2009 of 26 February 2009 on the Community Trade Mark, OJ L78, 24.3.2009, pp. 1–42.
[266]   Directive (EU) 2015/2436 of the European Parliament and of the Council of 16 December 2015 to approximate the laws of the Member States relating to Trade Marks OJ L 336, 23.12.2015, pp. 1–26 ('Trade Marks Directive').

and EU Trade Mark Regulation[267] contain the same proviso in Article 14(2).[268] The way in which the CJEU has interpreted the proviso 'in accordance with honest practices in industrial or commercial matters' is that it means 'a duty to act fairly in relation to the legitimate interests of the trade mark owner'.[269] The reference to acting 'fairly' begs the question of what is 'fair' in the trade mark context.[270] In *Gillette*,[271] the CJEU held that use of a trade mark is contrary to honest practices if it gives the impression of a commercial connection between the parties;[272] takes unfair advantage of the trade mark's distinctive character or repute, or denigrates that mark; or where the third party presents its product as an imitation or replication of the product bearing the trade mark. In other words, the CJEU defined the 'honest practices' proviso according to the very activities that constitute trade mark infringement. As commentators have remarked, this 'would seem to rule out the availability of the defences in almost every case',[273] and if there is to be a meaningful defence, 'the parameters of what would constitute honest practices must not be just a repetition of the elements that establish an infringement action'.[274] By way of contrast, however, in *Gerolsteiner*,[275] the CJEU did not assume that the likelihood of aural confusion between the registered word mark 'GERRI' for mineral water and non-alcoholic beverages, and the use of 'KERRY SPRING' as an indication of geographical origin for bottled mineral water meant that the use was not in accordance with honest practices.[276] Instead, the court accepted that there may be phonetic similarity and that it would require 'the national court to carry out an overall assessment of all the relevant circumstances', which included 'the shape and labeling of the bottle[s]'.[277]

It is argued that 'honest practices' offer little guidance for how 'fair practice' might be interpreted. This is because, although 'honest' has been defined as acting 'fairly' by the CJEU, the content given to 'fairness' has, in some cases, been determined by the very acts that constitute trade mark infringement. There are two problems with

---

[267] Regulation (EU) 2017/1001 of the European Parliament and of the Council of 14 June 2017, OJ L154, 16.6.2017, pp. 1–99 ('Trade Marks Regulation').

[268] Recital 21 of Regulation and Recital 27 of Directive 2015/2436 also refer to honest practices in industrial or commercial matters.

[269] Case C-63/97 *Bayerische Motorenwerke A.G. v. Deenik* EU:C:1999:82, [1999] 1 CMLR 1099, [61]; Case C-100/02 *Gerolsteiner Brunnen GmbH & Co v. Putsch GmbH* EU:C:2004:11, [2004] RPC 39, [24]; Case C-228/03 *Gillette Co v. LA-Laboratories Ltd Oy* EU:C:2005:177, [2005] FSR 37, [49]; Case C-558/08 *Portakabin Ltd, Portakabin BV v. Primakabin BV* EU:C:2010:416, [67].

[270] Ilanah Fhima, 'The Public Interest in European Trade Mark Law' [2017] *IPQ* 311, 324.

[271] Case C-228/03 *Gillette Co v. LA-Laboratories Ltd Oy* EU:C:2005:177, [2005] FSR 37, [49].

[272] See also Case C-558/08 *Portakabin Ltd, Portakabin BV v. Primakabin BV* EU:C:2010:416, [69].

[273] Fhima (2017), 324. See also Ilanah Simon, 'Nominative Use and Honest Practices in Industrial and Commercial Matters – A Very European History' [2007] *IPQ* 117.

[274] Po-Jen Yap 'Honestly, Neither Celine nor Gillette Is Defensible!' [2008] *EIPR* 286, 287.

[275] Case C-100/02 *Gerolsteiner Brunnen GmbH & Co v. Putsch GmbH* EU:C:2004:11, [2004] RPC 39.

[276] *Gerolsteiner Brunnen*, [25].

[277] *Gerolsteiner Brunnen*, [26].

this approach, the first being that the wrongs identified (e.g. commercial connection, unfair advantage of or denigration of a mark) do not map on to rationales of copyright law. Second, if the methodological approach of defining 'fairness' according to the acts that constitute copyright infringement (e.g. reproduction, communication to the public) were to be adopted, this would (as it has done in the EU trade mark context) risk undermining the scope of, and role for, the quotation exception.

The EU Trade Secrets Directive,[278] when identifying lawful versus unlawful acquisition, use or disclosure of trade secrets, refers to conduct that is in conformity with or contrary to 'honest commercial practices',[279] clearly linking back to the unfair competition notions referenced in Article 10bis Paris and Article 39 TRIPS. Nowhere is 'honest commercial practices' defined in the EU Trade Secrets Directive. However, we might assume that the conduct stipulated in Article 4(2)(a) as prohibited (i.e. 'unauthorised access to, appropriation of, or copying of any documents, objects, materials, substances or electronic files under the control of the trade secret holder, containing the trade secret or from which the trade secret can be deduced') *is* contrary to honest commercial practices. This does not define the circumstances exhaustively because Article 4(2)(a) refers to 'any other conduct . . . considered contrary to honest commercial practices'. As commentators[280] have noted, the flexible and broad proviso of 'honest commercial practices' leaves considerable interpretative space for EU member states, which may cut against the harmonization objective of the Directive, unless an autonomous interpretation is developed by the CJEU. In terms of the usefulness of the concept in informing 'fair practice' for the quotation exception in Article 10(1) Berne, there is not much that can be transplanted. This is, in part, because of the vagueness of the concept and the fact that, even in relation to the prohibited conduct that is identified, it is unclear whether the 'unauthorised' nature of the acts must involve tortious, contractual or criminal wrongdoing or knowledge of such wrongdoing.[281]

As such, it is reasonable to conclude that the notion of 'honest practices', as seen in international treaties and EU trade mark and trade secrets law, is of no real assistance when it comes to determining what 'fair practice' means in relation to Article 10(1) of Berne.[282] Instead, it is preferable to use a pluralistic notion of fairness drawn from the rationales of copyright protection, freedom of expression and distributive justice.

---

[278]   Directive (EU) 2016/943 of 8 June 2016 on the Protection of Undisclosed Know-How and Business Information (Trade Secrets) against their Unlawful Acquisition, Use and Disclosure [2016] OJ L157/1.

[279]   See Article 3(1)(d) and 4(1)(b) EU Trade Secrets Directive.

[280]   (2014) IIC: International Review of Intellectual Property and Competition Law: Max Planck Institute for Innovation & Competition Research Paper No 14–11, [10]; Trevor Cook, 'The Proposal for a Directive on the Protection of Trade Secrets in EU Legislation' (2014) 19 *Journal of Intellectual Property Rights* 54, 55; Anna A Wennakoski, 'Trade Secrets under Review: A Comparative Analysis of the Protection of Trade Secrets in the EU and in the US' [2016] *EIPR* 154, 161.

[281]   Sharon K Sandeen 'Implementing the EU Trade Secrets Directive: A View from the United States' [2017] *EIPR* 4, 6.

[282]   But note that Ohly (2018), 114–116 suggests unfair competition law might inspire a different approach to defining copyright infringement with a 'black list' of core infringements, economic rights combined with a market effects clause and a general clause on unfair use.

IV FAIR PRACTICE — A MATTER OF RULES OR STANDARDS?

Tying together the strands of the above analysis, an independent, pluralistic inter-pretation of 'fair practice' would lead to several considerations being assessed. These are (i) the nature and purpose of the quotation, (ii) the size of the quotation and its proportion in relation to the source work, (iii) the harm to the market of the source work, (iv) the integrity interests of the author of the source work and (v) the nature of the claimant's copyright work.

The nature and purpose of the quotation can be tied to economic harm, free speech and distributive justice considerations. Where the quotation is expressive in nature, it will be relevant to consider the artistic, political or commercial nature of the speech – in other words, the *value* of the speech. In addition, from a distributive justice point of view, it will matter if the nature or purpose of the quotation benefits certain disadvantaged groups, such as those with disabilities or lacking educational opportunities, or non-profit institutions. From an economic point of view, if the quotation use is commercial in nature, then this might indicate its substitutability for the source work; however, this consideration is probably best considered as part of the harm to the market for the work.

The size of the quotation and its proportion to the source work are considerations that really tie to the economic and moral (Lockean) justifications for copyright protection. The suggestion is that the larger the size of the quotation and the greater its proportion to the source of the work, then the more likely the target use that includes the quotation is likely to substitute for the source work.

The harm to the market for the source work is justifiable under the economic and moral (Lockean) justifications for copyright protection. The challenge, for national legislatures or more likely national courts, will be whether to take account of actual or potential harm. As discussed previously,[283] there are different views on whether economic harm should be considered as actual harm (what loss has occurred or foreseeably will occur) or potential harm (what loss could occur if the copyright owner hypothetically operated in that particular market). Although we argue there is a pluralistic, normative meaning to 'fair practice', we do not think it is possible to point to an autonomous approach to measuring economic harm. Rather, this will be a matter that would be legitimately left to the discretion of Berne Union Members. Meanwhile, harm to the integrity interests of the author reflects the moral (Kantian) justification for copyright protection and involves, we argue, taking an objective approach to the issue.

The nature of the claimant's work is another factor that would draw upon the pluralistic norms of harm and freedom of expression that have been discussed previously.

Finally, the presence of industry custom or standards will only have a role to play where they are sufficiently certain, representative and aspirational, whereas it should

---

[283] Section III, Part A, p. 155, above.

be irrelevant to assessing 'fair practice' that there is good or bad faith conduct by the defendant.

Having made the case for this pluralistic and autonomous interpretation of fair practice in Article 10(1) Berne, the next question is whether the provision proscribes rule-based notions of fairness or requires the use of standards in crafting quotation exceptions at the national level. This section examines whether Article 10(1) requires a standards-based approach to fair practice or a rules-based one, and concludes that Article 10(1) lends itself to an open textured (or standard) based approach to fair practice.

The language of standards and rules is an unfamiliar one in the international copyright law setting. It stems from the law and economics literature[284] and has tended to focus on national law and the relative balance between legislatures and the judiciary. In the copyright context, there has been significant discussion of the value of rules versus standards in relation to exceptions – particularly fair use.[285]

The difference between rules and standards is said to relate to the degree of precision in their definition.[286] This, in turn, impacts the discretion that is left to enforcers of the law.[287] Rules, in their pure sense, are applied consistently without variation – an example of a rule is a speed limit of thirty miles per hour.[288] Whereas a pure standard 'is a legal pronouncement that specifies no triggering facts that have defined legal consequences', an example being the reasonable care standard of negligence.[289] However, rules and standards exist on a spectrum and so it is possible to have qualifications to rules and for standards to develop rule-like interpretations. As Professor Korobkin describes, 'Just as a pure rule can become standard-like through unpredictable exceptions, a pure standard can become rule-like through the judicial reliance on precedent'.[290] Another way of distinguishing between rules and standards is whether the triggering circumstances can be specified ex ante or whether ex post evaluations of particular factors need to be made.[291]

Rules are described as having the value of predictability or certainty and, as such, avoiding the 'chilling effect' of an uncertain law on socially valuable behaviour.[292]

---

[284]   Classic discussions may be found in E Erlich and R A Posner, 'An Economic Analysis of Legal Rulemaking' (1974) 3 *J Legal Stud* 257; L Kaplow, 'Rules versus Standards: An Economic Analysis' (1992) 42 *Duke L J* 557; P Schlag, 'Rules and Standards' (1985) 33 *UCLA L Rev* 379. Combining an economic and behavioural analysis approach is R B Korobkin, 'Behavioral Analysis and Legal Form: Rules vs Standards Revisited' (2000) 79 *Or L Rev* 23.

[285]   See e.g. P Leval, 'Toward a Fair Use Standard' (1990) 103 *Harvard L Rev* 1105; N Elkin-Koren and O Fischman-Afori, 'Rulifying Fair Use' (2017) 59 *Arizona L Rev* 161, and E Hudson, 'Implementing Fair Use in Copyright Law; Lessons from Australia' (2013) 25 *Intellectual Property Journal* 201.

[286]   Erlich and Posner (1974), 258.

[287]   Hudson (2013), 212.

[288]   Erlich and Posner (1974), 258.

[289]   Korobkin (2000), 27.

[290]   Korobkin (2000), 29. See also Hudson (2013), 213.

[291]   Korobkin (2000), 30.

[292]   Erlich and Posner (1974), 263; Schlag (1985), 400; Korobkin (2000), 35 *et seq*; Hudson (2013), 220.

Although designing a rule may be more costly than designing a standard, the application of a rule will create savings over time where there is frequent, identical or repeat conduct that needs to be regulated.[293] However, rules can risk both over and under inclusion because of the limits of language and human foresight in specifying the rule.[294] In addition, there is the risk of rules becoming obsolete through changes in circumstances (such as technological developments).[295]

Standards, on the other hand, are less at risk of becoming obsolete since 'a standard does not specify the circumstances relevant to decision or the weight of each circumstance but merely indicates the kinds of circumstances that are relevant'.[296] They are apposite where behaviour subject to the law is infrequent and variable[297] and where flexibility and individualisation are important.[298] But there is the risk that lack of certainty will chill desirable behaviour, particularly for those users that are risk averse.[299] Further, while there are fewer costs involved in designing a standard there are more costs associated with compliance with a standard 'because it generally is more difficult to predict the outcome of a future inquiry'.[300]

Although the nomenclature of rules and standards is unfamiliar in an international copyright setting, the Berne Convention features examples of both rules and standards. The minimum term requirement in Article 7 Berne is the clearest example of a pure rule. Article 7 indicates that the duration of protection will be at least fifty years from the author's death, measured from 1 January following the year of death. Berne also has examples of standards – the three-step test in Article 9(2) probably being the best example because it involves an assessment of whether the exception is a special case, conflicts with the normal exploitation of the work and whether there is unreasonable prejudice to the legitimate interests of the author.

Within national law, the rules versus standards debate raises the issue of what should be determined by the legislature and what needs to be interpreted and applied by the judiciary, whereas, with an international copyright convention such as Berne, the considerations relate to the degree of autonomy permitted to the state. The issue here is whether Berne Union Members would have to implement 'fair practice' as a standard or whether it could be implemented as a rule. This view is taken regardless of whether the signatory is a country that approaches treaties as self-executing or as requiring domestic implementation. This is because, even in those countries (mainly civil law countries and US) where public international obligations

---

[293] Kaplow (1992), 621; Korobkin (2000), 32–3.
[294] Erlich and Posner (1974), 268.
[295] Erlich and Posner (1974), 277.
[296] Erlich and Posner (1974), 277.
[297] Kaplow (1992), 621.
[298] Schlag (1985), 400; Korobkin (2000), 33.
[299] Hudson (2013), 220.
[300] Kaplow (1992), 621.

are self-executing, there are rules of referral that are rarely self-executing and will require domestic legislation to give effect to them.[301] Article 10(1) would fall into this category.

The meaning of fair practice in Article 10(1) that has been advocated lends itself to a standard-like formulation. This could be implemented by identifying 'fair practice' as a requirement of the quotation exception and leaving the rest to judicial interpretation. There are several examples of jurisdictions that already adopt this approach.[302] Alternatively, it could be done by setting out in the national legislation the factors or circumstances that should be weighed in determining whether there is 'fair practice'.[303] Notably, as discussed previously, some civil law countries (such as France, Germany, Italy and Spain) do not explicitly mention 'fair practice' in the text of their quotation exception, although courts might take into account some fairness considerations. However, various common law copyright countries do explicitly indicate factors in copyright legislation to assess what is 'fair' use or 'fair' dealing, for the purposes of quotation.[304] At a minimum, Berne Union countries would have to expressly recognise the requirement of 'fair practice' or 'fairness' in their copyright or authors' right provisions dealing with quotation. While it may be ideal explicitly to set out the factors relevant to evaluating fair practice in authors' rights or copyright legislation, this is not required if it is the case that courts will

---

[301] Ricketson and Ginsburg (2006), [5.05]–[5.06], 182–3.

[302] For example, see Andorra, Law on Copyright and Neighboring Rights, Art 8 'reproduction of a short part of a published work, in the form of quotation . . . provided such reproduction is compatible with fair practice'; Burundi, Law No. 1/021 of December 30, 2005, on the Protection of Copyright and Related Rights in Burundi, Art 26 'provided that such quotations are compatible with fair practice'; Cyprus, Law on Copyright and Related Rights of 1976 (Law No. 59/1976, as amended up to Law No. 18(I)/1993), s7(f) 'quotation of passages from published works if they are compatible with fair practice'; Greece, Law No. 2121/1993 on Copyright, Related Rights and Cultural Matters (as amended up to Law No. 4281/2014), Art 19 'provided that the quotation is compatible with fair practice'; Malaysia, Copyright Act 1987 (Act 332, as at 1 January 2006), s. 13(m) 'the making of quotations from a published work if they are compatible with fair practice'; Niger, Decree No. 93-027 of March 30, 1993, on Copyright, Neighbouring Rights and Folklore, Art 10, 'such quotation is compatible with fair practice'; Republic of Korea, Copyright Act (Act No. 432 of January 28, 1957, as amended up to Act No. 12137 of December 30, 2013), Art 28 'It is permissible to quote a work . . . in compliance with fair practices'; Senegal, Law No. 2008-09 of January 25, 2008, on Copyright and Related Rights, Art 44 'short quotations that are compatible with fair practice'; Sri Lanka, Intellectual Property Act (Act No 36 of 2003), s. 12(3) 'reproduction, in the form of a quotation, shall be permitted. . .provided that the reproduction is compatible with fair practice'; Uganda, The Copyright and Neighbouring Rights Act 2006, s 15 'fair use . . .where the quotation is compatible with fair practice'; Zimbabwe, Copyright and Neighbouring Rights Act (Chapter 26:05), s. 31 'the quotation is compatible with fair practice'.

[303] For example, as in Dominica, Copyright Act 2003 (Act 5 of 2003), s. 65 requiring that reproduction in the form of a quotation is 'compatible with fair practice' and s. 66: 'For the purpose of determining whether an act done in relation to a work constitutes fair practice, the court determining the question shall take account of all factors which appears to it to be relevant, including (a) the nature of the work in question; (b) the extent and substantiality of that part of the work affected by the act in relation to the whole of the work; (c) the effect of that act upon the potential market on the commercial value of the work'.

[304] See Section II, Part A, above.

anyway weigh these considerations as part of their assessment of the exception that deals with quotation. Courts in civil law countries have shown some tendency to do this already.[305] What is crucial is that the considerations that have been identified – pertaining to economic and moral harm, distributive justice and freedom of expression – *are*, in fact, part of the judicial assessment of fair practice.

The pluralistic notion of 'fairness' that has been advocated here also means that there will be leeway at domestic level as to the relative emphasis that is given to these various fairness considerations, but it would not allow them to be ignored. Moreover, there would also be discretion as to how the content of these factors is defined where the norms of harm, distributive justice and freedom of expression include different policy choices. For example, one could point to the ways in which speech interests are assessed and valued when considering the nature and purpose of the quotation. In this situation, 'fair practice' requires the *expressive* purpose of the quotation to be considered, as opposed to prescribing how speech interests are taken into account, for example, by treating political speech as more valuable than commercial speech. Similarly, while courts should assess the harm to the copyright author/owner, we suggest that both economic and moral harm should be considered, but not the relative weighting between the two. Further, different jurisdictions might take divergent approaches to whether economic harm relates to harm to the actual or potential market for the work. However, there are some considerations that should *not* be relevant to the autonomous, pluralistic notion of fair practice that has been proposed – namely, 'honest commercial practices' and good or bad faith – and courts should be wary of relying on custom or trade norms.

---

[305] See Section II, Part A, above.

7

The Consequences of Global Mandatory Fair Use

As has been argued, Article 10(1) Berne mandates a quotation exception that we describe as global mandatory fair use. It is global because of the reach of Berne and TRIPS. It creates a mandatory exception because of the clear language of the provision and its *travaux*.[1] It relates to 'use' that is not limited by type of work, type of act, or purpose and which 'quotation' should be understood broadly.[2] Finally, it is 'fair' use because the conditions of Article 10 – namely, the work having been lawfully made available to the public,[3] attribution,[4] proportionality,[5] and fair practice must be satisfied.[6] In particular, the requirement of 'fair practice' embraces a range of normative considerations relating to economic and moral harm, distributive justice, freedom of expression and, in limited situations, custom.

This chapter considers some of the consequences of global mandatory fair use. To begin, it considers how Article 10(1) Berne differs from the three-step test and how this international obligation could lead to different ways of assessing national exceptions, such as fair use.[7] It then turns to examine how certain national copyright exceptions fail to comply with the obligations in Article 10(1) and calls for their reform. Next, this chapter considers how Article 10(1) should influence the judicial interpretation of exceptions and the relationship between the quotation and parody exceptions. Finally, it is suggested that Article 10(1), properly understood, could lead to a liberalising of industry guidelines and practices.

I ARTICLE 10(1) BERNE IN CONTRAST TO THE THREE-STEP TEST

Having explored the various elements of Article 10(1) Berne in detail in earlier chapters, this section seeks to tease out the differences between Article 10(1) Berne

---

[1] Chapter 3, Section I.
[2] Chapter 4, Section I (no limit by purpose); Chapter 3, Sections II and III (no limit by works or rights); Chapter 5 (definition of quotation).
[3] Chapter 4, Section II.
[4] Chapter 4, Section III.
[5] Chapter 4, Section IV.
[6] Chapter 6.
[7] On the non-applicability of the three step test, see Chapter 3, Section IV.

and the three-step test and show how this may impact on national copyright exceptions – in particular, the 'fair use' exception in section 107 US Copyright Act 1976. In so doing, we see that Article 10(1) has both a liberating and a constraining effect.

There are several important differences between the three-step test and the mandatory quotation exception in Article 10(1) Berne. These relate to (i) the acceptable scope of the exception, (ii) the normative value of the exception and the interests taken into account, (iii) the unpublished nature of the work that is used, (iv) the treatment of moral rights of authors, (v) the cumulative nature of the requirements and (vi) whether the exception supports 'free' exceptions. In exploring these differences, we adopt, for the sake of argument, the WTO Panel's interpretation of the three-step test in the 'Fairness in Music Licensing case'.[8] We recognise there has been much debate about the scope of the three-step test[9] and critique of the WTO Panel's Decision (much of which we agree with);[10] nevertheless, this decision is taken as the current benchmark for the scope of the three-step test in international copyright law.[11] We also illustrate

---

[8] WTO Panel Report, United States – Section 110(5) of the Copyright Act 1976, (15 June 2000), WT/DS/160/R.

[9] See e.g. C Geiger, D Gervais and M Senftleben, 'The Three Step Test Revisited: How to Use the Test's Flexibility in National Copyright Law' (2014) 29 *Am U Intl L Rev* 581 (suggesting that a global, as opposed to cumulative, approach to the three-step test should be used); Kamiel J Koelman, 'Fixing the Three Step Test' (2006) 28(8) *EIPR* 407; M Senftleben, *Copyright, Limitations and the Three-Step Test: An Analysis of the Three-Step Test in International and EC Copyright Law* (Kluwer 2004); Christophe Geiger, Jonathan Griffiths and Reto M Hilty, 'Towards a Balanced Interpretation of the "Three Step Test" in Copyright Law' (2008) 30(12) *EIPR* 489; Huaiwen He, 'Seeking a Balanced Interpretation of the Three-Step Test – An Adjusted Structure in View of Divergent Approaches' (2009) 40(3) *IIC* 274.

[10] See e.g. D Brennan, 'The Three Step Test Frenzy – Why the TRIPS Panel Decision Might Be Considered Per Incuriam' (2002) 2 *IPQ* 212; Robert Burrell and Allison Coleman, *Copyright Exceptions: The Digital Impact* (Cambridge University Press 2005), 217 (saying that the decision 'does little to clarify the position'); Graeme B Dinwoodie and Rochelle C Dreyfuss, *A Neofederalist Vision of TRIPS: The Resilience of the International Intellectual Property Regime* (Oxford University Press 2012), 80 (describing the Panel's approach as formalistic, which 'anatomized the Exceptions provision, mistook accounting for judging, and also relied heavily on dictionary definitions'); Daniel J Gervais, 'Towards a New Core International Copyright Norm: The Reverse Three Step Test' (2005) 9 *Marquette Intellectual Property L Rev* 1, 14 *et seq*; Sarah E Henry, 'The First International Challenge to the U.S. Copyright Law: What Does the WTO Analysis of 17 U.S.C. 110(5) Mean to the Future International Harmonization of Copyright Laws under the TRIPS Agreement?' (2001) *Penn State International L Rev* 301, 323 ('The Panel's reasoning serves more to muddy the waters surrounding acceptable exceptions, rather than to clear them'). Matthew Kennedy, 'Blurred Lines: Reading TRIPS with GATT Glasses' (2015) 49 *Journal of World Trade* 735, 744, 747–8 (pointing out the difficulties of interpreting TRIPS using trade law jurisprudence and critiquing the interpretation of the WTO Panel); Henning Grosse Ruse-Khan, *The Protection of Intellectual Property in International Law* (Oxford University Press 2016), 433, [12.45] (describing as 'most problematic' the Panel's approach of defining 'all relevant terms in Article 13 in great detail – rather than limiting itself to identify the range of possible understandings that a VCLT interpretation allows'); Annette Kur, 'Of Oceans, Islands, and Inland Water – How Much Room for Exceptions and Limitations under the Three-Step Test?' (2009) 8 *Rich J Global L & Bus* 287, 323–4.

[11] As Justin Hughes, 'Fair Use and Its Politics – At Home and Abroad' in Ruth L Okediji (ed.), *Copyright Law in an Age of Exceptions and Limitations* (Cambridge University Press 2017), ch. 8, 234–74, 245, states, 'this WTO decision … serves as the pragmatic authoritative interpretation of the provision'.

how Article 10(1) Berne has potentially different consequences to the three-step test by utilising the US 'fair use' exception.

A *Acceptable Scope of the Exception*

The WTO Panel explicitly denied that, according to the three-step test, the purpose of exceptions must be legitimate in a 'normative sense'. Instead, it indicated that the scope of an exception must be 'clearly defined' and 'narrow in scope and reach'.[12] According to the WTO Panel, 'clearly defined' means that the scope of an exception must be 'known and particularized'.[13] With regard to an exception being 'narrow in scope and reach', the Panel stated 'an exception or limitation must be limited in its field of application or exceptional in its scope. In other words, an exception or limitation should be narrow in a quantitative as well as a qualitative sense. This suggests a narrow scope as well as an exceptional or distinctive objective.'[14]

In the context of the case, the Panel decided that the 'business' exception failed the first step because, although defined with certainty, it was too broad in

---

Examples of scholars treating it as such include Sabine Jacques, *The Parody Exception in Copyright Law* (Oxford University Press 2019), 51, (using the WTO Panel as guidance on the three-step test within TRIPS); Jo Oliver, 'Copyright in the WTO: The Panel Decision on the Three-Step Test' (2002) 25 *Colum J L & Arts* 119, 170 ('the panel decision will provide valuable guidance to legislatures enacting legislation to comply with the Treaty, as well as to those interpreting that legislation'); Hao Dong and Minkang Gu, 'Copyrightable or Not: A Review of the Chinese Provision on "Illegal Works" Targeted by WTO DS362 and Suggestions on the Legal Reform' (2009) 4 *Asian J WTO & Int'l Health L & Pol'y* 335, 355 *et seq* (using the DS160 WTO Panel decision interpretation of the three-step test to assess the compliance of Article 4(1) of the Copyright Law of the People's Republic of China 1990, which is about denying protection to illegal works, with international copyright law); Juan He, 'Developing Countries' Pursuit of an Intellectual Property Law Balance under the WTO TRIPS Agreement' (2011) 10 *Chinese J Int'l L* 827, 850 (noting that TRIPS Panel Decisions, including DS 160, have interpreted the 'three-step' test in a manner that favours rightsholders and that this can constrain developing countries); Biruk Haile, 'Scrutiny of the Ethiopian System of Copyright Limitations in the Light of International Legal Hybrid Resulting from (the Impending) WTO Membership: Three-Step Test in Focus' (2012) 25 *J Ethiopian L* 159 (assessing Ethiopian copyright limitations in light of the WTO Panel interpretation of the three-step test); Sarah E Henry, 'The First International Challenge to the U.S. Copyright Law: What Does the WTO Analysis of 17 U.S.C. 110(5) Mean to the Future International Harmonization of Copyright Laws under the TRIPS Agreement?' (2001) *Penn State International L Rev* 301, 324–7 (analysing how national exceptions may not be compliant with the WTO Panel Decision). Although contrast Australian Law Reform Commission, *Copyright and the Digital Economy* (Report No 122) (Sydney, ALRC, 2013), 117, suggesting that the 'precise meaning of each step of the test is far from certain' given the one WTO Panel decision on the three-step test as it relates to copyright. It is also interesting to note that the WTO Panel Decision was not overtly discussed in the UK in the *Gowers Review of Intellectual Property* (December 2006), although the three-step test is mentioned at [4.88] and was part of assessing how to reform UK copyright exceptions in light of the Gowers Review: see e.g. *Taking Forward the Gowers Review of Intellectual Property: Proposed Changes to Copyright Exceptions* (Intellectual Property Office Newport 2008).

12   WTO Panel Report, United States – Section 110(5) of the Copyright Act 1976, (15 June 2000), WT/DS/160/R, [6.112].
13   WTO DS 160/R, [6.108].
14   WTO DS 160/R, [6.109].

scope.[15] Particularly pertinent was the fact that 'a substantial majority of eating and drinking establishments and close to half of the retail establishments [were] covered by the exemption'.[16] By way of contrast, the 'homestyle' exception was seen as limited to only a small percentage of such establishments and applicable only to dramatic musical works, such as operas, operettas and musicals.[17]

Thus, the three-step test, as interpreted by the WTO Panel, requires an exception to be limited in scope and reach and to have sufficient certainty. It is on this basis that some commentators have queried the legitimacy of US 'fair use' in section 107 of the US Copyright Act 1976.[18] This has led some scholars to argue that section 107 of the US Copyright Act 1976 satisfies the criterion of 'certain special cases' because of the developed US case law that fits into clusters and is relatively predictable.[19] Implicit in this argument is that the first step is the domain of both the national legislature and the national courts.[20] Indeed, Professor Justin Hughes has argued that 'the fair use doctrine is a *mechanism* to allow *specific* judicially created exceptions to copyright liability' and thus credibly satisfies the three-step test.[21] Opponents argue, however, that fair use is too open-ended to satisfy the first step and query those jurisdictions that have introduced fair use, but without the jurisprudential history attaching to section 107.[22]

---

[15] WTO DS 160/R, [6.131]–[6.133].

[16] WTO DS 160/R, [6.133].

[17] WTO DS 160/R, [6.143] and [6.148].

[18] See Hughes (2017), 242: 'The real issue is the first step' and also Okediji (2000), 126.

[19] Michael J Madison, 'A Pattern-Oriented Approach to Fair Use' (2004) 45 *William & Mary L Rev* 1525; Barton Beebe, 'An Empirical Study of U.S. Copyright Fair Use Opinions, 1978–2005' (2008) 156 *U Pa L Rev* 549; Pam Samuelson, 'Unbundling Fair Uses' (2009) 77 *Fordham L Rev* 2537. Contrast how the International Intellectual Property Alliance ('IIPA') argues that 'fair use' has been improperly imported into South African copyright law because 'the country lacks the decades of legal precedent that have served to define, refine and qualify the fair use doctrine in the United States': IIPA, '2019 Special 301 Report on Copyright Protection and Enforcement' (7 February 2019), 72, available at https://iipa.org/files/uploads/2019/02/2019SPEC301REPORT.pdf (accessed 7 February 2020). This is a regularly raised objection by the IIPA to countries that 'import' fair use as explained in Niva Elkin-Koren and Neil W Netanel, 'Transplanting Fair Use Across the Globe: A Case Study Testing the Credibility of U.S. Opposition' (11 May 2020) *Hastings Law Journal*, forthcoming. Available at SSRN: https://ssrn.com/abstract=3598160 (accessed 9 June 2020). The authors argue that this objection is misplaced.

[20] M Senftleben, 'The International Three-Step Test: A Model Provision for EC Fair Use Legislation' (2010) 1 *JIPITEC* 67, 76 [52].

[21] Hughes (2017), 253–4.

[22] Okediji (2000), 150, 'local judicial institutions may not be developed enough to exercise a balanced application of the doctrine'. See also Burrell and Coleman (2005), 270–1, stating that 'the key issue is whether the fair use defence is confined to "certain special cases"' and Rami Olwan, 'The Adoption of the American Fair Use in Gulf States: A Comparative Analysis of Authors' Exceptions in Common Law and Civil Law Countries' (2016) 38 *EIPR* 416, 432–3, expressing concern about civil law jurisdictions in Gulf states being able to utilise or develop judicial precedent. Cf. David Tan, 'The Transformative Use Doctrine and Fair Dealing in Singapore' (2012) 24 *Singapore Academy of Law Journal* 832, who argues that adopting US jurisprudence is a solution, and Elkin-Koren and Netanel (2020), who demonstrate how Israeli courts have developed a sophisticated and independent

This debate becomes redundant once one appreciates the relevance of Article 10(1) Berne. As we have argued, this provision mandates a quotation exception – one that is open-ended as to the range of purposes or uses of the quotation. The concept of 'quotation' is broader than has often been appreciated and can encompass many forms of expressive and transformative uses that, it has been said, lie at the heart of fair use under US law.[23] Although not every act that would count as 'fair use' under section 107 of the US Copyright Act 1976 can be described as 'quotation' (in particular, the technology-related uses, such as accessing interface information to ensure functional interoperability,[24] or private use[25]), a great deal of what US fair use encompasses reflects its obligations under Article 10(1); the remainder can likely be easily justified under Article 9(2) and the other exceptions in Berne (as understood in the light of the three-step test).[26]

B *The Normative Value of the Exception*

According to the WTO Panel, the normative basis of an exception is not especially relevant to determining consistency with the first limb of the three-step test. Compatibility with the first limb can occur even if an exception 'pursues a special purpose whose underlying legitimacy in a normative sense cannot be discerned'.[27] Even so, the Panel indicated that 'public policy purposes stated by law-makers when enacting a limitation or exception may be useful from a factual perspective for making inferences about the scope of a limitation or exception or the clarity of its definition'.[28] Interestingly, this approach is not about assessing the normative value of the exception, but rather takes a functional approach (i.e. using the normative basis as a technique for identifying the clarity and scope of an exception). For example, in relation to the 'homestyle' exemption, the WTO Panel avoided making a 'value judgment on the legitimacy' of the exception, but did give some weight to the public policy purposes 'for drawing inferences about the scope of an exemption and the clarity of its definition'.[29] In the Panel's view, the legislative history, which pointed to the public policy purpose of protecting small business, often run by immigrants, women and minorities, supported the conclusion that the exception had a narrow scope.[30] In reaching this conclusion, the WTO Panel did not consider

---

jurisprudence on fair use, informed both by Israel's previous legal tradition of fair dealing and US case law, and observing that unrestrained copying has not arisen as a result.

[23] Such as parody: *Campbell* v. *Acuff-Rose Music* 510 US 569 (1994), 510 US 569 (1994).

[24] *Sega Enterprises Ltd* v. *Accolade Inc*, 977 F. 2d 1510 (9th Cir. 1992). See also *Oracle Am., Inc.* v. *Google, Inc.* 750 F.3d 1339 (2014) (certiorari denied by Supreme Court – see (2015) 135 S Ct 2887).

[25] Such as time-shifting: *Sony* v. *Universal City Studios, Inc*, 464 US 417 (1984).

[26] For example, private copying for the purpose of time-shifting could be justified according to the three-step test.

[27] WTO DS 160/R, [6.112].

[28] WTO DS 160/R, [6.112].

[29] WTO DS 160/R, [6.157].

[30] WTO DS 160/R, [6.156]–[6.157].

the normative value of the exception relative to the interests of the rights holder.[31] In this way, it stripped out possible countervailing interests of social and public importance.

Similarly, in considering the second limb of the test, the WTO Panel replicated this approach. Although it pointed to empirical and normative understandings of 'normal' exploitation, it focused wholly on the economic harm to the rights holder and did not actually engage in a normative assessment of 'normal exploitation'.[32] The Panel described the empirical component as related to 'areas of the market in which the copyright owner would ordinarily expect to exploit the work, but which are not available for exploitation because of this exemption'.[33] The normative aspect was intended to take 'into account technological and market developments'[34] and to ascertain which forms of exploitation would likely and plausibly 'acquire considerable economic or practical importance'.[35] The Panel stressed that 'not every use of a work, which in principle is covered by the scope of exclusive rights and involves commercial gain, necessarily conflicts with a normal exploitation of that work'.[36] However, as already mentioned, it did not really articulate when this might be and concentrated its attention on an empirical enquiry into the economic harm suffered by rightsholders.[37] Commentators have criticised the Panel's preoccupation with the interests of rights holders, not least because it excludes important countervailing interests, such as access to information, promotion of competition, along with the interests of creators.[38] It has been suggested that perhaps the Panel assumed that the test would 'automatically balance user and producer interests appropriately'[39] because it derived from Article 9(2) Berne, but this ignores the ramification of transposing the

---

[31] See also Dinwoodie and Dreyfuss (2012), 62, referring to the fact that the Panel failed to consider 'the relative economic value and social importance of each use or the question of the value of a particular form of exploitation to users relative to right holders'.

[32] Jane C Ginsburg, 'Toward Supranational Copyright Law? The WTO Panel Decision and the "Three Step Test" for Copyright Exceptions' (2001) 187 *RIDA* 3, 17.

[33] WTO DS 160/R, [6.177].

[34] WTO DS 160/R, [6.178].

[35] WTO DS 160/R, [6.180].

[36] WTO DS 160/R, [6.182].

[37] WTO DS 160/R, [6.208]. This is criticised by Dinwoodie and Dreyfuss (2012), 63.

[38] Geiger et al (2008), 490; Grosse Ruse-Khan (2016), [12.48], 434–5. Contrast André Lucas, 'For a Reasonable Interpretation of the Three-Step Test' (2010) 32 *EIPR* 277, 279, arguing that the second step has always been restricted to the economic sphere and should not take into account other interests. Note that the three-step test for patent exceptions in Article 30 TRIPS expressly refers to the legitimate interests of the patent owner *and* of third parties. The WTO Panel has thus explored the scope of legitimate interests in this context. See WTO Appellate Body Report, Canada – Patent Protection of Pharmaceutical Products (17 March 2000) WT/DS114/R. It is perhaps, therefore, unsurprising that it did not do so in relation to Article 13 TRIPS, which does not explicitly mention the legitimate interests of third parties.

[39] Graeme B Dinwoodie and Rochelle C Dreyfuss, 'Designing a Global Intellectual Property System Responsive to Change: The WTO, WIPO and Beyond' (2009) 46 *Houston L Rev* 1187, 1207.

measure into TRIPS, 'where it applies to all user activities, to all markets, and to all of the principal intellectual property regimes'.[40]

By way of contrast, Article 10(1) Berne treats the normative underpinnings of the quotation exception as particularly important. For example, as we have argued, freedom of expression and other normative justifications, relating to economic and moral harm, along with distributive concerns, play a key role in determining 'fair practice'. This approach of using normativity to judge what constitutes 'fair practice' involves assessing the value of the use itself. Moreover, it creates a means of ensuring that the interests of users, and the public more generally, are weighed alongside the interests of authors or rights holders. The three-step test is fixated on empirical economic harm to the author or rights holder, whereas the quotation exception takes account of a range of interests, only one of which is economic harm to the rights holder, in its requirement of 'fair practice'.

This feature of Article 10(1) Berne, when translated into a national context, such as US fair use, could point to justifications for certain considerations, such as transformative use. Transformative use is a key consideration under US fair use[41] and one that has itself undergone a transformation in the past decade or so.[42] According to its original advocate, Judge Pierre Leval,[43] the basis for transformative use supporting 'fair' use is that it promotes copyright's rationale of stimulating creativity to the benefit of society.[44] As such, Judge Leval argued that this requires quotation that is 'of the transformative type that advances knowledge', in contrast to where it 'merely repackages, free riding on another's creations'.[45] This view of transformative use was adopted by the US Supreme Court in its decision in *Campbell* v. *Acuff-Rose*.[46] However, in more recent years, US courts have, on occasion, taken an expansionist view of what counts as transformative use and how this may be weighed as part of all four factors. An illustrative example is *Cariou* v. *Prince*,[47] where the Court of Appeals

---

[40]   Dinwoodie and Dreyfuss (2009), 1208.

[41]   Indeed, some have argued that is *the* key consideration: see Neil W Netanel, 'Making Sense of Fair Use' (2011) 15 *Lewis & Clark L Rev* 715, 745, describing how, in the period before 2010, if the use was transformative, this 'infuse[d] the court's analysis of factors three and four'. Contrast (based on US case-law to 2005) Beebe (2008), 604, 'courts and commentators have exaggerated the influence of transformativeness'.

[42]   For an enlightening empirical analysis of the role of transformative use in fair use cases until 1 January 2017, see J Liu, 'An Empirical Study of Transformative Use in Copyright Law' (2019) 22 *Stan Tech L Rev* 163.

[43]   P Leval, 'Toward a Fair Use Standard' (1990) 103 *Harvard L Rev* 1105.

[44]   Leval (1990), 1111.

[45]   Leval (1990), 1116. Lloyd L Weinreb, 'Fair's Fair: A Comment on the Fair Use Doctrine' (1990) 103 *Harv L Rev* 1137, 1140–4, criticised this view.

[46]   510 US 569 (1994), 114 S Ct 1164 (1994). Liu (2019), 174, notes that after *Campbell* the popularity of transformative use in fair use litigation in the US 'started to skyrocket'. Elkin-Koren and Netanel (2020), 61, observe that the Israeli Supreme Court 'fully embraced the transformative use approach that currently dominates U.S. fair use law' in C.A. 3425/17 *Société des Produits Nestlé v Nespresso Club Ltd* (SC 7 August 2019). A redacted translation of this case is found at 'George Clooney – What Else. . . (Nespresso v. Espresso Club)' (2020) 51 *IIC* 262–72.

[47]   714 F. 3d 694 (2d Cir. 2013). Another example is *Authors Guild v. HathiTrust* 755 F. 3d 87 (2d Cir. 2014).

for the Second Circuit held that transformative use does not require 'comment on the original [work] or its author', can serve purposes other than those identified in section 107[48] and is to be judged according to how the defendant's use may 'reasonably be perceived' as opposed to the defendant's stated intentions.[49] Further, in assessing the other fair use factors, the court relied heavily on the transformative *purpose* to assess whether the market was harmed and to counteract the quality and quantity of what was copied.[50] Decisions such as *Cariou* have attracted criticism for collapsing the four fair use factors into a consideration of transformativeness,[51] and subsequent cases have not always adopted such a generous view of transformative use.[52]

Transformative use or purpose sits comfortably with the notion of 'quotation' in Article 10(1), according to our interpretation. When it comes to the requirement of 'fair practice', there is also a place for transformative use, particularly if account is taken of freedom of expression or distributive justice considerations. Some types of transformative use may better align with freedom of expression than others, such as 'directly commenting on or criticizing the original work' or 'using the original work to comment on something else',[53] whereas, changing the purpose of the work, say from an entertainment to educational purpose, or to create a social benefit, may fit better with distributive justice concerns. Importantly, however, the 'fair practice' assessment in Article 10(1) Berne would not allow this one factor to 'stampede' other considerations, such as economic and moral harm to the author. Therefore, to the extent that US fair use can be legitimately criticised for this 'stampeding' trend,[54] we suggest this is inconsistent with 'fair practice' within Article 10(1).

---

[48] *Cariou*, 706. The court described the 'entirely different aesthetic from Cariou's photographs' contrasting the 'serene and deliberately composed portraits' with the 'crude and jarring works' of Prince. (706)

[49] *Cariou*, 707.

[50] *Cariou*, 709–10.

[51] J C Ginsburg, 'Exclusive Rights, Exceptions, and Uncertain Compliance with International Norms' (2014) 242 *RIDA* 175, 251, and J C Ginsburg, 'Fair Use For Free, or Permitted-But-Paid?' (2014) 29 *Berkeley Tech L J* 1383, 1445. Liu (2019) has also criticised the courts for being inconsistent in what they consider as 'transformative' – he notes that in cases of physical and purposive transformation of a work courts find transformative use, but that there is variability in the finding of transformative use in instances of physical but no purposive transformation, or purposive but no physical transformation. In addition, there have also been findings of transformative use where there is no physical or purposive transformation.

[52] See *Kienitz* v. *Sconnie Nation* 766 F. 3d 756, 758 (7th Cir. 2014), criticising the *Cariou* decision. *Kienitz* was referred to in *TCA Television Corp* v. *McCollum* 839 F. 3d 168, 181 (2d Cir. 2016), but the Second Circuit Court of Appeal did not seek to defend its decision in *Cariou*). See also *Brammer* v. *Violent Hues Productions* 922 F. 3d 255 (4th Cir. 2019), where use of a photograph to illustrate tourist attractions was held not to be transformative and *Fox News Network* v. *TVEyes Inc* 883 F. 3d 169 (2d Cir. 2018), where recording large quantities of television programming into a text searchable database was transformative but outweighed by the effect on the plaintiff's market.

[53] See Tan (2012), 846–7.

[54] Beebe (2008), 605, noting that 'in those opinions in which transformativeness did play a role, it exerted nearly dispositive force not simply on the outcome of factor one but on the overall outcome of the fair use test'. See also Liu (2019), observing that courts have shown a tendency to treat 'transformative use

C *The Unpublished Nature of the Source Work*

The three-step test applies to works that are published or unpublished,[55] although the unpublished status of a work may impact on whether there is a conflict with the normal exploitation of the work and may prejudice the legitimate interests of the author (namely, her divulgation right).[56] In contrast, Article 10(1) Berne has a clear condition that the work from which the quotation is taken has lawfully been made available to the public.[57]

For acts that fall within the scope of section 107 of the US Copyright Act 1976 and within the scope of 'quotation' in Article 10(1) Berne, this means that the status of the work as not having been made available to the public is crucial. Yet the rider to section 107 (added in 1992 by amendment)[58] states: 'The fact that a work is unpublished shall not itself bar a finding of fair use if such finding is made upon consideration of all the above factors.'[59] This provision, arguably together with the decision of the Second Circuit in *Wright v. Warner Books, Inc*[60] (which preceded the amendment to section 107), signalled a turning point that 'ended the concerns about the feared possibility of a per se rule flatly prohibiting the use of unpublished material in the fair use analysis'.[61] It reversed the Supreme Court decision in *Harper & Row, Publishers Inc v. Nation Enterprises*,[62] whereby the unpublished status of the work was treated as 'a critical element of its "nature"' and weighed heavily against fair use because of the importance of the right of first publication and the impact this would have on the market for the work.[63] To ensure compatibility with Article 10(1) Berne, there may be no need to revert to the position reflected in *Harper & Row*, since this decision focused on the *unpublished* nature of the work, whereas Article 10(1) Berne refers to works that are lawfully made available to the public. However, where the work had not been lawfully made available to the public (and the use fell within Article 10(1), as opposed to Article 9(2) Berne) there would be a need to treat the use as presumptively unfair.

---

as a shortcut to fair use' (167) and observing at 240: 'a finding of transformative use overrides findings of commercial purpose and bad faith under factor one, makes irrelevant the issue of whether the original work is creative or unpublished under factor two, stretches the extent of copying permitted under factor three towards 100% verbatim reproduction, and precludes the evidence on damage to the primary or derivative market under factor four even though there exists a well-functioning market for the use'.

[55] Sam Ricketson and Jane C Ginsburg, *International Copyright and Neighbouring Rights: The Berne Convention and Beyond* (2nd ed., Oxford University Press 2006), [13.28], 777–8.

[56] Ricketson and Ginsburg (2006), [13.29], 778.

[57] Chapter 4, Section II, pp. 71–77.

[58] Roger L Zissu, 'Fair Use: From Harper & Row to Acuff Rose, May 13, 1994' (1994) 42 *J Copyright Soc'y USA* 7, 10.

[59] Pub. L. No. 102–492, 106 Stat. 3145 (1992).

[60] 953 F. 2d 731, 20 U.S.P.Q. 2d 1892 (2d Cir. 1991).

[61] Zissu (1994), 11.

[62] 105 S Ct 2218, 2226–8 (1985), treating the unpublished nature of President Ford's memoirs as a key factor weighing against fair use.

[63] *Harper & Row*, 2232. See further David B Goroff, 'Fair Use and Unpublished Works: Harper & Row v. Nation Enterprises' (1984) 9 *Colum-VLA Art & L* 325.

D *The Treatment of Moral Rights of Authors*

For the three-step test, as interpreted by the WTO Panel, the focus of the assessment is *economic* harm to the right holder, and there is only a slim possibility that authorial interests, such as moral rights, will be taken into account, whereas Article 10(1) Berne more explicitly and directly respects the moral rights of authors. This is done in several ways. The first is that Article 10(1) does not operate as an exception to moral rights in Article 6*bis* Berne.[64] The second is that Article 10(1) reinforces the right of attribution via Article 10(3). Finally, in assessing 'fair practice', the integrity interests of the author may be a relevant consideration.

Why, then, are moral rights virtually ignored by the three-step test, as interpreted by the WTO Panel? This requires us to consider the Panel's interpretation of the third step. The Panel held that 'interests' were not confined to actual or potential economic harm.[65] 'Legitimate' was held to mean 'lawfulness' but also to have a normative component, 'in the context of calling for the protection of interests that are justifiable in the light of the objectives that underlie the protection of exclusive rights'.[66] The Panel indicated that 'one – albeit incomplete and thus conservative – way of looking at legitimate interests is the economic value of the exclusive rights conferred by copyright on their holders', but went on to indicate that they are not 'necessarily limited to this economic value'.[67] However, the Panel failed to elaborate upon what may have been other legitimate interests. Rather, in defining unreasonable prejudice, it indicated that this threshold would be breached if 'an exception or limitation causes or has the potential to cause an unreasonable loss of income to the copyright owner'.[68] The Panel maintained this economic focus in the way in which it assessed the 'business' exemption.[69]

The fact that the Panel indicated that legitimate interests are not 'limited to right holders of the Member that brings forth the complaint'[70] might indicate that moral rights interests are pertinent.[71] This seems unlikely, however, given that Article 6*bis* Berne is specifically excluded from incorporation into TRIPS.[72] Article 13 TRIPS may be contrasted with Article 9(2) Berne, where moral rights are clearly part of

---

[64] See Chapter 3, Section III, Part B, pp. 57–60. Cf Ricketson and Ginsburg (2006), [13.30], 778, who observe that Article 9(2) Berne only governs exceptions and limitations to the right of reproduction and does not extend to moral rights protected under Article 6*bis*. So, in that sense, Article 9(2) and Article 10(1) Berne are similar.

[65] WTO DS 160/R, [6.223]

[66] WTO DS 160/R, [6.224]

[67] WTO DS 160/R, [6.227].

[68] WTO DS 160/R, [6.229].

[69] Dinwoodie and Dreyfuss (2012), 64, stating that the Panel 'merely reiterated its arithmetic arguments'.

[70] WTO DS 160/R, [6.231].

[71] Andrew F Christie and Robin Wright, 'A Comparative Analysis of the Three-Step Tests in International Treaties' (2014) 45(4) *IIC* 409, 429, pointing out that the legitimate interests of a creator include moral rights, whereas transferees of copyright will not have these interests.

[72] André Lucas, 'For a Reasonable Interpretation of the Three-Step Test' (2010) 32(6) *EIPR* 277, 277; Ricketson and Ginsburg (2006), [13.104], 855 and Senftleben (2004), 225-226.

Berne (in Article 6*bis*), and thus 'interests' in step three may include economic and non-economic considerations.[73]

An impact of Article 10(1) Berne for the US fair use doctrine is that the latter may have to pay greater attention to the conditions of attribution of source and authorship.[74] At present, attribution is not a requirement of fair use; nor does it usually tend to be weighed as part of evaluating 'fairness'.[75] To ensure compatibility of 'quotation' uses with Article 10(1), US fair use would need to take heed of attribution of source and author. Given the open-ended nature of section 107, there would be nothing stopping courts relying on attribution as a separate factor in appropriate cases or, as Professor Ginsburg suggests, as part of factor one – the nature of the use.[76] However, Professor Beebe has observed that judges rarely consider factors beyond those four listed in section 107[77] and Professor Ginsburg has observed that authorship attribution has been given little weight.[78] However, this would not prevent future courts from taking a more robust approach.[79] Even so, it may be preferable to make legislative adjustments to section 107 to indicate that attribution *is* a factor that ought to be considered by courts.

More significantly, the approach to the right of integrity may need to change. Currently, the right of integrity (such as it is under US law) is subject to specific exceptions in section 106A(c) and also subject to the fair use exception in section 107.[80] Looking at the congressional history, various challenges were made to the extension of fair use to moral rights. For example, Professor Ginsburg questioned whether there was any public policy or public benefit underlying the extension of fair use to moral rights and whether it was ever fair to deny attribution or to attribute falsely.[81] Congress acknowledged that 'the modification of a single copy or limited

---

[73]   Ricketson and Ginsburg (2006), [13.24], 774. See also Senftleben (2004), 222.

[74]   See also Jane C Ginsburg, 'The Most Moral of Rights: The Right to Be Recognized as the Author of One's Work' (2016) 8 *Geo Mason J Int'l Com L* 44.

[75]   Cf Catherine J Cameron, 'Reinvigorating U.S. Copyright with Attribution: How Courts Can Help Define the Fair Use Exception to Copyright by Considering the Economic Aspects of Attribution' (2013) 2 *Berkeley J Ent & Sports L* 130, who discusses the few cases where attribution has played a role in fair use.

[76]   Ginsburg (2016), 72–3.

[77]   Beebe (2008), 563–4, referring to a sample of fair use cases from 1978–2005.

[78]   Ginsburg (2016), 73.

[79]   See also Ginsburg (2016), 73. Indeed, Elkin-Koren and Netanel (2020), 65–7, note that in Israeli decisions on fair use, lack of attribution has usually weighed against there being fair use. Although the authors query whether this will continue to be the case after the Israeli Supreme Court decision in C. A. 3425/17 *Société des Produits Nestle* v. *Nespresso Club Ltd* (SC 7 August 2019).

[80]   See Section 107, 'Notwithstanding the provisions of Sections 106 and 106A, the fair use of a copyrighted work . . . '.

[81]   Visual Artists Rights Act of 1989: Hearing before the Subcommittee on Courts, Intellectual Property, and the Administration of Justice of the Committee on the Judiciary, House of Representatives, One Hundred First Congress, First session, on HR 2690, p. 89, 18 October (1989). See also Mr Peter Karlen, Moral Rights in Our Copyright Laws: Hearings on S. 1198 and S. 1253 Before the Subcommittee on Patents, Copyrights and Trademarks of the Senate Comm. on the Judiciary, 101st Cong. pp. 105–6 (1989).

edition of a work of visual art has different implications for the fair use doctrine than does an act involving a work reproduced in potentially unlimited copies'.[82] However, these differences were not explored and Congress hastily inserted the fair use limitation to federal moral rights based on an assurance from the US Copyright Office that there was no conflict between fair use, copyright and moral rights.[83] Scholars have criticised the application of fair use to moral rights.[84] There is an additional, compelling reason to those cited by these scholars – namely, the fact that the mandatory quotation exception does not operate as an exception to infringement of the moral rights contained in Article 6*bis* Berne. Therefore, to ensure that 'fair use' is consistent with Article 10(1) Berne, it would seem necessary to revisit the question of whether, and, if so, to what extent, section 107 is applicable to moral rights.

E *The Cumulative Nature of the Requirements*

Whether the three-step test is cumulative in nature (i.e. the steps are taken in sequence and each must be satisfied) has been debated by scholars. Some favour seeing the three-step test as an integrated whole. Professors Geiger, Gervais and Senftleben, for example, argue that '[w]hile the steps can be considered sequentially ... it should not be overlooked that the test constitutes a single analytical whole and serves the ultimate goal to strike an appropriate balance'. As such, all steps should be considered, even if one is not met.[85] Several scholars share this view of approaching the three-step test as elements in an overall, comprehensive assessment.[86] Others have suggested that in order to reflect a balanced test, the order of the steps could be reversed. This would enable a focus on 'legitimate interests' of the author or rights holder, which would open up a policy space in

---

[82] H.R. Rep. No. 101-514 at 22 (1990).

[83] Visual Artists Rights Act of 1989: Hearing before the Subcommittee on Courts, Intellectual Property, and the Administration of Justice of the Committee on the Judiciary, House of Representatives, One Hundred First Congress, First session, on HR 2690, 77, 18 October 1989. See also Moral Rights in Our Copyright Laws: Hearings on S. 1198 and S. 1253 before the Subcommittee on Patents, Copyrights and Trademarks of the Senate Comm. on the Judiciary, 101st Congress, p. 234 (1989).

[84] Dane S Ciolino, 'Rethinking the Compatability of Moral Rights and Fair Use' (1997) 54 *Wash & Lee L Rev* 33. See also Jane C Ginsburg, 'Copyright in the 101st Congress: Commentary on the Visual Artists Rights Act and the Architectural Works Copyright Protection Act of 1990' (1990) 14 *Colum-VLA J L & Arts* 477, fn. 26; Peter H Karlen, 'What's Wrong with VARA: A Critique of Federal Moral Rights' (1992–1993) 15 *Hastings Comm & Ent L J* 905, 912–13, and Rebecca Stuart, 'A Work of Heart: A Proposal for a Revision of the Visual Artists Rights Act of 1990 to Bring the United States Closer to International Standards' (2007) 47 *Santa Clara L Rev* 645, 683.

[85] Christophe Geiger, Daniel Gervais and Martin Senftleben, 'The Three Step Test Revisited: How to Use the Test's Flexibility in National Copyright Law' (2014) 29 *Am U Intl L Rev* 581, 585.

[86] Christophe Geiger, Jonathan Griffiths and Reto M Hilty, 'Towards a Balanced Interpretation of the "Three Step Test" in Copyright Law' (2008) 30(12) *EIPR* 489, 493, 495; Annette Kur, 'Of Oceans, Islands, and Inland Water – How Much Room for Exceptions and Limitations under the Three-Step Test?' (2009) 8 *Rich J Global L & Bus* 287, 340.

which to discuss competing interests at stake, including those linked to the underlying justification of the exception.[87] Closely linked is the suggestion that the third step should become the focal point of analysis.[88] Another suggestion is to retain the cumulative, sequential structure of the three-step test, but adopt different interpretative approaches for each step.[89] Other commentators have suggested that there is undue concern about a sequential approach because, practically speaking, the second and third steps inevitably overlap and intertwine.[90] However, some scholars, such as Professor Lucas, vehemently reject a global or overlapping interpretation of the elements of the three-step test, seeing this as 'directly contrary to the wording of the text' and the Stockholm Revision *travaux*.[91]

The WTO Panel in the 'Fairness in Music Licensing case' adopted the view (albeit without there being any argument on this point) that the three-step test is cumulative in nature, so that failure to meet the first limb would be fatal.[92] Thus the failure of the 'business' exemption in section 110[5](B) of the US Copyright Act 1976 to meet the first condition in Article 13 TRIPS meant that the exception failed overall.[93] Similarly, because the 'homestyle' exception complied with the first step, the Panel considered it necessary to analyse and apply the second and third steps (and also found these met). In addressing these steps, the Panel noted that they are 'closely related' and overlap in their field of operation.[94]

Article 10(1) Berne may be contrasted with the Panel's approach to the three-step test in Article 13 TRIPS. Recall that quotations shall be permissible according to Article 10(1): (i) 'from a work which has already been lawfully made available to the public'; (ii) provided that their 'making is compatible with fair practice'; and (iii) 'their extent does not exceed that justified by the purpose' and (iv) that according to Article 10(3) 'mention shall be made of the source, and of the name of the author, if it appears thereon'. It is argued that, based on the text of the provisions, each of these conditions is distinct. However, this does not mean that all the conditions must be approached sequentially and that no overlap exists between them. Granted, the conditions of a work having been lawfully made available to the public and attribution of author and source appear as straightforward prerequisites without overlap. However, overlap exists between the requirements of quotation, fair practice and

---

[87]   Christophe Geiger, 'The Three-Step Test, A Threat to a Balanced Copyright Law?' (2006) 37 *IIC* 683, 697.

[88]   Martin Senftleben, *Copyright, Limitations and the Three-Step Test: An Analysis of the Three-Step Test in International and EC Copyright Law* (Kluwer 2004), 132, 192–3.

[89]   Huaiwen He, 'Seeking a Balanced Interpretation of the Three-Step Test – An Adjusted Structure in View of Divergent Approaches' (2009) 40(3) *IIC* 274.

[90]   Hughes (2017), 242.

[91]   André Lucas, 'For a Reasonable Interpretation of the Three-Step Test' (2010) 32(6) *EIPR* 277, 281.

[92]   WTO DS 160/R, [6.74], 'As both parties agree, these three conditions apply cumulatively; a limitation or an exception is consistent with Article 13 only if it fulfils each of the three conditions.'

[93]   WTO DS 160/R, [6.160]. Although the Panel nevertheless considered steps two and three and found that they also were not met; see [6.190]–[6.211] and [6.237]–[6.266].

[94]   WTO DS 160/R, [6.161].

proportionality, and it is important to be aware of this. As was argued earlier in the book, what constitutes a quotation should be understood broadly: it relates to all types of works, may be a transformative use, is not restricted to certain purposes and may be of any length. Proportionality targets whether the length of the quotation is justifiable according to its purpose. Fair practice involves a consideration of whether the quotation is consistent with a pluralistic notion of 'fairness', and this may involve examining the nature or purpose of the use, the type of expressive use, the nature of the work quoted, the size of the quotation and its proportion in relation to the source work, harm to the market of the source work and the integrity interests of the author of the source work. From this outline, it is apparent that the length of a quotation is relevant to both the proportionality and fair practice requirements but should not be a barrier to whether a particular use is deemed a 'quotation'. Further, the purpose or use of the quotation should not determine its status as 'quotation', but this will be relevant to judging proportionality and also fair practice. Thus, it is crucial not to exclude certain uses as 'quotation' based on these criteria, but instead to factor them into the assessments of proportionality and fair practice. In addition, the relationship between these two latter requirements is important, and logically speaking, it makes more sense to consider proportionality before fair practice. This is because, based on the *travaux*, proportionality is really only concerned with judging the appropriate length of quotations. As the *travaux* make clear, 'fair practice' is also concerned with assessing the length of quotations, but this, we argue, is part of a broader assessment of whether the quoted use is *fair*. Given that the normative considerations for assessing fairness are more wide ranging, it makes sense to only apply a light filter at the proportionality stage, and to interrogate more fully the length of the quotation alongside all the other relevant factors at the fairness stage.

The impact of Article 10(1) Berne including overlapping considerations, as opposed to the WTO Panel view that the three-step test is sequential or cumulative in nature, mainly relates to how national legislatures implement the quotation exception and how national courts should interpret exceptions. For national legislatures, quotation may be defined broadly (and certainly should not be restricted to short quotations for specific purposes) and their proportionality and fairness judged according to several factors. As such, an open-ended, multifactor exception, such as fair use in section 107 of the US Copyright Act 1976, would be permissible. There would, however, as argued previously, need to be a clearer indication that the failure to attribute and whether the work has been lawfully made available, are relevant considerations.[95] Moreover, courts, in interpreting a national fair use exception consistently with Article 10(1) Berne, would need to engage in weighing and assessing relevant factors. Thus, an exception that is structurally organised along the lines of US fair use could give effect to Article 10(1).

---

95 Chapter 7, Section I, Parts C and D, pp. 198–201.

F *Free-Use Exceptions*

A further distinction that can be made between the three-step test and Article 10(1) Berne is that the former permits free-use as well as royalty-based exceptions, whereas the latter is simply 'free use'.[96] Currently, US fair use is an unremunerated exception, and Article 10(1) Berne justifies this to the extent that quotation uses fall within section 107. It also provides potential resistance to the argument that certain existing fair uses, in fact, should be permitted but paid[97] and the suggestion that therefore substantial incompatibility exists between the third limb of the three-step test and US fair use.[98]

II CHANGES TO NATIONAL EXCEPTIONS

Once the scope and force of Article 10(1) Berne is understood, it becomes apparent that several jurisdictions have failed properly to implement this international obligation. The next section looks at instances of this non-compliance.

A *Specific-Quotation Exceptions*

Numerous civil law jurisdictions and the occasional common law jurisdiction feature specific quotation exceptions. Unfortunately, some of these exceptions limit the purposes for which quotation may be made. For example, Portugal permits quotation for 'criticism, discussion or teaching', while Belgium permits quotation only for 'criticism, polemic, review, education or in scientific works'; Korea allows quotation 'for purposes of news reporting, critique, education and research, etc' and China permits quotation 'for the purpose of introducing or commenting on a certain work, or explaining a certain point'.[99] In Greece, a statutory quotation exception is limited to circumstances where the act of quotation is 'necessary in order to support

---

[96] See Chapter 6, Section II, Part A. See also Bernt Hugenholtz and Ruth L Okediji, *Conceiving an International Instrument on Limitations and Exceptions to Copyright*, Amsterdam Law School Legal Studies Research Paper No 2012-43, at http://ssrn.com/abstract=2017629 (accessed 28 January 2020), at 51, describing quotation as an 'uncompensated limitation'; Raquel Xalabarder, 'On-line Teaching and Copyright: Any Hopes for an EU Harmonized Playground?' in Paul Torremans (ed.), *Copyright Law: A Handbook of Contemporary Research* (Edward Elgar 2007), ch. 15, 397, 'no compensation applies', and Pascale Chapdelaine, *Copyright User Rights: Contracts and the Erosion of Property* (Oxford University Press 2017), 37, fn. 43.

[97] In particular, non-profit educational and library uses, as opposed to private uses and mass digitization, which are the examples discussed by Jane Ginsburg, 'Fair Use For Free, or Permitted-But-Paid?' (2014) 29 *Berkeley Tech L J* 1383, 1445–6.

[98] Jane Ginsburg, 'Exclusive Rights, Exceptions, and Uncertain Compliance with International Norms' (2014) 242 *RIDA* 175, 261–3.

[99] Código do Direito de Autor e dos Direitos Conexos 1985, Article 77(1)(g) (Portugal); Article XI.189 of Book XI, Title V of the Code of Economic Law (Authors and Related Rights) (updated 19 June 2019) ('criticism, controversy, or review') (Belgium); Copyright Act (Act No. 432 of January 28, 1957, as amended up to Act No. 12137 of December 30, 2013), Art 28 (Republic of Korea); Copyright Law of the People's Republic of China of February 26, 2010 (amended up to the Decision of February 26, 2010, by

one's own opinion, or to criticize the opinion of another'.[100] It thus did not cover the use of extracts from the claimant's book on Herodotus in the defendant's educational text because 'the extracts are not used to support the defendant's opinion or to criticise the plaintiff's opinion'.[101]

Limitations by purpose are by no means the only limitations on the right to quote that can be seen in national law. Some countries limit the availability of the freedom to quote to particular works: Austria, for example, refers only to literary or musical works,[102] while Lithuania's quotation exception is limited to 'a relatively short passage of a literary and scientific work'[103] and Zimbabwe only permits quotation of literary and musical works.[104] Some national laws require a faithful representation of a quoted author's work. In Estonia, it is provided that the quotation is only permissible if the idea of the work as a whole is conveyed correctly.[105] In Mexico, quotation is only permitted 'without altering the work'.[106]

Some national laws purport to qualify the scope of the quotation expression by a 'quantitative' limit. The most obvious example of such a country is France, where the exception is limited to '*les courtes citations*'.[107] The most dramatic applications of such a restriction are to be found in the cases that indicate that the complete

---

the Standing Committee of the National People's Congress on Amending the Copyright Law of the People's Republic of China), Art 22 (China). See also Argentina, Law No. 26.570 of November 25, 2009, amending Law No. 11.723 of September 28, 1993, on Legal Intellectual Property Regime, Art 10 ('for didactic or scientific purposes, comments, criticisms or notes') (Argentina); Armenia, Copyright and Related Rights Law of 15 June 2006, Article 22 ('for scientific, research, polemic, critical and informational purposes') (Armenia); Brazil, Law No. 9.610 of February 19, 1998 (Law on Copyright and Neighboring Rights), Art 46 ('for the purposes of study, criticism or debate') (Brazil); Cambodia, Law on Copyright and Related Rights, Art 25 ('short quotations justified by the critical, polemical, pedagogical, scientific or informative nature of that work') (Cambodia); Latvia, Copyright Law (as amended up to 31 December 2014), Section 20 ('for scientific, research, polemical, critical purposes') (Latvia); France, IP Code 1992, Article L122–5(3)(a) (referring to the 'critical, polemic, educational, scientific, or informative character of the work in which they are incorporated') (Malta); Malta, Copyright (Amendment) Act No. IX of 2009, s. 9 ('quotations for purposes such as criticism or review'). See further Lionel Bochumberg, *Le Droit de Citation* (Masson 1994) ch. 2 (characterterising the different approaches as open and closed).

[100] Greek Copyright Act 1993, Article 19.

[101] *Re Quotations in Students' Text Books* (1 January 1990) [1992] ECC 56 (Protodikion (District Court), Athens) (in English) (decided under Copyright Act 2387/1920, as amended by Act 4301/1929). A level of ambiguity, however, is introduced in the reasoning of the Court when it added that 'instead, the defendant presents the extracts and the passages as his own with no mention of the plaintiff's name'. It may be that the case can be seen as one where the attribution requirement was unmet.

[102] Austria, Federal Law on Copyright in Literary and Artistic Works and Related Rights (Copyright Act) (as amended up to Federal Law Gazette (BGBl) I No. 99/2015, Section 46. See Westkamp, (2007), 113. See also South Africa Copyright Act 1978, Section 12(3).

[103] Lithuania, Law on Copyright and Related Rights No. VIII-1185 of 18 May 1999 (as amended on 7 October 2014 – by Law No. XII-1183), Article 21.

[104] Zimbabwe, Copyright and Neighbouring Rights Act (Chapter 26:05), s. 31.

[105] Copyright Act 2004 (consolidated text of 1 February 2017), Article 19(1).

[106] Ley Federal Del Derecho De Autor, 24 December 1996 (as amended), Article 148 (Mexico).

[107] Article L122–5(3)(a) of the France IP Code. For commentary, see Yves Gaubiac, 'Freedom to Quote from an Intellectual Work' (1997) 171 *RIDA* 2.

reproduction of a work of art, whatever its format, cannot in any case be deemed to be brief quotation.[108] Greece also restricts its quotation exception to 'short extracts', Serbia to 'short excerpts' and Sri Lanka, although it has a 'fair use' exception, explicitly stipulates that quotations of short parts of a work shall be permitted.[109] The Copyright Law of Trinidad, which (unusually for a former British colony) operates a quotation exception, limits the quotation to 'a short part of a published work'.[110]

Some national laws, including the laws of France, Spain, Morocco, the Czech Republic, Lithuania and Poland (to cite just a few), seem to insist on incorporation of a quotation into 'another work'.[111] Article L. 122–5(3)(a) of the French I.P. Code exempts 'analyses and brief quotations justified on the grounds of the critical, polemic, educational, scientific, or informative character of *the work in which they are incorporated*'. Some French case law suggests that the 'quoting text' must be able to operate effectively without the 'quoted text'.[112]

Some jurisdictions also require that the quoting work comment upon or 'refer back' to the quoted text.[113] For example, the Serbian Copyright Law requires that the quoted part is 'integrated into another work without alterations, for the sake of

---

[108]   See *Fabris v. Sté Sotheby's et autres* (1990) 145 *RIDA* 339 (C d'A Paris); *Fabris v. Loudmer* (Cass, 1st Ch Civ) (1991) 148 *RIDA* 119, (1992) 23 *IIC* 294; Cass (full court), 5 November 1993, (1994) 159 *RIDA* 320; Martin Senftleben, 'Internet Search Results – A Permissible Quotation?' (2013) 235 *RIDA* 3, 71–3 (discussing how this operated to exclude search results in the form of thumbnails from the French conception of 'quotation').

[109]   Greek Copyright Act 1993, Article 19; Serbia, Law on Copyright and Related Rights (Official Gazette Republic of Serbia No. 104/2009, 99/2011, 119/2012 and 29/2016), Art 49, and Sri Lanka, Intellectual Property Act (Act No 36 of 2003), s. 11 (fair use) and s. 12(3) (quotation). Examples of other national laws with a similar limitation include: Greek Copyright Act, Article 19 ('Quotation of short extracts of a lawfully published work . . . . shall be permissible . . . ') (WIPO translation); Lithuania, Law on Copyright and Related Rights No. VIII-1185 of 18 May 1999 (as amended on 7 October 2014 – by Law No. XII-1183), Article 21 ('a relatively short passage of a literary and scientific work'); Romanian Law No. 8 of March 14, 1996 on Copyright and Neighbouring Rights, Art 33(1)(b); Spanish Copyright Act, Article 32 ('fragments of the works of others'). A similar condition formerly operated in Belgian law but was deleted on implementation of EU Information Society Directive: Westkamp (2007), 129.

[110]   Trinidad, Act 8 of 1997 (as amended), s 10.

[111]   Spanish Copyright Act, Article 32 ('It shall be lawful to include in one's own work fragments of the works of others . . .'); Morocco Law and Copyright and Related Rights, 15 February 2000, Law 2-00, Article 14 (quotation 'in another work'); Czech Republic, Article 31a Copyright Act 2000 ('included in one's own individual work'); Lithuania ('in the form of a quotation . . . in another work'); Polish Copyright Act 84 of 4 February 1994 (as updated), Section 29.1 ('It shall be permitted to quote, in works *constituting an independent whole* . . . '). Indeed, Lionel Bochumberg, *Le Droit de Citation* (Masson 1994) ch. 3 treats incorporation of a quotation in a second work as a 'universal standard.' Cf. Chapter 5, Section III, Part A, pp. 110–113 for examples that suggest this does not accord with the ordinary meaning of the term 'quotation'.

[112]   See P Kamina, 'France' in L Bently (ed.), *International Copyright Law and Practice* (LexisNexis 2019) § 8[2][i], citing Paris, 4th ch, 14 June 2000, Juris-Data no. 121281 (in relation to an anthology of extracts of texts).

[113]   In fact, such a requirement was rejected at the intergovernmental conference itself. See pp. 27–28, above. There, the Swiss delegation proposed a limitation 'to the extent that they serve as an explanation, reference or illustration in the context in which they are used', corresponding to that which had been suggested in the Committee of Experts. The matter was discussed in the Main Committee but was ultimately defeated 27–10. *Records*, 591.

illustration, confirmation or reference'.[114] Even where such a requirement is not embedded in legislation, it has at times been recognised in jurisprudence.[115] For example, German case law had insisted that there be 'some inner relation with the quoting text: for example, the quotation may clarify a larger context or illustrate the quoting text',[116] only for the Constitutional Court in its 2000 *Germania III* decision to reject such a requirement where material was reused as background incident in a play, because to require such an inner relation would unduly limit the playwright's constitutionally guaranteed 'freedom of art'.[117] Quite how far this moved German jurisprudence is unclear.[118] In *Thumbnails I*,[119] for example, the BGH rejected the

---

[114]   Serbia, Law on Copyright and Related Rights (Official Gazette Republic of Serbia No. 104/2009, 99/ 2011, 119/2012 and 29/2016), Art 49.

[115]   Kamina, 'France', citing Paris, 1re ch, 10 September 1996, (1997) 171 *RIDA* 3. However, when faced with a different set of circumstances, the Cour de Cassation found that there was no need for discussion, and that the quotation exception was available where brief segments from works were brought together and classified in a database: *Le Monde* v. *Microfor*, Cass. civ. I, 9 November 1983, [1984] ECC 271, [7] (in English); Cass., Full Court, 30 October 1987, (1988) 135 *RIDA* 78, [1988] ECC 297 (in English) (excusing the creation of a database of the titles of articles that appeared in the newspaper *Le Monde* and *Le Monde Diplomatique* on the basis that the database was a work of an 'an informative character', and therefore one qualifying under the exception for quotation even though there was no 'personal comment or explanation' by its author). Kamina, ibid., [FRA-134], refers to the case as controversial and notes that '[t]he courts have resisted this reasoning in different fact situations.'

[116]   M Gruenberger, 'Germany' in L Bently (ed.), *International Copyright Law and Practice* (LexisNexis 2019) § 8[2][i].

[117]   *Germania 3*, BVerfG (Federal Constitutional Court), 29 June 2000, 2001 GRUR 149, *reversing* OLG (Court of Appeal) Munich, 26 March 1998, 1998 ZUM 417, translated and analysed by Christophe Antons and Elizabeth Adeney, 'The Germania 3 Decision Translated: The Quotation Exception Before the German Constitutional Court' [2013] *EIPR* 646.

[118]   In *Blühende Landschaften* (Blossoming Landscapes), BGH (Federal Court of Justice), Case No I ZR 212/10, Nov. 30, 2011, 2012 GRUR 819, the BGH overturned the Court of Appeal's finding that the incorporation of fifteen whole articles and ten photographs from the plaintiff's newspaper, *Märkische Oder Zeitung*, into a book based on the diary of a judge, *Blühende Landschaften*, was 'quotation'. Firstly, the BGH emphasised that, in general, there needed to be an 'inner connection' between the diary and the articles before they could be justified under Article 51 quotations. More specifically, 'quotations should serve as a reference or basis for discussion for independent explanations of the quoting person to facilitate intellectual discussion'. The BGH found that the Court of Appeal had failed to identify such inner connection. In this respect, it is notable that most of the articles and photographs featured as a documentary appendix rather than being integrated in any way within the judge's diary entries. Second, having regard to constitutional freedom of art that informed the *Germania III* decision (and which the BGH agreed requires a broader application of the quotation exception where the defendant's expression is an artistic, rather than purely communicative, one), the BGH found that the mere technical characterisation of the diary as a montage or collage did not make it an artistic work. This was because of the absence of creative choices on the part of the writer. Instead, the BGH indicated that the plaintiff's material was deployed as part of a descriptive communication of historical facts and their assessment by the defendant rather than primarily as 'a creative expression of his individual personality' ('nicht primär schöpferischer Ausdruck seiner individuellen Persönlichkeit ist').

[119]   *Thumbnails I*, BGH, Case No I ZR 69/08, 29 April 2010, BGHZ 185, 291 Rn 26, discussed in Mathias Leistner, 'The German Federal Supreme Court's Judgment on Google's Image Search – A Topical Example of the "Limitations" of the European Approach to Exceptions and Limitations' (2011) 42 *IIC*

possibility of exempting Google's generation of 'thumbnails' – that is, low-resolution versions of images already available online, via the 'quotation' exception, because of the absence of any 'intellectual appraisal of the used work'. (The court held the service justified on the basis of implied consent.)

All of the restrictions examined previously are, in fact, incompatible with Article 10(1) Berne. Thus the specific quotation exceptions in numerous jurisdictions would need to be amended to ensure compliance. Ideally, the best way of ensuring compliance is to replicate the terms of Article 10(1) as far as possible.

B *Fair Dealing Exceptions*

Numerous jurisdictions have fair dealing exceptions. Consider, for example, the 'fair dealing' exceptions in the laws of Australia, New Zealand, Canada, India, Jamaica, South Africa (and many other former British colonies),[120] each limited by a specified purpose.[121] In these countries, the obligation in Article 10(1) Berne Convention seems primarily to be reflected in the fair dealing exception for the purpose of 'criticism or review', which typically requires that such criticism or review be of the work, or another work (or, in some instances, the performance of a work).[122] This falls well short of permitting quotation for criticism in general,[123] let alone for other purposes, and is inconsistent with the clear terms of Article 10(1), and, evidently, with its legislative history.[124]

417; and Martin Senftleben, 'Internet Search Results – A Permissible Quotation?' (2013) 235 *RIDA* 3, 59.

[120] But not all: cf. Trinidad, Act 8 of 1997 (as amended), Section 10 (quotation exception).

[121] Copyright Act 1994, Section 42–3 (criticism, review, reporting current events, research or private study) (New Zealand); Copyright Act 1968, Section 40–2 (research or private study, criticism or review, parody or satire, reporting news), (Australia); Copyright Act 1957, Section 52(a) (private use, including research, criticism or review, reporting current events, and various exceptions for computer programs) (India); Copyright Act 1978, Section 12 (research or private study, criticism or review, reporting current events) (South Africa); Copyright Act 1985 (as amended), Section 29 (Fair dealing for the purpose of research, private study, education, parody or satire does not infringe copyright) (Canada); Nigerian Copyright Act, Cap C28, as codified in 2004 (Second Schedule), Section 6; Bermuda Copyright and Designs Act 2004, Sections 41–42. Cf. Singapore Copyright Act 1987 (revised in 2006), Section 35 (fair dealing exception with no limitation as to purpose) but retaining fair dealing for criticism or review in Section 36; CDPA 1988, Section 30(1ZA) added (1 October 2014) by the Copyright and Rights in Performances (Quotation and Parody) Regulations 2014, SI 2014/2356 and South Africa Copyright Act 1978, Section 12(3) refers to a specific quotation exception.

[122] Copyright Act 1994, Section 42 ('criticism or review, of that or another work or of a performance of a work') (New Zealand); Copyright Ordinance 2011, ch. 528, Section 39(1) (Hong Kong) (same); Copyright and Designs Act 2004 (Bermuda) (same); Copyright Act 1968, Section 41 ('criticism or review, whether of that work or of another work') (Australia); Copyright Act 1957, Section 52(a)(ii) (India) ('whether of that work or of any other work'); South Africa, Act 98 of 1978, Section 12(1)(b) ('of that work or another work').

[123] Cf Copyright Act 2001, ch. 130, Section 26(1) ('criticism or review') (Kenya); Copyright Act 2004, sched 2 (Nigeria) (same).

[124] This conclusion might be avoided where the concept of 'substantial part' itself is broadly interpreted to encompass fair uses. There is some support from commentators that this was the role which the

What can be said in favour of a fair dealing exception for criticism or review, however, in contrast to 'fair use', is that, generally speaking, attribution of source and the author *is* a requirement. Unfortunately, however, the requirement that the work has been made available to the public is often absent.[125] In this way, the fair dealing exception also lacks compliance with Article 10(1) Berne.

III JUDICIAL INTERPRETATION

A proper understanding of the mandatory quotation exception in Berne should also inform judicial interpretation of quotation exceptions and other exceptions that are intended to give effect to Article 10(1).[126]

An example that will be used here is the fair dealing for the purposes of 'quotation' exception, which was introduced in the UK as of 1 October 2014.[127] Section 30(1ZA) of the CDPA provides:

'Copyright in a work is not infringed by the use of a quotation from the work (whether for criticism or review or otherwise) provided that—

(a)   the work has been made available to the public,

(b)   the use of the quotation is fair dealing with the work,

(c)   the extent of the quotation is no more than is required by the specific purpose for which it is used, and

(d)   the quotation is accompanied by a sufficient acknowledgement (unless this would be impossible for reasons of practicality or otherwise).'

There are five components to the exception: first, the use must be by way of 'quotation'; second, that quotation must be of a work that has been made available to the public; third, the use must be no more than necessary to achieve its purpose;

---

concept was intended to take in the Copyright Act 1911, but gradually the courts shifted away from such approach: see Lionel Bently, 'Parody and Copyright in the Common Law World' in *Copyright and Freedom of Expression* (ALAI 2008), 360; Robert Burrell, 'Reining in Copyright Law: Is Fair Use the Answer?' [2001] *IPQ* 361, 370.

[125]   See the following, which require sufficient acknowledgment but not that the works used are made available to the public: New Zealand (Section 42 Copyright Act 1994); Australia (Section 41 Copyright Act 1968); South Africa (Section 12(1) Copyright Act 1978); Canada (Section 29 Copyright Act 1985); Nigeria (Section 6 Copyright Act 2004); and Singapore (Section 36 Copyright Act 1987). India does not appear to have either a requirement of sufficient acknowledgment or that the work is made available to the public; see Section 52 Copyright Act 1957.

[126]   On the ways in which judicial interpretation can operate to contract or expand the flexibilities within copyright exceptions see Burrell and Coleman (2005), 253–63, and Michael Geist, *The Copyright Pentalogy: How the Supreme Court of Canada Shook the Foundations of Canadian Copyright Law* (University of Ottawa Press 2013), ch. 5, 'Fairness Found: How Canada Quietly Shifted From Fair Dealing to Fair Use'.

[127]   SI 2014/2356, available at http://www.legislation.gov.uk/uksi/2014/2356/pdfs/uksi_20142356_en.pdf (accessed 28 January 2020).

fourth, the use must be 'fair dealing'; and fifth and finally there must be 'sufficient acknowledgment' of the source and its authorship.

This is a very important change in UK law, which had previously permitted quotation as part of the fair dealing for criticism or review, or reporting current events exceptions. The previous law not only required some form of criticism or review to be present, but in addition, the criticism or review was (i) of a work, (ii) of a performance of a work or (iii) of another work. Quotation under the previous fair dealing defence would not have been permitted if there was no element of criticism or review (as, for example, with a dictionary of quotations), nor if the criticism or review was simply to criticise a practice, the way somebody had behaved or political events.[128] Quoting material for such purposes would not have been permissible according to fair dealing for the purposes of criticism or review, but now in all likelihood might be permissible under the fair dealing-for-quotation defence.

Section 30(1ZA), on its face, appears consistent with Article 10(1) Berne. In particular, the second, third and fifth requirements of section 30(1ZA) coincide with the making available to the public, proportionality and attribution require-ments of Article 10(1) and (3). However, U.K. courts are likely to be faced with determining what amounts to a 'quotation' and also assessing 'fair dealing'. Under section 30(1ZA), fair dealing by quotation can be 'for criticism or review *or otherwise*'. On its face, the fair dealing by quotation can be for *any* purpose. As the Government announced, this 'permits the use of quotations for *other fair purposes*'.[129] According to the IPO's website[130] announcing the change, it was stated that the change extends 'the existing exception for "criticism or review" to cover all types of fair quotation'. On the other hand, it could be argued that the words 'or otherwise' should be interpreted *eiusdem generis*, so that the quotation defence is only available for purposes similar to 'criticism or review'.

Ultimately, the question of whether section 30(1ZA) is open-ended should be interpreted in light of EU copyright law, given that the section purports to imple-ment Article 5(3)(d) of the Information Society Directive.[131] Looking at Article 5(3) (d), this provision points even more clearly at open-ended purposes. Article 5(3)(d) refers to 'quotations for purposes *such as* criticism or review', which is clearly meant to be illustrative and without restriction. So, it would be perverse to limit 'otherwise' in section 30(1ZA) of the CDPA to purposes analogous to criticism or review. However, the opinion of Advocate General Trstenjak in *Painer* suggests a narrower interpretation of Article 5(3)(d). She indicates that '[t]here must also be a material reference back to the quoted work in the form of a description,

---

[128]   *Ashdown* v. *Telegraph Group Ltd* [2002] Ch 149, 171.
[129]   *Modernising Copyright* (2012), 28.
[130]   'Changes to Copyright Exceptions', 30 July 2014.
[131]   This should continue to be interpreted in light of the EU *acquis*, even after Brexit, according to Jane Parkin, 'The Copyright Quotation Exception: Not Fair Use by Another Name' (2019) 19 *OUCLJ* 55, 87.

commentary or analysis' (i.e. the 'quotation must therefore be a basis for discussion').[132] Further, she indicates that the quotation is reproduced without modification in identifiable form. However, and encouragingly, Advocate General Trstenjak accepted that the whole work could be quoted, albeit that this would be particularly relevant to the requirement of fair practice.[133] The Court of Justice in *Painer* did not address the Advocate General's view that quotations must refer back to the source work and be for the purposes of commentary or analysis. Therefore, it cannot be taken as having endorsed the Advocate General's opinion on this point. Moreover, the Court stressed that Article 5(3)(d) 'is intended to strike a fair balance between the right to freedom of expression of users of a work or other protected subject-matter and the reproduction right conferred on authors',[134] which suggests that the exception should be interpreted to give effect to freedom of expression and thus a narrow view of quotation should not be adopted. The ambiguity about the Court of Justice's interpretation of 'quotation' has now been resolved, to some extent, by the Court's rulings in the subsequent references in *Pelham v. Hütter* [135] and *Spiegel Online v. Volker Beck*.[136] However, as we shall see, the judicial interpretation of the quotation exception by the Court of Justice does not always align with what is mandated by Article 10(1) Berne.

Turning first to *Pelham*, this reference involved the use of a two-second sample of a rhythm sequence from the Kraftwerk song 'Metall auf Metall' in the song 'Nur Mir'. The alleged infringement was a reproduction of part of the sound recording (or phonogram) containing 'Metall auf Metall'. The Bundesgerichtshof referred a series of questions to the Court of Justice, which entailed asking, inter alia, whether the sample from the claimant's sound recording was a reproduction within the meaning of Article 2(c) of the Information Society Directive and if there was a quotation within the meaning of Article 5(3)(d) of the same Directive. The CJEU ruled that a sound sample from a phonogram would not constitute a 'reproduction' within Article 2(c) if, 'in exercising the freedom of the arts', as contained in Article 13 of the EU Charter of Fundamental Rights, it was used 'in a modified form unrecognizable to the ear, in a new work'.[137] The Court went on to indicate, as regards the quotation

---

[132] Case C-145/10 *Painer* v. *Standard Verlags GmbH*, EU:C:2011:239 (Advocate General's Opinion), [210].

[133] *Painer* (Advocate General's Opinion), [213].

[134] Case C-145/10 *Painer* v. *Standard Verlags GmbH* EU:C:2011:798, [2012] ECDR 6 (CJEU, 3rd Chamber), [134].

[135] Case C-476/17 *Pelham GmbH* v. *Hütter* EU:C:2019:624 (CJEU, Grand Chamber). For a discussion of the case at national level, see Bernd Justin Jütte and Henrike Maier, 'A Human Right to Sample – Will the CJEU Dance to the BGH-Beat?' (2017) 12 *JIPLP* 784.

[136] Case C-516/17 *Spiegel Online GmbH* v. *Volker Beck* EU:C:2019:625 (CJEU, Grand Chamber).

[137] *Pelham*, [31]. See also [36]. The Information Society Directive does not purport to harmonise the right to make adaptations of a work, but only of the reproduction, communication and distribution rights. The ruling in *Pelham* might be thought, implicitly, to make further harmonisation unnecessary, since it seems that all modifications that are recognisable to the senses fall within the scope of the 'reproduction right'. More startling still, the Court implies that the right would cover even uses of protected material that was unrecognisable, if the use was not an exercise of freedom of the arts.

exception in Article 5(3)(d), that 'quotation' should be interpreted consistently with the usual meaning in everyday language, the legislative context and the underlying rationale,[138] and that this pointed to the essential characteristics being

> the use, by a user other than the copyright holder, of a work or, more generally, of an extract from a work *for the purposes of illustrating an assertion, or defending an opinion or of allowing an intellectual comparison between that work and the assertions of that user,* since the user of a protected work wishing to rely on the quotation exception must therefore have *the intention of entering into 'dialogue' with that work,* as the Advocate General stated in point 64 of his Opinion.[139] (emphasis added)

The provided passage suggests that quotation involves the intention of entering into a dialogue with the protected copyright work; however, this begs the question of what 'dialogue' means in this context. Is it limited to illustration, defence of an opinion or intellectual comparison, as suggested in the above passage from the Court's ruling?[140] We would argue that it is not so limited since the Court also approves of the Opinion of Advocate General Szpunar, where he states: '[T]he quotation must enter into some kind of dialogue with the work quoted. Whether in confrontation, as a tribute to or *in any other way, interaction between the quoting work and the work quoted is necessary.*"[141] Arguably, this reference to 'in any other way, interaction' between the source and destination works is a broad concept, and the notions of 'confrontation' and 'tribute' – or indeed 'illustration', 'defence' or 'comparison' – may be seen as examples of that interaction but not *exhaustive* of what may constitute a dialogue. Thus, while, as we have argued in Chapter 5, Article 10(1) Berne precludes introducing a condition that a quotation requires a referencing back to the source work (even though such purpose will be relevant to the conditions of proportionality and fair practice),[142] it might be possible to interpret the Court of Justice's notion of 'dialogue' broadly so as to minimise the impact of incorrectly incorporating such a requirement.

The Court of Justice in *Pelham* also seemed to follow Advocate General Szpunar's conditions that the quotation must be 'unaltered and distinguishable' and incorporated into the quoting work 'without modification'.[143] This is evident from the following passages:

---

[138] *Pelham,* [70]. Note our criticism in Chapter 5, Section I, pp. 84–86, of an approach that relies heavily on dictionary meaning to inform 'ordinary meaning'.

[139] *Pelham,* [71].

[140] Cf Emily Hudson, *Drafting Copyright Exceptions: From the Law in Books to the Law in Action* (Cambridge University Press 2020), 279, who suggests that much will turn on the meaning of 'dialogue' and suggests that 'it might be difficult to point to any intellectual illustration, defence or comparison being made in the defendant's work'.

[141] Case C-476/17 *Pelham GmbH v. Hütter* EU:C:2018:1002 (Advocate General's Opinion), [64] (emphasis added).

[142] Chapter 5, Section IV, Part B, pp. 131–136, above. But the Polish Supreme Court of Appeal has already applied the ruling of the CJEU in *Pelham* to rule that a "press clippings" service could not rely on the quotation exception: August 9, 2019, II CSK 7/18 (unpublished).

[143] *Pelham* (Advocate General's Opinion), [65].

In particular, where the creator of a new musical work uses a sound sample taken from a phonogram which is *recognisable to the ear* in that new work, the use of that sample may, depending on the facts of the case, amount to a 'quotation', on the basis of Article 5(3)(d) of Directive 2001/29 read in the light of Article 13 of the Charter, provided that that use the intention of entering into dialogue with the work from which the sample was taken, within the meaning referred to in paragraph 71 above, and the conditions set out in Article 5(3)(d) are satisfied.

However, as the Advocate General stated in point 65 of his Opinion, *there can be no such dialogue where it is not possible to identify the work concerned by the quotation at issue.*[144] (emphasis added)

Having said this, it is worth observing that the Court referred to the sample being 'recognizable' or identifiable in the new work. This does not per se require that the quotation is 'without modification', as the Advocate General suggests, since a quotation can conceivably remain recognisable, even where changes have been made, as the examples discussed in Chapter 5 illustrate.[145] Consequently, the CJEU has *not* stipulated a 'without modification' requirement, but had it done so, it would have been inconsistent with the proper interpretation of Article 10(1) Berne.

As for the requirement of recognisability or identifiability, which proved critical when the case returned to the national court,[146] this begs a few questions. The first is whether the Court was referring to the same concept of recognisability that it used when discussing whether a 'reproduction' of a part of the phonogram had occurred. In relation to this issue, the Court ruled that where the 'sample is unrecognizable to the ear in that new work', it would not amount to a 'reproduction' within Article 2 (c) of the Information Society Directive.[147] This approach to recognisability assumes that the quotation is identifiable by the *listener* or *audience* of the work, as opposed to there being identification by the user of the copyright work of that material as a quotation.[148] The fact that the Court refer-s to *'recognisable to the ear in that new work'*[149] suggests that this question is being assessed according to the audience of the work. Second, according to this notion of recognisability, the question arises of *which audience* identifies the quotation and when the assessment

---

[144] *Pelham*, [72]–[73].

[145] E.g. Manet's, *Le Déjeurner sur l'herbe* and Maurice Denis' *Homage to Cézanne*, discussed in Chapter 5, pp. 105–107 and 116–117.

[146] *Metall auf Metall IV* (BGH), Case No I ZR 115/16 (30 April 2020) (rejecting the quotation defence on the basis that the audience would not recognise the sampled sounds as alien to *Nur Mir*).

[147] *Pelham*, [36].

[148] Jane Parkin, 'The Copyright Quotation Exception: *Not* Fair Use by Another Name' (2019) 19 *OUCLJ* 55, 72–3 for this distinction between identification by the user of the work and identifiability by the audience. She argues that the ordinary meaning of 'quotation' requires that the user of the quoted material must intentionally identify this material as being from another source, otherwise this is an instance of plagiarism. The focus is on how the user has presented the material, rather than how the audience perceives it, and the advantage is said to be that identification is 'fixed in time' (73) and questions relating to which audience and how much of the audience are avoided (74).

[149] *Pelham*, [72] (emphasis added).

is made. Is the audience the ordinary reader, viewer or listener, or does it refer to experts and must it be by a substantial section of that audience? Further, must the recognition occur contemporaneously with the release of the destination work, or is it acceptable that subsequently, at a different time and in a different context, there is recognisability of the source of the quotation?[150]

According to Jane Parkin, it is ill-advised to adopt a requirement of recognisability or identifiability by the audience along the lines of what the Court of Justice suggests. Instead, Parkin argues that the requirement should be one of identification, which focuses on how the user of the quoted material has presented this material, and this involves the use of indicators, such as quotation marks, visual framing, source acknowledgment or oblique references through the titling of a work. According to her, the requirement of acknowledging the 'source' of the work will usually mean the identification requirement is satisfied, and questions relating to which audience, how much of the audience, and time and context are avoided.[151] We would agree with Parkin, insofar as she advocates against a requirement of identifiability or recognisability by the audience, but we disagree that inherent in the meaning of 'quotation' is identification by the user of the quoted work such that the exception could not operate as a defence to subconscious infringement.[152] Rather, as we have argued in Chapter 5, ordinary understandings of 'quotation' do not necessarily point to the deliberate or intentional use of the material quoted, nor do those that require recognisability by an audience.

Turning next to the CJEU ruling in *Spiegel Online*,[153] this reference involved a controversy about an article authored by Volker Beck, an MP from 1994 to 2017 in Germany, which was published, he alleged, in a modified way to which he objected. In order to illustrate his point, Mr Beck published on his website the original (manuscript) version of his article and the published version. Spiegel Online made available for download on its website via hyperlinks these two versions, alongside an article that suggested Mr Beck had been misleading the public for years. The Bundesgerichtshof referred several questions to the CJEU. Relevant to our purposes here was question 5, which asked:

> Is there no publication for quotation purposes under Article 5(3)(d) of Directive 2001/29 if quoted textual works or parts thereof are not inextricably integrated into the new text – for example, by way of insertions or footnotes – but are made available to the public on the internet by means of a link in the form of pdf files which can be downloaded independently of the new text?

---

[150]   See Chapter 5, Section III, Part D, pp. 125–128, esp. 128. See also Parkin (2019), 74.
[151]   Parkin (2019), 74.
[152]   See Chapter 5, Section IV, Part A, pp. 128–129.
[153]   Case C-516/17 *Spiegel Online GmbH* v. *Volker Beck* EU:C:2019:625 (CJEU, Grand Chamber).

In answering this question, the Court reiterated its view in *Pelham* that 'the usual meaning of the word "quotation" in everyday language' involves use 'of an extract from a work for the purposes of illustrating an assertion, of defending an opinion or of allowing an intellectual comparison between that work and the assertions of that user'.[154] As was argued previously, and in Chapter 5, it is not inherent in the ordinary meaning of 'quotation' that there must be a purpose of this kind and this aspect of the ruling should not be followed by UK courts. Alternatively, if UK courts choose to follow this ruling, it would be preferable to adopt the notion of 'dialogue' referred to in *Pelham*, which can be interpreted more flexibly and generously, and the acts of illustration, defence or comparison simply constitute non-exhaustive examples of what can amount to 'dialogue'.

The Court in *Spiegel Online* went on to follow the Advocate General's Opinion in deciding that:

> neither the wording of Article 5(3)(d) of Directive 2001/29 nor the concept of 'quotation' ... require that the quoted work be inextricably integrated, by way of insertions or reproductions in footnotes for example, into the subject matter citing it, so that a quotation may thus be made by including a hyperlink to the quoted work.[155]

In reaching this conclusion, Advocate General Szpunar had noted that the quotation exception could apply to all types of works, including musical, audiovisual and artistic works and that the traditional methods of signaling quotation in text works (through use of quotation marks, or footnotes) would need to be adapted.[156] Similarly, the Advocate General reasoned that the incorporation of quotations in literary works could be adapted to include hyperlinks,[157] but that it did not extend to the entirety of a work that was independently downloadable and accessible.[158] This acceptance by the Advocate General that quotation applies to all types of works and different quoting practices is commendable and the Court of Justice can be seen to have implicitly approved of this interpretation. However, immediately ruling out an entire work from the meaning of quotation was a step too far by the Advocate General and not in keeping with Article 10(1) Berne. It is therefore important to note that the Court of Justice did not go as far as the Advocate General on this point, but indicated instead that the use 'must be made "in accordance with fair practice, and to the extent required by the specific purpose", so that the use of that manuscript and article for the purposes of quotation must not be extended beyond the confines of what it [sic] necessary to achieve the informatory purpose of that particular quotation'.[159] In other words, the Court advocated what we have argued is the correct

---

[154] *Spiegel Online*, [78].
[155] *Spiegel Online*, [80].
[156] Case C-516/17 *Spiegel Online GmbH v. Volker Beck*, EU:C:2019:16 (Advocate General's Opinion), [41]–[42]. See also *Pelham* (Advocate General's Opinion), [62].
[157] *Spiegel Online* (Advocate General's Opinion), [43].
[158] *Spiegel Online* (Advocate General's Opinion), [48]–[49].
[159] *Spiegel Online*, [83].

interpretation of quotation according to Article 10(1) of Berne (i.e. the concept of quotation can involve the use of *entire* work), and the size of the quotation is relevantly assessed as part of the proportionality and fair practice requirements in the exception.

Returning to section 30(1ZA) CDPA, this provision also requires that there is a 'fair dealing' and this should be seen as implementing the requirement of 'fair practice' in Article 5(3)(d) of the Information Society Directive and Article 10(1) Berne. As was discussed in Chapter 6, the fair dealing exceptions in the CDPA do not articulate fairness factors in the way that we see for fair use in the United States and other jurisdictions. However, factors have been judicially developed and include the extent of what has been used; the amount and importance of the work taken; the proportion of what has been used in relation to the rest of the work or the commentary, dishonest acquisition of the work, excessive use in relation to the purpose, commercially compet- ing with the claimant's work; and the unpublished nature of the work.[160] It is argued that these factors would need to be revisited by UK courts in light of the pluralistic notion of fairness that is contained in the 'fair practice' requirement. Importantly, these factors must not have a tunnel vision approach that focuses solely on the economic interests of authors or rights holders. For reasons that have been expressed earlier in Chapter 6, the nature and purpose of the quotation (including the type of expressive use) is a factor that UK courts would need to weigh, along with the harm to the integrity interests of the author. In addition, courts would need to omit consideration of dishonest acquisition of the work that is quoted (since this is an inappropriate factor to consider), excessive use in relation to the purpose (since this is covered by the proportionality requirement) and the unpublished nature of the work (since this is covered by the requirement that the source work that is being quoted must have been made available to the public).

IV MAKING SENSE OF THE PARODY EXCEPTION

Remarkably, in much of the literature discussing parody exceptions in copyright law, there is little discussion of which international provision underpins the existence of such an exception. The assumption appears to be that it is the three-step test.[161] For example, in her monograph on the parody exception, Dr Sabine Jacques discusses

---

[160] See *Hubbard* v. *Vosper* [1972] 2 QB 84; *Hyde Park Residence* v. *Yelland* [2001] Ch. 143; *Ashdown* v. *Telegraph News* [2002] Ch. 149. See Chapter 6, Section II, Part A.

[161] Mariko A Foster, 'Parody's Precarious Place: The Need to Legally Recognize Parody as Japan's Cultural Property' (2013) 23 *Seton Hall Journal of Sports and Entertainment Law* 313, 342–3, and Sabine Jacques, *The Parody Exception in Copyright Law* (Oxford University Press 2019), ch. 2; Conrad Visser, 'The Location of the Parody Defence in Copyright Law: Some Comparative Perspectives' (2005) 38 *Comparative and International Law Journal of Southern Africa* 321, 341–3 (discussing how a parody exception in South Africa would comply with the three-step test as interpreted by the WTO Panel in the 'Fairness in Music Licensing' case); and John C Knapp, 'Laugh, and the Whole World . . . Scowls at You: A Defense of the United States' Fair Use Exception for Parody under TRIPs' (2005) 33 *Denv J Int'l L & Pol'y* (discussing how fair use, insofar as it embraces parody, complies with the three step test in Article 13 TRIPS as interpreted by the WTO Panel).

the compliance of parody exceptions in France, the United Kingdom, Australia, Canada and the United States with the three-step test. She concludes that the compliance with the three-step test of the Australian parody exception is difficult to verify and dependent on the 'fairness' factors; that the US fair use exception does not comply with Article 9(2) Berne (because of the lack of protection for moral rights in the US); and that the UK, Canadian and French parody exceptions are compliant with the three-step test.[162] This fixation on assessing parody exceptions according to the three-step test is odd when one considers that the freedom of expression rationale is shared by quotation and parody[163] and probably shows the dominance of three-step test thinking when it comes to copyright exceptions and limitations.

A consequence of the broad scope of what may constitute 'quotation' and the fact that quotation may be for *any* purpose is that Article 10(1) Berne may embrace uses that are parody, satire, pastiche or caricature. These sorts of reuses, in other words, may be characterised as quotations, and as such, national parody exceptions ought to be considered for consistency with Article 10(1) Berne rather than the three-step test. For example, in the United States, it is well established that parodic uses fall within fair use.[164] As such, one needs to look at the consistency of US 'fair use' with Article 10(1) Berne, which we have done previously.[165] For other jurisdictions, the compatibility of specific, national parody exceptions with Article 10(1) Berne needs to be considered. We examine a couple of illustrative examples.

Australia introduced a fair dealing exception for parody or satire in 2006, via the Copyright Amendment Act 2006.[166] The origin of this change can be linked to the restrictive interpretation of the fair dealing for criticism or review exception,[167] the 'Fair Use Inquiry' held in 2005[168] and submissions that called for new exceptions

---

[162] Sabine Jacques, *The Parody Exception in Copyright Law* (Oxford University Press 2019), ch. 2.

[163] For parody, see Jacques (2019), 17, and the sources cited in fn. 113, and the discussion in ch. 5. According to Jacques (2019), freedom of expression is the rationale for parody exceptions in common law copyright and civil law authors' rights traditions. For quotation, see Chapter 6, Section III, Part B, pp. 159–163.

[164] See *Campbell* v. *Acuff-Rose*, 510 US 569 (1994), 114 S Ct 1164 (1994).

[165] See Section I, above.

[166] Copyright Amendment Act 2006 (Cth) Sch 6 Pt 3 items 9A-9B, inserting Section 41A Copyright Act 1968 (for literary, dramatic, musical and artistic works) and Section 103AA (for audio-visual items). For discussion, see G Austin, 'EU and US Perspectives on Fair Dealing for the Purpose of Parody or Satire' (2016) 39 *UNSW L J* 684; S McCausland, 'Protecting "A Fine Tradition of Satire": The New Fair Dealing Exception for Parody or Satire in the Australian Copyright Act' [2007] *EIPR* 287; J McCutcheon, 'The New Defence of Parody or Satire under Australian Copyright Law' [2008] *IPQ* 163; B Mee, 'Laughing Matters: Parody and Satire in Australian Copyright Law' (2009/10) 20 *Journal of Law, Information and Science* 61; N Suzor, 'Where the Bloody Hell Does Parody Fit in Australian Copyright Law?' (2008) 13 *MALR* 218.

[167] As evidenced in *TCN Channel Nine Pty Ltd* v. *Network Ten Pty Ltd* [2002] FCAFC 146; critiqued in M Handler and D Rolph, '"A Real Pea Souper": The *Panel* Case and the Development of the Fair Dealing Defences to Copyright Infringement in Australia' [2003] *Melbourne University L Rev* 15.

[168] Attorney-General's Department, Issues Paper, *Fair Use and Other Copyright Exceptions: An Examination of Fair Use, Fair Dealing and Other Exceptions in the Digital Age* (May 2005).

for particular uses, such as parody.[169] Section 41A of the Copyright Act 1968 (Cth) states: 'A fair dealing with a literary, dramatic, musical or artistic work, or with an adaptation of a literary, dramatic or musical work, does not constitute an infringement of the copyright in the work if it is for the purpose of parody or satire.'

Some commentators have applauded the fact that this provision includes satire as well as parody, suggesting that it is broader than the position taken under US fair use, which privileges parody.[170] Not everyone, however, has welcomed the exception as a positive solution. Professor Jani McCutcheon has argued that a fair use exception would have been preferable and that 'it seems incongruous that so much rests on analysis and argument over a relatively elusive conception of what a parody or a satire is'.[171] While Ben Mee has argued that integrating the exception within a three-step test structure (as was originally proposed in the Bill) would have been preferable to relying on a fair dealing notion, that is a matter of 'impression and degree'.[172] Definitions of parody or satire are absent from the legislation and commentators have suggested that the distinction lies in the fact that parody is directed at a particular work, whereas satire uses a work to critique or ridicule more generally.[173] Or, as others have described, '[t]o call something a parody is to say something about its form: that it imitates and distorts some pre-existing work or genre. To call something a satire is to identify some critical purpose in the treatment of some person, practice or institution.'[174] Further, it has been argued that when the exception eventually comes to be interpreted by the courts, the requirements of 'parody' or 'satire' should be approached flexibly.[175]

---

[169] See submissions by Australian Subscription Television and Radio Association, SBS, ABC, Ten, Copyright in Cultural Institutions Group, CNMCCA and the Arts Law Centre of Australia as cited in McCausland (2007), fn. 32.

[170] McCausland (2007), 292, describing the express protection of satire as 'a world first'; McCutcheon (2008), 178, 'Australia appears to be the first country to expressly permit a fair dealing of a copyright work for a satirical purpose, thus affording broader protection than other jurisdictions, and in particular the US fair use defence, as presently interpreted'; Suzor (2008), 219, 'This duality is important because it provides a larger scope than the equivalent exception under US law', and at 242, 'The broad wording of the new exceptions relieves courts from the arduous task of distinguishing between parody and satire, something which literary critics, let alone judicial officers, find difficult to do'. Contrast Austin (2016), 713, who expresses some wariness over a broad interpretation of the exception.

[171] McCutcheon (2008), 187–8.

[172] Mee (2009/10), 81–2. Contrast Suzor (2008), 229, suggesting the existing exception is much simpler than the original proposal and does not impose an undue burden on the would-be parodist.

[173] Suzor (2008), 219; McCutcheon (2008), 167–8.

[174] C Condren, J Milner Davis, S McCausland and R. Phiddian, 'Defining Parody and Satire: Australian Copyright Law and Its New Exception: Part 2 – Advancing Ordinary Definitions' (2008) 13 *MALR* 401, 421. According to the authors, this definition is 'justifiable from a literary and technical point of view but also capture[s] the reality of what practitioners and reflective consumers understand by these terms'.

[175] Suzor (2008), 247; McCutcheon (2008), 188. Contrast Austin (2016). So far, the only interpretation has been in a decision prior to the enactment of the parody exception: *TCN Channel Nine Pty Ltd*

In terms of the consistency of the Australian parody/satire exception with Article 10(1) Berne, quotations for parodic or satirical purposes are unproblematic. Indeed, broad, flexible or even overlapping notions of parody and satire are acceptable according to Article 10(1) because quotations may be for *any* purpose. Distinguishing between the different types of artistic practice (i.e. parody or satire) should not be relevant to whether there is a relevant purpose for the fair dealing exception, and this would mean that courts would have to pay less attention to policing the boundaries of 'parody' versus 'satire' and their relationship to other concepts, such as burlesque, caricature or pastiche.[176] However, it may be that this type of differentiation becomes relevant to weighing the freedom of expression interest that is at stake, or the likelihood of economic or non-economic harm to the author. The advantage, however, of not having to pigeonhole uses as either 'parody' or 'satire' is that courts can maintain their focus on the expressive interests and potential harm at stake, rather than on definitional niceties. Likewise, this avoids what Dr Sabine Jacques has described as a 'battle' between 'users and right-holders of copyright works', where 'the former tend to favour a broad definition' of parody and 'the latter prefer a narrow and precise definition to best secure their interests'.[177]

Problematic, however, is the absence of any attribution requirement in section 41A of the Australian Copyright Act 1968 (Cth). Short of amending the legislation to include this requirement, courts would need to treat the absence of attributing the source and the author, where this information appears on the work that is parodied or satirised, as presumptively unfair. However, it would be open to the courts, as we argued previously, to interpret this requirement flexibly.[178] As such, in the case of parody or satire, it may be that through targeting or using well-known works that are recognisable to audiences, there is implicitly attribution. A further point is that unpublished works seem to fall within the scope of section 41A of the Australian Copyright Act 1968 (Cth), and this is also inconsistent with Article 10(1) Berne. For consistency to occur, where the work that is parodied or satirised has not been lawfully made available to the public, the court would need to treat this as a 'trump' factor (i.e. as presumptively unfair). It may be that, in practice, this does not arise as a problem because effective parodies or satires are ones that use works that have a cultural significance, and as such, these are likely already to have been made available to the public.

---

v. *Network Ten Pty Ltd* [2001] FCA 108 (Conti J), [17], and this was in *obiter*. Here Conti J used the Macquarie Dictionary to indicate that 'the essence of parody is imitation ... that burlesque is in the nature of vulgarizing parody ... whereas satire is described as being a form of ironic, sarcastic, scornful, derisive or ridiculing criticism of vice, folly or abuses, but not by way of an imitation or take-off'. The discussion of parody and satire did not occur in the appeal decisions: see [2002] FCAFC 146 and [2004] HCA 14.

[176]   For a discussion of these concepts and their boundaries, see Jacques (2019), ch. 1.

[177]   Jacques (2019), 16.

[178]   Chapter 3, Section III, Part B, pp. 59–60 and Chapter 4, Section III, pp. 77–78.

In addition, while 'fair dealing' under Australian copyright law might be reflective of elements of 'fair practice' in Article 10(1) Berne, it does not include the plurality of concerns that this concept covers. In particular, fair dealing tends to focus primarily on notions of economic harm and does not take into account, for example, the integrity interests of the author. Here, it is important to note that the right of integrity of the author remains intact – that is, section 41A does not operate as an exception to the integrity right (in contrast to US fair use). Even so, a relevant factor for 'fair dealing' should include the impact on the author's integrity interests.[179] The fair dealing factor 'purpose and character of the use' could allow for the freedom of expression interests of the defendant to be taken into account, although here it may be necessary to identify precisely those interests, rather than simply appealing to this as a broad principle.[180] Therefore, while the Australian parody/satire exception does not fully align with Article 10(1) Berne, with appropriate judicial interpretation of the fair dealing factors or legislative amendment, it could come closer to doing so.

In 2014, the United Kingdom introduced a new fair dealing exception for the purposes of caricature, parody or pastiche in section 30A of the CDPA,[181] in reliance on Article 5(3)(k) of the Information Society Directive.[182] This provision may be traced back to the Gowers Review of Intellectual Property, published in December 2006, which recommended the introduction of a new parody exception.[183] Subsequently, the UK Intellectual Property Office consulted, inter alia, on this recommendation, but later rejected the need for such an exception.[184] This attracted some rather robust criticism from academic commentators, such as Professor Ronan Deazley.[185] The proposed parody exception was later resuscitated[186] and introduced in 2014. Section 30A of the CDPA states: 'Fair dealing with a work for the purposes of caricature, parody or pastiche does not infringe copyright in the work.'

---

[179]   Suzor (2008), 247 has suggested that it would 'seem highly counter-intuitive for parliament to introduce broad exceptions to copyright infringement for parody and satire if a significant proportion of parodies and satires are likely to be restrained by the operation of the moral right of integrity'.

[180]   See Austin (2016), 711: 'simplistic invocation of the principle of freedom of expression does little to delineate the appropriate scope of fair dealing' and 712: 'to invoke freedom of expression does little in itself to advance the analysis of the scope of copyright defences'.

[181]   The Copyright and Rights in Performances (Quotation and Parody) Regulations 2014 No 2356 which came into force on 1 October 2014.

[182]   Which allows Member States to introduce exceptions to the rights of reproduction and communication to the public for 'use for the purpose of caricature, parody or pastiche'.

[183]   Gowers Review, [4.89]–[4.90], p. 68.

[184]   Taking Forward the Gowers Review of Intellectual Property: Proposed Changes to Copyright Exceptions (Intellectual Property Office Newport 2008), 38–44. Taking Forward the Gowers Review of Intellectual Property: Second Stage Consultation Copyright Exceptions (Intellectual Property Office Newport 2009), 45.

[185]   R Deazley, 'Copyright and Parody: Taking Backward the Gowers Review?' (2010) 73 MLR 785.

[186]   Arguably as a result of the Hargreaves Review, Digital Opportunity: A Review of Intellectual Property and Growth (May 2011), [5.32] and [5.35]–[5.36], 49–50.

Notably, the UK exception refers to parody, caricature *and* pastiche, language that differs from the Australian parody exception, but which is clearly modelled on Article 5(3)(k) of the Information Society Directive. While UK courts have not yet interpreted section 30A, the CJEU (Grand Chamber) ruling in *Deckmyn* has indicated that 'parody' has an autonomous EU meaning and the essential characteristics of parody are twofold: (1) to evoke an existing work while being noticeably different from it and (2) to constitute an expression of humour or mockery.[187] This interpretation would thus guide UK courts in their application of the parody exception. Dr Emily Hudson has argued that 'pastiche' may be understood broadly to cover all sorts of reuses, 'laudatory and non-critical imitation, such as creating a new work in the style of another artist or genre, and making a new work from a compilation or assembly of pre-existing works'.[188] She writes, '[T]he term pastiche can clearly extend to mash-ups, fan fiction, music sampling, appropriation art and other forms of homage and compilation.'[189] If Article 10(1) Berne underpins section 30A CDPA, we have no qualms with this broad interpretation of pastiche since the mandatory quotation exception, as we have repeatedly emphasised, is not limited to certain purposes. Whereas, if the basis for section 30A CDPA is the three-step test in Article 9(2) Berne and Article 13 TRIPS, then Dr Hudson's expansive interpretation of 'pastiche' may conflict with the first step 'certain special cases', at least as interpreted by the WTO Panel. A problematic aspect of relying on Article 10(1) Berne to justify section 30A CDPA is that this provision does not feature requirements of attribution and the work having been lawfully made available to the public. This would need to be rectified through legislative amendment or, as argued previously in relation to Australia, judicial interpretation. Further, courts would need to approach 'fair dealing' with a pluralistic notion of fairness in mind, which would affect the fairness factors that are considered.

The obvious question that arises is how to reconcile the fair dealing exception for quotation in section 30(1ZA) CDPA with the fair dealing exception for parody, caricature and pastiche in section 30A CDPA. More specifically, does the existence of a specific fair dealing quotation exception indicate that this is the *only* provision in the CDPA giving effect to Article 10(1) Berne? Or do both fair dealing for quotation and parody exceptions reflect the implementation of Article 10(1) Berne? The fact that section 30(1ZA) CDPA closely maps the requirements of Article 10(1) and 10(3) Berne, including the requirements of attribution and the work having been lawfully made available to the public, might suggest that this is the sole provision intended to implement the quotation exception. However, this is at odds with the fact that fair

---

[187] Case C-210/13 *Deckmyn* v. *Vandersteen* EU:C:2014:2132 (CJEU, Grand Chamber), [2014] ECDR 21, [20].

[188] E Hudson, 'The Pastiche Exception in Copyright Law: A Case of Mashed-Up Drafting?' [2017] *IPQ* 346, 347.

[189] Hudson (2017), 347.

dealing for the purposes of criticism or review, which previously was meant to implement Article 10(1) Berne, remains in the CDPA. Commentators have suggested that Article 5(3)(k) (parody), in contrast to Article 5(3)(d) (quotation), of the Information Society Directive is not linked to Article 10(1) Berne.[190] However, there is no solid basis for this view, and it rests on a misunderstanding of the true scope and potential of the mandatory quotation exception in Berne and the persistence of three-step test thinking. As such, it is argued that Article 10(1) Berne is more than capable of embracing parody and the ways in which parody exceptions are implemented in national laws. The attribution and made available to the public requirements are a way of promoting consistency with moral rights, although practically speaking, unpublished works are unlikely to be parodied or satirised, and the plurality of norms informing 'fair practice' are also likely to promote a more coordinated approach with the right of integrity.[191] Furthermore, the freedom of expression rationale underpinning parody[192] is shared and central to the mandatory quotation exception, and to the extent that national parody exceptions are implemented as imperative, this may be justified by the mandatory nature of Article 10(1) Berne, as was discussed in Chapter 3.[193]

V INDUSTRY GUIDELINES AND PRACTICES

As discussed in Chapter 6, guidelines issued by publishers' organisations tend to set unduly narrow and conservative limits for quotation, in terms of the types of works that may be quoted, the length of extracts that may be used and the purposes for which the quotation may be used.[194] These interpretations are, in many instances, contrary to the breadth and flexibility that Article 10(1) Berne permits. However, the guidelines do converge with the scope of the quotation exception insofar as they require attribution of the author of the quoted work and indicate that unpublished works may not be quoted without permission.

Once the scope of the mandatory quotation exception is properly understood, this could lead to publishing guidelines being revisited. Granted, publishers, as usually commercial entities, may be more likely to adopt conservative guidelines in order to

---

[190] M M Walter and Silke von Lewinski, *European Copyright Law: A Commentary* (Oxford University Press 2010), 1049, [11.5.58], clearly link Article 5(3)(d) of Information Society Directive to Article 10(1) Berne but at [11.5.67], 1055, do not link Article 5(3)(k) to any particular provision in Berne. See also Mireille van Eechoud, P Bernt Hugenholtz, Stef van Gompel, Lucie Guibault and Natalie Helberger, *Harmonizing European Copyright Law: The Challenges of Better Lawmaking* (Kluwer 2009), 99, suggesting that Article 5(3)(k) is inspired by the three-step test. Cf Guibault (2002), 106, who links both quotation and parody to freedom of expression, implicitly suggesting that might be justified on the same basis in Berne. However, at 32–3, she treats parodic uses as distinct from quotation.

[191] On the importance of aligning parody exceptions with moral rights regimes, see Jacques (2019), ch. 6.

[192] See fn. 162, above.

[193] Chapter 3, Section I, Part A pp. 29–38, above.

[194] Chapter 6, Section III, Part D, pp. 173–178, above.

minimise the risk of litigation.[195] In addition, the notion of 'fair practice', which contains a plurality of considerations and ideally should be operationalised as a standard in national laws, might also trigger the desire for cautious rule-like interpretations. Yet, even in the context of these concerns, there is scope for loosening the existing guidelines.

One such example of a user organisation taking a somewhat more nuanced approach and one that may allow users to benefit more effectively from the quotation exception in section 30(1ZA) of the CDPA is Channel 4. The Guidelines issued by Channel 4 on 'fair dealing' in the UK[196] note that '[i]t seems clear that programme-makers will be able to fair deal with quotations from all types of copyright works', although they also note that, in relation to photographs, this is likely to be acceptable only in 'exceptional circumstances'. The guidance also states that there are 'no set limits in terms of how big or small, or long or short, a quotation can be relative to the work from which it is taken, so this will have to be considered on a case-by-case basis'. It goes on to indicate that 'any quotation that is used should be directly relevant to the purpose for which the quotation is being used, and particular attention should be paid to any proposed fair dealing with a quotation, where anything other than a "short extract" of the original work is intended to be taken'. The guidance acknowledges that 'short extract' in the case of an artwork or photograph is not clear and that '[q]uoting from a painting or sculpture, or photograph is likely to involve showing the entire work, albeit briefly'. Finally, the guidance suggests that a clear 'editorial purpose' or reason should underpin the use of the quotation. Given that there has not yet been judicial interpretation on section 30 (1ZA) (a point which Channel 4's guidance acknowledges), this set of guidelines is to be applauded for leaning away from an entirely risk-averse approach and more towards taking advantage of the quotation exception. Our position is that *all* the relevant quotation guidelines, particularly from the publishing industries, would do well to be revisited and to move towards more permissive guidance.

Of course, this goal is simpler to state than it is to achieve.[197] However, some encouragement about the potential for change in approach to quotation in practice may be taken from the development of codes of best practice regarding fair use that have emerged in the United States. Professors Patricia Aufderheide and Peter Jaszi discuss[198] how they have helped facilitate communities of users, including

---

[195] See Rothman (2007), 1905–6, discussing litigation avoidance customs.
[196] https://www.channel4.com/producers-handbook/c4-guidelines/fair-dealing-guidelines (accessed 28 January 2020).
[197] Although it may be particularly difficult to achieve in the music industry, where 'fair use' has not made an impact in music copyright litigation in the United States, even though it might have been expected to do so: see E Lee, 'Fair Use Avoidance in Music Cases' (2018) 59 *Boston College Law Review* 1873 and E Lee and A Moshirnia, 'Does Fair Use Matter? An Empirical Study of Music Cases' (2020) 94 *S Cal L Rev* (forthcoming).
[198] See Patricia Aufderheide and Peter Jaszi, *Reclaiming Fair Use: How to Put Balance Back in Copyright* (2nd ed, University of Chicago Press 2018).

documentary filmmakers, dance historians, media literacy teachers, online video makers, creators of open-access university courseware, librarians, archivists and journalists, to develop codes of best practice in relation to fair use of copyright material. In their work, Professors Aufderheide and Jaszi had noticed that these types of user/creator groups needed to 'quote copyrighted material in order to do their work well', but the licensing arrangements did not suit their needs because they were often targeted at highly professional organisations. Professors Aufderheide and Jaszi map their journey in assisting these various groups of users and suggest practical steps for developing codes of practice.[199] These steps include identifying the sorts of problems encountered by the community with relation to copyright material, working out the ways in which fair use might be applicable, testing these understandings against legal advice and then seeking endorsement and wide circulation of the code.

What is proposed here is that a similar approach could be taken in relation to the application of the quotation exception and perhaps some obvious communities to tackle first would be librarians and publishers of scholarly works. Indeed, the empirical work conducted by Dr Emily Hudson suggests that UK libraries and cultural institutions might be receptive to developing guidelines that explore the full breadth of the quotation exception. In her work, Dr Hudson observes that although institutions 'were still finding their way in relation to quotation ... interviewees did not view section 30(1ZA) as technical and unknowable, or as limited to the paradigmatic example of short snippets of literary content in quotation marks' and that 'the breadth of the drafting was praised'.[200] The enthusiasm with which the new quotation exception in UK law has been embraced by cultural institutions points to communities where it would be worthwhile encouraging codes of best practice where the benefits of the exception are fully mined.[201]

---

[199]   Ibid, Chapter 9, 'How to Fair Use'.
[200]   Hudson (2020), 280.
[201]   Indeed, Hudson (2020), 281 notes that 'quotation had the most in common with how US interviewees described fair use' and, as Aufderheide and Jaszi discuss, fair use in the United States has been a fertile ground for developing codes of best practice.

8

Conclusion

Until now, the international legal norm created by Article 10(1) Berne has been relatively dormant and its potential overlooked by scholars, policymakers, judges, practitioners and legislatures: it is now time to harness its potential in the shaping of permitted uses of copyright material. Moreover, despite its clear terms, only a minority of national legal systems have implemented Article 10(1) in full.[1]

We might pause to reflect on why global mandatory fair use has remained dormant and why Members of the Berne Union have acted so openly to contradict their international obligations – something we refer to as 'dysfunctional pluralism'.[2] We suggest there are five inter-related explanations.

First, Article 10(1) Berne has been presented in some contexts and by some commentators as 'optional', not mandatory. The effect of this is that some Berne Union Members might have been led into thinking that in adding qualifications and conditions to the quotation exception, they were acting within the freedom left to them by the Berne Convention. However, as has been demonstrated in Chapter 3, Article 10(1) Berne is mandatory in nature, and as a result, the full scope of this exception, along with its conditions, must be implemented by Berne Union Members.[3]

Second, it has been assumed by some legislatures and scholars that Article 10(1) Berne is subject to the three-step test and that this not only justifies but actually demands the addition of such conditions. Chapter 3 has explained why this view is misplaced and the reasons why the three-step test does not govern the application of Article 10(1) Berne.[4] Three-step test thinking has dominated the landscape of copyright exceptions, and it is vital that this is resisted, given that it is unwarranted.

---

[1] Cf. Guido Westkamp, *The Implementation of Directive 2001/29/EC in the Member States* (2007), Part II, 44 (suggesting there are 'no significant deviations' from terms of Directive in implementation, though 'some minor peculiarities should be mentioned').

[2] See Lionel Bently and Tanya Aplin, 'Whatever Became of Global Mandatory Fair Use? A Case Study in Dysfunctional Pluralism' in Susy Frankel (ed.), *Is Intellectual Property Pluralism Functional?* (Edward Elgar 2019), ch. 1 (from which this chapter draws heavily).

[3] Chapter 3, Section I, pp. 29–38, above.

[4] Chapter 3, Section IV, pp. 60–68, above.

Third, it has been assumed that 'quotation' describes a rather narrow set of permitted practices, limited by reference to a textual/print conception of quotation.[5] As argued at length in Chapter 5, this view of quotation is not only contrary to the language of Article 10(1) and its *travaux*; it also does not comport with the ordinary meaning of 'quotation' and quotation practices.

Fourth, it might have wrongly assumed that some of the conditions are legitimate elaborations of the (for some countries awkward) notion of 'fair practice'. Yet, as was argued in Chapter 6, that is not the case because there are various norms that ought to inform an assessment of 'fair' practice. While these norms will allow for some flexibility for countries to assess 'fair' quotation, they do not justify national exceptions that are clearly contrary to the mandatory scope of Article 10(1).

Finally, the pluralistic implementation of Article 10(1) Berne by Union Members is underpinned by institutional difficulties with enforcing user freedoms in a state-based international legal order. Given that this final argument has not been addressed earlier in the book, we turn to discuss it now.

The final explanation for the dysfunctional pluralism that we have identified lies, we think, in failures in the 'transnational compliance procedures' in relation to copyright exceptions.[6] This failure reflects the weak position of users at both national and international levels. On the national level, as has been often noted, there is an asymmetry in the capacity of the various 'stakeholders' in copyright to participate in the legislative process: on the one hand, there are right holders who commonly form well-resourced groups to promote their interests with the legislature and executive;[7] on the other hand, there are users which, being large in number and widely distributed, are rarely able to co-ordinate effectively to resist extensions of copyright. The effect of this asymmetry is that rights holders lobby successfully for extended rights and longer terms, while users rarely are able to resist, let alone promote, new

---

[5]   This is true even amongst scholars who advocate for broad flexibilities for users. See e.g. Michael Geist, *The Copyright Pentalogy: How the Supreme Court of Canada Shook the Foundations of Canadian Copyright Law* (University of Ottawa Press 2013), ch. 5, 'Fairness Found: How Canada Quietly Shifted from Fair Dealing to Fair Use', [1] ('Some narrow limitations on copyright holders' rights, such as quotation, remain uncontroversial') and [9] ('The Berne Convention's Article 10 includes a specific, though somewhat limited, fair "practice" provision that focuses primarily on quotation, education use and attribution').

[6]   The term is from Harold Koh, 'Bringing International Law Home,' (1998) 35 *Houston L Rev* 623.

[7]   One such example is the petition for review of the eligibility of South Africa for the Generalized System of Preferences under 84 Fed. Reg. 11151 by the International Intellectual Property Alliance ('IIPA') to the US Trade Representative. The IIPA recommends that South Africa is put on the Priority Watch List because of its alleged weak copyright enforcement regime, which has been aggravated by the introduction of 'fair use' exception and a quotation exception that is not limited by purpose and thus 'risks causing substantial harm to rights holders and renders the proposed exception incompatible with the internationally-recognized three-step test for copyright exceptions and limitations'. See IIPA, '2019 Special 301 Report on Copyright Protection and Enforcement' (7 February 2019), 72, available at https://iipa.org/files/uploads/2019/02/2019SPEC301REPORT.pdf (accessed 7 February 2020). On 25 October 2019, the Office of the United States Trade Representative announced that GSP eligibility review of South Africa would occur – see https://ustr.gov/about-us/policy-offices/press-office/press-releases/2019/october/ustr-announces-gsp-enforcement# (accessed 7 February 2020).

exceptions. Where rare new exceptions do find support, they tend to be narrowly defined and highly qualified. It is these processes that broadly explain why exceptions, such as the right of quotation, end up in many national laws couched in a multiplicity of conditions and qualifications.

The matter is compounded because a similar structural failure also occurs at an international level.[8] While, in general, it is no longer the case (as it might have been at the time of the Stockholm Revision of Berne) that Members of the Berne Union are able to become signatories to texts that contain obligations, to ratify those treaties, and yet to ignore their prescriptions, because TRIPS gave teeth to Berne, this remains true for Article 10(1). In short, TRIPS works well for right holders, not users.[9] This is because the system depends on a nation-state recognising a commercial interest that is substantially affected by non-compliance such that it triggers the dispute resolution process. An example would be a right-holder group in country (A) that, because of non-compliance in country (B), is not benefiting from an expected revenue stream. All relevant right-holders in country (A) have an interest in causing country (B) to change its laws. However, it is much more difficult to envisage a parallel situation in respect to Article 10(1) Berne. That would require a national Government (A) to complain before the WTO that another contracting party (B) has not honoured its obligation to implement the mandatory exception, with the effect that businesses from (A) are unable to exploit their productions in country (B), or have been charged for unnecessary licences to do so.

Of course, it might be that international operators of internet 'platforms' might have an interest in ensuring that the quotation right is properly secured to users.[10] Indeed, one possible response that Google might have made to the Spanish reforms to the quotation right that required the payment of remuneration could have been to seek action from the USTR to commence dispute settlement at the WTO.[11] The

---

[8]   It is interesting that several EU countries, such as the Netherlands, modified their 'quotation exception' in order to comply with the EU's Information Society Directive, 2001/29/EC. As Article 5(3)(d) is not in significantly different terms from, and on its face is no stricter than, Article 10(1) Berne, such a response likely reflects different perceptions in the binding force of the two regimes.

[9]   Although notice how South Africa is seeking to 'use' TRIPS to its advantage. Presumably in response to the calls for it to be put on the Priority Watch List because of introducing a fair use and other new exceptions, South Africa has issued a communication in which it claims that 'fair use' is not in conflict with TRIPS and asking for other countries to discuss the flexibilities of the three-step test within TRIPS: see WTO Council for TRIPS, 'Intellectual Property and the Public Interest: The WTO TRIPS Agreement and the Copyright Three-Step Test: Communication from South Africa' 29 January 2020, IP/C/W/663, available at www.keionline.org/wp-content/uploads/W663.pdf (accessed 7 February 2020).

[10] Guy Pessach, 'Beyond IP – The Cost of Free,' (2016) 54 *Osgoode Hall L Rev* 225, (highlighting the reliance of new media enterprises on free availability of cultural material).

[11] In 2014, Spain, influenced by a previous initiatives in Germany, added a new Article 32(2) to its Copyright Act: 'The making available to the public by providers of digital services of contents aggregation of non-significant fragments of contents, available in periodical publications or in periodically updated websites and which have an informative purpose, of creation of public opinion or of entertainment, will not require any authorization, without prejudice of the right of the publisher

claim would, presumably, have been that the money paid over as remuneration by Google and other news platforms should be reimbursed. Instead, of course, as is well known, Google simply withdrew its Google News service.[12] Another possibility might be that the provider of an internet platform complains that its interests (and thus those of the State in which it is established) are affected because a particular national law does not allow users to take advantage of the quotation exception, so the platform is less well used and thus less popular. It is easy to see, however, that a national government might want to weigh the interests of the platform against other interests of content producers that benefit from the fact that third countries impose unlawful conditions on the quotation right. Unless a particular national economy comes to be dominated by the economic interests of platforms (whose business depends on user-generated content, the legitimacy of which in turn relies on the quotation exception), it is difficult to imagine a national government seeking to vindicate the quotation right in WTO proceedings.

Even if the failings of transnational compliance procedures pose significant obstacles to combating this 'dysfunctional pluralism,' the promise of global mandatory fair use is already to be found in the text of Article 10(1) Berne, and much therefore can still be realised by the concerted action of what Harold Koh referred to as 'transnational norm entrepreneurs' (including NGOs, academics and intellectual communities).[13] By highlighting the centrality of Article 10(1) Berne in international copyright law, and clarifying its status as mandatory, the attention of national policy actors can be diverted from obsession with the 'three-step test' and its constraints on what nation-states cannot do for users (including author-users) and refocused on what nation-states are *already obliged* to do for users. More specifically, pressure can be brought to bear at a national level by repeated emphasis on the illegitimacy of limitations and qualifications as to shortness and purpose. Once these legislative reforms are achieved, it will become possible to explore the breadth that the notion of 'quotation' in Article 10(1) offers. This could take the form of reconsidering the shape and role of US-style 'fair use' exceptions, along with parody exceptions, and how national courts do and should interpret the quotation exception. Finally,

---

or, as applicable, of other rights owners to receive an equitable compensation. This right will be unwaivable and will be effective through the collective management organizations of intellectual property rights. In any case, the making available to the public of photographic works or ordinary photographs on periodical publications or on periodically updated websites will be subject to authorization.' See R. Xalabarder, 'The Remunerated Statutory Limitation for News Aggregation and Search Engines Proposed by the Spanish Government; Its Compliance with International and EU Law' (30 September 2014) IN3 Working Paper Series, http://infojustice.org/wp-content/uploads/2014/10/xalabarder.pdf (accessed 10 June 2020).

[12] R Xalabarder, 'Press Publisher Rights in the New Copyright in the Digital Single Market Draft Directive', CREATe Working Paper 2016/15 (December 2016), 20–1; L Bently and M Kretschmer, 'Strengthening the Position of Press Publishers and Authors and Performers in the Copyright Directive,' Study for the European Parliament, PE596.810 (September 2017), esp. 29–36 (describing impact of law).

[13] Harold Koh, 'Bringing International Law Home' (1998) 35 *Houston L Rev* 623.

a proper understanding of Article 10(1) Berne may allow industry guidelines and best practices regarding quotation to be revisited and reformulated and, in so doing, move away from the current, highly restrictive, risk-averse practices that exist in many of the creative industries (such as the publishing and music industries).

This book seeks to provoke norm entrepreneurs and their interpretive communities, in particular Members of the Berne Union and those law-makers and policy-makers within them, to give full effect to a norm that has been on the books for fifty years, and thus, finally, to recognise global mandatory fair use. In so doing, we are not advocating the destruction of copyright or a blunt pro-user position. Instead, we are suggesting fresh perspectives that will hopefully lead to shifts in author/owner and user relations.

Bibliography

BOOKS AND BOOK CHAPTERS

Adeney E, *The Moral Rights of Authors and Performers: An International and Comparative Analysis* (Oxford University Press 2006).

Ades D, 'Web of Images', in Dawn Ades et al., *Francis Bacon* (The Tate Gallery in Association with Thames and Hudson 1985).

Allgrove B and Groom J, 'Enforcement in a Digital Context: Intermediary Liability' in Aplin T (ed.), *Research Handbook on IP and Digital Technologies* (Edward Elgar 2020) ch. 25.

Alloway L, '"Pop Art" since 1949' *The Listener* (London, 27 December 1962), reprinted in Kalina R (ed.), *Imagining the Present: Essays by Lawrence Alloway* (Routledge 2006).

Ap Siôn P, *The Music of Michael Nyman: Texts, Contexts and Intertexts* (Ashgate 2007).

Aplin T, *Copyright Law in a Digital Society* (Hart 2005).

Aufderheide P and Jaszi P, *Reclaiming Fair Use: How to Put Balance Back in Copyright* (University of Chicago Press 2011).

Aufderheide P and Jaszi P, *Reclaiming Fair Use: How to Put Balance Back in Copyright* (2nd ed., University of Chicago Press 2018).

Austin J F, *Proust, Pastiche and the Postmodern or Why Style Matters* (Bucknell University Press 2013).

Ballantine C, *Music and Its Social Meanings* (Gordon and Breach 1984).

Band J and Gerafi J, *The Fair Use/Fair Dealing Handbook* (Policybandwidth 2013).

Barendt E, *Freedom of Speech* (2nd ed., Oxford University Press 2005).

Baron J L, *A Treasury of Jewish Quotations* (Crown 1956).

Barthes R, *Image, Music, Text* (Fontana Press 1984).

Bartlett J (1820–1905) and Kaplan J, *Bartlett's Familiar Quotations* (17th ed., Little, Brown 2002; 1st ed. 1855).

Bently L, 'Parody and Copyright in the Common Law World' in *Copyright and Freedom of Expression* (ALAI 2008) 360.

Bently L, and Aplin T, 'Whatever Became of Global, Mandatory, Fair Use? A Case Study in Dysfunctional Pluralism' in Frankel S (ed.), *Is Intellectual Property Pluralism Functional?* (Edward Elgar 2019) ch. 1.

Bently L (ed.), *International Copyright Law and Practice* (LexisNexis 2019, annually updated).

Bercovitz A and Bercovitz G, 'Spain' in Bently L (ed.), *International Copyright Law and Practice* (LexisNexis 2019).

Bertrand A, *Droit d'auteur* 3rd ed (Dalloz 2010).

Biguenet J, 'Double Takes: The Role of Allusion in Cinema' in Horton A and McDougal S Y (eds.), *Play It Again, Sam: Retakes on Remakes* (University of California Press 1998).

Bjone C, *Philip Johnson and His Mischief: Appropriation in Art and Architecture* (Images Publishing Group 2014).

Bliss M, *Brian De Palma* (Scarecrow Press Inc 1983).

Blomqvist J, *Primer on International Copyright and Related Rights* (Edward Elgar 2014).

Bochumberg L, *Le Droit de Citation* (Masson 1994).

Bond A (ed.), *Francis Bacon: Five Decades* (Thames and Hudson 2013).

Boozer J, 'Crashing the Gates of Insight' in Kerman J B (ed.), *Retrofitting Blade Runner* (Bowling Green University Popular Press 1991).

Bouche N, *Intellectual Property Law in France* (2nd ed., Kluwer 2014).

Brandon J M, 'Battleship Potemkin' in Di Mare P C (ed.), *Movies in American History: An Encyclopaedia*, vol. 1 (ABC-CLIO 2011).

Browning D C, *Dictionary of Quotations and Proverbs* (Chancellor 1952).

Bureau de L'Union, 'Les Emprunts Licite', (1924) *Le Droit D'Auteur* 37.

Burkholder P, *All Made of Tunes: Charles Ives and the Uses of Musical Borrowing* (Yale University Press 1995).

Burkholder P in Sadie S and Tyrrell J (ed.), *The New Grove Dictionary of Music and Musicians* (Oxford University Press 2001) 6.

Burrell R and Coleman A, *Copyright Exceptions: The Digital Impact* (Cambridge University Press 2005).

Calinescu M, 'Rewriting' in Bertens H and Fokkema D W (eds.), *International Postmodernism: Theory and Literary Practice* (J Benjamins 1997) 243–8.

Chapdelaine P, *Copyright User Rights: Contracts and the Erosion of Property* (Oxford University Press 2017).

Chapin J, *The Book of Catholic Quotations* (John Calder 1957).

Christie I, 'Introduction: Rediscovering Eisenstein' in Christie I and Taylor R (eds.), *Eisenstein Rediscovered* (Routledge 1993) 1–30.

Cohen J M and Cohen M J, *The New Penguin Dictionary of Quotations* (Viking 1992).

Coke V D, *The Painter and the Photograph from Delacroix to Warhol* (University of New Mexico Press 1964).

Collins Pocket Dictionary of the English Language (Collins 1989).

Colombet C, *Propriété Littéraire et Artistique et Droits Voisins* (9th ed., Dalloz 1999).

Correa C M, *Trade Related Aspects of Intellectual Property Rights: A Commentary on the TRIPs Agreement* (Oxford University Press 2007).

Craig C J, *Copyright, Communication and Culture: Towards a Relational Theory of Copyright Law* (Edward Elgar 2011).

Crinson M, *Stirling and Gowan: Architecture from Austerity to Affluence* (Yale University Press 2012).

Crofton I, *A Dictionary of Art Quotations* (Routledge 1988).

Davidson C (ed.), *Robert A M Stern: Tradition and Invention in Architecture: Conversations and Essays* (Yale University Press 2011).

Davies G and Garnett K(eds.), *Moral Rights* (Sweet & Maxwell 2010).

Davies G and Garnett K (eds.), *Moral Rights* (2nd ed., Sweet and Maxwell 2016).

Davison M, *The Legal Protection of Databases* (Cambridge University Press 2003).

De Carvalho N P, *The TRIPS Regime of Antitrust and Undisclosed Information* (Kluwer 2008).

De Grazia M, 'Sanctioning Voice: Quotation Marks, the Abolition of Torture, and the Fifth Amendment' in Woodmansee M and Jaszi P (eds.), *The Construction of*

Authorship: Textual Appropriation in Law and Literature (Duke University Press 1994) 281–302.

De Grazia M, 'Shakespeare in Quotation Marks' in Marsden J I (ed.), *The Appropriation of Shakespeare: Post-Renaissance Reconstructions of the Works and the Myth* (St Martin's Press 1992) 57–71.

Desbois H, *Le Droit D'Auteur* (3rd ed., Dalloz 1978).

Dinwoodie G B and Dreyfuss R C, *A Neo-Federalist Vision of TRIPS: The Resilience of the International Intellectual Property Regime* (Oxford University Press 2012).

Distel A, Hoog M and Moffett C S, *Impressionism: A Centenary Exhibition* (Metropolitan Museum of Art 1974).

Douglas A and Strumpf M, *Webster's New World Dictionary of Quotations* (Macmillan 1998).

Drahos P, *A Philosophy of Intellectual Property* (Dartmouth 1996).

Drassinower A, *What's Wrong with Copying?* (Harvard University Press 2015).

Dusollier S, 'Realigning Economic Rights with Exploitation of Works: The Control of Authors over Circulation of Works in the Public Sphere' in P B Hugenholtz (ed.), *Copyright Reconstructed: Rethinking Copyright's Economic Rights in a Time of Highly Dynamic Technological and Economic Change* (Kluwer 2018) ch. 6, 163–201.

Dworkin G, 'Exceptions to Copyright Exclusivity: Is Fair Use Consistent with Article 9.2 Berne and the New International Order' in Hansen H (ed.), *International Intellectual Property Law and Policy: Volume 4* (Juris 2000) ch. 66.

Dyer R, *Pastiche* (Routledge 2007).

Edgar R, Marland J, Rawle S, *The Language of Film* (2nd ed., Bloomsbury 2015).

Ehrlich E and DeBruhl M, *The International Thesaurus of Quotations* (Harper Perennial 1996).

Elkin-Koren A C N and Salzberger E M, *The Law and Economics of Intellectual Property in the Digital Age: The Limits of Analysis* (Routledge 2013).

Ellickson R C, *Order without Law: How Neighbours Settle Disputes* (Harvard University Press 1991).

Emerson W, 'Quotation and Originality' in Emerson R W, *Letters and Social Aims* (Houghton Mifflin 1875).

Emery M, 'Argentina' in Bently L (ed.), *International Copyright Law and Practice* (LexisNexis. 2019).

Falce V, 'Italy,' in Bently L (ed.), *International Copyright Law and Practice* (LexisNexis 2019).

Farwell B, *Manet and the Nude: A Study in Iconography in the Second Empire* (Garland 1981).

Fergusson R, *The Hamlyn Dictionary of Quotations* (Hamlyn 1989).

Ficsor M, *The Law of Copyright and the Internet* (Oxford University Press 2002).

Ficsor M, *Guide to the Copyright and Related Rights Treaties Administered by WIPO* (WIPO 2003).

Finnegan R E, *Why Do We Quote? The Culture and History of Quotation* (Open Book Publishers 2011).

Fisher W, 'Theories of Intellectual Property' in Munzer S (ed.), *New Essays in the Legal and Political Theory of Property* (Cambridge University Press 2001) ch. 6, 165–99.

Fitzhenry R I, *Say It Again, Sam: A Book of Quotations* (Michael O'Mara 1996).

Fontenelle T, 'Introduction' in Thierry Fontanelle (ed.), *Practical Lexicography: A Reader* (Oxford University Press 2008).

Fordham M and De la Mare T, 'Identifying the Principles of Proportionality' in Jowell J and Cooper J (eds.), *Understanding Human Rights Principles* (Hart 2001) 27–90.

Françon A, *Cours de Propriété Littéraire, artistique et Industriel* (Litec 1999).

Fraser D (ed.), *Dictionary of Quotations* (Collins 1983).

Fried M, *Manet's Modernism: Or, The Face of Painting in the 1860s* (University of Chicago Press 1996).

Gabbard K, 'The Quoter and His Culture' in Reginald Buckner and Steven Wieland (eds.), *Jazz in Mind: Essays on the History and Meaning of Jazz* (Wayne State University Press 1991).

Garber M, *Quotation Marks* (Routledge 2003).

Gardiner R, *Treaty Interpretation* (2nd ed., Oxford University Press 2017).

Geist M, *The Copyright Pentalogy: How the Supreme Court of Canada Shook the Foundations of Canadian Copyright Law* (University of Ottawa Press 2013).

Geller P, 'Must Copyright Be for Ever Caught between Marketplace and Authorship Norms?' in Sherman B and Strowel A (eds.), *Of Authors and Origins* (Clarendon Press 1994) 159–201.

Gibson B, *The Instrumental Music of Iannis Xenakis: Theory, Practice, Self-Borrowing* (Pendragon Press 2011).

Ginsburg J and Treppoz E, *International Copyright Law: US and EU Perspectives, Text and Cases* (Edward Elgar 2015).

Girouard M, *Big Jim* (Pimlico 2000).

Godard J L, *Jean-Luc Godard par Jean-Luc Godard* (Cahiers du cinema 1985).

Goldstein P, *International Copyright: Principles, Law, Practice* (Oxford University Press 2001).

Goldstein P and Hugenholtz B, *International Copyright: Principles, Law, Practice* (Oxford University Press 2010).

Gombrich E H, *The Ideas of Progress and their Impact on Art* (Cooper Union 1971).

Goodman N, *Ways of Worldmaking* (Hackett 1978).

Goodwin J, *Eisenstein, Cinema, and History* (University of Illinois Press 1993).

Greenhalgh P, in *Francis Bacon and the Masters* (Fontanka Publications 2015).

Greenleaf G and Lindsay D, *Public Rights: Copyright's Public Domain* (Cambridge University Press 2018).

Grosse Ruse-Khan H, *The Protection of Intellectual Property in International Law* (Oxford University Press 2016).

Grønstad A, *Transfigurations: Violence, Death and Masculinity in American Cinema* (Amsterdam University Press 2008).

Gruenberger M, 'Germany' in Bently L (ed.), *International Copyright Law and Practice* (LexisNexis 2019).

Guibault L, *Copyright Limitations and Contracts: An Analysis of the Contractual Overridability of Limitations on Copyright* (Kluwer 2002).

Hanks P, 'Definition' in Durkin P (ed.), *The Oxford Handbook of Lexicography* (Oxford University Press 2016).

Harkins P, 'Microsampling: From Akufen's Microhouse to Todd Edwards and the Sound of UK Garage' in Danielsen A (ed.), *Musical Rhythm in the Age of Digital Reproduction* (Ashgate 2010) 177–194.

Heisner B, *Production Design in the Contemporary American Film: A Critical Study of 23 Movies and their Designers* (McFarland & Co 2004).

Henderson C W, *The Charles Ives Tunebook* (2nd ed., Indiana University Press 2008).

Henning-Bodewig F, 'International Unfair Competition Law' in Hilty R M and Henning-Bodewig F (eds.), *Law against Unfair Competition – Towards a New Paradigm in Europe?* (Springer 2007) ch. 2, 53–60.

Hoesterey I, *Pastiche: Cultural Memory in Art, Film, Literature* (Indiana University Press 2001).

Höpperger M and Senftleben M, 'Protection against Unfair Competition at the International Level' in Hilty R M and Henning-Bodewig F (eds.), *Law against Unfair Competition – Towards a New Paradigm in Europe?* (Springer 2007) ch. 3, 61–76.

Houston K, *Shady Characters: The Secret Life of Punctuation, Symbols, and Other Typographical Marks* (Norton & Co 2013).

Hudson E, *Drafting Copyright Exceptions: From the Law in Books to the Law in Action* (Cambridge University Press 2020).

Hughes J, 'Fair Use and Its Politics – at Home and Abroad' in Okediji R L (ed.), *Copyright Law in an Age of Exceptions and Limitations* (Cambridge University Press 2017) ch. 8, 234–274.

Hugenholtz P B (ed.), *Copyright Reconstructed: Rethinking Copyright's Economic Rights in a Time of Highly Dynamic Technological and Economic Change* (Kluwer 2018).

Iampolski M, *The Memory of Tiresias: Intertextuality and Film* (trans. Harsha Ram) (University of California Press 1998).

Iljadica M, *Copyright Beyond Law: Regulating Creativity in the Graffiti Subculture* (Hart 2016).

Jacobs S, *Framing Pictures: Film and the Visual Arts* (Edinburgh University Press 2011).

Jacques S, *The Parody Exception in Copyright Law* (Oxford University Press 2019).

Jencks C, 'Philip Johnson and the Smile of Medusa' in Emmanuel Petit (ed.), *Philip Johnson: The Constancy of Change* (Yale University Press 2009).

Joannides P, 'Bacon, Michelangelo and the Classical Tradition' in P Joannides, A Geitner, and T Morel (eds.), *Francis Bacon and the Masters* (Fontanka Publications 2015) 26–36.

Johnson S, *A Dictionary of the English Language* (W Strahan 1755) 1626 (reprint, New York, 1967).

Kahng E (ed.), *The Repeating Image: multiples in French painting from David to Matisse* (Yale University Press 2007).

Kamina P, 'France' in Bently L (ed.), *International Copyright: Law and Practice* (LexisNexis 2019).

Katz M, *Capturing Sound: How Technology has Changed Music* (University of California Press 2010).

Kilgarriff A, 'I Don't Believe in Word Senses', in Thierry Fontenelle (ed.), *Practical Lexicography: A Reader* (Oxford University Press 2008) ch. 9, 135–51.

Klopmeier and Arend in Stoll P T, Busche J and Arend K (eds.), *WTO-Trade Related Aspects of Intellectual Property Rights* (Martinus Nijhoff 2009) 253–67.

Kolker R P, *Film, Form, and Culture* (4th ed., Routledge 2016).

Knapp L F (ed.), *Brian De Palma: Interviews* (University Press of Mississippi 2003).

Kur A, 'Limitations and Exceptions under the Three-Step Test – How Much Room to Walk the Middle Ground' in Kur A and Levin M (eds.), *Intellectual Property Rights in a Fair World Trade System: Proposals for Reform of TRIPS* (Edward Elgar 2011) ch. 5, 208–61.

Kur A and Grosse Ruse-Khan H, 'Enough Is Enough – The Notion of Binding Ceilings in International Intellectual Property Protection' in Kur A and Levin M (eds.), *Intellectual Property Rights in a Fair World Trade System – Proposals for Reform of TRIPS* (Edward Elgar 2011) ch. 8, 359–407.

Kuspit D, 'Some Thoughts about the Significance of Postmodern Appropriation Art' in Brilliant R and Kinney D (eds.), *Reuse Value: Spolia and Appropriation in Art and Architecture from Constantine to Sherrie Levine* (Ashgate 2011) 237.

Kvifte T, 'Digital Sampling and Analogue Aesthetics' in Melberg A (ed.), *Aesthetics at Work* (Unipub 2007) 193.

Lacasse S, 'Intertextuality and Hypertextuality in Recorded Popular Music' in Talbot M (ed.), *The Musical Work: Reality or Invention?* (Liverpool University Press 2000) ch. 2.

Ladas S P, *Patents, Trademarks and Related Rights* (Harvard University Press 1975).

Landau S I, *Dictionaries: The Art and Craft of Lexicography* (2nd ed., Cambridge University Press 2001).

Levy E, *Cinema of Outsiders: The Rise of American Independent Film* (New York University Press 1999).

Lewis H, 'No Rules, Just Art' in *The Architecture of Philip Johnson* (Bullfinch Press 2002).

Lewis H and O'Connor J, *Philip Johnson: The Architect in His Own Words* (Rizzoli 1994).

MacDonnel D E, A *Dictionary of Quotations in Most Frequent Use: Taken from the Greek, Latin, French, Spanish and Italian Languages* (3rd ed., G.G. and J. Robinson 1799).

Masiyakurima P, 'The Free Speech Benefits of Fair Dealing Defences' in Paul L C Torremans (ed.), *Intellectual Property and Human Rights: Enhanced Edition of Copyright and Human Rights* (Kluwer 2008) ch. 9, 235–56.

Mauner G L, *Manet, Peintre-Philosophe: A Study of the Painter's Themes* (Pennsylvania State University Press 1975).

Masouyé, C, *WIPO Guide to the Berne Convention for the Protection of Literary and Artistic Works* (Paris Act, 1971) (WIPO 1978).

Masouyé, C, *WIPO Guide to the Rome Convention and Phonograms Convention* (WIPO 1981).

Mazziotti G, *EU Digital Copyright Law and the End-User* (Springer 2008).

McKean J, *Leicester University Engineering Building: James Stirling and James Gowan* (Phaidon 1994).

McLeod K and Dicola P, *Creative Licence: The Law and Culture of Digital Sampling* (Duke University Press 2011).

McMurtrie D C, *Concerning Quotation Marks* (Privately Printed 1934).

Merges R P, *Justifying Intellectual Property* (Harvard University Press 2011).

Metzer D, *Quotation and Cultural Meaning in Twentieth Century Music* (Cambridge University Press 2003).

Miyakawa F, *Five Percenter Rap* (Indiana University Press 2005).

Moreham N A and Warby M, *Tugendhat and Christie: The Law of Privacy and the Media* (3rd ed., Oxford University Press 2016).

Morris Y S, 'The Legal Implications Surrounding the Practice of Video Sampling in the Digital Age' in Greenfield S and Osborn .G (eds.), *Readings in Law and Popular Culture* (Routledge 2008) 274–309.

Murray S O and Roscoe W, *Islamic Homosexualities: Culture, History, and Literature* (New York University Press 1997).

The New Shorter Oxford English Dictionary (Oxford University Press 1993).

Ng-Loy, Wee Loon, *Law of Intellectual Property of Singapore* (rev. ed., Sweet & Maxwell 2009).

Nicol A, Millar G and Sharland A, *Media Law & Human Rights* (2nd ed., Oxford Uniersity Press 2009).

Nimmer M B and Nimmer D, *Nimmer on Copyright* (Matthew Bender 1996).

O'Grady J, 'Introduction' in A J Ayer and J O'Grady (eds.), A *Dictionary of Philosophical Quotations* (Blackwell 1992).

Ohly A, 'European Fundamental Rights and Intellectual Property' in Ohly A and Pila J (eds.), *The Europeanization of Intellectual Property Law: Towards a European Legal Methodology* (Oxford University Press 2013) ch. 8, 145–63.

Ohly A, 'A Fairness-Based Approach to Economic Rights' in P B Hugenholtz (ed.), *Rethinking Copyright's Economic Rights in a Time of Highly Dynamic Technological and Economic Change* (Kluwer 2018) ch. 4, 83–119.

Okediji R L, 'Reframing International Copyright Limitations and Exceptions as Development Policy' in Okediji R (ed.), *Copyright Law in an Age of Limitations and Exceptions* (Cambridge University Press 2016) ch. 14, 429–95.

Okpaluba J, 'Digital Sampling and Music Industry Practices, Re-Spun' in Bowrey K and Handler M (eds.), *Copyright Law in the Age of the Entertainment Franchise* (Cambridge University Press 2014) ch. 4, 75–100.

Owens C, 'Philip Johnson: History, Genealogy, Historicism' in Kenneth Frampton, *Philip Johnson: Processes. The Glass House, 1949 and The AT&T Corporate Headquarters, 1978* (Institute for Architecture & Urban Studies NY 1978).

Petersen K, 'Shakespeare and Sententiae: The Use of Quotation in Lucrece' in Maxwell J and Rumbold K (eds.), *Shakespeare and Quotation* (Cambridge University Press 2018) ch. 2.

Randall J (ed.), *Anthology of Quotations: Over 12,000 Quotations Arranged by Theme* (Bloomsbury 2002).

Rathbone E E, Robinson W H, Steele E, and Steele M, *Van Gogh Repetitions* (Yale University Press 2013).

Rawls J, *A Theory of Justice* (rev. ed., Oxford University Press 1999).

Reese-Lawrence A, *James Stirling: Revisionary Modernists* (Yale University Press 2012).

Reff T, *Manet, Olympia* (Allen Lane 1976).

Reinbothe J and von Lewinski S, *The WIPO Treaties 1996* (Butterworths 2002).

Ricketson S, 'The Berne Convention: The Continued Relevance of an Ancient Text' in Vaver D and Bently L (eds.), *Intellectual Property in the New Millennium: Essays in Honour of William R. Cornish* (Cambridge University Press 2004) ch. 15, 217–33.

Ricketson S and Ginsburg J, *International Copyright and Neighbouring Rights: The Berne Convention and Beyond* (2nd ed., Oxford University Press 2006).

Ricketson S and Ginsburg J, 'The Berne Convention: Historical and Institutional Aspects' in Gervais D J (ed.), *International Intellectual Property: A Handbook of Contemporary Research* (Edward Elgar 2015) ch. 1, 3–36.

Riley D W, *My Soul Looks Back, 'Less I Forget: A Collection of Quotations by People of Color* (Harper Perennial 1995).

Roth L M, *Understanding Architecture: Its Elements, History, Meaning* (The Herbert Press 1993/1994).

Russell J, *Francis Bacon* (Thames and Hudson 1993).

Sadler G, 'A Re-examination of Rameau's Self-Borrowings' in Heyer J H (ed.), *Jean-Baptiste Lully and the French Baroque: Essays in Honor of James R. Anthony* (Cambridge University Press 1989) 259.

Said E, *Beginnings: Intention and Method* (Columbia University Press 1985).

Samuelson P, 'Justifications for Copyright Limitations and Exceptions' in R L Okediji (ed.), *Copyright Law in an Age of Limitations and Exceptions* (Cambridge University Press 2016) ch. 1, 12–59.

Senftleben M, *Copyright, Limitations and the Three-Step Test: An Analysis of the Three-Step Test in International and EC Copyright Law* (Kluwer 2004).

Senftleben M, 'Quotation, Parody and Fair Use' in Hugenholtz B, Quaedvlieg A and Visser D (eds.), *A Century of Dutch Copyright: 1912–2012* (DeLex 2012) 354–5.

Shiffrin S V, 'Lockean Arguments for Private Intellectual Property' in S R Munzer (ed.), *New Essays in the Legal and Political Theory of Property* (Cambridge University Press 2001) 138–67.

Shorter Oxford English Dictionary on Historical Principles, vol. 2 (6th ed., Oxford University Press 2007).

Silbey J, *The Eureka Myth: Creators, Innovators, and Everyday Intellectual Property* (Stanford University Press 2015).

Simpson J A and Weiner E S C (eds.), *The Oxford English Dictionary* (Clarendon 1989) vol. XIII.

Sinnreich A, *Mashed Up: Music, Technology and the Rise of Configurable Culture* (University of Massachusetts Press 2010).

Slocum B G, *Ordinary Meaning: A Theory of the Most Fundamental Principle of Legal Interpretation* (University of Chicago Press 2013).

Stam R, *Film Theory: An Introduction* (Blackwell 2000).

Stamatoudi I, 'Greece' in Bently L (ed.), *International Copyright: Law and Practice* (LexisNexis 2019).

Steinberg L, 'The Glorious Company' in Lipman J and Marshall R, *Art about Art* (Whitney Museum 1978) 8–31.

Stern R, *Modern Classicism* (Thames and Hudson 1988).

Stoll P T, Busche J and Arend K (eds.), *WTO-Trade Related Aspects of Intellectual Property Rights* (Martinus Nijhoff 2009).

Sylvester D, *Interviews with Francis Bacon* (3rd ed., Thames and Hudson 1987).

Tafuri M, 'L'Architecture dans le Boudoir: The Language of Criticism and the Criticism of Language' in Hays K M (ed.), *Architecture Theory since 1968* (MIT Press 1998).

Tant R, 'Archive' in Gale M and Stephens C (eds.), *Francis Bacon* (Tate Publishing 2008).

Taylor R, *The Battleship Potemkin: The Film Companion* (I. B. Tauris 2000).

Trachtenberg M and Hyman I, *Architecture: From Prehistory to Postmodernism* (2nd ed., Pearson 2001).

Tucker P H, *Manet's Le déjeuner sur L'herbe* (Cambridge University Press 1998).

Tullio de Mauro, *Grande Dizionario Italiano dell'uso* (Torino 1999).

Urbina F J, *A Critique of Proportionality and Balancing* (Cambridge University Press 2017).

Van Eechoud M, Hugenholtz P B, Van Gompel S, Guibault L and Helberger N, *Harmonizing European Copyright Law: The Challenges of Better Lawmaking* (Kluwer 2009).

Veneciano J D, 'Louis Armstrong, Bricolage and the Aesthetics of Swing' in O'Meally R G, Edwards B H, and Griffin F J (eds.), *Uptown Conversation: The New Jazz Studies* (Columbia University Press 2004) 256–78.

Von Lewinski S, *International Copyright Law and Policy* (Oxford University Press 2008).

Voorhoof D, 'Freedom of Expression and the Right to Information: Implications for Copyright' in Geiger C (ed.), *Research Handbook on Human Rights and Intellectual Property* (Edward Elgar, 2015) ch. 17, 331–53.

Wadlow C, *The Law of Passing Off: Unfair Competition by Misrepresentation* (5th ed., Sweet & Maxwell 2016).

Walsh V, 'Real Imagination in Technical Imagination' in Gale M and Stephens C (eds.), *Francis Bacon* (Tate Publishing 2008).

Walter M M and Von Lewinski S, *European Copyright Law: A Commentary* (Oxford University Press 2010).

Weber B, 'Cool Head, Hot Images' in Knapp L (ed.), *Brian De Palma – Interviews* (University Press of Mississippi 2003).

Wendell Holmes Jr O, *The Common Law* (Little, Brown 1881).

Williams J, *Rhymin' and Stealin'* (University of Michigan Press 2013).

Wittgenstein L, *Philosophical Investigations* (4th revised ed., Wiley-Blackwell 2009).

Worby R, 'Foreword', in P Ap Siôn, *The Music of Michael Nyman: Texts, Contexts and Intertexts* (Ashgate 2007).

Xalabarder R, 'On-line Teaching and Copyright: Any Hopes for an EU Harmonized Playground?' in Torremans P (ed.), *Copyright Law: A Handbook of Contemporary Research* (Edward Elgar 2007) ch. 15, 373–401.

ARTICLES

Abercrombie S, 'A Few Good Buildings: Reading the Obituaries of Philip Johnson' (2005) 74 (2) *The American Scholar* 117.

Adeney E, 'Appropriation in the Name of Art: Is a Quotation Exception the Answer?' (2013) 23 *AIPJ* 142.

Ambasz E, 'Popular Pantheon' (December 1984) *Architectural Review* 35.

Antons C and Adeney E, 'The *Germania 3* Decision Translated: The Quotation Exception before the German Constitutional Court' [2013] *EIPR* 646.

Ap Siôn, 'Hidden Discontinuities and Uncanny Meaning' (2014) 33(2) *Contemporary Music Review* 167.

Aprill E P, 'The Law of the Word: Dictionary Shopping in the Supreme Court' (1998) 30 *Ariz St L J* 275.

Arnold R, 'Reflections on the Triumph of Music: Copyrights and Performers' Rights in Music' (2009) (20 October) Oxford Intellectual Property Invited Speaker Seminar.

Aronsson-Storrier A, 'Copyright Exceptions and Contract in the UK: The Impact of Recent Amendments' (2016) 6 *Queen Mary Journal of Intellectual Property* 111.

Austin G, 'EU and US Perspectives on Fair Dealing for the Purpose of Parody or Satire' (2016) 39 *UNSW L J* 684.

Barthelmess S, 'Richard Meier's Stadthaus Project at Ulm' (1990) (Spr) 44 (3) *Jo Architectural Education* 2.

Bate S and Abramson L, 'To Sample or Not to Sample' [1997] *Ent L R* 193.

Beaudoin R, 'Counterpoint and Quotation in Ussachevsky's *Wireless Fantasy*' (2007) 12(2) *Organised Sound* 143.

Beebe B, 'An Empirical Study of U.S. Copyright Fair Use Opinions, 1978–2005' (2008) 156 *U Pa L Rev* 549.

Behrens R, 'Review of "Eisenstein: The Master's House"' (2004) 37(3) *Leonardo* 252.

Benoliel D, 'Copyright Distributive Justice' (2007) 10 *Yale J L & Tech* 45.

Bently L, 'Copyright and Quotation in Film and TV' CREATe Working Paper (June 2020).

Bently L and Sherman B, 'Great Britain and the Signing of the Berne Convention in 1886' (2001) 48 Jo Copyright Soc'y USA 311.

Bergström S, 'Current Problems Concerning Broadcasting in the International Field' (1958) 51 *EBU Review (B)* 21–6; (1959) 25 *RIDA* 120.

Bergström S, 'Kommitté I. Revisionen av Bernkonventionen' (1968) 37 *NIR* 7.

Bergström S, 'Report of the Work of the Main Committee I' [1967] *Copyright* 183.

Bicknell J, 'The Problem of Reference in Musical Quotation: A Phenomenological Approach' (2001) 59 *Journal of Aesthetics and Art Criticism* 185.

Bodelsen M, 'Gauguin's Cézannes' (1962) 104 *Burlington Magazine* 204.

Bohannan C, 'Copyright Harm, Foreseeability, and Fair Use' (2007) 85 *Washington University L Rev* 969.

Bracha O and Syed T, 'Beyond Efficiency: Consequence-Sensitive Theories of Copyright' (2014) 29 *Berkeley Tech L J* 229.

Bradshaw D, 'Fair Dealing and the Clockwork Orange Case: "A Thieves' Charter"?' [1994] 5 *Ent L R* 6.

Brennan D, 'The Three Step Test Frenzy – Why the TRIPS Panel Decision Might Be Considered *Per Incuriam*' [2002] *IPQ* 212.

Brudney J and Baum L, 'Oasis or Mirage: The Supreme Court's Thirst for Dictionaries in the Rehnquist and Roberts Eras' (2013) 55 *William & Mary L R* 483.

Bruno G, 'Ramble City: Postmodernism and Bladerunner' (1987) 41 *October* 61.

Burkholder J P, 'The Uses of Existing Music: Musical Borrowing as a Field' (1994) 50 *Notes* 851.

Burrell R, 'Reining in Copyright Law: Is Fair Use the Answer?' [2001] *IPQ* 361.

Cabay J and Lambrecht M, 'Remix Prohibited: How Rigid EU Copyright Laws Inhibit Creativity' (2015) 10 (5) *Journal of Intellectual Property Law & Practice* 359.

Cameron C J, 'Reinvigorating U.S. Copyright with Attribution: How Courts Can Help Define the Fair Use Exception to Copyright by Considering the Economic Aspects of Attribution' (2013) 2 *Berkeley J Ent & Sports L* 130.

Capdevila-Werning R, 'Can Buildings Quote?' (2011) 69 *Jo Aesthetics and Art Criticism* 115.

Carrier D, 'Manet and His Interpreters' (1985) 8(3) *Art History* 320.

Carter S L, 'Custom, Adjudication and Petrushevsky's Watch: Some Notes from the Intellectual Property Front' (1992) 78 *Va L Rev* 129.

Casteels M, 'Works of Art and the Right of Quotation' (1954) 11 *RIDA* 81.

Chon M, 'Intellectual Property "from Below": Copyright and Capability for Education' (2007) 40 *UC Davis L Rev* 803.

Chon M, 'Intellectual Property and the Development Divide' (2006) *Cardozo Law Review* 2821.

Chon M, 'Intellectual Property Equality' (2010) 9 *Seattle Journal for Social Justice* 259.

Christie A F and Wright R, 'A Comparative Analysis of the Three-Step Tests in International Treaties' (2014) 45(4) *IIC* 409.

Christoffersen J, 'Straight Human Rights Talk – Why Proportionality Does (Not) Matter' (2010) 55 *Scandinavian Stud L* 11.

Cianciardo J, 'The Principle of Proportionality: The Challenges of Human Rights' (2010) 3 *J Civ L Stud* 177.

Ciolino D S, 'Rethinking the Compatability of Moral Rights and Fair Use' (1997) 54 *Wash & Lee L Rev* 33.

Clay J, 'Ointments, Makeup, Pollen' (trans. John Shepley) (1983) 27 *October* 4–5.

Cohen J E, 'Copyright and the Perfect Curve' (2000) 53 *Vand L Rev* 1799.

Condren C, Davis J M, McCausland S and Phiddian R, 'Defining Parody and Satire: Australian Copyright Law and Its New Exception: Part 2 – Advancing Ordinary Definitions' (2008) 13 *MALR* 401.

Cook T, 'The Proposal for a Directive on the Protection of Trade Secrets in EU Legislation' (2014) 19 *Journal of Intellectual Property Rights* 54.

Cooter R C, 'Three Effects of Social Norms on Law: Expression, Deterrence and Internationalisation' (2000) 79 *Oregon L Rev* 1.

Cornu M and Mallet-Poujol N, 'Le droit de Citation Audiovisuelle: Légitimer la Culture par L'image' [1998] *Legicom* 119.

Crews K D, 'The Law of Fair Use and the Illusion of Fair Use Guidelines' (2001) 62 *Ohio St L J* 599.

Crinson M, 'Melnikov in Leicester – A Mythology' (2013) 4 *Leuchtturmprojekte* 48.

Cunningham C D, Levi J N, Green G M, Kaplan, J P, 'Plain Meaning and Hard Cases' (1993) 103 *Yale L J* 1561.

Dal Co F, 'The Melancholy Experience of Contemporaneity' (1993) 2 (September/October) *ANY (Architecture New York)* 26.

Damme I V, 'On Good Faith Use of Dictionary in the Search of Ordinary Meaning under the WTO Dispute Settlement Understanding – A Reply to Professor Chang-Fa Lo' (2011) 2 *Journal of International Dispute Settlement* 231.

Damstedt B G, 'Limiting Lock: A Natural Law Justification for the Fair Use Doctrine' (2003) 112 *Yale L J* 1179.

Dean W, 'Bizet's Self-Borrowings' (1960) 41(3) *Music and Letters* 238.

Deazley R, 'Copyright and Parody: Taking Backward the Gowers Review?' (2010) 73 *MLR* 785.

Deazley R and Mathis J, 'Writing about Comics and Copyright' CREATe Working Paper 2013/9 (December 2013).

Derclaye E and Favale M, 'Copyright and Contract Law: Regulating User Contracts: The State of the Art and a Research Agenda' (2010) 18 *J Intell Prop L* 65.

Derclaye E and Taylor T, 'Happy IP: Replacing the Law and Economics Justification for Intellectual Property Rights with a Well-Being Approach' (2015) *EIPR* 197.

Derclaye E and Taylor T, 'Happy IP: Aligning Intellectual Property Rights with Well-Being' (2015) *IPQ* 1.

Dinwoodie G, 'A New Copyright Order: Why National Courts Should Create Global Norms' (2000) 149 *U Pa L Rev* 469.

Dinwoodie G B, 'The Development and Incorporation of International Norms in the Formation of Copyright Law' (2001) 62 *Ohio St L J* 733.

Dinwoodie G B and Dreyfuss R C, 'Designing a Global Intellectual Property System Responsive to Change: The WTO, WIPO and Beyond' (2009) 46 *Houston L Rev* 1187.

Dong H and Gu M, 'Copyrightable or Not: A Review of the Chinese Provision on "Illegal Works" Targeted by WTO DS362 and Suggestions on the Legal Reform' (2009) 4 *Asian J WTO & Int'l Health L & Pol'y* 335.

Dotan A, Elkin-Koren N, Fischman-Afori O, Haramati-Alpern R, 'Fair Use Best Practices for Higher Education Institutions: The Israeli Experience' (2010) 57 *J Copyright Soc'y USA* 447.

Dratler J, 'Distilling the Witches' Brew of Fair Use in Copyright Law' (1988) 43 *U Miami L Rev* 233.

Dreyfuss R C and Lowenfeld A F, 'Two Achievements of the Uruguay Round: Putting TRIPS and Dispute Settlement Together' (1997) 37 *Va J Int'l L* 275.

Duro P, 'Quotational Art: Plus Ça Changes: Plus C'est La Meme Chose' (1991) 14 *Art History* 294.

Easterbrook F H, 'Text, History, and Structure in Statutory Interpretation' (1994) 17 *Harv JL & Pub Pol'y* 61.

Elkin-Koren N and Fischman-Afori O, 'Rulifying Fair Use' (2017) 59 *Arizona L Rev* 161.

Elkin-Koren N and Fischman-Afori O, 'Taking Users' Rights to the Next Level: A Pragmatist Approach to Fair Use' (2015) 33 *Cardozo Arts & Ent L J* 1.

Elkin-Koren N and Netanel Neil W, 'Transplanting Fair Use Across the Globe: A Case Study Testing The Credibility of U.S. Opposition' (May 11, 2020) *Hastings Law Journal*, Forthcoming. Available at https://ssrn.com/abstract=3598160.

Ellickson R C, 'Of Coase and Cattle: Dispute Resolution among Neighbors in Shasta County' (1986) 38 *Stan L Rev* 623.

Ellickson R C, 'The Evolution of Social Norms: A Perspective from the Legal Academy' (1999) (1 July) Yale Law School Working Paper No. 230.

Elmahjub E and Suzor N, 'Fair Use and Fairness in Copyright: A Distributive Justice Perspective on Users' Rights' (2017) 43 *Monash U L Rev* 274.

Epstein R A, 'Some Reflections on Custom in the IP Universe' (2008) 93 *Va L Rev Brief* 223.

Erlich E and Posner R A, 'An Economic Analysis of Legal Rulemaking' (1974) 3 *J Legal Stud* 257.

Estival D and Pennycook A, 'L'Académie Française and Anglophone Language Ideologies' (2011) 10 *Language Policy* 325.

Fabiani M, 'Le droit de Reproduction et La revision de la Convention de Berne' (November 1964) *Le Droit D'Auteur* 286.

Fauchart E and Von Hippel E, 'Norms-Based Intellectual Property Systems: The Case of French Chefs' (2008) 19 (2) *Organization Science* 187.

Fhima I 'The Public Interest in European Trade Mark Law' [2017] *IPQ* 311.

Field T, 'From Custom to Law in Copyright' (2008) 49 *IDEA* 125.

Fisher W W, 'Reconstructing the Fair Use Doctrine (1988) 101 *Harv L Rev* 1659.

Foster M A, 'Parody's Precarious Place: The Need to Legally Recognize Parody as Japan's Cultural Property' (2013) 23 *Seton Hall Journal of Sports and Entertainment Law* 313.

Frampton K, 'Leicester University Engineering Laboratory' (1964) 34(2) *Architectural Design* 61.

Frampton K, 'James Stirling: A Premature Critique' (1993) 26 *AA Files* 3.

Frankel S J and Kellogg M, 'Bad Faith and Fair Use' (2013) 60 *J Copyright Soc'y USA* 1.

Friedman B, 'From Deontology To Dialogue: The Cultural Consequences Of Copyright' (1995) 13 *Cardozo Arts & Ent L J* 157.

Garro A M, 'Codification Technique and the Problem of Imperative and Suppletive Laws' (1981) 41 *Louisiana L Rev* 1007.

Gaubiac Y, 'Freedom to Quote from an Intellectual Work' (1997) 171 *RIDA* 2.

Gaubiac Y, 'La liberte de citer une œvure de l'spirit', Paris, 1re ch., 10 September 1996, (1997) 171 *RIDA* 3

Geiger C, 'The Three-Step Test, A Threat to a Balanced Copyright Law?' (2006) 37 *IIC* 683.

Geiger C, Gervais D and Senftleben M, 'The Three Step Test Revisited: How to Use the Test's Flexibility in National Copyright Law' (2014) 29 *Am U Intl L Rev* 581.

Geiger C, Griffiths J and Hilty R M, 'Towards a Balanced Interpretation of the "Three Step Test" in Copyright Law' (2008) 30(12)*EIPR* 489.

Geiger C and Izyumenko E, 'The Constitutionalisation of Intellectual Property Law in the EU and the Funke Medien, Pelham and Spiegel Online Decisions of the CJEU: Progress, but Still Some Way to Go!' (2020) 51 *IIC* 282.

Geller P, 'Can the GATT Incorporate Berne Whole?' (1990) 12 *EIPR* 423.

Geller P, 'Copyright History and Future: What's Culture Got to Do with It?' (2000) 47 *Jnl Copyright Society of USA* 209.

Gerbrandy S and Klaver F, 'La Revision de la Convention de Berne' (1967) 52 *RIDA* 5.

Gervais D J, 'Making Copyright Whole: A Principled Approach to Copyright Exceptions and Limitations' (2008) 5 *U Ottawa L & Tech J* 1.

Gervais D J, 'The Compatibility of the Skill and Labour Originality Standard with the Berne Convention and TRIPS Agreement' [2004] *EIPR* 75.

Gervais D J, 'Towards a New Core International Copyright Norm: The Reverse Three Step Test' (2005) 9 *Marquette Intellectual Property L Rev* 1.

Gervais D J and Derclaye E, 'The Scope of Computer Program Protection after SAS: Are We Closer to Answers?' [2012] *EIPR* 565.

Ghosh S, 'The Merits of Ownership; Or How I Learned to Stop Worrying and Love Intellectual Property Review Essay of Lawrence Lessig, The Future of Ideas, and Siva Vaidhyanathan, Copyrights and Copywrongs' (2002) 15 *Harv J L & Tech* 453.

Ginsburg J C, 'A Tale of Two Copyrights: Literary Property in Revolutionary France and America' (1990) 64 *Tull L Rev* 991.

Ginsburg J C, 'Achieving Balance in International Copyright Law (Review of Reinbothe J and von Lewinski S, *The WIPO Copyright Treaties*, 1996)' (2003) 26 *Columbia Journal of Law and the Arts* 201.

Ginsburg J C, 'Copyright in the 101st Congress: Commentary on the Visual Artists Rights Act and the Architectural Works Copyright Protection Act of 1990' (1990) 14 *Colum-VLA J L & Arts* 477.

Ginsburg J C, 'Copyright without Walls? Speculations on Literary Property in the Library of the Future' (1993) 42 *Representations* 53.

Ginsburg J C, 'Creation and Commercial Value' (1990) 90 *Columbia L Rev* 1805.

Ginsburg J C, 'Exclusive Rights, Exceptions, and Uncertain Compliance with International Norms' (2014) 242 *RIDA* 175.

Ginsburg J C, 'Fair Use For Free, or Permitted-But-Paid?' (2014) 29 *Berkeley Tech L J* 1383.

Ginsburg J C, 'International Copyright: From a 'Bundle' of National Copyright Laws to a Supranational Code?' (2000) 47 *J Copyright Soc'y USA* 265.

Ginsburg J C, 'The Most Moral of Rights: The Right to Be Recognized as the Author of One's Work' (2016) 8 *Geo Mason J Int'l Com L* 44.

Ginsburg J C, 'Toward Supranational Copyright Law? The WTO Panel Decision and the "Three Step Test" for Copyright Exceptions' (2001) 187 *RIDA* 3.

Goodman N, 'In Some Questions Concerning Quotation' (April 1974) 58 (2) *The Monist*, 294.

Gordon B, 'Three Designs by Johnson/Burgee' (1978) 164 *Architectural Record* 84.

Gordon W J, 'Fair Use as Market Failure: A Structural and Economic Analysis of the Betamax Case and its Predecessors' (1982) 82 *Colum L Rev* 1600.

Gordon W J, 'Fair Use Markets: On Weighing Potential License Fees' (2011) 79 *Geo Wash L Rev* 1814.

Gordon W J, 'A Property Right in Self-Expression: Equality and Individualism in the Natural Law of Intellectual Property' (1993) 102 *Yale L J* 1533.

Goroff D B, 'Fair Use and Unpublished Works: *Harper & Row* v. *Nation Enterprises*' (1984) 9 *Colum-VLA Art & L* 325.

Griffiths J, 'Copyright Law after Ashdown: Time to Deal Fairly with the Public' [2002] *IPQ* 240.

Griffiths J, 'Unsticking the Centre-Piece – The Liberation of European Copyright Law?' [2010] *JIPITEC* 87.

Haile B, 'Scrutiny of the Ethiopian System of Copyright Limitations in the Light of International Legal Hybrid Resulting from (the Impending) WTO Membership: Three-Step Test in Focus' (2012) 25 *J Ethiopian L* 159.

Handler M and Rolph D, '"A Real Pea Souper": The *Panel* Case and the Development of the Fair Dealing Defences to Copyright Infringement in Australia' [2003] *Melbourne University Law Review* 15.

Harbo T-I, 'The Function of the Proportionality Principles in EU Law' (2010) 16 *European Law Journal* 158.

Hatherley O, 'Konstantin Melnikov's Legacy' (28 August 2015) *Architectural Review*.

Hatherley O, 'Whose Modernist Icon Is it Anyway?' (23 April 2010) *Building Design* 9

He H, 'Seeking a Balanced Interpretation of the Three-Step Test – An Adjusted Structure in View of Divergent Approaches' (2009) 40 *IIC* 274.

He J, 'Developing Countries' Pursuit of an Intellectual Property Law Balance under the WTO TRIPS Agreement' (2011) 10 *Chinese J Int'l L* 827.

Heide T, 'Copyright, Contract and the Legal Protection of Technological Measures – Not the Old Fashioned Way: Providing a Rationale to the Copyright Exceptions Interface' (2002–2003) 50 *J Copyright Soc'y USA* 315.

Helfer L R, 'World Music on a U.S. Stage: A Berne/TRIPS and Economic Analysis of the Fairness in Music Licensing Act' (2000) 80 *BU L Rev* 93.

Hemmungs Wirtén E, 'Colonial Copyright, Postcolonial Publics: The Berne Convention and the 1967 Stockholm Diplomatic Conference Revisited' (2010) 7 (3) *SCRIPT-ed* 532.

Henry S E, 'The First International Challenge to the U.S. Copyright Law: What Does the WTO Analysis of 17 U.S.C. 110(5) Mean to the Future International Harmonization of Copyright Laws under the TRIPS Agreement?' (2001) *Penn State International Law Review* 301.

Hepp F, 'The International Protection of the Plastic Arts' [1957] *Le Droit D'Auteur* 144.

Hesser T, 'Intellectual Property Conference of Stockholm, 1967: The Official Program for Revising the Substantive Copyright Provisions of the Berne Convention. The Fifth Annual Jean Geiringer Memorial Lecture on International Copyright Law' (1967) 14 *Bull Copyright Soc'y* 267.

Hesser T, 'Some Questions Concerning the Future Revision of the Berne Convention' (January 1962) *Droit D'Auteur* 11.

Hettinger E C, 'Justifying Intellectual Property' (1989) 18 *Philosophy and Public Affairs* 31.

Holm-Hudson K, 'Quotation and Context: Sampling and John Oswald's Plunderphonics' (1997) 7 *Leonardo Music Journal* 17.

Hudson E, 'Implementing Fair Use in Copyright Law; Lessons from Australia' (2013) 25 *Intellectual Property Journal* 201.

Hudson E, 'The Pastiche Exception in Copyright Law: A Case of Mashed-Up Drafting?' [2017] *IPQ* 346.

Hugenholtz B and Okediji R L, 'Conceiving an International Instrument on Limitations and Exceptions to Copyright' (2008) Amsterdam Law School Legal Studies Research Paper No 2012-43.

Hughes J, 'The Philosophy of Intellectual Property' (1988) 77 *Georgetown Law Journal* 287.

Hughes J and Merges R P, 'Copyright and Distributive Justice' (2016) 92 *Notre Dame L Rev* 513.

Jencks C, 'Contextual Counterpoint in Architecture' (2012) 24 *Log* 71.

Joo T W, 'Remix without Romance', (2011) 44 *Conn L R* 415.

Jutte B J and Maier H, 'A Human Right to Sample – Will the CJEU Dance to the BGH-Beat?' (2017) 12 *JIPLP* 784.

Kadens E and Young E A, 'How Customary Is Customary International Law?' (2013) 54 *William & Mary L Rev* 885.

Kaminski M E and Yanisky-Ravid S, 'The Marrakesh Treaty for Visually Impaired Persons: Why a Treaty was Preferable to Soft Law' (2014) 75 *U Pitt L Rev* 255.

Kapczynski A, 'The Cost of Price: Why and How to Get beyond Intellectual Property Internalism' (2012) 59 *UCLA L Rev* 970.

Kaplow L, 'Rules versus Standards: An Economic Analysis' (1992) 42 *Duke L J* 557.

Karlen P H, 'What's Wrong with VARA: A Critique of Federal Moral Rights' (1992–3) 15 *Hastings Comm & Ent L J* 905.

Kennedy M, 'Blurred Lines: Reading TRIPS with GATT Glasses' (2015) 49 *Journal of World Trade* 735.

Kennedy R, 'Was it Author's Rights All the Time?: Copyright as a Constitutional Right in Ireland' (2011) 33 *DULJ* 253.

King E, '"Small Scale Copyrights?" Quotation Marks in Theory and Practice' (March 2004) 98 (1) *The Papers of the Bibliographical Society of America* 39.

Kirchmeier J L and Thumma S A, 'Scaling the Lexicon Fortress: The United States Supreme Court's Use of Dictionaries in the Twenty-First Century' (2010) 94 *Marq L R* 77.

Knapp J C, 'Laugh, and the Whole World ... Scowls at You: A Defense of the United States' Fair Use Exception for Parody under TRIPs' (2005) 33 *Denv J Int'l L & Pol'y*.

Koelman K J, 'Fixing the Three Step Test' (2006) 28(8) *EIPR* 407.

Koh H, 'Bringing International Law Home' (1998) 35 *Houston L Rev* 623.

Korobkin R B, 'Behavioral Analysis and Legal Form: Rules vs Standards Revisited' (2000) 79 *Or L Rev* 23.

Kuenzli K M, 'Aesthetics and Cultural Politics in the Age of Dreyfus: Maurice Denis's *Homage to Cézanne*' (2007) 30 *Art History* 683.

Kur A, 'Of Oceans, Islands, and Inland Water – How Much Room for Exceptions and Limitations under the Three Step Test?' (2009) 8 *Rich J Global L & Bus* 287.

Lacey L J, 'Of Bread and Roses and Copyright' [1989] *Duke L J* 1532.

Landau M, 'Fitting United States Copyright Law into the International Scheme: Foreign and Domestic Challenges to Recent Legislation' (2007) 23 *Ga St U L Rev* 847.

Landes W and Posner R, 'An Economic Analysis of Copyright Law' (1989) 18 *J Legal Studies* 325.

Leaffer M, 'The Uncertain Future of Fair Use in a Global Information Marketplace' (2001) 62 *Ohio State Law Journal* 849.

Lee E, 'Fair Use Avoidance in Music Cases' (2018) 59 *Boston College L Rev* 1873.

Lee E and Moshirnia A, 'Does Fair Use Matter? An Empirical Study of Music Cases' (2020) 94 *S Cal L Rev* (forthcoming).

Leistner M, 'The German Federal Supreme Court's Judgment on Google's Image Search – A Topical Example of the 'Limitations' of the European Approach to Exceptions and Limitations' (2011) 42 *IIC* 417.

'Les Emprunts Licite' [1924] *Le Droit D'Auteur* 87.

Leval P, 'Toward a Fair Use Standard'(1990) 103 *Harvard L Rev* 1105.

Litman J, 'Lawful Personal Use' (2007) 85 *Texas L Review* 1871.

Lo C-F, 'Good Faith Use of Dictionary in the Search of Ordinary Meaning under the WTO Dispute Settlement Understanding' (2010) 1 *Journal of International Dispute Settlement* 431.

López J M, 'Derecho de Autor, Revistas de Prensa y Press Clipping' (2008) 215 *RIDA* 2.

Lucas L, 'For a Reasonable Interpretation of the Three-Step Test' (2010) 32(6) *EIPR* 277.

Liu D, 'Copyright and the Pursuit of Justice: A Rawlsian Analysis' (2012) 32 *Legal Studies* 600.

Liu J, 'An Empirical Study of Transformative Use in Copyright Law' (2019) 22 *Stan Tech L Rev* 163.

Lunney Jr G S, 'A Tale of Two Copyrights' (February 26, 2020). Available at SSRN: https://ssrn.com/abstract=3544757.

MacLeod M, 'Architecture and Practice in the Reagan Era' (February 1989) 8 *Assemblage* 22.

Madison M J, 'A Pattern-Oriented Approach to Fair Use' (2004) 45 *William & Mary L Rev* 1525.

Masouyé C, 'Perspectives de revision de la Convention de Berne' (1964) 43 *RIDA* 5.

Masouyé C, 'The Next Stockholm Conference' (1962) 34 *RIDA* 2.

McAdams R H, 'The Origin, Development and Regulation of Norms' (1998) 96 *Mich L R* 338.

McCausland S, 'Protecting "A Fine Tradition of Satire": The New Fair Dealing Exception for Parody or Satire in the Australian Copyright Act' [2007] *EIPR* 287.

McCutcheon J, 'The New Defence of Parody or Satire under Australian Copyright Law' (2008) *IPQ* 163.

McGowan D F, 'A Critical Analysis of Commercial Speech' (1990) 78 *Cal L Rev* 359.

Mee B, 'Laughing Matters: Parody and Satire in Australian Copyright Law' (2009/10) 20 *Journal of Law, Information and Science* 61.

Melville R, 'Francis Bacon' (December 1949–January 1950) 20 (120–1) *Horizon* 419.

Munro C R, 'The Value of Commercial Speech' (2003) 62 *Cambridge Law Journal* 134.

Nesbet A, 'Inanimations: Snow White and Ivan the Terrible' (1997) 50(4) *Film Quarterly* 20.

Netanel N W, 'Making Sense of Fair Use' (2011) 15 *Lewis & Clark L Rev* 715.

Netanel N, 'The Next Round: The Impact of the WIPO Copyright Treaty on TRIPS Dispute Settlement' (1997) 37 *Va J Intl L* 441.

Ng A, 'Copyright and Moral Norms' (2012–2013) 14 *Loy J Pub Int L* 57.

Okediji R L, 'The Limits of International Copyright Exceptions for Developing Countries' (2019) 21 *Vand J Ent & Tech L* 689.

Okediji R L, 'Towards an International Fair Use Doctrine' (2000) 39 *Colum J Transnat'l L* 75.

Oliar D and Sprigman C, 'There's no Free Laugh (Anymore): The Emergence of Intellectual Property Norms and the Transformation of Stand-Up Comedy' (2009) 94(8) *Virginia L Rev* 1787.

Oliver J, 'Copyright in the WTO: The Panel Decision on the Three-Step Test' (2002) 25 *Colum J L & Arts* 119.

Olwan R, 'The Adoption of the American Fair Use in Gulf States: A Comparative Analysis of Authors' Exceptions in Common Law and Civil Law Countries' (2016) 38 *EIPR* 416.

Olwan R, 'The Ratification and Implementation of the Marrakesh Treaty for Visually Impaired Persons in the Arab Gulf States' (2017) 20 *J World Intell Prop* 178.

Parish J, 'Sampling and Copyright – Did the CJEU Make the Right Noises?' [2020] 79 *Cambridge Law Journal* 31.

Parkin J, 'The Copyright Quotation Exception: *Not* Fair Use by Another Name' (2019) 19 *Oxford University Commonwealth Law Journal* 55.

Pavot D, 'The Use of Dictionary by the WTO Appellate Body: Beyond the Search of Ordinary Meaning' (2010) 4(1) *Journal of International Dispute Settlement* 29.

Pessach G, 'Beyond IP – The Cost of Free' (2016) 54 *Osgoode Hall L Rev* 225.

Posner E A, 'Standards, Rules, and Social Norms' (1997) 21 *Harv J L Public Pol'y* 101.

Post R C, 'The Constitutional Status of Commercial Speech' (2000) 48 *UCLA L Rev* 1.

Radin M J, 'Property and Personhood' (1982) 34 *Stanford L Rev* 957.

Randall M H, 'Commercial Speech under the European Convention on Human Rights: Subordinate or Equal?' (2006) 6 *Human Rights L Rev* 53.

Randolph A R, 'Dictionaries, Plain Meaning, and Context in Statutory Interpretation' (1994) 17 *Harv J L & Pub Poly* 71.

Recht P, 'Pseudo-Quotation in the Field of the Plastic and Figurative Arts' (1957) 17 *RIDA* 84.

Recht P, 'Should the Berne Convention include a Definition of the Right of Reproduction?' [April 1965] *Copyright* 82.

Reese R A 'Innocent Infringement in U.S. Copyright Law: A History' (2007) 30 *Colum Journal of Law and the Arts* 133.

Reese-Lawrence A 'The Return of the Dead: Stirling's Self-Revision at Roma Interotta' (2011) 22 *Log* 22.

Reichman J H, 'Universal Minimum Standards of Intellectual Property Protection under the TRIPS Component of the WTO Agreement' (1995) 29 *Int'l Law* 345.

Richman B D, 'Norms and Law: Putting the Horse Before the Cart' (2012) 62 *Duke L J* 739.

Ricketson S, 'The Boundaries of Copyright: Its Proper Limitations and Exceptions: International Conventions and Treaties' [1999] *IPQ* 56.

Riis T and Schovsbo J, 'Extended Collective Licences and the Nordic Experience' (2010) 33 *Col Jo L & Arts* 471.

Rognstad O, 'Restructuring the Economic Rights in Copyright – Some Reflections on an Alternative Model' (2015) 62 *J Copyright Soc'y USA* 503.

Rosenblatt E L, 'A Theory of IP's Negative Space' (2011) *Columbia Journal of Law and the Arts* 317.

Rosenfield H N, 'Customary Use as "Fair Use" in Copyright Law' (1975) 25 *Buff L Rev* 119.

Rothman J E, 'Best Intentions: Reconsidering Best Practices Statements in the Context of Fair Use and Copyright Law' (2010) 57 *J Copyright Soc'y USA* 371.

Rothman J E, 'Custom, Comedy and the Value of Dissent' (2009) 95 *Va L Rev Brief* 19.

Rothman J E, 'The Questionable Use of Custom in Intellectual Property' (2007) 93 *Va L Rev* 1899.

Rothman J E, 'Why Custom Cannot Save Copyright's Fair Use Defense' (2007) 93 *Va L Rev Brief* 243.

Rubin P A, 'War of the Words: How Courts Can Use Dictionaries in Accordance with Textualist Principles' (2010) 60 *Duke L J* 167.

Sag M, 'Predicting Fair Use' (2012) 73 *Ohio St L J* 47.

Sag M, 'The Prehistory of Fair Use' (2011) 76 *Brooklyn L Rev* 1371.

Saka P, 'Quotation' (2013) 8 *Philosophy Compass* 935.

Samuelson P, 'Possible Futures of Fair Use' (2015) 90 *Wash L Rev* 815.

Samuelson P, 'Symposium: Intellectual Property and Contract Law for the Information Age' (1999) 87 *Cal L Rev* 1.

Samuelson P, 'The US Digital Agenda at WIPO' (1997) 37 *Virginia Journal of International Law* 369.

Samuelson P, 'Unbundling Fair Uses' (2009) 77 *Fordham L Rev* 2537.

Sandeen S K 'Implementing the EU Trade Secrets Directive: A View from the United States' [2017] *EIPR* 4.

Sanjek D, 'Don't Have to DJ No More: Sampling and the "Autonomous Creator"' (1992) 10 *Card Arts & Ent L J* 607.

Sarid E, 'Don't Be a Drag, Just Be a Queen – How Drag Queens Protect Their Intellectual Property without Law' (2014) 10 *FIU L Rev* 133.

Schauer F, 'Is Law a Technical Language?' (2015) 52 *San Diego L Rev* 501.

Schauer F, 'Statutory Construction and the Coordinating Function of Plain Meaning' [1990] *Sup Ct Rev* 231.

Schlag P, 'Rules and Standards' (1985) 33 *UCLA L Rev* 379.

Scoville R M, 'Finding Customary International Law' (2016) 101 *Iowa L Rev* 1893.

Senftleben M, 'Internet Search Results – A Permissible Quotation?' (2013) 235 *RIDA* 3.

Senftleben M, 'The International Three-Step Test: A Model Provision for EC Fair Use Legislation' (2010) 1 *JIPITEC* 67.

Shaver L, 'Copyright and Inequality' (2014) 92 *Washington University L Rev* 117.

Simon I, 'Nominative Use and Honest Practices in Industrial and Commercial Matters – A Very European History' [2007] *IPQ* 117.

Sokolowski R, 'Quotation' (1984) 37(4) *The Review of Metaphysics* 699.

Special Issue, (2014) 33(2) *Contemporary Music Review on Music Borrowing and Quotation*.

Strauss S, 'Why Plain Meaning?' (1997) 72 *Notre Dame L Rev* 1565.

Strömholm S, 'Droit Moral – The International and Comparative Scene from a Scandinavian Viewpoint' (1983) 14 *IIC* 1.

Strömholm S, 'Svante Bergström' [1981] *SvJT* 398.

Stuart R, 'A Work of Heart: A Proposal for a Revision of the Visual Artists Rights Act of 1990 to Bring the United States Closer to International Standards' (2007) 47 *Santa Clara L Rev* 645.

Subotnik E E, 'Intent in Fair Use' (2014) 18 *Lewis and Clark L Rev* 935.

Sunstein C R, 'Social Norms and Social Roles' (1996) 96 *Colum L Rev* 903.

Suzor N, 'Where the Bloody Hell Does Parody Fit in Australian Copyright Law?' (2008) 13 *MALR* 218.

Tan D, 'The Transformative Use Doctrine and Fair Dealing in Singapore' (2012) 24 *Singapore Academy of Law Journal* 832.

Thumma S A and Kirchmeier J L, 'The Lexicon Has Become a Fortress: The United States Supreme Court's Use of Dictionaries' (1999) 47 *Buff L R* 227.

Tournier A, 'Le Comité d'experts de Genève' (1964) 42 *RIDA* 27.

Tsakyrakis S, 'Proportionality: An Assault on Human Rights?' (2009) 7 *Int'l J Const L* 468.

Van Houweling M S, 'Distributive Values in Copyright' (2005) 83 *Texas L Rev* 1535.

Vaunois A, 'Letter de France' (March 1925) *Le Droit D'Auteur* 29.

Vaver D, 'The National Treatment Requirements of the Berne and Universal Copyright Conventions' (1986) 17 *IIC* 577.

Visser C, 'The Location of the Parody Defence in Copyright Law: Some Comparative Perspectives' (2005) 38 *Comparative and International Law Journal of Southern Africa* 321.

Wadlow C, 'Regulatory Data Protection under TRIPs Article 39 (3)and Article 10*bis* of the Paris Convention: Is There a Doctor in the House?' (2008) *IPQ* 355.

Wauwermans P, 'Lettre de Belgique', (June 1895) *Le Droit D'Auteur* 75.

Weinreb L L, 'Fair's Fair: A Comment on the Fair Use Doctrine' (1990) 103 *Harv L Rev* 1137.

Weinreb L L, 'Fair Use' (1999) 67 *Fordham L Rev* 1291.

Wennakoski A A, 'Trade Secrets under Review: A Comparative Analysis of the Protection of Trade Secrets in the EU and in the US' [2016] *EIPR* 154.

Williams J, 'Theoretical Approaches to Quotation in Hip-Hop Recordings' (2014) 33(2) *Contemporary Music Review* 188.

Wilmington M, 'The Rain People' (January–February 1992) 28 (1) *Film Comment* 17.

Wolf S, 'Proportionality in EU Law: A Balancing Act' (2012–13) 15 *Cambridge Yearbook of European Legal Studies* 439.

Wong M W S, 'Transformative User-Generated Content in Copyright Law: Infringing Derivative Works or Fair Use' (2009) 11 *Vanderbilt Journal of Entertainment and Technology Law* 1075.

Xalabarder R, 'Press Publisher Rights in the New Copyright in the Digital Single Market Draft Directive', CREATe Working Paper 2016/15 (December 2016).

Xalabarder R, 'The Remunerated Statutory Limitation for News Aggregation and Search Engines Proposed by the Spanish Government; Its Compliance with International and EU Law' (30 September 2014) IN3 Working Paper Series. http://infojustice.org/wp-content /uploads/2014/10/xalabarder.pdf.

Yanisky-Ravid S, 'The Hidden Though Flourishing Justification of Intellectual Property Laws: Distributive Justice, National Versus International Approaches' (2017) 21 *Lewis & Clark L Rev* 1.

Yap P-J, 'Honestly, Neither Celine nor Gillette Is Defensible!' [2008] *EIPR* 286.

Yen A C, 'Restoring the Natural law: Copyright as Labor and Possession' (1990) 51 *Ohio State L J* 517.

Yu P K, 'Customizing Fair Use Transplants' (2018) 7 *Laws* 1.

Yu P K, 'Fair Use and its Global Paradigm Evolution' (2019) 2019 *U Ill L Rev* 111.

Zervigón' A, 'Remaking Bacon' (1995) 54(2) *Art Journal* 87.

Zimmerman C, 'Stirling Reassembled' (2007) 56 *AA Files* 30.

Zissu R L, 'Fair Use: From Harper & Row to Acuff Rose, May 13, 1994' (1994) 42 *J Copyright Soc'y USA* 7.

NEWSPAPER ARTICLES

Campbell R, 'Architect James Stirling: Controversial, Daring, Amazing' *The Boston Globe* (Boston, 30 June 1992).

Cork R, 'A Master of Mind and Matter' *The Times* (10 October 1995) 34.

Goldberger P, 'Philip Johnson Is Dead at 98: Architecture's Restless Intellect' *New York Times* (New York, 27 January 2005).

Huxtable A L, 'Architecture: Bigger – And May Be Better: The Outlook in Architecture' *New York Times* (New York, 26 August 1978) 83.

Huxtable A L, 'Architecture View: "Towering" Achievements of '78' *New York Times* (New York, 31 December 1978) D21.

Huxtable A L, 'Johnson's Latest – Clever Tricks or True Art?' *New York Times* (New York, 16 April 1978) 26.

Huxtable A L, 'The Troubled State of Architecture' *New York Review of Books* (1 May 1980) 22.

OTHER SECONDARY SOURCES

Australian Law Reform Commission, *Copyright and the Digital Economy* (Report No. 122) (Sydney, ALRC, 2013).

Attorney-General's Department, Issues Paper, *Fair Use and Other Copyright Exceptions: An Examination of Fair Use, Fair Dealing and Other Exceptions in the Digital Age* (May 2005).

Board of Trade, *Report of the Copyright Committee* (1951–2) (Cmd. 8662).

Bodenhausen G H C, *Guide to the Application of the Paris Convention for the Protection of Industrial Property*, WIPO Publication No. 611 (1969).

Ficsor M, *Guide to the Copyright and Related Rights Treaties Administered by WIPO* (WIPO 2003).

Gowers Review of Intellectual Property (UK, December 2006).

Taking Forward the Gowers Review of Intellectual Property: Proposed Changes to Copyright Exceptions (Intellectual Property Office Newport 2008).

Taking Forward the Gowers Review of Intellectual Property: Second Stage Consultation Copyright Exceptions (Intellectual Property Office Newport 2009).

Hargreaves Review, *Digital Opportunity: A Review of Intellectual Property and Growth* (May 2011).

Masouyé C, *Guide to the Berne Convention for the Protection of Literary and Artistic Works* (WIPO 1978).

Okpaluba J, 'Digitisation, Culture and Copyright Law: Digital Sampling, A Case Study' (PhD thesis, King's College London, 2000).

Ricketson S, *WIPO Study on Limitations and Exceptions of Copyright and Related Rights in the Digital Environment* (2003) SCCR 9/7.

Westkamp G, *The Implementation of Directive 2001/29/EC in the Member States*, Part II (2007).

WIPO, *Guide to the Berne Convention* (1978).

WIPO, *Records of the Diplomatic Conference on Certain Copyright and Neighboring Rights Questions, Geneva 1996*, vol. 1 (WIPO 1999).

WIPO, *Records of the Intellectual Property Conference of Stockholm, June 11 to July 14, 1967*, vol. I and vol. II (WIPO 1971).

WIPO, *Implications of the TRIPs Agreement for Treaties Implemented by WIPO* (WIPO 1996).

Xalabarder R, *Study on Copyright Limitations and Exceptions for Educational Activities in North America, Europe, Caucasus, Central Asia and Israel* (WIPO, 5 November 2009), SCCR/19/8.

Index

Cambridge Intellectual Property and Information Law

TITLES IN THE SERIES (FORMERLY KNOWN AS CAMBRIDGE
STUDIES IN INTELLECTUAL PROPERTY RIGHTS)

Sebastian Haunss
  Conflicts in the Knowledge Society: The Contentious Politics of Intellectual Property
Helena R. Howe and Jonathan Griffiths
  Concepts of Property in Intellectual Property Law
Rochelle Cooper Dreyfuss and Jane C. Ginsburg
  Intellectual Property at the Edge: The Contested Contours of IP
Normann Witzleb, David Lindsay, Moira Paterson and Sharon Rodrick
  Emerging Challenges in Privacy Law: Comparative Perspectives
Paul Bernal
  Internet Privacy Rights: Rights to Protect Autonomy
Peter Drahos
  Intellectual Property, Indigenous People and Their Knowledge
Susy Frankel and Daniel Gervais
  The Evolution and Equilibrium of Copyright in the Digital Age
Edited by Kathy Bowrey and Michael Handler
  Law and Creativity in the Age of the Entertainment Franchise
Sean Bottomley
  The British Patent System and the Industrial Revolution 1700–1852: From Privileges to Property
Susy Frankel
  Test Tubes for Global Intellectual Property Issues: Small Market Economies
Jan Oster
  Media Freedom As a Fundamental Right
Sara Bannerman
  International Copyright and Access to Knowledge
Andrew T. Kenyon
  Comparative Defamation and Privacy Law
Pascal Kamina
  Film Copyright in the European Union (second edition)
Tim W. Dornis
  Trademark and Unfair Competition Conflicts
Ge Chen
  Copyright and International Negotiations: An Engine of Free Expression in China?
David Tan
  The Commercial Appropriation of Fame: A Cultural Critique of the Right of Publicity and Passing Off
Jay Sanderson
  Plants, People and Practices: The Nature and History of the UPOV Convention
Daniel Benoliel
  Patent Intensity and Economic Growth
Jeffrey A. Maine and Xuan-Thao Nguyen
  The Intellectual Property Holding Company: Tax Use and Abuse from Victoria's Secret to Apple
Megan Richardson
  The Right to Privacy: Origins and Influence of a Nineteenth-Century Idea
Martin Husovec
  Injunctions against Intermediaries in the European Union: Accountable but Not Liable?
Estelle Derclaye
  The Copyright/Design Interface: Past, Present and Future